R⟋ 1952.

DATE DUE

THE SERPENT-WREATHED STAFF

the serpent-wreathed staff

by
**ALICE
TISDALE
HOBART**

THE BOBBS-MERRILL COMPANY, INC.
INDIANAPOLIS   *Publishers*   NEW YORK

With profound gratitude
I
dedicate this book
to the two who have been
inextricably woven into this
and all the other novels I have written

DR. JOEL GOLDTHWAIT

who because of his great knowledge and understanding
brought me out of invalidism and
made possible for me the arduous work of writing
and

MRS. ANNE STODDARD

who recommended to the Century Magazine
my first fiction and throughout
all the years since has without
stint given me the benefit of her
sensitive and perceptive mind

CARVED on the doors of medical buildings and hospitals, stamped on seals and charters, used as the insignia of the Medical Corps, printed on the title pages of books is the caduceus, the sign and symbol of healing—a staff, two wings at its top, two serpents entwining it. A symbol with the power of a symbol to convey vast areas of experience.

In the ancient temples of the East the living serpent was used in the rites of healing. In time it gave place to the serpent symbol. Into the hieroglyphics of Egypt the entwined serpents were woven. On the walls of the temples of India are the opposed and balanced serpents, male and female, the bearers of life and healing. The Hebrews had the emblem—the brazen serpent raised on a pole by Moses so that the people might look upon it and be healed. From ancient Babylon the symbol, a rod wreathed with two serpents, was carried to Greece.

For long centuries the symbol disappeared, then reappeared. Mysteriously it made its way across Europe until it reached England. In its long journey at times doves hovered over it, once griffins, and in Greece the wings of the herald were added. Sometimes it was a bare staff, but always serpent entwined. Finally tipped with wings it came to America.

✦ 1 ✦

EARLY on a June morning in 1942 Dr. Samuel Towne went quietly out of his house, crossed the lawn, and passed through an opening in the lilac hedge which surrounded his garden. Although the darkness was not entirely dispelled by the pale light of the approaching dawn, from long habit he walked sure-footedly along the faintly discernible paths until he reached a bed of roses. Taking a trowel from the pocket of the loose cotton jacket he was wearing, he knelt and began loosening the soil around the bushes. He had come to his garden this morning because he had found through past experience that when he had a problem, either medical or personal, which perplexed him he was often able to solve it if his hands were close to the earth.

Today marked a change in his life for which he thought he had prepared himself, but when he woke this morning he realized he had not. In appreciation of his services to the hospital which he had helped to found forty years ago the lately completed orthopedic wing for children was to be given his name today at the annual commencement exercises of the medical students. The conferring of this honor upon him marked his retirement both as head of the hospital's staff and as dean of the medical school.

At seventy-seven he needed to slow down, but he felt that during the fifty years he had specialized in the baffling causes of arthritis he had acquired knowledge which still could with benefit be drawn upon by the younger doctors at the hospital had he been given a position of consultant. What he had learned through years of study about the mechanics of the body and the manifestations of arthritis which result from wrong use of the human machine was not yet, he knew, fully understood by his fellow specialists.

Furthermore, the physician who was to take his place considered disease an entity in itself, something Dr. Towne vigorously denied. Although he believed the body was a machine that when damaged demanded the most scientific care, he believed also the spirit transcended it and must be enlisted in the fight against disease. This placed a double responsibility on the physician, something his successor considered an unnecessary drain, especially on the surgeon. Dr. Towne feared that the very core both of his knowledge and his philosophy would be lost, thus negating his fifty years of effort.

At sixty, when he had announced at the height of his reputation in surgery that he would no longer operate, he had felt no such frustration.

Yet the two resignations were part and parcel of each other. In giving up surgery he had been actuated by the same pride he imagined a singer had in stopping before the voice showed its aging. He wished no tremor of his hand to be remembered. It was time he relinquished the surgeon's knife to younger and surer hands. But ideas, he had found, were not so easily passed on. No, he was not reconciled to his retirement.

He rose from his knees and looked off to a knoll beyond the garden crowned with pines. Against the now faintly illumined sky the tall pointed trees were a black pinnacle, a thrust of triumph that had often brought him to victory—but not this morning.

He walked over to a break in the hedge, through which he could survey the valley lying at the foot of the low hill on which his house and garden had been built. The rising sun was sending its first rays up from a low ridge of hills on the other side of the valley. Shielding his eyes from the blinding light, Dr. Towne gazed at the city below him spread along the banks of the river which ran the length of the valley. During his lifetime the city had grown from a village into a great industrial center, its character changed from the personal into the impersonal. Most of the men and women who now inhabited it were without roots in the community. Perhaps it was time, after all, for him to give way to physicians whose roots, too, were not in the valley and whose philosophy of medicine was less personal than his own. Then his lifelong experience made him recoil from any such idea. He knew better than to hand man over completely to the machine age. Man was more than a beautiful mechanism.

His branch of the Townes had come to this valley in upper New York State a hundred years ago. The medical history of many of its original families, passed down to him from his father and grandfather who had been physicians, had convinced him that every patient was under some pressure from the family which left a mark on the spirit and which was transmitted either for good or evil to the body.

He liked to think of the family as an organism susceptible to disturbance by internal and external forces but possessing some special sensitivity to adjust itself to all sorts of mishaps, again and again regaining its balance after catastrophe. Otherwise it would be destroyed by the colossal forces always playing upon it.

His own family at its founding in America, brought to tragedy by violent forces of fear and intolerance, yet healing its terrible hurt. Vividly he remembered the farmhouse in Vermont where he had visited his grandparents. On the shelf over the great fireplace in the kitchen stood two candlesticks from the homestead in Salem, Massachusetts, from which Rebecca Towne had been taken to be executed for witchcraft. Her son Samuel, who had left Salem soon after his mother's death to settle in Vermont, had brought the candlesticks with him. Treasured heirlooms, they now stood on the mantel in Dr. Towne's parlor. A large family the Townes had become, spreading over America—strong men and women, their prototype the woman who had died in sturdy defense of her own and her neighbors' innocence.

His thoughts turned to his immediate family whom he had left asleep back there in his house which had sheltered him from the day of his birth, but his son only during his youth—if it had ever really been a shelter to him. Had the period in Dr. Towne's own life when he had been regarded as unorthodox by his profession left a permanent mark on his son Francis? Recognized now as an authority in his field of medicine, Samuel Towne of late had found the years he had been scoffed at, ridiculed and all but driven out of the profession for his revolutionary ideas on the treatment of arthritis, fading into his success. But had those early years faded for his son? the old man asked himself in this moment of self-examination. Francis was as aloof on his arrival yesterday as he always had been. His father had expected something more on this first return since his mother's death.

Remembering that he had never made it easy for the boy Francis, Samuel Towne felt remorse. Not considering what a sensitive boy might be going through at school at the hands of his mates, the doctor had fought his own battle, sometimes with bitterness, sometimes with glee at the discomfiture of his colleagues. His defiance of those who opposed him in the profession had resounded at times through the state—needless defiance sometimes, he thought now in the quietude of success and age.

As soon as he was through college, Francis, refusing to take up medicine, had accepted a teaching position in a Midwest city, where he had married and brought up his two sons. Both had become doctors. The older, named after his grandfather and called young Sam, had started his practice in the city where he was born. Alan, six years Sam's junior, had a year ago become his brother's partner. Dr. Towne had hoped that one or both of his grandsons would join him. He thought wistfully of how through them he could have passed on his peculiar understanding of man's bony structure, teaching them to use his experience to correct deformities without operating. But they, like the specialist who had been chosen to replace him, were more interested in surgery that would cure deformities after they had occurred than in the slow and less dramatic treatment that would prevent them. Nevertheless, their grandfather took pride in the accomplishments of his grandsons. Both had graduated with honors.

Too, the old man was proud of their instant response to the call for doctors in the armed forces. Immediately after Pearl Harbor Alan had written that he and Sam had decided, since they were surgeons, one of them should give his services, and that Alan, who had no family, should be that one. Later Alan had written of his engagement to an English girl he had met when he was serving a residency at a hospital in New York City. Later still he had suggested that, as all the family wished to be present when the new wing of the hospital was given the Towne name, he would like to be married at his grandfather's house.

Dr. Towne knew nothing about Esther Oglethorpe except that her father was a noted English philosopher and that he and his wife had been killed in an automobile accident while he was on a lecture tour here in America two years ago. She had arrived with Alan late the evening before. His first impression of her was that she looked more French than English and was very reserved. He hoped she'd make Alan a good wife. Sam had married well. Odd, though, after choosing a doctor for a wife Sam had not been willing that she should practice.

Suddenly Dr. Towne realized he was tired and that he had been standing for a long time looking with unseeing eyes at the valley beneath him. As he turned back into the garden, a sudden puff of wind blowing across it filled his nostrils with the mingled scent of earth and flowers. He felt the dew-moistened air on his cheeks and hands, familiar and dear sensations associated with many such mornings. It was in this garden he had come closest to breaking down the barrier between himself and his son, for Francis shared with him the need to live close to the earth. Year after year the doctor had come here, gaining refreshment in working with living, growing plants or sitting quietly on a semicircular bench backed by the bole of a great maple.

It was here he had been sitting that autumn day almost two years ago now. The year was dying; he wanted to die with it. That constant agonizing search which had gone on ever since his wife's death he could no longer endure. The cold of the stone seat had crept up through his hands resting on it and along his arms into his chest. Cold, cold. "Sarah, I cannot go on without you," his heart had cried out, "and I cannot find you!" He must have slept, for there was a flurry of brown leaves on the path, and Sarah, clad in the brown and white gingham dress she had worn on the day after their marriage, he saw coming toward him. A bowl of wild strawberries rested lightly against her slender hip. "I shall make thee a shortcake. Thee hath work to do." So had she spoken on that day when they were both young; now out of the vividness of a dream she spoke to him again. Slowly the cold had receded from his heart, and he had obeyed her summons to work.

No such vision of her today—only the memory of her in the last years crippled with a form of arthritis from which he knew not how to save her. Failure where he most poignantly desired success. Failure and retirement—hardly a message to take to the graduates of the medical school whom he was to address this morning. He rose, walked slowly over to a tool shed at the back of the garden. Taking a basket and clippers, he went again to the rose bed and cut the first buds of the season. Placed in his cool dark cellar, they would keep their freshness for Alan's wedding this evening.

He walked across the lawn toward his house. Alan, who had risen early, looked out of his bedroom window and saw him. Deeply conscious of love and respect for this tall erect gentleman in the faded blue cotton jacket with the sun on his white hair, Alan leaned out of the window in salute to him. Dr. Towne, looking up, smiled and waved his trowel.

At eleven that morning the auditorium was filled with the graduates and their families. On the stage many distinguished members of the profession were seated. They rose in respect to Dr. Towne, who with the president of the board was making his way up the crowded aisle. Samuel Towne raised his eyes to the wall behind the stage where a great bronze plaque of the caduceus he had some years ago given to the hospital was fastened. He had seen to it that the symbol of healing was correct in every detail—the small stylized wings topping the staff, the two serpents twined about the staff formalized, no longer a representation of a living thing but a symbol with the power of a symbol to convey vast areas of experience.

When Dr. Towne was seated the presiding officer rose and with genuine feeling expressed what he believed was undoubtedly the sentiment of everyone present. "No more fitting name than yours, Dr. Samuel Towne, could be given to the new wing for crippled children. By placing your name over its door it is our desire to do honor to your untiring service to this institution and to your patient and careful research in your special field of medicine. You have done much to lessen the suffering of little children."

As the applause died away Samuel Towne rose, laid his carefully prepared address on the desk. When he raised his eyes he found himself looking into the eyes of his family. They were sitting three rows back but directly in front of him: Francis in the center with Sam on one side of him, Alan on the other; on Sam's right his wife Josephine, and next to her their daughter Sarah, a girl of twelve; beyond Alan was Esther Oglethorpe, his fiancée.

Suddenly it seemed imperative to Dr. Towne that he speak directly to his grandsons. His impression last evening had been that even so early in their careers there was rigidity in their thinking. Dr. Towne had always fought against that attitude in the profession. Perhaps he could rouse Sam and, if so, Alan, who had always been the worshipful younger brother. Then Dr. Towne's thoughts turned to the untried doctors who were graduating today and who occupied the two rows of seats directly in front of him. He wished to say something to them, too, that would send them out free men unhampered by the thought-clichés of older men.

After thanking the trustees for the honor they had conferred on him, he paused, and those who had often heard him lecture knew it meant some change in the direction of his thought. "The address I intended to make seems to me unnecessary," he said. "You will find it printed in the state medical journal in next month's issue. But now, while we are together, I want to tell you something of my personal experience as a pioneer in a once-neglected field. You are well aware, many of you, that I have not always been considered orthodox. Some of you"—he turned to include the men seated on the platform—"do not consider me entirely so today. I want to tell you of the struggle of the unorthodox—what the hazards are and the rewards."

Young Sam, looking up at the tall distinguished-looking speaker, felt himself a battleground of emotion. He loved his grandfather and was proud of him to an extent but often uneasy for fear that so independent a personality might even yet do something to discredit himself and the family. Active opposition to Dr. Towne had died down years ago, but whispers flared up whenever there was the slightest reason to question his diagnosis of a case. Until this moment never had young Sam heard the man he was named after mention the years when the profession had treated him as little short of an outcast. Surely he wasn't going to reopen the controversy and give his colleagues advantage over him at the very moment when they were offering him their belated homage!

"I want you to understand," Dr. Samuel Towne was saying, "that such criticism as was meted out to me is fundamentally right. Every theory in medicine, if medicine is to remain healthy, must be beaten out on the anvil of skepticism. So do we weed out charlatanism."

How fine! thought Alan. He is turning the attacks made against him in the past to the advantage of medicine. But a glance at his father and brother, and Alan found his pride replaced by concern. Francis Towne seemed to have shrunk into himself. A stony expression had descended like a mask over his face, only a few moments before alive with happiness. Sam was biting his neat mustache, a habit he had when annoyed.

Then Alan felt himself responding to the challenge in his grandfather's words. "I warn you not to make skepticism a habit," he was saying. "Ours is a profession of adventure. Only so do we go forward. America's place in the forefront of medicine is not ours by right of any divine decree. We could lose that position as Germany lost it to us, as Austria lost it to Germany, France to Austria, England to France. Italy was the first to carry high the torch of modern medicine."

Dr. Towne had turned to the men sitting behind him. "As you know, in the twenties there was a great outpouring of money for medical education, something unequaled anywhere in the world at any other time." Again he faced the graduates. "That is what put us in the vanguard of medical knowledge. You are the last to benefit by it. The depression already has cut down that outpouring. War will cut it farther. You, recipients of those lavish gifts, have an added responsibility. Give of yourselves to keep the profession moving forward. Watch that you do not become money-changers in the temple of medicine. It is possible for us to close our minds to social and technical advances in medicine if it is not to our personal interest. It has happened in the past."

His voice rose, commanding and forceful. "There is another temptation peculiar to men of ability—and we are men of ability. We are the strong over the weak. Sickness is a universal experience. Because we hold power over sickness, let us not think ourselves superior. I ask for professional humility, respect for human life. To you who are about to go overseas— humility will especially become you. Don't think you know it all. The ancient civilizations, China and India, have made contributions to medical knowledge. I ask that you keep your minds open. Clouded in antiquity the responsibilities of priest and healer were one and the same."

6

Clapping broke out, young men and old applauding a man they respected even if they did not accept all his ideas.

Now for the last time Dr. Towne stepped forward to administer to the graduates the doctor's oath. They rose and repeated after him clause by clause the oath handed down from Hippocrates, "I swear by Apollo the physician" allegiance to fellow physicians—to succor them when in need—and continuing with the vows to the sick that reiterate the brotherhood of physicians. In Dr. Towne's thinking it should be broadened to the brotherhood of man.

As the graduates droned out the phrases he had a sense of failure. Perhaps it was futile for one who had passed through the disciplines which experience brings to convey to those who had not passed through those disciplines the meaning of an experience. And then, looking at his son, Samuel Towne had the suspicion that his motive in the address he had given had not been wholly noble—not entirely to bring a wider vision to these young men and his grandsons. Out of the troubled centers of his being had come his old sense of defiance. At whatever cost he would justify himself and his theories.

2

THE long June day was reaching toward twilight. In the dining room of Dr. Towne's house the white tablecloth and Dr. Towne's pale pink rose-buds in a silver bowl were the only objects plainly revealed. The heavy mahogany furniture and dark walls receded into the half-light of the late afternoon. An old woman in her Sunday black moved quietly about the table, placing the flat silver grown thin with use. "If Miss Sarah was here, that's the way she'd like it. Pity she couldn't see Mr. Alan married," she said, talking to herself.

In the parlor beyond, almost indiscernible in the shadows, Francis sat at the piano, playing softly the music he intended to play later at the wedding.

Upstairs Alan and Sam, in the bedroom they used to share as children when they came to spend the summer with their grandparents, were sitting by an open window where they could catch the afternoon breeze. Their white flannel coats lay on the bed.

"You haven't said yet, Sam, whether you approve of my girl. I'd like you to, you know," said Alan.

"She seems attractive. It gave me a bit of a jolt, I'll admit—this sudden desire of yours to get married before going overseas. I could wish you'd given it more consideration," said Sam, avoiding a direct answer to Alan's question.

"Oh, but I have!" Alan exclaimed. "I mean I've known her for some time, but I wasn't engaged to her until a few weeks ago. I told you about it immediately." He was all at once conscious that in setting himself right with Sam about not being hasty he had given his brother the impression of not confiding in him so momentous a decision. Ever since the death of their mother when they were children, the two brothers had always shared the important events in their lives.

"You see there was nothing really to tell," he added with a smile, Sam forgotten now, thinking of his unbelievable good luck in winning Esther Oglethorpe. It had not been easy.

"There's one thing I want to take up with you," said Sam, changing the subject. "It's about the office building. Some of the other doctors and I have been trying to get hold of it for our exclusive use. I've just had a telegram saying we have it. I've made a considerable investment in it in order to be among the group who will control its policies. Of course I had both of us in mind."

"I know," said Alan. "It's wonderful to have you to keep a foothold for me while I'm away. I wouldn't have felt I could marry just now if it weren't for that."

Both brothers were now silent, Alan looking often at his watch as the hour for his marriage drew nearer, Sam thinking about the telegram which set forward his plan to see the Towne brothers wealthy and important in the city of their birth. Physicians would be scarce with so many in the service. He welcomed the work ahead because it would bring both him and Alan nearer the goal he had set for them.

He began thinking of Esther as she had looked last evening in her simple sheer black dress, her black hair drawn smoothly back and knotted low at the back of her head. A single string of pearls around her throat set off her creamy skin. There was the slightest suggestion of the European about her. Sam shrewdly valued its effect in the Midwest city in which he and Alan planned to make their reputation. Esther was not beautiful, according to the American standard. Her face was too thin. When in repose it held a maturity which took away its youth; and youth to the average American was essential to beauty. Sam, trying to analyze that maturity, had come to the conclusion that it lay in what might be interpreted as a sense of responsibility, a French quality, and he understood she had some French blood. But when Esther smiled, suddenly her youth took over with startling effect; more interesting, that merging of maturity and youth, than mere girlish beauty in the eyes of the discriminating, Sam reflected. Yes, Alan had shown good taste in choosing her for his wife. "I do approve of your girl," Sam said, breaking the silence.

At the front of the house in the room where he had been born and spent so many nights with his wife Sarah, Dr. Towne was sitting by the window

8

which looked out on the lawn and watching the shadows lenghten across the grass. When he called "Come in" in answer to a light knock and the door was opened by his granddaughter-in-law Josephine, his eyes lighted up with pleasure. "I've scarcely had a word with you. I'd almost lost hope I was going to. Do sit down so we may talk quietly. And you're leaving this evening?" There was a note of disappointment in the old man's voice.

"Sam thinks he can't be away longer. Don't you think Esther is lovely, Grandfather?"

"Yes, but not more so than you. You're a very beautiful woman, Josephine." Dr. Towne looked with no little admiration at the tall vigorous woman standing before him.

"Just to you," she answered with a smile.

"No, to all who are discerning," he insisted sturdily.

She had been a favorite of his ever since the day in the children's ward, some fourteen years ago, when he had seen her sweep into her arms a small boy whose legs were drawn out of shape by arthritis. In his delight as she hugged him close to her the child had voluntarily straightened the bent legs ever so slightly—something so far, fearful of the pain, he had refused to attempt.

"Do you do this often?" he had asked her.

"Yes," she had replied quite simply. "Affection helps."

After Jo's graduation Dr. Towne had seen to it that she was given one of the internships in the hospital. She was strong and forceful. She needed to be to endure the ordeal the men students had put her through, but these qualities were balanced by warmth and generosity. Samuel Towne felt deep gratification that it was he who had introduced her to Sam when he had come east to see his grandfather about a loan to help him get started.

Looking at her now, he had a sense of the waste it was, in time of war especially, for her not to use her professional skills. "Josephine, I don't want to interfere," he said, "but now that so many doctors will be going overseas, have you thought of taking up your profession again?"

At his words Josephine looked distressed. "I don't know, Grandfather. Sam seems to think——"

"You don't need to explain, my dear. I shouldn't have meddled. It's something between you and Sam, of course."

"It's all right, Grandfather. I'm glad you brought it up. I must go now." She stooped to kiss him on the forehead. "It's almost time for the wedding. I must see if I can help Esther and get Sally ready. She's with Esther, worshiping at the shrine of romance." Jo's voice as she spoke these last words was tender and sweet.

When she entered Esther's room Jo's attention went directly to her daughter, who was sitting on a stool with one foot resting on top of the other, the skirt of her dress fallen between her widespread knees in awkward childish fashion. Her elbows rested on her knees; her chin was cupped in her hands; her eyes were on Esther in bridal white, standing before the mirror fastening in place a pair of intricately designed earrings. Jo hadn't expected Sally to be so carried away. She laid her hand on her daughter's shoulder, saying, "Alan's a lucky man, isn't he, dear?"

"I'll say he is!" exclaimed Sally, not taking her gaze from the bride.

Esther turned to face the two. "It's my mother's wedding dress," she said in explanation of the style of thirty years ago.

"And this lovely veil?" asked Jo, picking up the fragile lace from the bed, thinking that only from Europe came such exquisite handmade work.

"My grandmother's and then my mother's."

Deftly Jo lowered it over Esther's head. It fell to the hem of her dress behind; in front it covered her face, which, reflected in the mirror, had looked white and still. "It must be a strain to be plunged so intimately into a family of strangers, but you're really one of us. The ties are close but good," said Jo very gently.

With sudden intuition Esther comprehended that the ceremony which was to make her Alan's wife was also a ritual by which she was taken into the family. She appreciated now Alan's desire to have all the family participate. She looked quickly at Jo. Their eyes met in understanding. With astonishment Jo noticed that the stillness, which she now suspected was caused by apprehension, had gone from Esther's eyes. So she has felt herself on probation, Jo thought, wondering a little that one with her background was so sensitive to the family's scrutiny.

As a clock in the lower hall struck the hour of six, Alan and Sam went down the stairs, along the hall which extended the length of the house, out a door at the back that opened on the lawn, and walked across the grass to a great elm that stood at the entrance to the enclosed garden. The minister joined the two men. He was the only outsider except Lydia, the old housekeeper, who stood on the veranda overlooking the scene.

Francis now increased the volume of his music, and Sally, dressed in her first long dress, at a nod from her mother started slowly down the stairs, her bouquet tightly clasped in her hands, counting one, two, three to each step, just as her father had instructed her to do. Often he had explained that to her and her alone fell the duty of carrying on the traditions of the family. Precision and accuracy were family qualities. Suppose she should stumble now when on her rested the responsibility to lead the wedding procession. One, two, three. Were the rest following? She mustn't look back. Then she heard her mother's reassuring whisper behind her: "It's perfect, Sally. We're coming."

Grandfather, who had been standing in the door of his room, came forward now and offered his arm to Esther. She raised her eyes and smiled. Silently they made the journey through the house. As they crossed the lawn Dr. Towne felt the trembling of her hand where it rested on his arm. He felt compassion for the stranger come among them. "My child," he murmured.

Watching them come toward him, Alan laid his hand on the trunk of the old tree. In their childhood he and Sam had believed that it had special power to give them strength when they touched its bark. Now the action was an instinctive dedication of his strength to her whom he was about to marry and yet must leave within a week. Then letting go the tree, he took Esther's hand and repeated after the minister the ancient vows of constancy, ". . . for better for worse . . . in sickness and in health . . . till death us do part . . ."

The afternoon fast deepening into evening left Esther's face under her veil indistinct. She seemed all at once a stranger to him. In a moment of doubt he thought, Is it in our power to make each other happy? His decision to marry her was the most independent act of his life. As he put back her veil and looked into her eyes, his doubt vanished. In its place came confidence in the rightness of this marriage. He bent his head and kissed her.

The family as one unit, Esther walking between Alan and Francis, the others following, moved toward the square-built mansion which for a century had held the life of the family. When they entered the dining room, Grandfather Towne took Esther's hand and with the formality of his generation led her to the head of the table. "You are to sit here, my dear, opposite me. Sarah would have wished it so." He is giving me his benediction, thought Esther. How beautiful the acceptance into this American family! No faintest note of discrimination to mar their welcome. She wished now that she had not waited so long before consenting to marry the man she loved.

All at once the room, Alan, and his family were gone. She was in Warsaw, a very little girl standing by the window of her grandmother's house. Her eyes were just above the window sill. Down in the street she saw her mother running toward the house shielding her head with her hands against stones thrown at her. With a great effort Esther put from her this intrusion of the past upon the present and raised her head.

In the interim she saw that Jo had been seated with Sally next to her, but the three generations of Towne men were still standing. How strikingly alike they were—tall men, not one of them under six feet, highly intelligent-looking, with long narrow faces, deep-set steel-blue eyes, high-bridged noses with slightly flaring nostrils, prominent cheekbones! Father would have felt kinship with them, she thought. Despite being very American, they have retained something of their English heritage. Through Father I am united to them.

"Francis at Esther's right," Grandfather Towne was saying. As Francis seated himself he laid his hand protectingly over hers where it rested on the table. So Alan's father accepted her, too. She glanced at Sam taking his place at Grandfather's left opposite Jo. Last evening it had seemed to Esther that Alan's brother resented her. Now as their eyes met Sam smiled. Her last anxiety over her place in the family faded away.

Lydia, who had been waiting impatiently for what she called "all this unnecessary fuss" to be over, began passing the steaming hot dishes she had prepared. This was no wedding supper of chicken salad and coffee but a dinner such as she deemed necessary to sustain "the boys," as she still thought of Sam and Alan, on the journey each had ahead of him this evening. There was fried chicken, cornbread, rich gravy and mashed potatoes such as only she knew how to make, Alan assured her when she passed them to him.

Again Esther's attention was caught by another likeness of the Towne men. Their hands holding the thin old silver forks and spoons were strangely alike, although Grandfather's were blue-veined and old. But the shape was the same—large with a wide spread between fingers and thumb —the kind of hands she had often heard spoken of as musicians' hands. In this case, except for Alan's father, they were those of surgeons.

"Well, what do you make of us? You were studying us, weren't you?" asked Alan, who was sitting at her left.

"Yes," she answered quite simply. "I'm trying to find my way among you."

"We're just a typical American family," he answered, smiling.

"Typical nothing!" Sam, who had overheard the remark, countered. For an instant he leveled his challenge at Alan and then redirected it to his grandfather. "I've been thinking all day about something you said to the graduates this morning, sir. If I understood you correctly, you were urging us of all things to be humble before patients."

"Not exactly. I believe I cautioned against a feeling of superiority," Samuel Senior answered.

"Doesn't that amount to the same thing? Furthermore, you imply the necessity of personal contact with patients."

"Yes." The old man's eyes had a bright light in them which should have warned the younger man that he was treading on delicate ground.

But, used to having his opinions accepted in the professional world, Sam went on. "I maintain that the more impersonal the surgeon is, the more effective he is. I am interested only in a perfect operation. Often I never see the patient again. We are in the mechanical age; the personal relationship for the surgeon is an anachronism."

"You mean you take no cases that involve it?" asked his grandfather in a tone sharp with disagreement.

"I leave them to the psychiatrists."

"You believe there is then a place for psychology in modern medicine, Sam?" The elder man's tone was milder now.

Alan, listening intently, felt relief. His brother could end the argument here, but to his dismay he heard Sam say with just an edge of scorn in his voice, "If you believe in it, yes."

"And you don't?"

"It never killed anyone," Sam retorted with a shrug.

Grandfather Towne's expression was suddenly stern. "There was something else I said to the graduates you could well remember, Sam—not to make skepticism a habit."

Sam flushed. He had said more than he meant to. His grandfather's address that morning had touched the very quick of Sam's pride. It had grown upon him as the day went on that in the presence of a distinguished group of doctors come together to honor him the great Dr. Towne had gone out of his way to draw attention to the years when he had been all but read out of the profession. Sam could not understand why his grandfather should wish so to humiliate himself and his family. But the old man was the head of the family. His censure left Sam disarmed and vulnerable.

Alan, seeing his brother's discomfiture, went to his support. "Sam's an awfully busy surgeon, Grandfather."

"I gather so," answered the head of the family a trifle dryly.

"We're celebrating Alan's marriage," pleaded Francis with a gesture of weariness.

Samuel Towne looked at his son. Had he again widened the distance between them?

Suddenly there was a clap of thunder. Wind sent the curtains billowing out. Francis jumped for the open window, shut it as the rain poured against it. He turned, saying, "Smell the earth, Father!" Breathing in the odor of the rain-touched earth, father and son were drawn together.

The old housekeeper entered bearing the wedding cake and placed it before Esther. "It's Miss Sarah's recipe," she said. "I made it myself."

Dr. Towne lifted his glass of champagne. "To the new member of the family!" As the chorus of family voices rose around him the old man leaned forward slightly as if trying to catch each single cadence to hold it forever.

Jo, sensing how often hereafter when sitting alone in this room Grandfather Towne would relive this hour, felt annoyed with her husband for the discordant note he had introduced; then, raising her eyes, she met Sam's. Laced through the whole day had been the memory of her own wedding and of the lover Sam had been before he had become absorbed in his profession. And yet through the years there had been times when he had come out of his absorption—then tenderness, a beautiful wooing, a passionate interlude. Not for a long time had he seemed so conscious of her as at this moment. The resolve she had made after her talk with Grandfather to take up her profession fell away under the throbbing of her senses.

Sam's gaze drifted to his daughter. Her brown eyes, so like her mother's, were too brilliantly alive in her small pale face. Had the wedding put too great a strain on her now when she was just coming into adolescence? From a young child she had been sensitive to every change of atmosphere around her. She would need all her mother's time and attention as she grew into womanhood.

As soon as it seemed fitting he turned to Alan. "If we're going to make our train, we ought to get started. You're sure you don't mind dropping us off at the station?"

In another moment Samuel Towne and his son Francis were alone in the dining room. Then they, too, left, going out on the veranda. Soon Alan and young Sam joined the two older men. The porch light over the door shone down on them. Each was conscious that never again might they be together. The sense of family was strong upon them. Grandfather Towne laid his hand on his namesake's shoulder, hoping Sam would understand by the gesture that difference of professional opinion did not lessen the bond between them. Then Sally ran down the stairs, followed more slowly by Jo and Esther. A few minutes more and grandfather and father stood listening to the sounds of the car going down the drive. Behind them was the lighted but empty house which both, feeling suddenly alone, held back from entering, remembering Sarah, whom each in his own way had loved so deeply and who was not waiting to give them comfort tonight.

"You look tired, Father. Shouldn't you rest?" asked Francis.

"I'll have plenty of time to rest." It was the first time Samuel Towne had referred to the significance of the morning's events. As he spoke he had the sensation that, now the pressure of his activities had been removed, his mind was bleeding as his physical body would have bled if the air pressure about it were removed. All day he had been putting off this moment. When he had joined his family after his address to the students, he had waved aside any attempt to talk of his retirement, a certain brusqueness creeping into his tone which warned his family not to trespass. But now Francis realized his father was opening the doors of his heart to him. And Francis at last was ready to enter, for, in seeking to make plain to the students what was his high conception of the doctor's role, Dr. Towne had revealed himself at last to his son.

It had not been as Francis had thought all his life, that his father was looking for a fight. In fact, he now understood that conflict had been repugnant to Dr. Towne, not only because by nature he loved harmony, but because his great desire had been for recognition by the respected members of his profession. To be ostracized by them must have been suffering indeed. He had fought because he must. The ethics of the profession demanded the best he had to offer, no matter what the cost. In a revealing flash it came to Francis that his father had not been able to accept the recognition accorded him today at its face value, because he was still conditioned by the years when he had not been accepted.

"How about the garden?" asked Francis. "The moon is up." Pacing the garden path together, they talked first of war and Alan's coming part in it, then the First World War and the parts they had played in it. Francis, a conscientious objector, had driven an ambulance; he had never until this evening spoken of the dangers he had encountered. Now he felt his father would understand that he was not a shirker. And he broke another silence. "I've never told you, Father, how proud I was when you were made head of that great hospital in England during the war."

They stooped to pass under a maple with low-growing branches. A touch on a branch and raindrops held on the leaves spattered their faces and hands. "Ours were the healing arts," said Dr. Towne. Now at last each recognized the function of the other. "I think," he went on, "if your mother were here she would say there was still work for me to do. I intend to move my office over to the industrial district. They'll be short of doctors there."

"Fine," answered his son. He smiled. Father'll die with his boots on, he thought, proud at last of his father's fighting spirit.

Together they went back to the house, able to enter it now. "I'm not teaching until autumn. I thought I'd stay for the summer if you'd like me to," Francis proposed. Then he said good night.

3

IT WAS getting on toward morning when the moon, sinking toward the horizon, sent its slanting rays through the window of the hotel in the city down in the valley. They fell full on Alan's face, waking him. Finding that Esther was lying on the farther edge of the bed, he moved over, drew her into his arms. Startlingly real to him still was her cry in their first effort at union. "Haven't you been asleep, dear?" he asked.

"Not yet," she answered.

Lovingly he ran his fingers through her hair, then kissed her forehead, her eyes, her throat, her lips, silently trying to express a man's consideration for the woman he loves. Suddenly he lowered his head to her breast, seeking in her all the mingled needs a man has for a woman, searching out not alone the lover but the mother, yes and that other quality in woman which receives unto herself a man's dreams.

With delicacy, with understanding, she took his varied emotions into her keeping. Leaning over him, she kissed him much as a mother kisses her child, then quickly with passion.

In the quietude that followed their passionate embrace he felt an over-powering necessity to protect her. Already life had brought her much suffering. He must keep her from any further suffering. But how could he, three thousand miles away? Love shadowed by separation gripped him. What could he do in a week to safeguard her? Had Esther been discriminated against in Europe? Had anything happened since she had come to America? Had people not suspecting her heritage hurt her with their remarks? What would happen to her while he was away? He was under no illusions. America was as capable of intolerance as Europe. He of all men could never doubt it. It lay deep in the history of his family and of his own boyhood.

"Esther," he cried out in anguish, "I cannot leave you!"

Late the next morning they drove across the state line into Massachusetts, which they had chosen as the scene of their wedding journey. Esther wanted to see Harvard, where her father would have lectured had he not been killed. Somehow she had the feeling he would like her to go there in his place. Alan had a half-formed plan to take Esther to Salem, where the Townes had first settled in America. Why, when he had been uninterested in going there before, he should wish to go now was not clear to him. Since it was possible he might change his mind in the end, he had said nothing to her about a visit there.

With delight Esther looked up at the elms which formed sheltering green arches over the streets of the New England towns and at the thin-leafed shadows thrown on white-shingled walls of colonial houses and sharp-roofed Cape Cod cottages. Toward a clear blue sky rose the thin-spired steeples of white-painted churches. She felt an atmosphere of sobriety in the scene which fitted her mood; separation and war hung over her.

As they walked among the ivy-covered buildings at Harvard she murmured, "Father would have been at home here."

"Wasn't he in New York?" asked Alan. "I always thought he liked it."

"He appeared to like it for Mother's sake, knowing she wanted to be as far from Europe as possible, but he was homesick for England," Esther answered. "Let's not talk about that. Let's just enjoy the place for him."

They were standing before the statue of John Harvard. Beneath was the date of the founding of the college. "Sixteen thirty-six!" exclaimed Alan. "That's sixty years before——"

"Before what?" asked Esther.

He ignored her question, asking one of his own. "Esther, would you like to see the Towne homestead? It's not very far from here."

"Really!" she exclaimed. "I thought New York State was where your family had always lived."

"Only for the last hundred years," Alan answered. "The American family goes back three hundred."

"Was that why you wanted to come to New England, Alan? Why didn't you say so?"

"It's a leftover from my childhood to be reticent about my family. I'll try to explain as we drive. I've never visited the old homestead myself," he said, "but some time or other each member of the family does."

"Has Sam?" she asked.

"He's an exception. He believes we should forget about the past."

"But you don't?"

"So far I've not been able to."

Esther reflected how little she knew about the man she had married, or he of her. And they had less than a week in which to learn about each other.

When they came to the outskirts of Danvers Alan stopped to study a map he took from the glove compartment. "This all used to be Salem," he explained. Then he looked from the map to a low hill at the right. On its summit stood a weather-beaten clapboard house. "This must be it," he said, turning the car into a narrow lane that led up the hill. In the soft gravel the car skidded slightly. With a deft swing of the wheel he brought it back. He guided it carefully the length of the lane, stopped it in rough grass behind the house. Far off to the west green hills stood out sharply. Below them the land sloped away to a wide meadow and a running brook. A hedge of lilacs set the dooryard off from an old apple orchard and sloping fields.

Hand in hand they walked to the front of the house and stood before its battened door. Rounded nails marked the points of intersection of its diagonally squared surface. Above it, set into the clapboards, was an ancient sundial. Through all the two hundred and fifty years since that tragic day, thought Alan, it has recorded the time—minutes and hours, days and years passing, the family moving on out across America. Now on his honeymoon he stood here with his bride in the spring sunshine.

The caretaker, who had heard the car come up the lane, opened the door. "Would you like to come in?" she asked.

The old home is evidently a historical shrine, thought Esther. As the caretaker led them through the low-beamed common room and up the steep stairs to the bedroom above, gradually it became clear to her why. "She was lying sick here when they took her," the woman explained. "But she wouldn't recant, wouldn't beg mercy for a sin she knew she hadn't done. Not her. She could have pretended she was a witch, then recanted. Surely her Maker would have understood that it was only to save her frail old body from being hanged and her sons and daughters from terrible grief. Others did. But not her!"

It seemed incredible to Esther that witch hunting could ever have taken place in this quiet, restrained countryside. Now she understood Alan's half-finished sentence when they stood before the statue of John Harvard. Incredible that, sixty years after a college had been established in this new America, only a few miles away superstition had grown into uncontrolled violence. But what Esther didn't understand was why Alan found it so difficult to tell her the story. "A leftover from childhood," he had said, but how strange! Nobody would burden a little boy with tragedy such as this.

"Her grave is down below," said the caretaker as they came out into the sunshine, pointing to a small grove of pines.

When they had seated themselves on the new spring grass of the hillside where they could look down on the family burial plot, Esther asked, "Can you tell me about it now?"

"She's told you," Alan answered.

"I mean about your childhood."

"I didn't realize it would bring it all back to come here," he said. With startling clarity events not thought of for years leaped up in his mind. "A bit of the old witch in you," so the distant cousin who cared for him and his brother after their mother's death had taunted him when he defied her. "You've got it in your blood." When he would burst into tears and promise to be good, she would say, "You must get over being so sensitive, Alan. Take it the way your brother Sam does when I correct him. He wouldn't cry. You're a crybaby." Too afraid to tell his father of the torment to which the middle-aged spinster day after day put him, he accepted her bullying. As time passed she enlarged on her story. "They took her to a high hill where all could see her. They burned her, stood her on some faggots." Fire haunted his dreams.

"I was only six when my mother died," Alan said at last. "We had a housekeeper after that." Bit by bit he described the woman and her cruelty. "One day I couldn't bear it any longer. I broke away from her."

"Did she hold you?" Esther asked in horror, her fingers tightening on his.

"No, only with her eyes. I ran down the hall. I wasn't looking, and I ran straight into Sam. He jerked me round. 'What's the matter?' he demanded. He said he'd beat hell out of me if I didn't tell him. I told him all right, scared of him now, too. He took my hand and dragged me into his room. 'You got to pretend to do what she wants,' he told me.

"Before that he'd treated me as a bothersome baby brother. But from then on we were allies. We did everything mean we could to get even with the woman we both hated, but we lived in fear she might tell the other boys about the witch in our family. At school, too, Sam fought my battles, and he taught me how to get along. 'Be like the boys in our crowd. If you're different they won't like you,' he'd say. He insisted there was no difference between us and the boys he let me play with."

"How long did this go on?" Esther asked. She had turned away so he wouldn't see the tears in her eyes. He was too close to his childhood just now. He'd think she pitied him—that, he wouldn't be able to accept.

"Until we went to our grandparents' the next summer. One day I asked Grandmother whether we were different.

" 'Would you care if you were?' she asked. 'Great people usually are,' she said dryly."

He could see his grandmother now as she had looked that day twenty years ago when she had skillfully drawn his story from him. Her eyes, usually filled with gentle laughter, were strangely militant, like flashing swords. "For a Quaker she looked almost angry," he told Esther with a smile. "I thought she was angry with me, until she put her arm around me and drew me close."

Alan stopped speaking. He found he had very little memory of what Sarah Towne had said to him. He could not now remember whether at that time she had made him feel pride in his ancestry, or whether he had learned it from her the next winter, which she had spent with them, or whether it had come to him later after reading a book he had found in his father's library. He could still see the thin volume with the title printed in gold on the blue cover, *Saint Made Witch Victim*. All of these events were now fused in his mind. "Grandmother must have taught me to respect so brave an ancestress, even to be proud of her," he said at last, feeling that was as near as he could come now to sorting out his childhood emotions.

"Didn't she teach Sam to be proud of her, too?" asked Esther.

"Yes, but he didn't think much of the idea. 'You just be like the kids in

our crowd and nothing will happen to you' was the gist of what he dinned
into me."

Through the years Alan had kept to the pattern set by Sam. But now for
the first time he faced squarely the fact that in marrying Esther he had
departed from it on a venture of his own. If Sam knew of her Jewish
ancestors, he would consider Alan had broken with his group. Esther he
would consider an outsider.

Silently they rose and went down to Rebecca's grave. Together they read
the quaint verses cut into the stone of the monument:

> O Christian martyr who for truth could die,
> When all about thee owned the hideous lie,
> The world redeemed from superstition's sway
> Is breathing freer for thy sake today.

"I wish I could believe that," said Alan.

"For the family it's proved so," said Esther, thinking of her acceptance
last evening.

A soft wind sighed through the branches of the pines.

They went back to the car, driving on and on until the emotions of the
day dropped away from them. Suddenly they were very hungry. "Why, we
haven't eaten since breakfast!" exclaimed Alan. At a wayside inn they ate
and drank. By the time they finished twilight had settled over the countryside. Alan took a back road and drove slowly. "I've an odd feeling of being
at home here," he said.

4

THE MEN of Alan's unit, thirty in all, were from the medical school in New
York City from which he and Sam had graduated. When Alan met the
others at their port of embarkation, he was keenly interested in learning
what his colleagues were like; it was a probability that for months, maybe
years, he would be working with them. Two of them he found he knew
slightly, for they were from his own class. The rest were strangers to him,
older men who had been practicing for some time in widely scattered parts
of the country.

Alan found the group an odd mixture of highly skilled and mediocre
men with ranks not in accord with their abilities. He was a major while an
older man by the name of Gregg, long recognized as a leading surgeon, was
only a captain. Alan wondered how it had come about that he, still with his
reputation to be made, outranked his distinguished colleague. That Sam

had used his influence in certain high circles Alan did not suspect, nor did he know that Gregg, had he used his influence, would have been put in command of the unit with the rank of colonel. It was rumored among the doctors that their commanding officer, a loud-voiced man named Beck, had used his connections in Washington to get the appointment and the rank of colonel.

When the transport sailed with its load of four thousand enlisted men, officers, doctors and nurses, fresh in many minds were the poignant memories of the clinging arms of loved ones, a child's final kiss. Some felt despair as they sought futilely to fix in their memories the faces of those whom they loved. Months, even years, might pass before they would see them again. On the part of others there was as desperate an effort to forget those whom they were leaving and whom they did not love. Among the doctors there was anxiety over their futures. Unlike men who had worked for large organizations and who were guaranteed their former positions after the war was over, the physicians, members of a highly competitive profession, were worried over the advantage their colleagues at home would gain in their absence. Alan was better off than most of them in this respect, for Sam would be keeping a place for him against his return.

Free from such fears, his thoughts centered almost wholly on Esther. His union with her, snapped off in its very beginnings, had an element of violence about it. Night after night she appeared to him in his dreams, only to vanish when he was about to take her in his arms. He would awake with a feeling of almost physical injury. Often he rose and as quietly as possible left the cabin he occupied with three other doctors and went on deck, seeking privacy, but he would find that many others had had the same idea and that every available space was occupied.

As the ship steamed down the coast of Africa and around the Cape of Good Hope, its occupants gradually loosened their hold on home and business, the life of the ship becoming their life. The main topic of conversation for the doctors was the petty tyranny of their colonel—his insistence that they salute as they passed him, his reprimands for the slightest departure from correct dress even when the ship sailed through the tropics. Delayed by constant engine trouble, it was two hundred days before they disembarked at Karachi. Time and tediousness had worked to unify their resistance to the colonel.

And then, although in the midst of a strange land and a strange people, they were drawn back to their own country by messages received from their families. For Alan there were letters from his father and grandfather, several from Sam, but none from Esther. Anxiety spread like a mist over his mind. Could she be sick? Surely someone would let him know if she were. Was she lonely without people of her own? None of his family was near enough to guard her against the inroads of loneliness.

He remembered little of the journey from Karachi to Assam, whence they were to be flown to China. At the end of the seven days' train trip he mechanically took his seat in the plane for the flight over the Himalayas.

On and on they flew. Below them lay a series of serrated white peaks and plateaus. Six hours and the plane began circling down toward dun-colored fields marked into squares by dun-colored dykes and, set in the midst, a city unfamiliar and forbidding with its gray roofs and white houses half obscured by a gray pall of falling rain, the only relief anywhere a brilliant red cross atop a gray tiled roof.

As the plane jolted to its landing the colonel's voice sang out, "Here we are, boys! Into the jeeps, make it snappy!" Over a newly made road they bumped until they came to a series of one-storied buildings set around three sides of a square. An officer from headquarters of the Air Force came forward and saluted the colonel. "Officers' billets to the right," he snapped out with a flourish. After considerable fuss the colonel at last appointed each physician to his cubicle.

Thankfully Alan shut the door of his, put down his flight bag. Privacy at last after weeks of unsought intimacy! But almost immediately there was a knock.

"Come in," he shouted.

A grinning Chinese man entered. "Major Towne, my belong your boy." He held out a handful of letters. Most of them were from Esther. All Alan could do at first was to finger them. Then according to the dates he laid them in order on the army cot, chief furniture of the room. He read the latest first, determined to ration himself to one a day. But like a starving man he read the next and the next until he had finished them all.

Relaxed and at peace with himself, he joined the others in the mess hall, to find that they, too, seemed at ease, and that the colonel appeared to have lost his aggressiveness. After the meal Beck invited, not commanded, them to go with him to see the hospital. They passed along the aisles between rows of beds, looked in at an operating room fully equipped, but the place was empty and silent except for the sound of their own feet going up and down the corridors and the steady bombardment of the colonel's voice.

As the days went by a few of the beds were filled: some Chinese officers brought over from the mission hospital in the city, a couple of Americans attached to the ground troops at the airfield suffering from malaria, a paratrooper with a broken ankle. There were scattered cases of stomach ulcer, and eye, ear and nose difficulties.

It did not take the doctors long to realize that the war had passed them, leaving them in an oasis of dull routine. Nothing in their training, they found, had prepared them for this cessation of activity into which curiously enough war with all its momentum and violence had pushed them. They were not proof against the double hazard of boredom and homesickness. Not a few sought relief in clandestine love affairs with the nurses; methodical drinking proved the answer for others.

Reared in Puritan and Quaker disciplines exemplified for him in both his father's and grandfather's loving devotion to the women they had married, Alan drew back from such solutions. For him either would mean a desecration of his marriage.

21

As spring came on he began taking long walks into the country. Treading the dykes that surrounded the rice paddies, he watched with growing interest the careful tending of every possible inch of tillable land with inefficient tools but with startling results. In dyked and flooded paddy after paddy bright green rice blades pushed up vigorously through the black water, growing taller and taller from day to day, turning a darker and darker green. How had such vitality been preserved in soil used for centuries? He began to be curious over the Chinese people, who until now had seemed alien and uninteresting. What was the discipline which held them to such unremitting labor? The grim demands of poverty? Undoubtedly, but something more. Alan had detected even in his servant a philosophy which gave him a lively sense of participation in the universe around him.

Now Alan's thoughts slid to himself. For years he had been immersed in the demands of his profession—medical school, internship, residency, and lately practice with his brother. At times as he walked along the narrow dykes looking down on the lush green rice with only the sound of his own steps to break the stillness of this unmechanized countryside, he began to wonder if there was not something essential which had been left out of his years of preparation and practice of medicine. Was efficiency the complete answer? What inner resources did he have to call on at a time like this? His was a quest both of mind and spirit; but invariably when he left the countryside behind and entered the hospital grounds, the quest seemed no longer valid.

As spring changed into summer, walks in the countryside were no longer possible. The pale tropic sun generated vapor out of the early morning rains. Into the humid heat the brassy bowl of the sky shut the valley. Languor and boredom spread like disease among the men. Alan found even writing to Esther a burden. About the best he could do was to mirror the mood of her latest letter. "It is nice to think of you going up to see Grandfather over the week end," or "I liked it that you were wearing the red dress I'm so fond of."

One evening he joined a half dozen of the doctors going into the Chinese city to try out a restaurant one of them had recently discovered, which had been placed in bounds. The Chinese men around him, eating and drinking and playing the finger game, bored him; his companions, eating and drinking and attempting to play the finger game, bored him. On a pretext of an errand at the mission hospital he left the party and wandered from street to street.

In the close-packed cubicles which did duty for both shop and home men stripped to the waist leaned over their counters, their bare trunks glistening with sweat which acted like nourishing oil, making their skin sleek and satiny. The women sat in the doorways, their white cloth stockings loosened so that the air might reach their legs above their feet deformed by binding. Fanning vigorously, they nursed their babies, exchanging gossip with their neighbors.

The spring's experience came back to him—both earth and people after centuries still filled with gusto and life. What was their secret? Or did they have one worth probing for? On the bodies of naked children darting between the legs of the pedestrians and chair bearers there were sores and boils. A blind man tapped his way before him. A man with the grotesque legs of elephantiasis sat in a doorway. Among both men and women he saw signs of syphilis. Why had these people so full of vitality done nothing for their sick? Again that stirring of curiosity.

He decided to make his pretext of a call on the mission doctor more than a pretext. He hailed a ricksha man and gave him the name of the hospital. But by the time they reached the high wall that surrounded it Alan's curiosity had evaporated. He stood irresolute before the gate. Then, thinking now that he was here he might as well go through with it, he pulled the bell rope hanging on the gatepost. Almost immediately the gate was opened by an elderly American man.

"I was passing," Alan explained somewhat lamely, then added, "I'm a doctor attached to the American unit. Towne is my name."

"Phillips is mine, Dr. Phillips. Come in, won't you?" The old gentleman turned abruptly and, Alan following, walked past the hospital to a Western house and along a hall to a room at the right. Two chairs and a table such as Alan had seen in the poorer shops along the way stood in the middle of the room. Against one wall were some old-fashioned Wernike bookcases half filled with books. Such meager surroundings, so austere a life as this aging man evidently was living, roused in Alan violent protest. A doctor was supposed to amount to something, to be someone. "What good can you do here?" he blurted out.

"A little, I think." Dr. Phillips' voice was gentle, but Alan detected a quizzical look in the man's eyes as he asked, "What more do you do at home? As fast as you treat one, doesn't another take his place? Don't you support yourself on that theory? The only difference is you make money. I don't. Isn't that what you mean really?"

"The physician represents only one branch of medicine in America," Alan replied heatedly. "There is research, you know, on a salary basis—small salaries at that, usually."

"Precisely. But how much does the practicing physician like you help in holding up that umbrella over the public? I was home a couple of years ago. I gained the impression that doctors in America were for the most part interested in the business of returns. You're a union, or a very exclusive gentleman's club. I couldn't decide which."

"That's not fair. I'm an orthopedist. I don't know a specialist who doesn't give considerable time to patients who can't afford to pay his fees."

"Ah, yes, and he sends the rich man a bill that covers his—shall I say?—charity."

Alan was angry, forgetting that he had started this conversation. But there was no use being angry with a crank.

"You think me a crank, no doubt." Alan was startled at the old man's penetration, but before he could offer an apology Dr. Phillips went on. "I don't know whether you were sent to me tonight, but now that you're here

I'm going to take it that you were. I don't like what I hear about your outfit. It's not doing much to uphold the high calling of the profession. Perhaps you do not know that the Chinese are a gossipy people. Nothing that takes place at your hospital is secret."

"We're not a religious order," Alan retorted.

The faded blue eyes of the old doctor sharpened. "The profession used to possess one of the attributes of an order." His voice was cool and cutting. "I refer to service."

"What do you expect of thirty virile men—highly skilled, most of them—set down here to a life of idleness?" Alan demanded.

"Idleness! Men with brains seeing for the first time a civilization older by centuries than their own, finding nothing to interest them in it? Too superior to study some of the enigmas of sickness right here before their eyes?" the sharp, crisp little man demanded. "You're an orthopedist, you say. Have you ever seen arthritis here? If it isn't here, why isn't it? Young man, don't think that by divine right you will forever lead the procession which carries the torch of healing."

Stirring in Alan's mind was the memory of his grandfather's admonition given in his farewell address. Oddly enough the two old men used the same words, "torch of healing," and both warned against its passing into other hands.

"Here," said Dr. Phillips, who rose and went to his bookcase and unlocked it with a key he took from his pocket. "I'm going to lend you this book, but I want you to take care of it. It's out of print. It's the history of Chinese medicine. You didn't know there was such a thing, did you? Here's a book on Chinese philosophy and one on Buddhism. Better take them all along. The next time you're distressed by the idleness forced upon you, try using your brains."

Back at the hospital, Alan put the books on his table, intending to keep them a day or two, then return them to their owner with a polite note. He was tired and went immediately to bed, only to find himself wide awake trying to answer the preposterous accusations the old doctor had brought against the American medical profession. Finally, unable to sleep, Alan switched on his light and reached for the book nearest him, the history of Chinese medicine. Its first page stated that in 2800 B.C. Chinese medicine was founded by the Divine Husbandman who had examined the hundred herbs and established the art. So thousands of years before American civilization had existed the Chinese had begun the search for healing. Even before the Greeks had made their contribution the Chinese had called healing an art.

Then the sick of this city as he had seen them this evening passed before Alan. Art, yes, but without science, our science, they'll never get anywhere.

He closed the book and picked up the volume on the philosophies of East and West. Turning the pages, he found his attention caught by a chapter on pain and disease. The East, by nature passive, accepted disease; the West, active, fought it. The author contended the two made a harmonious total. Man's spirit, if he were to conquer disease, must be balanced delicately between too great acquiescence, which led to defeat, and too great struggle, which led to rebellion, the harmony of the opposites—inertia and energy, passive and active, material and spiritual. Had he, as surgeon, Alan asked himself, been more than a good mechanic tinkering with the mechanism of the human body as the garage man did with a car's mechanism? The body, he saw with a flash of insight, must have its spiritual opposite in order to be healed. As he read, his horizons seemed to widen until instead of this small valley with its limitations and frustrations he was in space unlimited.

It was daylight when he closed the book. He must get some sleep. He was to be officer of the day—twenty-four hours on duty. During the next twelve hours he found no time for reading, but when night came and the few patients in the hospital were asleep and he sat at the desk in the main office with nothing to do but be on call if he were needed, he again opened the book on the philosophies of East and West. Fascinated, he read on and on. The vague gropings he had experienced in the spring during his walks in the country seemed to take on meaning.

He felt a strong need to communicate with Esther, share with her this new unfolding world. How much did she know of this larger universe? A good deal, he imagined, closely associated as she had been with her father. In the quiet night he wrote to her. The actual happenings of life so difficult for each to report to the other, often so banal when reported, had been holding them apart. But in this timeless world of the spirit he felt himself reunited with her. He didn't even bother to date the letter. Time meant nothing now, nor space, both of which before had so cruelly separated them.

Esther had found only a shadowy Alan in the microfilm copies of his letters. Now, reading, she felt his presence transcending the tiny photographed words.

The men of Alan's outfit had meant little to him. He was merely a good fellow exchanging the time of day with them, sharing the surface events of their life together. Now he began to wonder if there weren't some among them who, like himself, had been stirred by the enigmas of this great country of China—Gregg, the famous surgeon, for instance.

At dinner one evening Colonel Beck made the remark, "Pretty poor human beings, these Chinese. You'd think after a few thousand years they would have learned a little about medicine, wouldn't you?"

"Didn't we get ephedrine from them?" asked Alan.

"Oh, that! What's one drug when you think of what we've done in research?" said the colonel.

"We?" Alan lifted his eyebrows.

After dinner on leaving the mess hall Gregg caught up with him. "Why are you so hard on the colonel?" he asked. "He's getting more out of this than most of us. Suppose he is playing a part, he does it with zest. That's something in the midst of this dull routine, which seems to be our part in the tragedy of war."

"Kidding himself that he's a big guy?"

"Does that hurt anyone?"

"You mean tragedy has found its buffoon in the colonel?" Alan retorted.

"I'd hardly go as far as that."

Alan at his own door, feeling a little ashamed before the older man's tolerance, felt a desire to set himself right. "Won't you come in?" he asked. "Perhaps I'm loading onto the colonel my own dissatisfaction." He stood aside for the older man to enter.

"I see you have some of the mission doctor's books," said Gregg, sitting down on Alan's cot.

"I'm not the only one then?" said Alan eagerly.

As they talked he learned that Gregg had not only visited Dr. Phillips, but through him had been in touch with a Chinese doctor.

"And the Chinese concept of disease—what do you think of it?" asked Alan.

"I am a Western surgeon" was Gregg's cryptic answer.

5

SUMMER advanced. The heat increased, and Alan's interest even in talking to Gregg flagged. A half hour after dawn the sky, hot and brassy, was like a heated tent cloth hung to the mountain peaks. One morning Alan sat on the side of his bed waiting for his Chinese servant to bring him coffee. He was still leaden with the heavy sleep come at dawn, after hours of wakefulness when the moist heat of the night had crowded down on his already heat-saturated body. Suddenly he heard the air raid bell, warning of the approach of enemy planes, and then almost simultaneously, the sound of their propellers and the crash of bombs. He hastily drew on his thin trousers and shirt and hurried down the corridor to the main office.

Colonel Beck was already there, giving terse, clipped commands to the orderlies as the stretchers were taken from the ambulances just arriving from the airport. He turned to Alan. "You go ahead to the operating room. Gregg and I'll be there in a minute."

Under the hot lights shining down on the operating table all day the colonel and Gregg, with the younger surgeons assisting, amputated arms and legs, performed abdominal operations. Late in the afternoon when the last patient was carried from the operating room Alan admitted to himself that the colonel was a good surgeon.

But in the weeks that followed as Alan went about among the wounded he wished that a wiser man than Beck were head of the hospital. He thought of his grandfather, who, when he had been made head of a great English base hospital in the last war, had increased the recoveries to a high per cent. What did he do that wasn't done for these patients? his grandson asked himself more and more often as fall slipped into winter and winter into spring.

Some ingredient was lacking here that would help the men to recover. What was it that his grandfather was able to do for the wounded that none of them here with all their superb technique seemed able to do? The infection in wounds was much less than in the First World War due to advances in medical knowledge. But even when a patient's wounds healed quickly the man often remained sick. Sick in spirit from the terrible shock of modern warfare. Alan was beginning to think. Was the modern surgeon nothing but a good mechanic, as Alan had suspected that night nearly a year ago now, when he had been reading the philosophy of the East? Did his profession with all its modern scientific technique fail in getting at the root causes which govern recovery?

Well, if they were mechanics, they were certainly good ones, Alan reflected one day in the late spring as he studied the X rays taken of a young lieutenant's leg. The man had been brought in during the air raid with comminuted fractures in both legs just above the knee. Alan had expected the colonel to amputate, but with infinite patience he had used traction to get the fragments of the bone into alignment. In the tedious months that followed after the lieutenant had been immobilized in a cast Alan had marveled at the man's acceptance, seemingly inexhaustible, of both pain and boredom. It drove Alan one day to say, "You're the most patient man around here. What's your secret?"

"Perhaps I don't look at the delay the way you do," the young man answered.

Alan's curiosity was roused by his remark. "I see by your history you were majoring in philosophy before the war. Rather a long jump to being a bombardier, wasn't it?"

"I've never reconciled my two occupations, Major."

"You think it can be done?"

"No" was the man's laconic reply.

The conversation came back to Alan now as he studied the X rays.

There was a tap on his shoulder. "Too absorbed to recognize my step?"

Alan sprang to attention, gave the salute the colonel insisted on. "I was having a look at these X rays," he added in apology, annoyed with himself that he should feel it necessary to make an apology.

"Anything wrong?" Colonel Beck asked, looking over Alan's shoulder.

"Everything's O.K.," said Alan. "Only I can't get him to walk."

"Why do you say he can't? Of course he can. It's up to you to make him. You ought to be able by this time to recognize the shirker." The colonel threw down the films he had picked up. "If you can't do it, I can." He strode down the corridor to the ward, Alan following. "I've just been looking at your last X rays, Treadwell. Everything's all right. You should be back with your unit very shortly. I've left orders that you're to get up today."

The young officer neither answered nor showed by the slightest change of expression that he had heard the colonel.

Alan, wishing he could kick Beck who was now striding ahead of him out of the ward, had been intending to lead the young lieutenant slowly to the point where he would accept his recovery. He believed the man faced with horror the return to the destruction he was helping to carry on.

After the rounds of the ward Alan instructed the orderly to have the lieutenant taken to the tank. When he had been lowered into the warm water, Alan said in the gentlest of tones, "Try it, Treadwell. You can move your legs a little, certainly." There was no answer or movement. Alan spoke sharply. "Show a little spunk, Treadwell. There's nothing wrong with your legs. It's just that they're weak from lack of use."

"I'm not going to live," the lieutenant called out suddenly in a high-pitched tone.

Alan turned away with a feeling of distaste. "Take him back to his bed," he ordered. He wrote on his chart an order for a sedative to be given the lieutenant if he showed any further signs of hysteria.

That evening when the hospital was quiet, Alan, officer of the day, did not open the book he had brought with him. He was thinking of the lieutenant. He rose, intending to look in on him. Just then the night nurse entered. "He's dead, Dr. Towne—Lieutenant Treadwell." Doctor and nurse stood confronting each other. Accustomed as they were to death, both were shocked.

In the morning Colonel Beck reported the lieutenant's death due to an embolism of the lung, but Alan could not so easily dismiss the death of a healthy young man. A startling thought occurred to him. Had the man died because he wanted to? Had death been the only solution for him? Were the spirit and the body in too great conflict? He tried to close his mind against such unorthodox thinking. But he could not rid himself of the idea. If it were so, then he was in part to blame. In all the months when the lieutenant had had little to do but think, Alan had simply looked after the man's physical injury. There had been plenty of times when he might have offered him companionship, but other than that one question about Tread-well's former occupation he had never troubled himself to do so. If he had brought the lieutenant the books he himself was reading, he might have stirred so intelligent a man to less destructive thoughts than he had evidently been indulging in.

Alan was busy in his room the next evening when there was a knock on his door and Murphy, the most carefree, the gayest of the younger doctors, entered and took possession of Alan's cot, sprawling his six feet two over its length. "What in hell happened last night?" he asked, coming quickly to the point of his visit.

"What do you mean?" asked Alan.

"Oh, come on. It's no secret. Why the devil cover for that old fool Beck after the way he bullied the guy who died last night? I got it straight from my girl." He winked at Alan.

"What's it got to do with me?" Alan demanded.

Murphy settled himself a little more comfortably, indicating he intended to stay. "You think it could have been avoided."

Alan was startled. Had his thoughts been as apparent as that?

"We're due for an inspection in a day or two," Murphy added.

"What of it?"

"Nothing—except if we played it right we might bounce the colonel—show him up."

"But he's a good surgeon—which is more than you can say for most C.O.'s."

Murphy groaned. "You old New Englander!"

"I don't happen to be one. However, I don't want to frame the old bird. If that's being a New Englander, then I am one."

Alan saw now what Murphy was after. Colonel Beck evidently had had him up for behavior unbecoming to an officer. Alan squirmed inwardly when he thought of the solemnity the colonel had probably put into the interview, perhaps even threatened Murphy with a court-martial. Murphy's plan was to discredit the colonel before he was discredited.

"All you have to do," Murphy was saying, "is to tell the inspector what Beck said to the lieutenant. My eye, that's not framing the old blighter!"

Although Alan a moment before had rejected such a deal as shabby, it suddenly didn't seem so. A hot-air artist like the colonel had it coming to him.

Colonel Smith from the inspector general's office was about through with his investigation. It looked as if he'd better recommend that Beck be removed, maybe demoted. Two thirds of the doctors had brought in complaints against Beck. Yet somehow there seemed something phony about the whole thing. He couldn't put his finger on it. The day he arrived, Colonel Beck had met him at the airport, assured, even cocky.

"Glad to have you look us over" had been his first words. "We've got a pretty fine outfit here." He was as eager as a boy to show off his hospital. "As soon as you've rested," he said, "I'll take you round."

Then there had been that disconcerting incident. The nurse so punctiliously deferential as she accompanied them through the ward had suddenly gone to pieces. Colonel Smith had laid it to tension over his visit. But two or three like happenings later in the day pointed to a Nazi type of discipline. Had this colonel, so evidently childish in his love of uniforms and his insistence on all the spit and polish of the military, fallen victim to the enemy's philosophy? There had also been Major Towne's hint of some bullying of a patient by the colonel. "Get me Captain Gregg," the inspector called to his assistant. They had been close friends in civilian life.

On entering Captain Gregg solemnly saluted the inspector, as had all the others. Then he grinned.

"Sit down, Gregg. What kind of a story have you to tell? Have you any complaints?" the inspector asked, studying the gray-haired surgeon.

"Everything is going as well as you could expect," Gregg replied.

"That's not what the others say."

"I'm older than most of them. We can't all be paragons. I'd say offhand Colonel Beck has been made the goat."

"But isn't it the colonel's fault that a goat is needed?"

"One goat is as good as another. You'd simply be taking away the target for the men's dissatisfaction if you removed him. They'd find another if they didn't have him," said Gregg.

The inspector looked puzzled. Then he asked, "Why do they need a target?"

"The war has passed us by, for the most part," Gregg answered.

"You mean there's not enough to do here?"

Gregg nodded.

"What would you do about it?"

"Shuffle a few of the hotheads and two or three of the more skilled. With a full T-O, we're overstaffed."

"But not remove Colonel Beck?"

"If you're transferring the skilled, I suppose you'd transfer him," Gregg answered. "He should be operating every day. And for the same reason I'd transfer Major Towne."

The inspector again studied Gregg, who he knew had left a lucrative and distinguished practice. "When I recommend the other transfers, I think I'll suggest you be put in command here."

"Me!"

The inspector laughed. "Why not? I have an idea you are wasted, too."

It'll take some doing, he thought, but once in a while headquarters listens to my recommendations. There'll be some unhappy majors and lieutenant colonels if I get a captain jumped over their heads. But I kind of like to see the right man get the job.

❧ 6 ❧

THE PLANE taking the doctors to their new stations rose and quickly gained altitude. Alan looked down on the Valley. A few weeks ago it had stood for widening horizons and a greater communication with Esther, but of late it had shrunk to its original proportions, an imprisoned land from which he was now escaping.

Soon the Valley with its frustrations was behind him, barricaded by the lofty peaks of the Himalayas. The hospital in India to which he had been assigned was large and crowded to capacity, he understood. He had every reason to be elated, but he was not. The grapevine had it that Captain, now Lieutenant Colonel Gregg, had chosen the men to work with him, and he, Alan Towne, had not been one of them. Did Gregg suspect him of helping to frame Beck? Alan cursed himself for being a fool to fall into the trap Murphy had set for him—using him, that's what Murphy had been doing, getting him to tell the inspector how Beck had bullied the lieutenant just before his death, as if bullying Treadwell had anything to do with it. Sam had often pointed out to his brother the danger of deviation from well-established professional beliefs. What would Gregg think of such a remark? Alan remembered that once he had asked Gregg about the men's slow recovery, and Gregg had closed up, saying, "You're getting out of my specialty," or something like that. Gregg thought him a crackpot and so had kicked him upstairs. Alan flushed in humiliation. It was no comfort to him to look at Beck's great hulk squeezed into the bucket seat beside him or at Murphy sitting across from him, sulking over his assignment to a hospital in the jungle where there were only male nurses.

The plane dropped to its first landing in India. Here Alan left the others. When he reported for duty at the hospital in the near-by city, Colonel Reeves, the head of the hospital, asked, "Are you by any chance related to the famous Dr. Towne?"

"I'm his grandson."

"Splendid!" said Colonel Reeves. "I saw something of his work during the last war in the hospital in England. You'll have a chance to see his theories firsthand here. We are trying to hasten rehabilitation of men along the lines he worked out. We've gone somewhat farther, of course, during the years. I imagine your grandfather has carried his ideas a little farther, too. He's the kind that keeps growing. I think I'll let you help us out in the convalescent ward where we're working with men's minds as well as their bodies."

"I don't know too much about my grandfather's ideas of rehabilitation," Alan hastened to say. "I've always thought of him as a surgeon. He was a wizard at surgery. That's what I'm interested in. It's been a frustrating experience—these months when I've been shut off from much operating."

"Well, if that's the case, I'll assign you to the operating room," Colonel Reeves answered, disappointed. Unfortunately a genius does not pass it on to his descendants, he thought. Imagine a grandson of Dr. Samuel Towne having no more intellectual curiosity than that! Hasn't even taken the trouble to learn what an outstanding contribution his grandfather made to the recovery of wounded men!

Guess I rather jammed it through, thought Alan as he went out, but I've just got to operate.

He plunged into operating with unrelenting zeal despite the fact that India was entering its hottest season. Again he had little to write Esther. He couldn't keep telling her about operations he had performed, much as he would have liked to. He was pretty sure it would bore her, if the books she was sending him were any indication of where her interests lay, books which he was too tired to read after his long hours in the operating room. But his letters to Sam were the best he had ever written him.

He was making a brilliant record for himself. Only one or two of the surgeons in the hospital equaled him in speed or precision. But after two months of such concentration it began to tell on him. He would come from operating keyed to a high point of nervous tension. He laid it to his anxiety over the outcome of the war and his dislike of India—so passive, refusing its share of the burden of war. And when the monsoons began and rain fell in unrelenting torrents, the monotonous beat, beat of the falling rain was an added burden on his mind. He craved diversion as he never had before, but there was little available.

The native city was foul. Death and disease lurked in its unsanitary narrow streets. The foreign section was a superimposed fragile embroidery of the Occident. Its members, exclusive and arrogant, wished to have nothing to do with the heterogeneous array of men war had thrown into their midst. At the parties of the doctors and nurses Alan often found himself—by intent of the other doctors, he suspected—paired off with a laboratory technician who had the reputation of being about as responsive as the test tubes with which she worked. Alan was content, for he was not out for romance. He entertained himself trying to see if he couldn't break down her cool impersonality, but without success until one evening when, probing for a weak point in her armor, he said, "Why a girl like you should be named Shirley is beyond me. You haven't a ruffle or a furbelow anywhere in your nature."

"Is that meant for an insult?" she asked, flushing angrily.

"No, it's just that it's incongruous. You are the 'give us this day our daily bread' sort of person. Shirley is party stuff."

"Maybe you'd like my second name better. It's Martha," she answered. "The truth is," she went on, unbending a little, "my mother, who is romantic, named me Shirley. Martha is an old family name," she ended with pride, forgetting that always before she had hated it.

"Well, it's Martha from now on." Alan smiled down on her, feeling some satisfaction that he had broken through to the real flesh-and-blood person hiding behind the prim little spinster with the flossy name of Shirley. At least she had displayed enough red blood to get angry.

Martha was excited. Heretofore ignored by the other doctors, she was from now on singled out by Dr. Towne, the kind of man she had long dreamed of. Not only was he one of the outstanding surgeons in the hospital, he was distinguished-looking, if not handsome. His consideration of her she found enthralling. She had never experienced anything like it during the hard years she had struggled to make something of herself. Before she realized it she was deeply in love with him. The knowledge that Dr. Towne was married and in love with his wife had not prevented it, she told herself helplessly. In some curious, backhanded fashion she found satisfaction in imagining she occupied his wife's place, vicariously experiencing what she thought marriage to Alan would be like. The protective quality of his love for Esther fascinated her. Even here in far-off India he worried for fear something might happen to her—that she might need him and he not be there.

"Hasn't she any relatives she can go to?" Martha asked one evening.

"Not near ones," Alan answered. "But look, I should think you'd throw me out, always talking about my own affairs. I am concerned over Esther, but that's no reason to burden you with it."

"You're not burdening me," she answered simply.

It's awfully decent of her, he thought, and with that rare, almost naïve expansiveness which the self-contained person sometimes displays when he does let down the barriers, he rushed on to say, "You see, it's more than that she is alone. She doesn't know America too well and still has a pretty lofty idea of us—at least she did. Now that she's doing volunteer nursing in a hospital she may find out there's racial prejudice in America, too. She may find it hard to accept because of her great love for her mother."

"You mean she's a Jew?" exclaimed Martha.

"Of course you'll consider what I said was in confidence," Alan hastened to say. Something in Martha's expression had made him draw back. He felt for a moment as if he had betrayed Esther.

"Of course I will," Martha promised. She wouldn't have told it to anyone for the world. Vividly there came into her mind the section of the city where she had been brought up and where the feuds among the Jews, Catholics and Protestants were relived among their children. Her family's proud belief in its superiority had always been a warm cloak she drew around her as she went among her more prosperous but heretical neighbors. To her parents such a marriage as Dr. Towne's was considered a disgrace. Indeed she would keep this secret!

That night she did not sleep, struggling with confusion, doubt and humiliation. The friendship of which she had been so proud was nothing to be proud of after all. What would her people think of such a man? Finally she resolved not to see him any more. But when he dropped into the laboratory the next day she could not hold to her decision and accepted his invitation for the evening, an awful joy taking hold of her. During the day she persuaded herself that Esther was an adventuress who had taken advantage of Alan's chivalry. It was right, Martha told herself, to set aside the rigid ideas of marriage she had been brought up with, in order to rescue Alan from such a woman. It was right for her to break up a marriage like that, win him for herself if she could.

Martha had been reared in a hard world where one fought with all the weapons at one's disposal. Now that it was right for her to win Alan away from his wife, she began exploiting his kindness, telling him of her struggle to get an education. Hardship which she had met with fierce independence, she believed now had been almost impossible to bear.

"My dear," he said very gently one evening, "you're the kind of woman who should be taken care of."

"You've taught me there is such a thing as kindness in the world," she answered quietly.

As the days slipped into weeks Alan ceased to speak of Esther. It was two years since their brief honeymoon. Although he often longed for her, his longing, so sharp at first, had gradually softened. India was at once taking toll of his strength and sharpening his senses. The flesh-and-blood Martha laid a spell over his days, days held suspended in sensuous India.

Then suddenly he was drawn back into his own world. One afternoon as he was leaving the hospital he was handed a cable from Sam telling of their father's death. Picture after picture of his father passed before him almost with the vividness of sight. "The good gray Francis," his mother had called him, growing grayer with the years. One final picture—the four Towne men standing together under the light on the veranda—the beautiful chiseled lines of his father's face, the quiet mouth, the steady quiet eyes.

When one, two, three days passed and Martha heard nothing from Alan and careful questions asked of the nurses revealed that he wasn't sick, she became frightened. She was losing him! Was it to one of the nurses? Why hadn't she led him on to a closer union? For surely he loved her. But she had always been a good girl, as her mother had trained her to be. Surely she'd be rewarded for that. Another day and she could bear it no longer. She called him, asking if anything was wrong.

"Oh, no," he said. "I just haven't been fit company for anyone."

"Let's find a quiet corner where you can tell me what's troubling you," she said when later he joined her.

Alan gratefully accepted the relief of talking to someone about his father. "I blame myself for making so little effort to be a companion to him. As I think of it now, there was a ground on which neither of his sons met him. It was a bit as if he tried to speak to both Sam and me, but it was in a key too high for either of us to hear. You know there are tones the human ear doesn't get. Perhaps it's so with the mind, too."

Panic seized Martha. He was talking of things she did not understand. He was leaving her world and going back to his own. "No, no," her heart cried out. "He's mine!"

They had been sitting in a corner of the veranda that ran around the women's dormitory, a two-story brick house built high off the ground, once the home of a British officer. They were sheltered here from any onlooker. Alan rose to go. Martha walked with him to the flight of steps which led down to the once carefully kept garden, now after the rains a jungle of trees and vines which shielded them. Alan started down the steps, then turned. "I can't tell you what you've meant to me tonight, Martha."

Suddenly she leaned forward and kissed him full on the mouth. He reached out and grasped her tightly, pressing his lips harder and harder against hers. Under the bruising pressure passion grown to intensity during its long denial swept through her, communicating its violence to Alan.

❧ 7 ❧

On Sam's first day in his office after his father's death he had to lengthen his office hours in order to deal with even the most urgent cases. At the end of the afternoon, going over the appointments his receptionist had made for the following day, he saw a chance of getting back to his regular schedule very soon. The training he had given his receptionist and nurses for clocklike precision in handling office calls by emphasizing the war and the shortage of doctors was standing him in good stead. When he found them slowing down, taking extra time with a patient, he reminded them of the men and women who daily stood in a long line in the lobby waiting a place in the elevators, waiting their turn in his and other offices throughout the building.

The suite he occupied at the top of the medical building was quiet now with the afterhours stillness which came when the door had closed behind his secretary, the last to leave before his own departure. Usually he prepared to leave at once but today he lingered, for he was waiting for Jo, whom he had asked to meet him here. He went to the windows that looked out over the city. How it had grown in his lifetime! He thought of the heated discussion a few years ago over changing its name. Some of the newcomers claimed that Athenia was an absurd name for a thriving industrial center, but the old residents had clung doggedly to it.

Looking down now over the panorama spread out below him this spring evening, Sam was inclined to believe that the oldsters were right. Athens, from which the name Athenia had come, had reached the highest culture ever attained in the ancient world; the United States had now reached the highest pinnacle of well-being in the world today, its citizens the best-housed, the best-clothed, the freest from disease of all the peoples of the world. The Athenia he looked at from his window, so nearly at America's center, could well stand as the symbol of the greatness of the industrial age and of its beauty, too, as Sam saw it. From his vantage point its long straight streets appeared to radiate from the medical building. To the left rose the smokestacks of many factories, gigantic, splendid columns, creating a rhythmic and balanced industrial Karnak, if not a Parthenon. To the right the exclusive residential district where he lived was hidden in the sharp spring green of its many trees. He held his gaze away from the old part of the city where his father had lived.

To look there would bring back the shock and grief of his father's death, which undoubtedly could have been avoided had he been willing to come to live with Sam. Since Alan had gone overseas Sam believed that his father had neglected himself. Not until he had let a cold drift far into pneumonia had he called his elder son. All that the finest specialists of the city then could do had been too late.

Francis Towne was a silent man whom Sam did not understand, a good deal like Grandfather Towne. He, too, lived alone and refused to let the family look after him. It had hurt Sam to see how old his grandfather looked at the burial of his only son. But there is nothing I can do about it, thought Sam. I'd better be planning for those who listen to me.

As soon as he heard from Alan he would put the old home on the market. The neighborhood had deteriorated rapidly in the last few years. It was mean and drab now. His father's house and garden were remnants of another day. Until Sam was twelve and Alan six the house had been a congregating place for Athenia's leading citizens. And then suddenly, with the illness of their mother, isolation had descended on it—no longer the coming and going of friends; instead, nurses and doctors who would not allow Sam to see his mother. After her death the house had become a hostile place presided over by the woman whom Alan and he had hated.

It seemed to him almost immediately old friends began moving away to new and more fashionable parts of the city. In all the years since, as he thought of it now, he had been hampered by his father's refusal to follow. The determination to win back for his family the position in Athenia lost at his mother's death had kept Sam always a little under strain. He wanted the best for Jo and Sally and, of course, Alan, who had always been his peculiar responsibility.

He was proud of this brother gayer than he, more brilliant than he, and above all able to make himself felt in any group—no matter how important —if he wished to. But Alan still needs guidance and protection, thought Sam, because of his natural kindness which he has not as yet learned how to manage and which often leads him to make friends with the wrong people.

The opening of the outer door of the suite echoed through the silent rooms. Sam turned from the window, recognizing Jo's step as she came down the passageway that led from the waiting room, past his examination rooms and laboratory, to his private office at the end of the corridor. "I'm here," he called out.

When Jo entered, she noticed how relaxed her husband seemed standing there leaning against the window frame. Was he less disturbed by his father's death than she had thought? Sam's feeling for his father she had never entirely understood. That his own happiness often seemed to be jeopardized by the older man's way of life, she had early grasped. Did Sam—unconsciously, of course—feel his future was more assured now? Was that binding sense of obligation to the family made less or greater by his father's death? She yearned to know.

Jo had not accompanied Sam in the journey back to New York State for the burial of her father-in-law. She would have liked to go. She believed it would have meant something to Grandfather Towne—and she hoped to Sam—to have her near, but she had agreed that Sally was too young for such a journey and also too young to be left behind. On Sam's return this morning he had stopped at the house only long enough to change and bathe after the night in the plane. Why he had called later asking her to come to the office this afternoon had puzzled her. Home would have seemed a more fitting place to tell her of the events of the last few days.

As if guessing her thoughts he said, "It may seem odd to you that I asked you to come to the office today of all days, but I wanted you to help me refurnish this room. You'd think I had enough to do right now with the added duty of settling up Father's estate without taking this on, wouldn't you?" he asked with a deprecating smile. "I hadn't realized until I got back today how shabby the whole place was. I'm thinking of taking a more active part than I have before in the management of the building, and I want a comfortable place for the doctors to meet who are deciding policy."

"Perhaps it's a relief for you to construct and plan just now," Jo answered, thinking, He feels free now to climb as high as he can, and that is very high. But he wants me to assure him it's the right thing to do at this time. He has been a dutiful son. He should without any sense of guilt allow his ambitions full play.

Jo understands, he thought gratefully, that I need to find some way to put aside my grief.

Together they made plans. "Why not turn this cupboard into a place where you could make coffee for yourselves? Your couch could go over here," she suggested. For an hour they were companions in the undertaking.

Afterward, walking down the corridor, she asked, "How would you like to go out to the Country Club for dinner? It's Thursday, you know. No maid at home." His moment's hesitation, she felt, was due to what always had seemed to her an exaggerated sense of propriety. "It's a beautiful evening. I think it would rest you," she urged.

"What about Sally?"

"She's off with some friends."

"My only objection," he said, taking her arm and falling into step with her. In the empty corridor their steps echoed rhythmically.

Making their way to their table, considerately placed by the headwaiter in a corner made secluded by a pillar that hid them from most of the diners, they passed many people they knew. As Sam took his seat opposite her, she said, "I hope you didn't mind. I forgot there'd be a crowd here this evening."

"Quite the contrary," he answered. "For some reason I feel especially welcomed here tonight. I hadn't realized we had so many friends among the members. Do you remember our first night here when we didn't know anyone in the whole dining room? Has it been worth your part—which is very great?" he asked. His strong fingers closed over Jo's hand where it lay on the napkin she was about to pick up. There was in that gesture and his question an acknowledgment of partnership never before made but for which all her married life she had longed.

"Yes," she murmured, her eyes saying what she could not trust her voice to express. Despite his passionate love for her, despite his constant need of her, she believed in some odd way she had always remained an outsider to him. He had constantly sought through some new renunciation on her part to reassure himself that she really belonged to him. He was at last placing her coequal with himself.

"Cocktails?" he asked.

When they were brought, he raised his. "To ourselves!" A conventional toast, but it held a peculiar meaning for Jo. She looked away. On the distant horizon the sun's brilliant disk was level with the wide stretch of lawn outside the window; its low-lying light set shimmering each individual blade of grass. A group of trees with their leaves still small were delicately defined against the rays shooting upward from the sun. Jo stared into the brilliance not more blinding than her hope. For the first time in their married life she believed that Sam had accepted her completely.

He lifted his head and smiled, then handed his order to the waiter, picked up his cocktail, sipped leisurely. She saw him anew this evening; his keen gray eyes, his heavy iron-gray hair brushed straight back from his temples, his graying heavy eyebrows and his hands, strong and intelligent—perhaps his most marked characteristic—all emphasized his maturity.

"Sam, you offered me something very precious a few minutes ago."

"Did I?" he asked.

"Yes, full partnership."

"Haven't you always had it?" he asked. "You've always been my first consideration, Jo dear. It's been sweet to take care of you. Sometimes I've thought you misunderstood why I didn't want you to practice. But you do understand now that I didn't want you out taking the knocks you'd have to. If I can protect you, give you the dignified position you deserve, it's all I ask. Now that I'm established I can do it in full measure."

The light was gone from the greensward outside the long windows and from Jo's eyes. She felt herself caught in the coils of his love. "Sam, let me explain a little about myself," she begged.

"After being married to you for fifteen years do you think it's necessary?" he asked. "Wouldn't I be a little dumb if by this time I didn't understand you?" His smile was edged with irony.

"I've only lately learned to understand myself," she answered. "I need to struggle, Sam, even to be hurt in order to mean what I should to myself and so to you. If I am protected too much, I lose my sense of your world."

"You're not content then just with our home?"

"Of late, no. When you were struggling to make an income and Sally was little I had enough at home to make my life vital, but not lately. I felt myself growing dull and irritable. I wasn't meaning anything to you."

"Oh, but you've never been like that, at least not more than every woman is at times. Little things don't bother me as long as I know you really have nothing to worry about."

Jo was affronted by his attitude of sureriority. She would not let him rule her, as always before. This time she must see it through. "Sam, it is good for everyone to work. I've been helping out in a clinic for a year. Not for pay," she hastened to add, seeing his eyes pin-point with opposition, "and I've not gone under your name, thinking you might not like it. I've been known only as Dr. Jo. It's freshened me. I've felt vital, and I believe I've been able to mean more to you and to Sally."

Looking at him, knowing each change of mood, seeing the shuttered expression of his eyes, the tight set to his mouth telling of his complete withdrawal into himself, she realized she had gambled on his understanding and lost. But there was one more appeal she could make. "Every doctor's needed just now, Sam. There's such a shortage."

"You think me lacking in patriotism," he answered. "It's not enough that I let Alan go and am carrying a double load. You think I should come home to a wife who is too tired to take care of her house or her child."

"Have I ever neglected either?" asked Jo. "Have you noticed any difference this last winter?"

He did not reply, but during the rest of the dinner with studied nonchalance he held their conversation to surface matters—a funny story another doctor had told him, witty remarks about some of the people in the dining room. In spite of the sense of defeat settling over her, Jo had to smile, but she winced a little, too, for his witticisms were cruel, exposing the frailties even of their friends.

The dinner that had promised so much for her was over. As they rose Sam was aware as he had not been for some time of his tall, good-looking wife and how at their first meeting he had coveted her, wanting to make her the temple of his own proud soul, take possession of the innermost secret chamber. Tonight he had learned he never would. For an instant he wished her small, helpless and clinging, but he would not have wanted her then.

When they were in the car Sam suddenly dropped his flippant talk. "Suppose we drive for a little. There are things I should tell you about the changes Father's death will mean."

He's recovering from the shock, thought Jo with profound relief. We'll find a basis yet on which each of us can live to the full. Francis Towne not long before his death had given her hope that such an adjustment would sometime come about if she would be patient. For a little she had thought she hadn't been patient enough tonight, but after all it seemed to be coming out all right.

Her thoughts strayed from what Sam was telling her of how he planned to sell the old house as soon as he heard from Alan and plow the money back into the medical building to memories of her father-in-law. She had loved the quiet, self-effacing Francis Towne; she mourned his passing.

Then she was brought sharply back. Sam was saying, "Grandfather is working too hard. He's lost a good deal of weight. He's beginning to stoop. I begged him not to take any new patients."

"What did he say?" she asked.

" 'No new problems? I'd die.' "

"It sounds just like him, doesn't it?" she answered. With a catch in her voice she asked, "Is he really failing?"

"I asked Esther to run up to see him whenever she could. By the way, she looked tired. I don't think much of this nursing business. She has a month's vacation this summer. Why not ask her to spend it with us? Maybe you could persuade her to go to live with Grandfather."

"You'd like me to work on her to give up her nursing. Me of all people, when I——" She stopped in the middle of her sentence, seeing where Sam had been leading her.

"Don't you want her to visit us?" he asked. "You said something about your life being dull with just me."

"Oh, Sam," she exclaimed, "you know I didn't say any such thing!"

Later in the evening Jo came into the room Sam called his retreat, where he sat by his desk. "Here, Sam," she said, "I've written Esther. I thought you might like to add a word."

Carefully he read the letter. He picked up a pencil and crossed out a word here and there. "I think that will do," he said at last, handing it back.

"Do you regard me as a child bringing my homework for your approval?" she asked. "Is it to that status you have relegated me? Oh, Sam, don't let us quarrel!" she pleaded.

Looking up, he saw her lips were quivering. Well, she had hurt him first. Then he was angry. "For God's sake," he said, "don't act like a child, or one of those clinging kind of women!"

"I have no intention of doing so," she answered.

"One moment," he said. "I've given up the idea of letting Sally go to camp this summer."

"But, Sam, she's counting on it!"

"She'll want to be home if Esther comes."

It was clear to Jo that Sam was arranging the household in such a way that she would have no time for work in the clinic. Yes, she'd be busy. Sally, deprived of camp, would take a good part of her time if the child were to be kept happy. All her friends would be away. But it was idle to protest if Sam had made up his mind. Somehow he would persuade Sally that she would rather be at home.

ℒ 8 ℒ

On a day in late July Jo and Sally drove to the railway station early in order to find a parking place before Esther's train arrived. Sam was to come directly from the office. Sally moved between the platform and the entrance, fearful her father would not arrive in time. The headlights of the diesel engine appeared in the distance, grew larger, and still there was no sign of her father. Half child, half woman, she seemed to Jo—her hat on one side just as it had always been when as a little girl she was excited, her brown eyes large with childlike delight.

Jo was giving only scant attention to the incoming train and Sam's arrival, so intent was she on her daughter. Her thin little face had filled out in the last months. Her long, pointed chin, her mouth—once much too large for her face—now seemed more in proportion to the rest of her features. But the greatest change was in her figure. The flat chest of childhood was gone. On their latest buying expedition Sally had shyly chosen dresses that showed her firm little breasts to advantage. She was going to make a splendid woman, warm and tender, passionate too, if only she could be allowed to grow naturally. A sudden memory of her daughter as a very little girl flashed through Jo's mind. Sally was so small at the time that she had stood on a stool to whisper in her mother's ear, "I want a baby." Mistaking the child's meaning, Jo had whispered back, "I think I'm going to have one for you," and Sally had whispered, "I know, but I want one myself." Perhaps if the baby had lived Sally would have found satisfaction for the urge toward motherhood she evidently felt even at that age.

"Car 77. It's clear down at the other end of the train." Sam, unnoticed by Jo, had arrived. Taking her arm and Sally's, he hurried them the length of the platform. Sam was right, thought Jo, watching Esther as she came down the steps of the train: she looks tired. And then that surprisingly sudden renewal of vitality Jo had noticed take place in Esther on her wedding day had taken place as she drew Sally to her.

Soon they were seated in the car, Sam at the wheel, Sally beside him. Odd, thought Jo, sitting with Esther on the back seat. Sally had asked on the way down if she might have the coveted place by Esther.

"It'll not be nearly so hard for Alan on his return if Esther makes a place for herself now among our friends, and she no doubt will," Sam said to Jo as they waited in the living room for Esther to join them for dinner. Watching her a few minutes later come down the stairs and enter the room,

Sam shrewdly evaluated her effect on the women in the bracket of society in which he and Jo now moved. Esther was dressed much as she had been when he had first met her over two years ago now—a sheer black dress, a string of pearls around her throat which intensified the creamy color of her skin. That slight suggestion of the European about her did indeed give her distinction, something that would not be lost on his friends.

"What a lovely room!" Esther exclaimed.

Each chair, each table acquired through the years took on a new meaning for Sam as he recounted their history. "Do you call this Early American?" she asked.

"Oh, no, the crude attempts of the pioneers never interested me," he answered. Esther remembered then that Alan had told her Sam never visited the homestead in Massachusetts and had said he thought that part of their family history was well forgotten.

"This came a little later when there was more wealth, more refinement," Sam went on, touching with obvious pleasure the hand-rubbed surface of a table. "I'm glad you like it. If the room has distinction, I think you enhance it."

Esther was for the moment taken aback by the compliment and the unwonted warmth in his voice. The fastidious Sam, she had felt, had been reevaluating her since her arrival, against his own environment, a kind of final test of his acceptance of her. It would seem he had finally made up his mind that she was a fitting mate for his beloved brother.

While Alan had been in that valley surrounded by the Himalayas he had seemed so near to her that he was like a shining armor protecting her, but since he went to India she had lost the sense of his presence. Now in this room with its four walls shielding her and with Sam's final approval of her, she had a comforting sense of being once more in touch with Alan. Here was Sam, who idolized his younger brother, ready to include her in his affections, anxious to place her within the family circle and within the community to which she and Alan would belong when he returned.

Jo, watching the little scene, saw that Sam was at his best. There was this evening something of that quality of easement from strain she had noticed on the day after his father's funeral, but which she had destroyed when she revealed to him she had been working. Would Esther's coming set things right between them?

"Jo, Sally isn't going out, is she?" asked Sam. Where he stood he could see several girls coming down the stairs and going toward the front door.

Jo did not need to answer. Sally's clear voice rose above the others, saying good-by to her friends. "Have a good time at camp for me."

"See you in the fall," they called back. "Too bad you can't come, but of course if your father needs you——"

Into the silence of the living room Sally came. She looked at her mother. Had she heard what the girls said? Was the secret she shared with her father out?

"Of course your old father needs you," said Sam, drawing her to him, covering for her and himself.

During the long days of summer when the tempo of war increased and consequently anxiety over its outcome, the family drew closer and closer together. Good for all of them except Sally, Jo thought. She was beginning to fear that Sally was growing up too rapidly, assuming responsibilities she shouldn't have to carry. She often wished the child was at camp, away from the impact of war. One day she talked to Esther about it. "Am I too anxious?" she asked. "She's always been a sensitive child."

"I saw something like it among the children in England during the first year of the war."

"Then you have noticed it," said Jo.

"Sally was a child, of course, when I first met her," Esther answered.

"And you think she isn't now?" urged Jo.

"If she were more with girls of her own age——"

"Probably I'm overanxious," Jo interrupted, then added lightly, "Mothers usually are."

Doesn't she see that Sam demands more than a child can give? Esther wondered.

One evening Sam said to Esther, "I thought coming this summer would give you a chance to see how you can help Alan when he gets back. Medicine is about the most competitive business there is. In order to succeed both socially and professionally Alan will need to save himself wherever he can. He is apt to let his sympathies carry him too far. He must learn how to dismiss any individual at the end of the period allotted to him. We're surgeons. It's not up to us to solve a patient's emotional problems."

Sam was quick to see that he had puzzled Esther by these remarks. Possibly she wasn't so intelligent as he had thought her. "Does all this bewilder you?" he asked.

"A little," she answered. "I was trying to relate what you said to what I had seen of medicine in Europe. It's so different. Perhaps it isn't regarded so much as a business over there. Usually you see a doctor in a room in his own house. He isn't in a hurry——"

"Ah, there it is!" said Sam. "We're much farther advanced here in the United States. We're miles ahead scientifically. Someday, when I'm not pressed as I am just now, would you like to see how we do it here?"

"I'd love to," Esther hastened to say, feeling she had lost a little ground with him and wanting to get it back.

It was several days before he alluded to the matter again. In the meantime Jo took her to luncheons with her friends and to play golf at the Country Club. Esther noticed how often Jo's mind seemed to be elsewhere. Her interest is really in her profession, she decided, noting how often Jo led her to talk of her work as a volunteer nurse in the hospital in New York, and then would tell of her own experiences as an intern. "I know what you're asking yourself," Jo said during one of their conversations: "why I am idle when there's such a shortage of doctors. Last winter when I was——" She suddenly broke off.

"When you were what?" asked Esther.

"I didn't mean to mention it, but you're too clever not to guess where my interest lies. I might as well confess. I did work in a clinic last winter."

People come alive when she tells about them, especially children, thought Esther, as Jo, after a little urging, told of her experiences at the clinic. "You're not working there now. Is it because I'm here? I wouldn't for the world interfere. Sally and I could entertain ourselves. I'd hate to think I was the cause of a good doctor not helping out at a critical time like this."

"I wouldn't be doing it anyway. It seemed wiser to give it up for the summer. You won't say anything about all this before Sam, will you? He doesn't look at it as I do."

They had been crossing the golf course together. As if to prevent any further discussion, Jo strode ahead. When she turned, Esther thought she looked as carefree as all the rest of the women playing golf this morning. To the outside world she was a woman of leisure, the wife of a successful doctor—and that evidently was what Sam wanted her to be.

Esther was puzzled when that evening Sam proposed that she go with him to his office the next morning. It did not seem to fit in with his idea of what a wife's role should be.

Sally was perched on the arm of her father's chair at the time. "Oh, let me come, too, Daddy," she begged.

"You'd be bored after a half hour," said her father.

"I'm fourteen, and I'm going to be a children's doctor like Mother."

"Look here, you get that notion out of your head. Before she was married your mother had to earn her living. You don't and never will."

"You don't want me to?" she asked, an anxious note in her voice.

She's too eager to please him, thought Esther. We all are! The idea startled her.

The next morning Sam seated her at the desk by the side of his reception-ist where she could watch the smooth flow of men and women pouring through his consulting rooms. Several times she caught glimpses of him seeing a patient in or out. Does he never weary, she asked herself, of wearing that impersonal authoritative look, or has he worn that mask so long it's become his real self?

A man came to the desk to ask the receptionist if by any chance he might see Dr. Towne on urgent business. The girl studied him for a moment before answering, her expression seeming to say, "And who are you any-way?" He lost assurance even before she said in a cool tone, "Dr. Towne is busy just now."

"Maybe it's really urgent," Esther whispered as the man turned to leave.

"Nuts," said the girl. "Everyone thinks his troubles are urgent. Dr. Towne has to be protected. That's my job. He's worked to the limit. So was Dr. Alan before he left." Now Esther understood why she was here. Sam wanted her to understand that a busy doctor needed to come home to the quiet atmosphere which he believed only a wife with leisure could provide. He probably thought as little of her nursing as he did of his wife's help at the clinic.

At noon as Sam was showing Esther about the building he broached the subject, suggesting that the work she was doing was too strenuous. "When Alan gets home you don't want him to find you tired out. I doubt if the war lasts much longer," he said. Then before she could answer, he changed the subject.

At luncheon he was a gracious host. He charmed her with his vivid description of the city's past. He described its early settlers, how most of them had come from New England, how his mother and a group of friends had interested themselves in better music for the city, started what later had developed into a local orchestra. "Athenia is America at its best," he ended. "We think of ourselves here as maintaining the finest American traditions— English, like yours, for the most part. Of course the factories are bringing in the southern Europeans. We need them as workers, but not in the upper strata. We pride ourselves that the Jews, who have made themselves important in some of our cities, aren't so here. We carry the ball. Not," he hastened to add, "that there's really any objection to them. I have no racial feeling. We just don't need them."

Luncheon was finished, and they had risen as he spoke these words. "Why you're shivering!" he exclaimed, solicitously helping her on with her lightweight coat. "This air conditioning is kept too low. I must mention it to the management."

"I'm not really cold," Esther managed to say, thankful that he could not see her face. "It's been wonderful of you to take so much time to initiate me into the mysteries."

Sam scowled. Mysteries—he didn't like the word. He had never known her to be flippant. Did she mean to be now? He looked at his watch. "I arranged with Jo to call for you. It's just time."

Esther felt lightheaded and out of herself as she thanked Sam somewhat effusively and took her seat beside Jo in the car. So they didn't know! It was a wonder she hadn't given herself away long ago. She had taken it for granted Alan had at least told his brother about her Jewish ancestry. Why, Sam was Alan's confidant in all things.

"Shall we drive out to the Club?" Jo asked.

"That would be lovely!" exclaimed Esther.

Jo looked at her curiously. Her voice didn't sound natural. "Listen, my dear," she said, "you and Alan will be living your own lives when you come here. You don't have to copy us. In his love for the members of his family Sam is anxious to save them from mistakes. Don't be afraid to make a few." Words of bravado, thought Jo, knowing she wasn't able to follow her own advice.

For Alan's sake, Esther was thinking, I must see my visit through in the position he has placed me. He must have some good reason for not telling his family. I mustn't let Alan down. I must trust him. . . . It wasn't easy, for the disturbing thought kept coming to her that Alan hadn't wanted them to know about her mother. She had knowledge of too many peoples to doubt that racial prejudice could creep in anywhere, that America was no exception. It would have been naïve of her not to recognize that fact. If she had been so naïve, the girls with whom she was associated at the hospital would long ago have enlightened her by their casual remarks about Jews. She had accepted this attitude as more or less natural, but Alan's family she had thought of as being above prejudice. Now Sam had expressed that prejudice. Where then did Alan really stand?

The day for Esther's return to New York had come. The family was at the station to see her off.

"We'll have both you and Alan back very soon, please God," said Sam. "I believe the war isn't going to last much longer, but in the meantime I'd like to place a family responsibility on you, Esther. I know you go to see Grandfather occasionally. What would you think of giving up your nursing and going to stay with him?"

"I doubt if he'd want me," Esther answered.

"Well, perhaps not, but go up as often as you can. Try to get him not to work so hard."

"I'll try," she answered, "but I doubt if there's anything I can do." I—I whom Sam wouldn't accept if he knew! Again that out-of-herself feeling, a tragic sense of being rejected—and by her husband's family. She was climbing the steps of the Pullman now; at the top she turned and waved.

9

WHILE Esther had been with them Sam had managed to push to the back of his mind the fact that Jo had deceived him by taking up her profession without letting him know. But after Esther had gone he found suspicion of his wife consuming more and more of his thoughts. He'd be operating or examining a patient, and suddenly he'd wonder what she was doing. He began to use Sally more and more to check on her mother's activities. Gradually Sally came to suspect that there was some reason for her to watch her mother. It was a heady potion at once exhilarating and destroying.

These late summer days were hot, and Jo sometimes grew impatient with her daughter, who seemed to have no resources of her own. She knew Sally should have gone to camp with the other girls, but after all Sam had given her the choice of whether to go or stay for Esther's visit. Now she must accept the consequences of her decision. But the more Jo tried to make Sally independent, the more the girl clung to her. It isn't good, Jo thought. I shouldn't be so important to her. One day she said, "I'm going to put you on your own this morning while I play golf with some friends."

After her mother had gone, Sally followed her. She was discomfited when her mother's trail led to nothing more alarming than the Country Club. There was no mystery to solve! Out of her disappointment and her loneliness and a momentary doubt of her father the young girl built her own exaltation—her father loved her more than he loved his wife.

A little contrite, feeling she had been harsh, Jo hurried home after the first nine holes. She found her daughter walking up and down before the long glass in Sam's room attired in her mother's most beautiful morning gown, a recent gift from Sam. She hasn't dressed up in my clothes for years, thought Jo. She must have been hard put for entertainment. She is really lonely. It worried her mother.

At last Sally was back at school. Her friends were in and out of the house. There were laughter and giggling and a great deal of talk of boys. Then Jo began to think of taking up her work at the clinic. She must, with the shortage of doctors, and yet she put off from day to day the inevitable controversy with Sam.

With Sally at school, Sam's suspicion of Jo took on larger and larger proportions. You'd think I was afraid she was carrying on an affair with some other man, he thought. Suddenly it struck him that perhaps she was. Jo was attractive to men. If she deceived him in one thing, might she not in another?

That afternoon he left his office early. He had to know what she was doing. As he had suspected, she was not at the house, but in a few minutes he heard her car and after a little her voice in the kitchen saying to the maid, "It certainly takes a long time to market these days. I've been all the afternoon at it." Had she, or was she establishing an alibi even with their servant? He had to know.

When Jo entered the living room and saw him her eyes lighted up with pleasure. "How awfully nice, Sam!" she exclaimed.

But his heart was sore, and he could not accept such easy assurance of her love. Before he realized it, he was voicing in one sentence all his pent-up misery. "I can't live like this!"

"What do you mean, Sam?" she asked. Then she did know what he meant. "No," she answered soberly, "you can't, and certainly I can't. If you don't wish to trust me——"

"If I don't wish to trust you!" he exclaimed. "It's just what I want to do. But I must have some assurance."

"Assurance of what?"

"After the clinic business, how can you ask that? How do I know that you haven't——"

"That I haven't gone back? Well, I haven't, but I think I ought to, Sam. You know every doctor counts just now. I feel I must help out even if you don't approve."

"So that's what you've been working toward, a breaking up of our marriage! No wonder I distrusted you!"

"After all we've been to each other for years," she cried, "you're actually accusing me of planning to do a thing like that! Just because we differ doesn't mean our marriage is going on the rocks. You haven't any right to accuse me of such a thing." How to make him trust me! she thought in despair, realizing for the first time that his distrust of her cut deep into the fabric of their marriage.

"I'm not accusing you. It's what you've done that accuses you. But I'm not going to let you wreck Sally's life. I'm going to keep her with me if I have to fight for her in every court in the land. She is a Towne, and she's going to stay one."

"I've just served the purpose then of carrying on the Towne family?" Jo asked bitterly. Quickly she left him. Once in her own room, she closed the door leading into his.

The afternoon turned into evening. She heard Sam's light tap on the door. "Have you forgotten that we're going out to dinner?" he called out. "We mustn't be late." She caught herself wanting to laugh at the incongruity. Here with their marriage going to pieces Sam was worried about not being on time for a party! But she rose and dressed quickly. When she went downstairs she found him in the hall waiting for her. "We can just make it," he said.

At the dinner the conversation centered for a while on the local drive for funds to help the crippled children of the city. "I don't suppose you'd have time to be on the committee, Dr. Towne," said a rich and philanthropic woman, instigator of the plan.

"I'll take time," Sam answered. "It's something I can heartily endorse. The strong should care for the weak. Society is just a larger family."

The hostess, not wanting her guests to be too serious, now introduced a lighter subject. Amid the banter and the laughter Jo, although going through with her part in it, felt strangely alone. In spirit she was already divorced from Sam. His offer to help raise money to relieve the suffering of children, set against his refusing the service that she as doctor could render to those same children actually suffering from lack of physicians' care, was to her a cynical betrayal of the ideals of their profession.

Sam, glancing at her in animated conversation with their host, felt himself a battleground of admiration and rage. Jo was everything he wanted in a wife, and yet it was she who threatened the very structure of his success, success she had helped to create! Wealth marked his rise to the top of his profession. For his wife to work gave the impression that he needed her help financially. It was nothing short of wantonness for her to insist on doing it. This was intolerable.

The next morning after Sam had gone, Jo went to her room and shutting the door against interruption determined to solve the problem she had been struggling with all night. To bow to Sam's wishes would be complete subservience, a surrender of herself such as she could not agree to. If she didn't—— What then was to be her course?

As on the evening before, there was a light tap on her door, but this time it was Sally asking if she might come in. With a deep sigh she dropped down beside her mother on the bed. In spite of her troubled thoughts, Jo smiled, thinking, It's a wonderful copy of the way Sam sometimes makes known his desire for sympathy. "Well, out with it, my dear—whatever it is!"

Sally spoke in a voice so low Jo could hardly hear her. "I know about the clinic. I don't think you should have done what Daddy didn't want. He's so busy and so tired."

Jo felt genuine anger toward her daughter. What right had Sally to act as her judge? Then Jo's anger was turned against her husband for placing his burdens on a mere child. She put her arm about Sally, drew her closer. "I don't think either of us can keep Daddy from being tired," she said.

"I heard a little what you and Daddy said yesterday afternoon."

"You shouldn't have been listening, Sally. It isn't any of your business."

"But it is. Please don't go away!" cried the girl. She burst into tears and sobbed out hysterically the perplexities of the summer.

So that is what I have been doing to my child! thought Jo, trying to quiet Sally. Many small happenings of the past summer took on significance. She understood now the burden Sam in his insecurity had placed on shoulders too young to bear it. Surely it was not too late to set right the harm done. Then the crippled children at the clinic inadequately cared for filed before her. Should she choose one child or the many? But Sally was her own child. She could never forgive herself if Sally were hurt. Gently she stroked the girl's hair. "You don't need to worry, dear. I'm not leaving you. It takes a lot of adjustment for two people to live together. What you heard last night doesn't mean anything."

"Really it doesn't?"

"Really it doesn't," Jo answered. "Your stiff-necked mother has just got to bow her head a little."

"Oh, Mummie, I was afraid!" Again Sally burst into tears.

Jo called Sam at his office, explaining she was going to be downtown and would like to drive home with him. She meant to have no eavesdropping on this conversation. Once they were in the car, she brought up the subject so painful to both of them. "For Sally's sake," she said, "if you'll put aside your distrust of me, I'll give you my word . . ." She hesitated and then went steadily on. "I'll try to be the kind of wife you want." In panic at the cost to herself such a promise entailed, she added, "Until Sally is grown up and married."

"Very well," he said, "I'll go through with it."

"To satisfy Sally it will have to be an awfully good imitation of the real thing," she said.

"An awfully good imitation," he answered with the emphasis on his final word.

In the weeks that followed Jo set herself to conform in every way to the standards which meant so much to Sam. She joined several clubs to which he had often urged her to belong; she did more entertaining, asking the couples that would give them prestige. She bought more expensive clothes. Gradually she found Sam's suspicions of her falling away. Not that he showed his satisfaction; it was Sally's happiness that mirrored Sam's returning trust.

In time Jo's estimate of her husband became less harsh. Her sharp disappointment in him softened into understanding. Proud, reserved and separate, he had always fought, but with the years more desperately, to mold the family in his own likeness. She pitied him, for she was beginning to see he was a lonely man—in that loneliness lay the need to possess someone which dominated him—and she was afraid for Sally. If she, Jo, his wife, a doctor in her own right, conformed enough to his ideal, could Sally go free? To this she set herself.

When her sense of frustration became too great to be borne she would arrange to have luncheon with her old friend Naomi Pratt, a child specialist. She would go down early, berate her friend for not being ready, then put on a doctor's coat and for a half hour or hour help the overworked specialist. "It's only so I can get you out to luncheon," she would say.

Naomi Pratt's shrewd kindly eyes studied her friend and she put off the luncheon hour so that Jo might work a little longer.

❧ 10 ❧

THE BROWN mosquito net, standard equipment of the Army, was tucked tightly around Alan's bed. Feeling stifled, he jerked at the net, trying to loosen it, thinking irritably it was a bit ironical to protect him against malaria when he was already so full of parasites he doubted if another could find room in him. He lay on his back for a little, then on his left side, then his right. This aftermath of restlessness seemed almost worse than the fever and chills of the attack itself. He rang for the night nurse. "Is a sedative in order?" he asked.

"I'll speak to Dr. Gertz."

What a break, he thought, that Gertz should be on duty tonight! In the weeks that Alan had been sick he had come to rely on Gertz. When through the meshes of the net he looked into the man's steady black eyes, he felt his terrible restlessness already abating a little.

"Finding it hard to sleep?" Gertz asked. "I've ordered a hypo for you."

In the detachment from life which the drug induced Alan stood away from himself and his passion for Martha which had possessed him ever since the night he had become her lover. He saw himself plainly now in the light of the Puritan and Quaker traditions in which he had been reared—his disloyalty to Esther voiced in the words of Sam's last letter telling him of her visit. "I know you've been sick, but perhaps you could manage to write to her oftener. She never said anything, but several times I caught her look of disappointment when the mail arrived and there was no letter from you."

As the drug took over, Alan floated free of his anxiety and fell into a heavy sleep. But when he awoke he saw in all its starkness the dilemma in which he had placed himself. Martha, he knew, was not the ordinary adventuress. He believed she loved him. But surely she did not expect him to divorce Esther. Certainly, he argued, he had made plain to her that his final responsibility was to his wife. Too, his relationship to Sam was precious to Alan. He didn't want to lose his brother's respect, which he believed he would if he deserted Esther. But how can I break with Martha? I'm not ready to just yet, miserably he owned to himself.

Dr. Gertz, when he came to see him before going off duty, said, "I've news for you. As soon as we can get a place on a plane we're sending you home."

When Alan made no response he added, "I've worked hard to get this through."

"I'm sorry, Doctor. Of course I'm grateful. But——"

"But what?"

"It's this confounded malaria. I'm not up to thanking you properly."

"Make your plans. There should be a place for you within a few days." Dr. Gertz walked away. Meddling, he supposed, but if Towne didn't get free soon from this Martha Green who came to see him, that wife of his back home would be out of luck. Besides, malaria could kill. Well, the orders were in now. He was going home whether he wanted to or not.

That afternoon when Martha made her usual visit, the first thing Alan said to her was "I'm being sent home, Martha."

"You're not!" she exclaimed. "You can't be! Why should you? How did you work it?"

"I didn't. They've decided I won't get over the malaria until I get out of this climate."

"Of course you can get over it here!" There was a rough quality in her voice which Alan had never heard before, and it roused opposition in him.

"Martha, listen. I acknowledge I've been a cad to you. But it doesn't follow that I should be one to my wife, too."

"I've always gone straight. I can't ever go home if you let me down," she pleaded.

"I've explained often how I feel about Esther."

"Not for a long time."

"You knew that she is pretty much alone in a strange country and needs me," he insisted.

"Because she's a Jew! So you make a good American girl like me take the rap."

"So that's it, is it?" His voice was cold and cutting.

Sensing she had offended him, quickly Martha sought to get back what she had lost. "I didn't mean to talk against her. It's just that it's not so bad for her as for me. She's got your name. If you leave her, it won't ruin her. It will me. You've got to promise you won't go back on me." She began to sob hysterically.

"Hush," said Alan, "the whole ward will hear you. I'll try to arrange something."

A nurse watching from a distance came to the foot of his bed. "You'd better go now," she said to Martha. "He needs rest." Swiftly and efficiently she went about changing his hospital gown soaked with sweat.

∾ 11 ∾

ON HER return to New York Esther put off visiting Grandfather Towne. Once she had delighted in such visits, but now she dreaded to subject herself to his penetrating gaze. Sometimes she thought of telling the wise old man her family's story, and asking his advice what to do. Surely he didn't share Sam's idea about her mother's people. But would she then be letting Alan down if Dr. Towne should feel as she did, that Alan should not have hidden her identity? Finally she received a note from Dr. Towne asking why she had not been to see him. The visit could no longer be delayed.

On her next free week end she took a train scheduled to arrive at noon in order that the doctor should not have to break into his office hours to meet her, a courtesy he had insisted on in her previous visits. But when the train left New York three hours late she was concerned that after all she would interfere with his work. En route the train lost another hour, which meant that it would be after five when she arrived, a good time for him; but when the train pulled in she looked in vain for the tall white-haired Dr. Towne. Finding no taxi, she went into the station and telephoned his office.

"Is there any urgent need to speak to him?"

Esther realized it would be difficult to get past the secretary who was answering her. "I'm Mrs. Alan Towne, his granddaughter. Dr. Towne was to meet me."

"Oh, come down and take him home. Maybe you'll be able to put some sense into him. I can't."

Esther recognized that the words came from an old and privileged associate who believed she had the right to be exasperated because the doctor ignored her advice. Undoubtedly he won't listen to me either, thought Esther, as she waited at the curb for a taxi. She grew impatient as the cabs whirled by, all filled. Finally one pulled up before her. "Where you want to go, miss?"

She gave the number. "And I'm in a hurry," she added.

"Sure, sure, I'll get you there in a jiffy. You a patient of his?" the driver asked.

"No, a member of the family," Esther answered, determined to say no more. She was not yet used to this easy American manner of the chance acquaintance.

"Sure ought to be proud. The doctor's a regular guy. He cured my wife." He began to recount in great detail each step of his wife's sickness and recovery—as much a matter of the woman's spirit as her body, Esther reflected. "He shouldn't be working at this hour," the man added as he drew up before the building. Everyone seems to want to take care of Grandfather, Esther thought as she went up the steps that led to the brownstone residence in which Dr. Towne had taken a suite of offices.

"I'll tell him you're tired," said the white-haired secretary a little grimly, "and that he ought to take you home." She looks tired herself, Esther thought.

When she saw Dr. Towne come through the hall accompanying a young woman to the door, her original sense of security in being a member of the Towne family came back to Esther. No prejudice could lurk behind a face like that, no mask as there had been when Sam looked at a patient, but instead understanding. When the young woman reached the outer door she turned suddenly. "I must ask you something, Doctor. I've—I've not had courage to before."

"And why not?" he asked.

"I want to go overseas. I've a chance to go with other entertainers to the European front."

The doctor was standing with his back against the doorframe of the wide opening that led from the hall into the reception room where Esther was sitting. "How long?" he asked.

"Twelve weeks," the woman replied. Esther, watching with interest, thought that she detected an all but imperceptible tightening of the muscles around Grandfather Towne's mouth, but in a tone almost casual he said, "Yes, you may go."

As the door closed behind the woman he did not move, seemingly deep in thought. Then, as if adjusting a newly accepted burden, he straightened his shoulders and crossed the room to Esther. "My dear, I'm sorry to have kept you waiting." He bent and kissed her. As they faced the door to leave he saw his secretary. "You here yet?" he said with some surprise. "I told you to go home an hour ago."

"Umph," said the woman. "I leave when you do."

"It's beautiful in the country," Grandfather Towne said to his granddaughter, turning the car toward the hills and his home. The sun was about to sink, and its rays shining through the branches of the maples turned the leaves not yet fallen into transparencies of color. Esther felt herself sustained by the beauty and quiet all around her, enhanced by the serenity of the old man at her side.

When finally they entered the drive that led to the house she broke into his contemplation. "That woman you allowed to undertake so much—is she as frail as she looks?"

"Yes," he answered.

"But still you let her go."

"Let's put it this way," he said. "I'm taking a risk. The trip may even set back her recovery. That, I think I can repair. It's better than to harm her spirit."

"And you'd harm it if you said she couldn't go?"

"When she came to me she had been told she would in time be bedridden; she walked with difficulty. I believed I could make her well if I could rid her mind of the concept of disease and helplessness. It's been a hard fight. If I limited her now—do you see?"

They had reached the house. As he opened the front door he said, "I'm not able to get the help I had since Lydia left to care for her grandchildren; the daughter is working in a war plant. I've closed off all the rooms downstairs except the kitchen and my library." The old-fashioned folding doors into the double parlors were shut. So was the door that led into the dining room across the hall.

As he showed her to her room he said, "Dinner is at seven in the library. A woman comes in to get it. But don't expect too much."

Esther looked around the room she had occupied the night before her wedding. Her marriage to Alan had seemed a haven then, but now her trust in him had been shaken. Why had he not told his family about her? Was it because he felt some modicum of shame that she was part Jew? She no longer felt she was close to Alan. He had almost ceased to write her. When he did there was only a perfunctory rehearsal of the bare facts of his life. In the two years they had been separated had he forgotten her? Her heart felt squeezed in a vise. But gradually here in the house of his ancestors some spell was cast over her. The memory of her young husband during the week of their honeymoon came back to her—his gentleness, his protectiveness, yes, and his sincerity. Sternly she took herself to task. To doubt his loyalty to her was disloyalty toward him.

She went over to the window, opened it, and leaned out. A light wind blowing through the tree under which she had stood to be married set its dry leaves rustling. She heard a louder rustling. Scarcely discernible in the dusk she saw the man she now claimed as grandfather scuffling through the fallen leaves. Then she lost sight of him as he entered the part of his garden beyond the lilac hedge.

Seated at a small table by the fireplace, sharing with him the simple meal, Esther was aware of the old man's weariness. She believed he had given a great deal of himself this afternoon when he had sent a frail woman out to do what in her condition only the strength of the spirit could accomplish.

Surely if it were fair for her to ask it he could steady her, too, against the inroads of doubt.

Dr. Towne glanced around the room filled with memories of his wife and his son. On his desk stood a framed picture of the two. It was the one he liked best, taken at the time when the young boy's career promised to continue his own. "A man dreams a lot when his boy is small," he said.

Then Esther saw that he had wanted his son to be a doctor. Francis Towne's death had intensified the father's longing for the companionship of his son in his chosen profession. It is I, she thought, who should give him strength, not ask strength of him. She began telling him of Alan, letters written from that mountain valley in the Himalayas.

Samuel Towne's weariness, his sense of loss in the death of his only son, began to leave him. The continuation of himself and his work he had sought in Francis might yet come through Alan! "And now that he is in India, what has he written you?" he asked eagerly. "India has much to offer him."

"Has it?" asked Esther, startled. She rose and stood looking down into the fire, her back toward him, trying to still the tumult arising within her.

"Is anything wrong, my child?" he asked, his weariness returning as he sought to pull himself back from this new hope in Alan.

"I don't know," she answered. "He does not write—often." Suddenly Esther felt she must put the test to some member of his family. "Perhaps I should never have married him. It was asking too much of him."

"Why do you say so?"

She swung round to face him. "You, too, then know nothing about me?" she demanded.

Dr. Towne was at once alert, his weariness submerged in the physician, recognizing in her voice, as he had in countless other voices through the years, that she was close to the breaking point. Quietly he spoke. "Esther, you held nothing back when you consented to marry Alan, I am sure. You are too honest for that. Alan married you because he loved you."

"And you—do you accept me for my own sake?" She sought an answer in the face of the old man. When she got none, despair took over.

Dr. Towne studied more closely than he had before this young woman so recently come into his family. English but with some French blood, too, he had thought. After forty years he had learned to watch for subtle racial characteristics in the men and women who came to consult him. He had found that deep in the racial mixtures of the American people lay conflicts often leading to sickness. Now he saw pass across Esther's face a cast of the spirit—the age-old inheritance of a hunted race. It declared to him what had not been apparent before, what he might not now have recognized had she not given him the clue. "The Jews"—he spoke the word naturally—"are among the imaginative people of the world. Creative people. They have produced great musicians, painters, doctors, yes, and the great discoverer of the spirit of man, Christ. I welcome what you bring. It can enrich the family. It is the mingling of races which has made America great. I hope you agree with me that America is great."

"But in your family there is no mingling. I am the first. Is that not true?" she demanded.

"Yes," he said, "but your contribution is not less welcome because of that."

Gradually as he went on talking he saw her English reserve, of which he had been so conscious at their first meeting, re-established. That, too, is a splendid heritage, he thought, listening to her beautifully modulated voice, seeing the grace of her slight body as she told him of her father and mother and their life together. She was far from the breaking point now.

And then suddenly he saw that her hands had tightened on the arms of her chair. Her mind was doubling back. She was making a return journey to despair. "Alan—why does Alan not write to me?" she cried.

Here was the fear he had met so often in women since the war began. In the violent breaking off of union by the departure of their husbands they came to feel that they had been betrayed. Sometimes the betrayal was real, sometimes imagined. Either way it often made reconciliation impossible on the man's return. "When did you hear from Alan last?" he asked, determined to bring her real fear into the open.

"Six weeks ago." Her words were scarcely audible. "Can it be because I am part Jewish?"

Dr. Towne raised his hand, indicating silence. He spoke sternly. "You are laying on your mother's race a sense of inadequacy you do not wish to take yourself. I have seen many women face what you are facing. You do not wish to acknowledge that for some reason Alan just now does not need you so much as you would like. To think that you are not sufficient to him is intolerable, so you raise this barrier of race between you. I warn you if you do that you may not be able to pull it down when you want to. You do not know what Alan is facing or thinking. War is a terrible thing. Sometimes men in the midst of it find their marriages shrinking for the time being into unimportance. Don't ask of Alan more than he can give."

All but overcome with his own weariness, he rose, saying, "Put out the light when you go to bed." At the door he turned. "Try to understand, Esther." Then he was gone.

Esther watched the coals in the open fire turn to ash and fall away. It was long past midnight when she went to bed to sleep dreamlessly under the roof of Alan's forefathers.

After that she came to stay with Dr. Towne whenever she could, finding in this wise old man's strength the strength for belief in Alan.

As fall passed into winter she realized that Grandfather Towne was growing steadily more frail. She began to think of giving up her nursing to do what Sam had wanted—spend the rest of the winter with Grandfather—but she doubted if he would hear of such a thing.

⚘ 12 ⚘

It was a cold January day, and it was snowing. It seemed foolish to try to make the journey to upstate New York. The trains were running hours late. "I must go. He needs me," Esther kept telling herself, ignoring how much she needed him. Still she had not heard from Alan, but surely once she was in the presence of the old man she would be able to trust Alan, even though he was silent.

She decided not to send a wire, as she usually did, to say that she was coming. If the train were too late for her to call him at the office, she would take a taxi, or, failing that, try to get a room at a hotel in town for the night. When at nine o'clock in the evening she got off the train, she found a cab without too much difficulty. As it turned into the drive leading to the Towne house she saw with relief that there was a light in the library.

The snow had not been swept from the steps leading up to the front door, but there were the doctor's footprints, dark against the whiteness. He was too tired, she supposed, to clean the steps. Suddenly thankful she had come, she decided to surprise him if the door wasn't locked, and he rarely locked it until he went upstairs. Quietly she opened it. As soon as she had caught her breath after pushing her suitcase into the hall, she called out, "It's I, Grandfather. Esther!"

Her words echoed against the closed doors to the parlor and library, then died away in the silence which followed. Why did he not answer? He must be here. The light in the library made a bright line under the library door. She crossed the hall and opened it. Dr. Towne was sitting before his desk, his white head fallen forward on the green blotter, his strong, heavily veined right hand hanging inert over the chair arm.

"He's asleep," she said to herself, knowing it was not so. She went to his side, gently touched his brow, sunken with age but with the white hair springing vigorously from it. It was cold, so very cold. Mechanically she drew her hand away from the untenanted body beside her. A sharp cry escaped her.

A long while afterward, it seemed to her, she heard the telephone ringing insistently time after time. She picked up the receiver from the telephone on the desk.

"Hello!" A voice strangely unfamiliar, strangely familiar, answered. "I want to speak to Dr. Samuel Towne."

"Alan! I—— Alan, this is Esther."

"Esther! I called your apartment. The girl at the desk said you were away. She didn't know where you were."

Emotions crowded in upon Esther—Alan so near . . . she here in his grandfather's house with its dead occupant . . . an overpowering desire to protect Alan from shock in the loss of the head of his family, whom he dearly loved.

"Grandfather hasn't been well. I came up to look after him," she managed to say.

"Anything serious?" An anxious note crept into Alan's voice.

Suddenly the need to lean on her husband dominated all Esther's other emotions. "Grandfather . . . I found him just now . . . at his desk . . . he is dead. I don't know what to do." Her composure was gone. Sobs shook her.

Alan's voice came over the wire strong and sure. "Call Dr. Peterson— H. J. Peterson—ask him to take charge until I can get there. I'll ring off so that you can get him."

"Alan, Alan!" Esther called, but he had gone.

Neither busses nor airplanes were running because of the storm; the next train to upper New York would not leave until early morning. It would be afternoon before Alan could reach his grandfather's house. He telephoned Sam, and then an old friend living not far from his grandfather, asking if she would stay with Esther until he or Sam arrived. Then he called Army headquarters to arrange for more time before he reported at the hospital.

After finding a seat in the crowded train, he tried to forget in sleep the tangle of events in which he was caught. He had intended to go to Esther immediately on his arrival and, before anything personal developed between them, ask her to release him in order to keep his promise to Martha. Instead he must meet Esther deeply entrenched in the family. Any way he turned he felt blocked. Esther, Martha—the accusing eyes of both confronted him. At last he slept, his head bent forward, his chin, the long Towne chin, resting on his chest.

Late the next afternoon Esther opened the front door of the old homestead to him. Thin, gaunt, his face flushed with fever, his shoulders sagging under the weight of his flight bag, he stood before her, showing no joy at seeing her, making no gesture of affection.

"I must get to bed, Esther," he said. "I'm in for an attack of malaria." Dread of the hours ahead when he would be racked by fever was nothing to the relief he felt in the bulwark sickness gave him against any commitment to Esther.

With his hand resting on her shoulder, they went up the stairs. "Here," she said, opening the door to her room. He hesitated, seeing her dressing gown over the back of a chair. "Until I get over this, put me in the spare room, Esther."

"It's cold in there," she answered. "We're short of coal. I'll sleep here on the couch so I can take care of you."

The fever mounted, and he was shut off into a world of suffering. Here he dwelt indifferent to Esther, indifferent to Sam when he arrived a few hours later, indifferent both to Esther's and Sam's ministrations—both seemed equally gentle, equally demanding.

Dr. Towne's funeral could not be kept private, as Sam would have had it. The people of the city claimed that for an hour or two the doctor belonged to them. Their spokesman was his old secretary. Somehow she triumphed over Sam. In the white meeting house of the Quakers the casket was placed on the day of burial. Notice had been given that there were to be no flowers. The simplicity of the Quaker belief and the simplicity of the physician who had in humility served the community year after year barred the ostentation of floral tributes. Men, women and children filed in and out, looking for the last time into the face of the man who for fifty years had been a strong rampart to them against sickness and often despair.

At the grave hollowed out of the frozen earth Esther and Sam stood a little apart from the multitude who, huddling under black umbrellas, thronged the white slopes surrounding the small valley of the dead. A wet snow was falling, darkening the afternoon almost to twilight. The minister's voice was loud and clear.

> "Because man goeth to his long home,
> and the mourners go about the streets;
> Or ever the silver cord be loosed,
> Or the golden bowl be broken,
> Or the pitcher be broken at the fountain,
> Or the wheel broken at the cistern.
> Then shall the dust return to the earth
> As it was;
> And the spirit shall return unto God
> Who gave it."

The clods of frozen earth fell heavily onto the lowered coffin. Sam put his arm protectingly about Esther. She shivered. "We must go back to Alan," he said, thinking how much there was for him to arrange before his train left at midnight. His strong sense of the proprieties had held him back from opening the will until after the funeral. He had arranged to have the lawyer meet him immediately on his return.

Late in the evening Sam went to Alan's room and sat down beside the bed. "I'm sorry I can't stay to do everything. But you don't need to worry. All you have to do, old man, is get well. Dr. Peterson has made arrangements for you to report to the Army hospital as soon as you are able. I hope you will be let out of the Army soon. When that time comes I certainly will be glad to have you back. Now for Grandfather's will." Slowly Sam read so that the sick man might take in its full meaning. "I had no idea," he said as he finished, "that Grandfather had accumulated so much money." Sam's respect for him had obviously increased. "Even with his house and garden left to the city for a recreation center, you and I—well, certainly we're not beggared."

As he rose to go he said, "Some one of the family will have to see to Grandfather's personal belongings. What about Esther? Do you mind if she stays to do it after you've gone to the hospital?"

Alan saw nothing to do but acquiesce in Sam's plan, but he did it with resentment and anger, knowing it made Esther just a little more a part of the family, and so it would be more difficult for him to cut the ties that bound him to her.

As the outside door closed behind Sam, Alan heard Esther come slowly up the stairs and enter his room. "I want you to get a good rest tonight, dear," he said. "I can be left alone, now that the fever is gone."

"You'd rather?" she asked.

"I'd rather."

"Is anything wrong other than the malaria?" she asked. "Be honest with me, Alan."

"Please understand," he pleaded. "I'm not myself just now. There's not a drop of red blood in me."

Esther went into the guest room. Hastily she undressed, slipped into bed, drew herself into a ball in order that the heat of her body need warm only a small portion of the cold sheets. Some time in the night she awoke. Alan had called this the "spare room," a term new to her. It seemed symbolic now of her position in his life. A storm was in the making. Pellets of hard snow hit the windowpanes. A shutter somewhere banged in the wind.

Across the hall Alan lay awake, unable to put aside his responsibility to his wife. The devotion of his father and his grandfather to the women they had married was the pulse beat of the old house, holding Alan to its steady rhythm. Tenderness, protection—these things the men of his family had given to their wives. A peculiar responsibility was his; to ask Esther for a divorce would be a cruel blow from which he believed it would be almost impossible for her to recover. He had to remember how she had held back from marrying him until he had finally convinced her it made no difference to him that she belonged in part to a people who had borne many rejections. His leaving her could well be interpreted by her as such a rejection. In so doing he might injure her beyond any healing.

The storm had increased in intensity. The wind shook the house, sent the windows rattling. The snow drove against the glass of the windowpanes. He longed to ride out on the storm away from the disciplines in which he had been reared. Everything wild and undisciplined in him called out for Martha.

The door of his room opened, and he saw Esther silhouetted against the lighted hall. "It's an awful storm, Alan. I thought perhaps you'd be cold."

"Are you frightened, dear?" he asked as she put another blanket over him.

"A little," she answered.

"You mustn't be," he said. "It's just a good up-country New York storm." As he spoke the rebellious throbbing in his veins subsided. He reached out and took her hand. "Esther, I am not myself yet, but this is true: I love you. Now go back to bed." He could go no further tonight.

The three-day storm was over. The sun shone in blinding brilliance on the snow this morning. Alan was downstairs for the first time. Tomorrow he was to leave for the hospital. Sitting at his grandfather's desk in the library he went about writing a letter to Martha. When he had finished it and sealed the envelope he sat back exhausted, his shirt wet with sweat. He waited for his strength to come back. Slowly he rose, put on his overcoat, then sat down, overcome by weakness. He must mail the letter to Martha. Once it was sent, he could not go back on his decision. He reached the door, opened it. The cold, brisk air revived him. Now the steps. Now the street. Now the mailbox.

Dr. Peterson, who had offered to accompany Alan to the Army hospital, stood with Esther and Alan in the hall. "Well, we'd better be off," he said.

Quietly Esther and Alan kissed each other good-by. "You're sure you don't mind staying here?" he asked her. "You're certain it isn't asking too much of you?"

"Not if you wish it," she answered.

The door closed behind him. The only sound to reach Esther from the white and silent world outside was the clack of the chains on the doctor's car as they drove down the driveway. Then that sound, too, was lost in the distance. She was alone here in the house of Alan's ancestors, appointed by the two brothers to sort and evaluate the intimate family possessions. Sam's reason for such a request she could understand. As a member of the family she was regarded by him as an instrument to serve it. But why had Alan consented? If he loved her, he would have arranged to have her near him. She had only the few words he had spoken to her the night of the storm as evidence of his love. Since then he had retreated, it seemed to her, behind his malaria. She felt lost, unable to find her way in this American family. In Grandfather Towne she had felt she had a guide into its twisting labyrinths. Without him she was like a blind person groping her way.

Day after day she went about her task, clearing the attic of the accumulation of generations—children's toys, discarded furniture, trunks filled with carefully stored relics, soldiers' uniforms, wedding dresses, immortelles shaped into the words "Mother" and "Father." Sam, going over the house with her before he left, had found packets of yellow letters in the attic which he told her to destroy unless they definitely connected the family with great events, such as the Revolutionary or Civil War. To judge she must read them all. Had Sam planned this, she began to wonder, to bring her, an English girl, more intimately into the family? If so, she was falsely accepting his trust.

Sitting before the fire during many long evenings she read of the struggles and accomplishments of this old American family—its life on the farms and in the towns of America. One pack, worn by much reading, contained letters written to old Samuel Towne by his mother while he was in Germany studying medicine, anguished letters telling him that his beloved younger brother, evidently wild, had run away. No trace of him was ever found, Esther learned from other records.

Down through the house she went, sorting, discarding, preserving, filling packing boxes for shipping, until at last she reached Grandfather Towne's library. Here no decision to make. His will stated that his medical books should go to Sam, and his diary and the pewter candlesticks that were relics of the family's tragedy to Alan.

Now the long task was finished. Gradually as the weeks passed Esther had come to feel her identity merging with the identity of Alan's family. Tomorrow she would leave to join him at the Army hospital where, fully recovered, he had been made a member of the staff.

The first hint of spring was in the air. The piled-up snow of the long winter was gone. Late in the afternoon she went for a last walk in the garden, passing on her way the great elm where she had stood to be married, then going on through the opening in the lilac hedge, treading the paths so often trod by generations of Townes. As she came back through the hedge she had a frightening sense of the empty house, the family gone from it. Fearfully she raised her eyes. The windows blazed in the setting sun, and every room seemed alight.

ᕰ 13 ᕰ

ALAN left the hospital well before Esther's train was scheduled to arrive. No possible accident must prevent him from meeting her. Walking up and down the platform, dreading their reunion yet longing for it, he tried to erase from his mind the years of the war. His decision about Martha had not brought him the peace he had expected. He was troubled about his own part in the affair, although he had come to see that she, too, was in part responsible. Furthermore, he had not been able to rid himself of the fear that she might seek him out when the war was over and demand he fulfill his promise to her, appeal to Esther if he did not consent. There was a tenacity about Martha that gainsaid easy defeat.

Watching Esther come down the steps of the train, he thought she looked older and tired. The family had asked a good deal of its newest member. And then he knew he was going to ask something more of her, something infinitely harder. To tell her about Martha was to destroy Martha's power over their lives. This he must do before they again began life together.

When they reached the room he had secured for them in the crowded boardinghouse he made his confession. "I want everything to be straight between us," he ended, "even if you can't fully understand that I loved you all the time."

What he was saying seemed to be something Esther had known for a long time, in fact ever since her talk with Grandfather Towne. She had feared she might always have to live with this knowledge locked up, something both she and Alan would know but never would mention. At first as he spoke she felt only relief that this ghost of another woman was gone, and then the ghost became a reality, a woman whom Alan had allowed to take her place. She must know what she was like. Slowly she spoke. "I could forgive you if I knew——"

"I'm not asking you for forgiveness. I'm asking for your understanding," Alan broke in and stood waiting.

Into the room came the noises of the household, a girl's voice high-pitched with excitement. "She's here! Isn't it romantic? After they've been separated so long."

And an old woman's voice: "Yes, I've a room to rent, but you say you have a baby."

A man answering: "Please take my wife in. I've got my orders. I'm leaving tonight."

And just below the window a man pleading: "Give us a kiss. I'm awful lonesome."

Esther rose and came to Alan where he stood by the door. They held each other close.

Later as they lay in each other's arms the barriers against understanding, accumulated in their long separation, seemed to dissolve. But not wholly, they found in the days which followed. Their so different environments, different experiences had bitten deep into the unquestioned acceptance of each other during their honeymoon week. The innocent happiness of that time was gone.

When Alan was off duty they took long bus rides to the edge of the city, seeking the precious privacy the war-filled city denied them. In the woods, on country roads, gradually they found their lives touching again—not at every point, but enough.

And then on September 2 the war was over, and like thousands of others they were free to go home.

ℒ 14 ℒ

EARLY one crisp morning in January 1946 Sam drove his car down the avenue which led to the medical-dental building. As he passed its front en route to the basement garage he glanced up to admire the good lines of the tall structure and the handsome carving of the caduceus over the entrance, repeated, he knew, on the bronze doors of the elevators which flanked the lobby. The lobby was usually empty at this time, but later during the doctors' office hours it would be crowded with patients packed solidly down one side of a rope, slowly inching their way toward the elevators. On the other side of the rope would be a mass of people hurrying to reach the exit.

After parking his car in the garage Sam took the doctors' private elevator, reflecting, as he was shot quickly to his offices on the top floor, that the lines of patients in the lobby were as great today as during the war. The anxiety on the part of some of the occupants of the building lest their practice be drastically cut with the return of doctors from the front had not been justified.

During the war Sam's practice had trebled, and with it his income. And his ambition—that had trebled, too. He was no longer content simply to be recognized as one of the leading surgeons of the city; he desired a national reputation which he hoped would bring him influence in shaping medical policies for the nation. Alan would be carried up with him.

Sam was driving himself with ruthless disregard of his health. At eight in the morning five days a week he entered the hospital where he frequently operated until one o'clock. After a brief intermission for lunch, often a sandwich eaten hastily before leaving the hospital, he saw patients at his office. Eliminating every moment of waste, he went from one consultation cubicle to another. Both his nurses and his receptionist had long been trained to save him every possible moment. His evenings he spent in writing and in keeping up with the latest publications of his profession. He had a book in mind. Already articles in medical journals on operating techniques had brought him to the attention of surgeons in other cities.

And now when he was so busy he was worried about Alan. He had been back several months, but as time went on he had seemed to fit less and less well into Sam's world. It had not been so in the first weeks after his return. In fact, for the month when the two families had lived together before Esther and Alan secured an apartment, Sam had thought that war had strengthened the ties of brotherhood. The brothers had often left the house together in the morning, and occasionally were able to return together in the evening. Alan was eager to know everything that had happened while he was away. He was deeply interested in the improvements Sam had made in his operating technique and anxious to put at his brother's disposal his knowledge of certain operations tried out with success by the Army. At night when they all sat around the dinner table Sam had had a sense of gathering his family under his care.

But gradually a change had come about in Alan. Sam had noticed first that his brother was restless. Lately he had acted as if he were actually dissatisfied. But why? He had the right to operate in one of the hospitals where Sam was accredited, although a doctor was not usually granted that privilege for several years after he set up practice in the city. Sam had used his influence in Alan's behalf, stressing his brother's splendid war record.

Some of his operations Sam had turned over completely to Alan. What more could Alan want than this full partnership?

Hoping a financial stake in the medical building might make Alan more contented, Sam had asked him to come to the office this morning in order that they might talk it over. Alan was late. Sam's fingers drummed nervously on the blotter as he sat waiting at his desk. At last he heard a key in the door. A moment later Alan came in, looking tousled. That he had not taken more time over his dressing disturbed Sam.

"I'm sorry I'm late. The hospital called me in the night to check on Mrs. Patterson. I didn't have time to go home and change."

"Everything all right?" Sam asked, completely the physician now.

At Alan's assurance Sam's concern shifted from patient to brother. "You should have telephoned me. My wanting to see you wasn't so immediate as all that." He was conscious anew how much his younger brother meant to him. Alan has no comprehension how close our ties are, he reflected.

"That's all right," said Alan en route to the corner where Jo had installed the apparatus for coffee making. "Want some?" he asked.

"No, thanks, but get yourself a cup. What I have to say can wait."

The tone of his brother's voice made Alan realize he was being too casual. He should show more interest in why he had been asked to come down so early. It had seemed almost impossible of late not to upset his brother without meaning to. "Go ahead, shoot!" After he had put the coffeepot over the flame he stretched out on the couch and lighted a cigarette.

"It's this." Sam swung his chair around. "I've been worried of late over your inability to settle into the professional groove."

Alan winced a little at the word groove, uttered so solemnly. That's just what he had hoped to avoid.

"I've been thinking perhaps you need to feel more a part of things here. I've put most of what Grandfather left me plus a chunk of my savings into this building." At Alan's low whistle Sam felt he had at last gained his brother's interest and hurried to capitalize on it. "There's a chance to buy out one of the original investors. I thought you might like to get in on the ground floor, do as I have—invest what Grandfather left you."

"Who's getting out?" asked Alan.

"Ferguson," Sam answered.

"Ferguson!" There was a note of surprise in Alan's voice, also regret. "Too bad to have him go. He's a good man. One of the best, I'd say."

"I don't know that I entirely agree with you there," Sam answered, "but let that go. If you buy him out, you and I would be hard to block in any policy we decided on. We'd have a pretty good chance of killing any suggestion which—well, which didn't seem wise."

"You mean dictate to the others."

"Why do you always put the worst interpretation on what I say? What's gone wrong between us?" Sam asked.

Oh, hell, thought Alan, now I've certainly put my foot in it! How'll I make him understand it's nothing personal if I refuse?

65

All at once both of them were conscious that the coffee was boiling over. They jumped up and collided. Sam backed away. Alan reached out, grabbed the pot, welcoming the extra moments thus given him to make his decision. After pouring out a cup of coffee he sat down opposite Sam, who had again seated himself at the desk.

"I'm not so sure you'd find me the person you want in Ferguson's place. Are you certain I'd always vote with you? You know I often disagree with you."

"But that's in private. We're brothers. We'd stand together in public, wouldn't we?"

Alan scratched his head. "I might as well tell you I don't agree with some of the decisions that have been made lately."

"What, for instance?"

"Well, about Ferguson. I don't imagine he's getting out because he wants to. Is it because he opposed some of your decisions? This is the best office building in town."

"That's only a guess on your part. What else?" Sam demanded.

"Refusing offices to some of the boys back from the war."

"How do you know anybody's been kept out? The board, in fairness to the men turned down, are sworn to secrecy. We don't want to make our ruling militate against them elsewhere. It might become a stigma."

"Oh yeah?" Alan was angry. "My eye, stigma! Awfully kind of you. Well, I happen to know that the guy who got me out of that beastly Indian climate when I was so sick with malaria is one of them. In fact, I intended to ask you to get the men in power here to reconsider their rejection of him. I'd have spoken to you before about him, but I didn't know he was in town until I ran across him yesterday."

"He failed to qualify or else he wouldn't have been turned down."

"He happens to have one of the finest records in the armed forces. His name is Gertz. The fact that he's a Jew wouldn't have anything to do with his failure to qualify, would it?" Alan demanded. "I'm sorry I said that," he hastened to add. "I have no right to lay that kind of prejudice at your door."

"It looks as if we'd just better not discuss Dr. Gertz," Sam answered.

Noticing that his brother had evaded the challenge that he state his position on racial prejudice, Alan thought he had been wiser than he realized at the time of his marriage in not taking Sam into his confidence.

"Look, it's a great opportunity for you," Sam pleaded. Getting no answer, he played his last card. "I had thought in time we could make this building a memorial to Grandfather. Give it his name eventually when we own a majority of the stock."

A man certainly never knows to what use his money may be put after his death, Alan reflected. Grandfather would turn over in his grave if we did a thing like that—have his name blazoned over the entrance to a building that barred the way to any good doctor. He was always giving young men a break. "I guess you'll have to count me out on the deal," he said aloud, "but that needn't make any difference between us, Sam. We can't always see things alike," he added, hoping to soften the refusal.

On their ride to the hospital Alan had an uneasy sense of disloyalty to his brother, but when they started the day's operations it left him. Now again he could be the admiring brother respecting Sam's skill. But during the afternoon as Alan carried out the efficient office routine—half hour for new patients, fifteen minutes for old ones—he had to face the fact that he found it more and more difficult to enter wholeheartedly into partnership with Sam. Slowly he came to see that the conversation that morning had focused his growing discontent—something that until now he had laid to the effect of war, kidding himself that soon he would settle into his previous unquestioning acceptance of Sam's leadership.

For three years Alan had made his own decisions. However good or bad they were—and some he owned were pretty bad—they had given him an independence which was very precious to him. Precious or not, in the light of all Sam had done for him had he a right to that independence? Maybe he hadn't, but clearly it was impossible for him to give the blind allegiance he had heretofore given—he no longer thought as Sam did. His instinctive rebellion against the proposal that he invest in the building with the implication that he follow the accepted policy didn't promise well for future understanding between him and Sam.

As soon as his office hours were over Alan left for home to avoid any further discussion. Esther was out. When he went from the living room into the bedroom, he was impressed with its sense of order and quiet which he had taken for granted before. There were none of the conventional signs supposed to mark a woman's habitation, no elaborate dressing table with face creams, powders and perfumes. He remembered hearing her tell a friend who exclaimed over the lack of such a display, "I don't know. They always seem to me like brushes and brooms, things that should be kept in a cupboard. A bedroom shared with one's husband should be, well, not a workshop."

Alan had a sudden realization that the whole apartment looked as if it had been intelligently prepared for his home-coming—a trifle conceited perhaps for him to think so, but awfully nice—little touches hard to define. His chair at just the right angle so that the light was good for reading, the papers on his desk in the position in which he had left them the night before. Nothing sloppily sentimental about Esther's care of him, like putting his slippers out. Rather, her concern for his comfort seemed to grow out of a respect for his place in their home. It gave him an odd feeling of security. No matter how much unavoidable proximity there was in a small apartment like theirs, she would never use it to force her way of life on him, never invade his privacy. He was grateful, sensing that it was some such freedom he desired in his relationship with Sam.

Hearing Esther's step in the hall, then the sound of bundles put down preparatory to unlocking the door, he hastened to the door and opened it for her.

"You surprised me!" she exclaimed, her expression showing her pleasure in having him home at such an early hour.

He picked up her bags of groceries, carried them to the kitchen. "I've something I want to talk over with you."

When they were seated she thought he was about to speak, but then he seemed to be reconsidering. Esther waited, her heart pounding. Here might be another step in their adjustment to each other begun the evening she had joined him at the Army base. He had been a pretty difficult person to live with since his return to Athenia. Over the reason for his evident unhappiness, sometimes expressed in moodiness, sometimes in irritation, she had pondered many unhappy hours. The old haunting fear that he regretted his marriage had reasserted its power over her. Now as she looked across at him it seemed to her that the dark mood he had so often been under of late had lifted.

"You know, dear," he said at last, breaking the silence, "I don't know whether you've noticed it, but I haven't been myself lately. I haven't understood why until today."

"Yes, I knew something was troubling you," she said, thinking, If only it doesn't have anything to do with me!

"What I'm beginning to see is that following my profession may mean something different from what I originally thought it would." At his words relief swept over Esther, growing as he went on to say, "The truth is, since I came back I have hated every day in Sam's office. Well, no, not quite that— I mean after the first few weeks. I suppose I was dumb, but it wasn't until today that I realized what was wrong. Sam gave me a great chance this morning—to buy into the medical building."

"And you didn't take it!" exclaimed Esther.

"No. Faced with such a possibility, I suddenly found out why I was so discontented. I don't enjoy just seeing patients for half an hour, or fifteen minutes and tinkering with one bone or even all the vertebrae in their spines when I know there's often a hell of a lot wrong with their minds, too."

Esther's heart gave a leap. This was the man who had spoken to her in letters from that high valley in the Himalayas, and again when she had joined him at the hospital. The eager outgoing spirit which he had displayed then had helped greatly in their first efforts at adjustment. But here in Athenia he had seemed a different man.

Alan's thoughts also had gone back to the Army hospital. After he had been assigned to the staff, there had been a slow opening of the doors of his mind. Sitting in on the staff meetings, he had been amazed at first at the attention given by the other doctors to a psychiatrist, also a member of the staff. The man had a powerful attraction for Alan, hard to explain, for until now he had shared Sam's skepticism as to the value of psychiatry. When this quiet-spoken, unobtrusive man sat among them the discussions over patients were lively, spirited and full of understanding. It came to be accepted that men crippled in body need not be crippled in mind, and that it was the combined responsibility of all the doctors to see that if possible none was so crippled.

One day, with the brilliance and suddenness of lightning, Alan had turned upon himself this inquiry into the inner maladies of patients. The Alan Towne of the staff of the Army hospital surveyed the Alan Towne stationed in India—a cringing man trying to escape the original thinking he had done high in the Himalayas. All that followed—and here came the blinding truth—Martha and even the malaria had been a part of his scurrying efforts at retreat from himself. He would not be afraid from now on, he had promised himself, no matter where his thinking took him. But when he had returned to Athenia, then he had tried to fit his mind to Sam's, accepting the routine beliefs of his profession. Only this morning had he realized how stultifying was safety thus gained.

He looked up. He had been on a long journey from this room and Esther. How explain to her the indescribable complexities of an experience? "I haven't thought it all out," he said. "I think I'd like to set up an office in one of the suburban districts outside the city, get some doctors I know to go in with me. I believe one I knew overseas would jump at the chance. He's having a hard time getting started." Alan caught himself up at this point. He wasn't going to tell Esther that Sam had been instrumental in refusing Gertz an office in the medical building. It was a hurt deep within him that his brother should have had a part in that. "Dr. Gertz is a splendid internist. Then there's Eichel. You remember he was one of the assistant general surgeons at the Army hospital, Esther. I had a letter from him a few days ago. He's not been able to get hospital privileges anywhere. I believe I could arrange it so that he'd get into one hospital here in the city. The three of us would be a pretty good combination to start with. We'd get other specialists to join us later."

The idea was growing in Alan's mind as he talked. "We could try among us to treat the whole man, not just an organ, by pooling our knowledge of patients. It's not a new idea. You know we did something like this at the Army hospital."

Break with Sam! Esther saw it would lessen the threat to her marriage. Sam would no longer govern Alan. But was such a break possible without injury to one or both of the brothers? Esther had come to accept the strong feeling that bound the two together, even though she knew it held hazards for her. She wondered if Alan had considered what it would mean to break that tie. "Have you talked this over with Sam?" she asked.

At her question the plans and ideas growing in Alan's mind, which had crowded out the uneasiness he felt when he thought of leaving Sam, returned. "Of course it's too late. It wouldn't be fair after what Sam has done for me. Let's forget it!"

With consternation Esther realized that Alan's voice had taken on a submissive quality. If he did not branch out for himself now, she believed he would become Sam's second self, his own mind closed, shut off from further growth in order to keep untroubled his admiration for Sam. In time

Alan would take all his views from his brother. But if he followed the course which meant freedom from Sam's very orthodox thinking, might he not wreck himself? Would he always be wise? Probably not. No man branching out for himself ever was. She remembered her father saying, "Growth has its dangers—and its weaknesses." But the alternative was worse.

"It's an experiment, of course," she said, "and therefore a risk, and it will hurt Sam. That you must face. It will hurt him terribly. But you can't be your brother's keeper."

"I thought it was the other way around. I thought he was mine," Alan said, looking startled. "I don't know. Perhaps I'd better think about it some more."

"Please promise me that before you decide you'll talk to Jo."

"Why Jo? According to Sam, she isn't——" He stopped. He hadn't any right to give away Sam's confidence.

"She isn't what?" When Alan didn't answer, Esther went on. "I see a great deal of her."

"You've never told me about it."

"We became friends when I was out here before. When I came back—well, we just started in where we'd left off. Jo understands your brother. Perhaps someday he'll understand her—and how much he loves her. Perhaps sooner if you're out of the picture," Esther added with sudden insight.

"Umph," Alan said with a wry smile. He didn't particularly like such an interpretation of his relationship to Sam.

Without either of them realizing it, daylight went from the room. Finally they could no longer see each other's faces. Alan found it easier now to explain to Esther the steps which had led up to today's new conception of his professional role. While he talked it came to him that what he wanted to do was not so new to him as it had seemed at first. "I think it goes back to Grandmother—this idea of mine," he said. "Not long before her death I spoke to her about joining Grandfather—learn from him if I could how he worked with the minds as well as the bodies of his patients. I wonder now why I didn't do it. Maybe, if Grandmother had lived, I'd have had the strength to do it."

"Would it have taken special strength to join a man as respected as your grandfather?" asked Esther, surprised.

"At that time, yes. I feared the originality of his thinking. Going with Sam seemed—how shall I say it?—a safer bet."

Esther marveled that in spite of Alan's association through the years with the searching mind of his grandfather he had chosen to follow Sam's more conventional thinking. She did not believe Alan lacking in courage. She fumbled toward something her father had read to her—from Santayana, she thought. "A man is more gregarious"—ah, she had it now—"in his mind than in his body. . . . He can with pleasure go by himself for a walk, but he's afraid to be alone with his thoughts." That's what Alan will learn, she reflected; not to feel he needs Sam at his side when he thinks. And then we'll both be safe.

～ 15 ～

As ALAN waited for Jo, whom he had invited to have luncheon with him downtown, he began to feel ill at ease. Since his return he had never been alone with her; he had not wanted to be after what his brother had told him. He'd never seen a more loving husband than Sam. Whatever had happened, it wasn't Sam's fault, Alan was certain—that is, he had been until his talk with Esther.

The door into the restaurant opened, and Jo came toward him. Now that he had put aside to some extent his resentment against her, he was aware that the lines of her face showed the marks of spiritual struggle. His new understanding of human beings under stress, gained at the Army hospital, made him able to recognize in some measure how great her struggle had been. Her expression and quiet bearing showed she had won at least a partial victory.

"I'm sorry to have kept you waiting," she said in the direct manner characteristic of her. She gave no explanation, simply assumed that he would understand that she would not purposely be late to an appointment. Not until they were at the table and he had given their order did she speak again. "You must have some reason for asking me to luncheon," she said, smiling.

"It's about Sam," he began. "About me and Sam," he corrected, noticing a noncommital look pass over her face, an expression almost automatic as if she had grown used to the necessity of guarding her relationship to her husband.

Briefly Alan explained that he wanted to give up his partnership with his brother, set up for himself.

"You want my opinion as to the feasibility of your project?" she asked.

"I'd like to know this: After all Sam has done for me, have I the right to go against what he wants of me?"

"I'm a strange one to answer that question for you, am I not? I think you've blamed me for doing just that sort of thing to Sam myself."

"Yes, I have—up until a day or two ago. Maybe I do now, but I feel you're the only one who knows just how much I'd hurt him."

"You'll hurt him a great deal, if that's what you want to know. But will you hurt him less by staying on—I mean in the long run? Are you prepared to give all Sam asks? And if you aren't——" She did not finish her sentence.

Alan said nothing, although the silence between them was growing awkward.

Finally Jo put the issue to him squarely. "If you haven't failed Sam already, are you sure you can avoid doing it sometime?"

Alan was angry with her, for he thought she was attempting to justify her own action by implying that Sam always asked too much.

"You've begged the question," he said stiffly. "I'm not asking you what Sam expects of either me or you. I'm asking you how much in your estimation I owe him."

"If you think I'm trying to blame Sam for what happened between us, you're mistaken," she answered.

For a moment Jo had his admiration, then he felt himself hating her for her part in destroying the image of his brother that he was so carefully trying to treasure. She was a cold, hard woman, giving Sam nothing in return for his devotion to her. Through the rest of the meal he was elaborately polite, knowing that by this very politeness he was hurting her.

As they stood on the walk outside the restaurant, waiting for a taxi, she turned and looked straight into his eyes. "One thing I want you to know," she said: "As a surgeon Sam will always command your respect, as he does mine." Quickly she entered the taxi which had just pulled up to the curb.

Alan was not certain from this last remark whether she meant to influence him to stay or leave Sam, but as he walked away he knew that sometime during their talk he had decided to go through with his project; and he knew, too, he must tell Sam this afternoon before his sense of obligation to his brother again took over.

16

Driving home that evening Sam felt weighed down by the pressure of interference with his way of life increasing around him. First his wife, now his brother threatened the ideal he had set up for the family. Alan separated from him would be a liability both to himself and to the family. He would probably lose money, going out for himself in one of the outlying districts of the city. The doctors already there would resent the intrusion. Sam didn't know that he'd blame them. Why did Alan want to leave an assured practice for an uncertain one? Sam saw his brother sinking back into the place in the community their father had held. "I won't let him," he promised himself fiercely. "I'll take care of him as I always have, even if he is letting me down."

As Sam entered his house he looked toward the stairs, expecting to see his daughter rushing to meet him as usual, outdistancing her mother who followed more slowly. Tonight the two were coming down hand in hand. He realized with a pang that Sally was no longer a little girl, but a woman, if a very young one. Her hair was arranged in a new way which made her look older. She was wearing a white off-the-shoulder dress; its skirt billowed around her feet. "Very charming, my dear. Did you think I was in need of a special celebration, or something of the sort?" he asked, going forward to greet her.

She gave him a pat on the shoulder, then kissed him. "You've forgotten, Father," she chided him gently. "It's the dance I told you about."

"So you didn't dress up for me!" His tone was light, but his daughter, sensitive to his every mood, recognized the disappointment in his voice.

The doorbell rang. "Better answer it, Sally. It's probably for you," said her mother.

"I want Chester to know you." Sally took her father's hand, trying to pull him with her.

"I'm too tired tonight," said Sam, turning toward his study.

Sally was troubled, but delight in her first evening dress took over as she opened the door and saw the admiration in the eyes of the young man who stood there, heard his exclamation, "Hi, beautiful!"

Looking toward Sam's retreating figure he added, "Do I meet the folks?"

Jo stepped forward, saying, "You can talk to Sally's parents some other time. You're late, you'd better be off." She put her hand on the boy's sleeve saying, "Take good care of Sally."

In a whirl of white they ran down the steps to his car.

Without Sally at the table the dinner was a silent one for her parents. The delicate web she wove over their lives was swept away, leaving them stripped of subterfuge. Still concerned over her talk with Alan, Jo was unable to steady Sam as she often did when he needed reassurance.

Sam scarcely touched the well-cooked meal, nibbled at the green salad. Before the dessert was served he arose abruptly.

"You've eaten almost nothing!" Jo exclaimed anxiously.

"I'm not hungry."

"What's wrong, Sam?"

"Alan's leaving me." His voice hurt her, so filled was it with pain and bewilderment. For the moment Jo felt she was to blame for all his suffering.

Sam paced up and down in his study. How had he failed in his role of older brother? Step by step he reviewed his care of Alan, going back to the time he'd let him, a kid whom the older boys didn't want, trail them around. He hadn't broken with Alan today; he didn't intend to, despite his younger brother's crazy, half-baked ideas.

I'll have to save him in the end. Nothing to do now . . . wait until he sees what it will mean to get along without any influence . . . decide then what is the best course to take.

A sudden temptation—he'd prevent any doctors from out of town who joined Alan from getting hospital privileges—that would settle things and quickly. . . . No, even if he seemingly took no part in such a step, Alan would guess he was responsible.

At last, wearied of his thoughts and his pacing, Sam sat down at his desk, rested his head in his hand, listening for Sally to come home.

It was late, very late, when he heard his daughter come in, heard her talking to her mother, but he did not go out to speak to her.

When the house was still he went upstairs. Softly he opened the door into his wife's room. "Are you awake, Jo?" he asked.

"Yes."

He went over and sat down on the side of her bed, reaching for her hand in the dark. How awful, thought Jo—tonight of all nights for him to take the first step toward reconciliation!

❧ 17 ❧

It was not until late in March that the three doctors, Towne, Gertz and Eichel, completed a careful study of Athenia's Southeast District, recommended to them by the State Medical Board as a part of the city that was not overstaffed with doctors. The district consisted of a once independent town almost as old as the city itself. Originally it had been a mere crossroads, a store or a shop on each corner which serviced the surrounding farm community. Later, medium-income people from the city had bought land in the neighborhood in order to give their children better surroundings than they could afford in Athenia. The houses they had put up were good, substantial two-story structures. The lawns were ample, the wide streets tree-shaded. The schools were excellent. There was a local hospital of which the residents were justly proud.

In time factories had encroached on the southeastern edge of the village, and the near-by streets had deteriorated. There the houses were unpainted and shabby. The occupants, many of them Negroes, were poor.

But directly south of the old town a vigorous new suburb was growing up on farm land recently bought by a real-estate firm. Moderately priced houses were being built on the tract.

The three men had driven out this morning to look over the new suburb. They found houses identically placed in identical positions on identical-looking streets. Occasionally a business block broke the monotonous repetition. Then on and on the streets stretched, each house like the one next to it, all cut from the same pattern—low, one-storied, the front windows covered by narrow verandas looking out on small grassplots.

"I'd say this is hardly the place for us if we want to get rich," Eichel volunteered.

"Certainly none of us had better think about being rich for a long time," Alan replied. "We might as well face it. It's going to be slow."

"We expected that, didn't we?" said Gertz, thinking of his own futile efforts to get a start in the months since he had been back in civilian life.

"I heard yesterday," said Alan, "of a store on the business street next to the old town that would make good offices. I'd like you to see it. That is, if you are agreed that we'll settle for this district."

"I'm for it," said Gertz. "It's a growing community. I doubt if we can do better."

"If we show an interest in the building do you think Corwin would try to prevent us from getting it? He seems to be kingpin among the doctors around here," Eichel said. "He wasn't exactly cordial when we called on him."

"I don't think he'd go that far," said Alan. "What he'll do, probably, is keep us from getting privileges in the local hospital. The first thing to decide is do we or do we not settle in this district? How about it, Eichel?"

"It's O.K. with me," Eichel answered, but not without misgivings.

There were many things about the setup he didn't care for. He didn't go along with all Towne's ideas, and he didn't think much of such a middle-class neighborhood. But he had to get a start somewhere. He hoped by joining Towne to be allowed to operate in one of the finest hospitals in the city of Athenia. Dr. Samuel Towne, a surgeon he deeply respected, would certainly help his brother out to that extent. Eichel was a great believer in influence.

"I suppose for the time being we'll have to live in the city and drive out," said Gertz.

"If we can't do better. But I imagine we're all agreed it's not the way to get established. Our wives can help us a lot in the community. Besides, it's a pretty long drive," Alan answered.

All three were wondering how they'd manage. So far they had heard of nothing in the neighborhood either to rent or buy. Even the houses under construction in the new division, they had been informed, were sold.

A month later the three doctors opened their offices in the store Alan had mentioned. Gertz and his wife and baby were living in the flat on the second floor—a temporary measure until they could find a house. Eichel, who had four children, had finally bought an abandoned two-room district school, ten miles out in the country, which he was remodeling.

Not long after they had decided to settle in the Southeast District, Alan in driving about the old village had noticed an empty and shuttered house. It certainly belonged to the Gay Nineties—a veranda ran around three sides; its roof was edged with an intricate lace pattern done in wood. An old-fashioned iron fence some four feet high, each picket arrow-shaped at the top, surrounded the house and lawn. Evidently the place had once been somebody's country estate. In time the growing city had overtaken it.

Such a house would be hard to sell in a small-salaried community, Alan concluded, and therefore the price might be within his reach. On inquiry he learned that the owner, a very old lady, had died the year before and that as soon as the estate was settled the house would be put on the market, for none of her family cared to live in this part of the city. A few days later the agent called him, saying the house was now for sale. Before the hour was up Alan and Esther were inspecting it.

Esther liked it from the moment she entered it. Inside it was not unlike houses she had been used to in England. However, the financial obligation involved seemed to her a tremendous undertaking just as they were starting out. The agent was talking so much she could hardly think. She was grateful when Alan turned to him and said, "My wife and I need to talk this over alone."

"O.K. I'll go out on the front porch, but you know we haven't an exclusive on this. It's a bargain, and it's my advice you don't waste time if you want it."

"What do you think of it, Esther?" asked Alan.

"I like it. In fact, I like it very much, but isn't it more than we can afford?"

"I could easily make the down payment out of Grandfather's money."

"What about its tying you to your undertaking?"

"Yes, but shouldn't it? If I have an eye out all the time for something better, do I make myself really a part of the community? Wasn't that the reason for coming?" he demanded.

"I've only one more objection," said Esther. "If you can answer it, I'm for the house. Won't such a rather grand setting separate us from the community? And how do you think your partners will feel about it?"

Alan looked slightly taken aback. Then his face brightened. "I think I can answer that. A doctor is a special person. He is a bit apart. People want him to be, in a way. They want him to be a personage. They rate one another a bit too on material assets—houses, cars and so forth."

"But isn't it the doctor's practice that is supposed to bring all this about? It's obvious you couldn't buy the house on your practice."

"Well, hardly. You're just too logical sometimes," he answered a little ruefully.

"I'm sorry, dear. I just thought you ought to consider it from every angle."

"There's another angle you, my dear woman, should consider. We want a family. The environment has to be right, doesn't it? We're buying for the future, aren't we?"

I'm really happy, thought Esther. Her last fears over how Alan regarded their marriage were now swept away.

"But not unless you really think it's the thing, Esther." Alan glanced from her to the agent, who was walking nervously back and forth on the veranda. As he passed the window Alan saw he was actually biting his nails. Maybe there really was need for haste, and Esther was holding back.

"Your decision is not to buy, hang onto the apartment in town?" Alan was disappointed.

"Oh, no! My decision is for the house and has always been," said Esther.

"Come on! We've wasted enough time, if the back of the agent tells anything," cried Alan.

Six weeks had passed since a plaque bearing the three doctors' names had been placed on the wall at the side of the entrance to their offices. People going by glanced at it, but no one came in. This morning a man was heard reading aloud:

> "Dr. Alan Towne
> Dr. A. C. Eichel
> Dr. N. S. Gertz

"There's a Dr. Towne in the city, a famous surgeon. A friend of mine went to him," he said to his companion. "Don't suppose they're any relation."

"Too bad we can't carry an ad saying the Dr. Towne is your brother," said Eichel, who had been chewing the rag with Alan, as he put it.

Gertz, hearing his partners' voices, came in from his office. "If the Hippocratic oath we all had to take meant anything—you know, the idea of brotherhood and all that—the established doctors would give us a break," he volunteered.

"You kidding?" asked Eichel. "Medicine is a business. We're their competitors, aren't we? What gets me is that we can't advertise like any other businessmen."

Alan, sitting with his chair tipped back against the wall, surveyed his partners. Eichel, who was perched on the corner of Alan's desk, was stout, squat, had strong, capable-looking hands, a round face, prominent blue eyes and full mouth, a man of action. Gertz, who was pacing up and down, was about Eichel's height, but slight, delicate-boned. His face, when in repose more that of a dreamer than a doer, just now was tense and strained.

Eichel, except for his white coat, looks like a well-to-do businessman who knows his way around, thought Alan. If any of us breaks, it won't be Eichel. He looks durable.

"Suppose we carried a dignified notice in the papers giving our credentials so that the public would know we're able, well-trained men. What's wrong with that?" demanded Eichel.

"What's wrong with it?" Alan exclaimed. "Nothing. Only you know as well as I do it's not considered ethical in this area. So what?"

"I've done a lot of thinking since I was released from the Army," Gertz cut in. "The odds are against any doctor just starting in unless he has money. The oligarchy—and both of you know there is one—plays it both ways. They've made the profession a kind of exclusive gentlemen's club. To belong to it you musn't declare you're out to earn a profit. At the same time it's a union and a pretty tough one at that."

"Union! You mean unions," said Eichel. "I did a lot of general surgery while I was in the Army. Just let me try it now. Take a few cases belonging to another specialist and where'd I be? Out."

"You're not so badly off as I am," said Gertz. "Some of the O.B.'s say a general practitioner shouldn't deliver babies. My work is more and more curtailed every year. And yet a lot of women can't possibly afford to pay a hundred and twenty-five dollars to an obstetrician."

"Especially ones on the other side of the track," Alan put in, thinking of the rundown neighborhood that lay along the eastern edge of the district. "And they can't afford what I can do for them either."

"So we continue to sit on our tails and go home to our wives every night to report unemployed," said Eichel.

"There ought to be some way for doctors like us and sick people to get together," Alan observed.

Neither of his partners made any answer. Each was thinking of his personal problem. Gertz could hear his baby's fretful crying. The rooms upstairs were hot and breathless even now in May. He was beginning to wonder if he had asked too much of his wife. She had always lived in New York, and, although since the baby's birth she had given up her musical career, she had continued, until they came here, to live in the atmosphere of music. Singing was as natural to her as breathing, but here above the office she could not sing without being heard on the street. She had accepted this curtailment of her musical life for her husband's sake. But what she couldn't accept was any threat to the baby's comfort.

Eichel's thoughts jumped back to what his wife Gertrude had told him last night. She was pregnant again. He felt a bit ashamed to tell the other doctors about it. They'd think he really should have planned better. But it wasn't their affair. One of ten children, he had grown up defending the big family. He guessed he could justify his own growing family if he had to. Think of the pleasure the children would have in one another. Scenes from his own childhood came back to him. Only he'd see that Gertrude stopped having children before she was worn out as his mother had been. Gertrude had looked tired last night, but that was because she had no help. He'd have to get a strong woman to help her. That meant drawing again on his fast diminishing bank account—pretty big when he had returned from overseas, for he had saved a good deal of his pay, but reduced to a dangerous low in the months it had taken him to get even this slight foothold.

Alan, watching the two men silent and absorbed in their own thoughts, felt slightly embarrassed thinking of his own backlog. Still he was carrying the office expenses at present.

Gertz, looking at Alan, wondered exactly why he had left his brother and gone into this venture. He and Eichel were doing it because it offered the best opportunity to get a start. Towne very evidently was actuated by some other motive. There had been a great change in him since leaving India. Of course he was sick then, thought Gertz. He's gone through some kind of struggle since. I hope it wasn't over that girl who hung around the hospital. Anyway, he's come out on top. He's a man to trust. Nathan Gertz had a sudden feeling close to affection for Alan. Because of him he and Eichel weren't fighting alone. Aloud he said, "I had a letter from a friend this morning who has been trying to get established on the West Coast. He's just about decided to give it up and go into a medical insurance firm. They want a doctor on the staff."

At his words there was a definite change in the atmosphere of the room. "The very idea of having to give up my profession makes me shudder!" exclaimed Eichel.

"Profession! You claimed it was a business!" the others protested.

"All right, all right," said Eichel. "Anyway, we've got one another to kid, and that's a lot."

Alan brought his chair down with a thud. My God, he thought, what a futile conversation for three highly trained doctors to be indulging in! After all, we knew what we were getting into. Why gripe about it? We all know specialization is good if it isn't carried too far.

The people moving up and down the street weren't giving even a curious glance in Alan's direction. A general store down the street was having a sale. Everyone's attention was on it. Suddenly a wave of homesickness threatened to engulf Alan for what he had given up so nonchalantly. He had to acknowledge that he had not fully considered the difficulties involved in his venture. Until now Alan had not grasped Sam's bitter fight to arrive. It was such a struggle Sam had wished to spare him. He looked at his watch. This was the time when he and Sam used to work together in the operating room, minds and hands co-ordinating with the perfection of a delicately adjusted mechanism. How much did men deteriorate under prolonged unemployment? What had he done to himself?

❧ 18 ❧

LIVING miles apart, the men's wives had little opportunity to share with one another their anxieties.

Mrs. Eichel, an energetic, capable German woman, short and solidly built, had faced without flinching the problem of turning the two-room schoolhouse into a habitable place to live. In the first few weeks she performed enormous tasks, untiring until she had the old building scrubbed, repainted, and with enough partitions put in to give the various members of her family a decent amount of privacy. By the end of the first month she had created a home, but in so doing she had exhausted her strength. Now she had begun to worry about the coming baby, the prospect of a hot summer with four children to care for and the necessity to economize in every way, the Lord knew for how long.

It had been a drastic curtailment of her own life for Brenda Gertz to leave her mother's comfortable apartment in New York, where she had lived while her husband was overseas, for the small apartment with the limited conveniences the owner of the building had put in. With high courage she arranged to store the baby grand piano her mother had sent her, since it was an impossibility to get it up the narrow stairs or through any of the windows.

At first nothing had seemed too much of a sacrifice if she and Nathan might be together and she might share with him the delight in their son born while he was overseas. Her greatest problem was her need to sing and the necessity not to for fear those passing on the street would hear her. She was haunted at times with the feeling that the world of music, her natural environment, was slipping away from her. Let it go, she strongly told herself; the important thing at present is for Nathan to get established. But, as the weeks went by and Nathan still had not a single patient, she began to doubt her decision to help him strike out on his own, leave behind the opportunity of entering the office of her mother's brother, a fashionable New York physician specializing in the care of wealthy women.

It was late in April when Esther and Alan—the title deeds cleared—had the peculiar joy of entering the house which they envisioned would be their permanent home. Through the years it would grow in beauty and comfort. Until Alan was making a sufficient income they had decided to furnish only a part of the house—two bedrooms upstairs, one for themselves and one for guests; downstairs, a living room and the big old-fashioned kitchen which they would use also as a dining room. The two rooms across the hall from the parlors could easily be shut off. Their one extravagance was to have the partition taken out between the parlors and to redecorate the large living room thus created. To its furnishing Esther spent hours and days in the secondhand shops of the city. Under the guidance of Jo she bought a few pieces to go with the Victorian sofa and table which Grandfather Towne had left her in a codicil attached to his will. On the white marble mantelpiece at the end of the long room she placed the heirloom candlesticks.

The two women by tacit agreement said nothing of the break between the brothers—for break it really seemed to be. Jo did not explain that for the present she felt it was better not to ask Alan and Esther to come in for dinner. Esther did not blame her for not asking them, but in her heart she did blame Sam for making it hard for Alan just now. She believed Alan missed his brother's affection and advice more than he cared to own.

May was well on its way. Esther was not seeing much of Jo now, for their shopping had been brought to a sudden stop after Alan had said one evening he thought he'd have to be prepared to carry the other doctors for a much longer time than he had expected.

Trying to fill up the vacancy in her life made by the sudden cessation of her homemaking and Jo's daily companionship, Esther began taking long walks in the country, a custom once shared with her father. She liked the countryside and felt at home in America until on her return she passed down the streets of the Southeast District. This suburban life was alien to anything she had known in England or America. She felt unanchored, adrift in this puzzling small-town American life. Now she, too, like the other wives, began to wonder if it had been a mistake to encourage her husband in his undertaking. It had seemed simple to her for him to set up practice in a region insufficiently staffed with doctors. Now she was beginning to doubt it. One day when she felt unusually lonely and unsure of herself, she heard the telephone ringing as she entered the house. She ran across the hall to catch up the receiver, so eager was she to communicate with someone. To her delight she heard Jo's voice answering her hello. Jo was asking them to drop in for dinner that evening!

Esther hastened to call Alan. "Why, yes," he said. The surprise and happiness in his voice took from her the soreness of heart she had felt toward Sam.

Promptly at five Alan drove up to the house, ran up the steps and into the hall, calling, "Ready, Esther?"

"Coming," she called back. Almost immediately she appeared at the top of the steps. How proud he was of her! In his choice of a wife even Sam could find nothing to criticize.

Jo met them at the door as naturally as if this were a usual occurrence.

"Sam telephoned a few minutes ago he'd be a little late and to start the cocktails," she said, leading the way into the living room. "Will you make them, Alan? You're better at it than I am."

Alan was glad of the chance to busy himself. He had not seen his sister-in-law since their luncheon together, and he felt they both needed time to erase the memory of how they had parted that day. After handing Jo and Esther their cocktails he left them to talk, sat down in Sam's easy chair, lighted a cigarette, picked up the evening paper and settled back with the good feeling that he was again among his own people. He read through even the advertising section and still no Sam.

"I wonder what's keeping him. He's rarely as late as this," said Jo. There was an awkward silence, all three realizing that Sam was busier because of the lack of Alan's help. At last they heard the front door open and shut. Alan tensed a little in an effort to be natural when his brother came in, but it was Sally who entered the room.

"Oh, hello," she said, standing by the door, looking from one to the other. "Where's Father? Isn't he coming home for dinner?"

"Why did you think he wouldn't?" asked her mother.

"Oh, I don't know." Sally glanced at Alan.

Soon Sam came in. "Where have you been?" exclaimed Jo.

"It's nothing to be alarmed about," he said. "A pretty sick patient I couldn't turn over to my assistant."

"Who is the lucky man?" Alan felt a pang of jealousy—his place already filled. Then his good sense came to the rescue. Of all things, he thought, going off and leaving Sam, and then being upset when he doesn't sit around mourning my departure! I'd better get myself in hand.

"Your office full?" asked Sam.

"Patients not crowding one another exactly," Alan answered lightly.

"Save your shop talk," said Jo. "Let Sam get his hands washed so we can have dinner."

Sam, turning to leave, paused for a moment, then went over and laid his hand on his daughter's shoulder. "Come along, Sally," he said. "We both look as if we could do with a little tidying up."

They were nearly through dinner when Sam interrupted the general conversation to say, "I wonder, Al, while you are getting established if you'd care to be the doctor at the railway terminal near you. It's a new project just getting under way. They're looking for someone to handle their accident work. I'm not much in favor of this sort of thing usually, but as it's become a recognized thing you might as well profit by it. I know the railway officials. I think I could get the appointment for you. You'd have to be on call when there was an accident, go in an hour a day to look after minor injuries, testify in court if a case was brought against the railroad. I hesitated a little to suggest it to them until I had your reaction, knowing my suggestions are not always acceptable to you."

He hadn't meant to make any allusion to their divergence of opinion. It was a slip. Too bad if it put Alan on the defensive! After many wakeful nights Sam had come to the conclusion that the best way to handle his brother was to fall in with his plans for the time being. This industrial job would throw Alan into contact with keen and practical businessmen. It ought to stir his ambition. Once his ambition was awakened, he'd see the advantage of identifying himself with the leading doctors of the city. Sam wanted to keep the way open so it would be easy for Alan to join him again.

"The salary you'll probably receive would be enough to carry your office expenses, I imagine," Sam went on to say. "But watch your step. Don't get out of your speciality. You're there to take care of accidents while the men are at work. The management doesn't want to be accused of infringing on the local doctors."

Good old Sam! thought Alan. Although I hurt him going off the way I did, he is giving me my first break. "It's swell of you. Thanks a lot," he said. "I'll do my best."

At his acceptance Alan saw Jo exchange a glance of understanding with Sam. I believe they're working things out, he thought. She is definitely happier than she was the day I took her to luncheon—and more fulfilled. And then the startling thought came to him: I wonder if Sam finds her more necessary to him now that I'm not around. Esther's words, spoken the night he had told her of his intention to start out on his own, came back to him: "Someday Sam will find out how much he loves his wife, sooner perhaps if you're out of the picture." He had a sudden realization of the delicate balance of family relationships.

Esther too had noticed the glance that passed between Sam and Jo. It's Jo's doing, she thought, this reconciliation between the brothers. Somehow she's made Sam see that Alan needs him. Ruefully Esther reflected, I need not have stayed away from Jo, supposing I was hiding Alan's difficulties in getting started.

As they rose from the table Sam stood aside for the women to pass, then turned to Alan. "I'd like to suggest something if you won't take it as criticism."

"Of course not," Alan answered.

"Here goes then. Isn't your setup a little overbalanced? As you know, the custom is to keep the number of Jews in many medical schools and some hospitals, and even in setups like yours, to a strict quota. Now you have Gertz and Eichel in with you. If you take on anyone else, it would, I think, do away with a lot of criticism if you saw to it that he's a Gentile."

Alan laughed. "I'd like to see what Eichel would do if you said that before him. He's so German I think he shares your—shall I say?—slight bias."

"I'm relieved."

"If a witch hunt is ever on, you want to be sure I'm not among the hunted. Is that it?" asked Alan.

"There, I was afraid you'd take what I had to say as criticism, but it's a habit of mine to see you don't do anything too rash. It might interest you to know there's a term going around for men like you—'premature antifascist.'"

With a start Alan realized the women were lingering in the doorway, waiting for the brothers to join them. Devoutly Alan hoped Esther hadn't overheard the conversation. She gave no sign.

On their drive home he explained to her what a help the industrial position would be, telling her as he had not before how great had been his anxiety over their inability to get a start. Gradually he grew uneasy at her lack of response. "Are you tired, dear?" he asked.

"No."

Silence again, and then suddenly she said, "Why haven't you ever told Sam . . . about me?"

"Why should I? It's none of his business. Besides, what possible difference would it make? You are yourself, and he likes you."

"Would he if he knew? I think not."

"Esther, I'm awfully sorry you overheard what Sam said, but really I think you're making a lot out of a little."

Again there was silence, unbroken during the rest of the drive.

As Alan drove into the garage the glare from the headlights was reflected from the garage wall into the car. He saw Esther's face in the mirror. Her eyes held a strained look.

"Esther, dear," he said, putting his hand over hers, "don't take Sam too hard. You have to understand him. He hunts conformity the way a freezing animal hunts shelter. Sometimes I think it grew out of defending me against —well, against lots of things when we were boys."

"That's not the point, Alan. It's—it's that you have seen fit to keep secret the fact that I belong to a race not wholly acceptable to your brother."

"But why, Esther, do you want to complicate things for yourself? I don't want you hurt. Can't you understand?"

83

"And you think you've kept me from being hurt?"

"Maybe not always, but mostly. Don't get me wrong. What Sam thinks doesn't matter to me. I married you because I love you. I shall be proud to be the instrument to pass down in my family all of your heritage. It will enrich our Puritan stock. There is an idealistic strain in your mother's people I covet for my children. It's in you, and I hope to God it will be in them."

Esther's head was bowed to hide from her husband her distaste for his false declaration of admiration for the Jews, for false it seemed to her. Hollow words. Then it came to her that Grandfather Towne had said almost the same thing, and she had not felt that he was making a false statement. But Grandfather Towne would not have remained silent as Alan had this evening. Deep in her heart she believed Alan did not wish Sam to know the truth about her.

"Suppose we forget it," she said, stepping out of the car. Not waiting for him, she entered the house. Suddenly she remembered something else Grandfather Towne had said. "If you raise the barrier of race between you and Alan, you may not be able to pull it down when you want to." But she was not raising it. Sam and Alan were.

❧ 19 ❧

ALAN'S opportunity to become the doctor for the near-by Railroad Center freed all three of the partners from a state of mind which might be termed a professional claustrophobia—a growing fear that they would never break through the shut and barred doors of professional opportunity. But now a small entrance into the busy, active world of doctors was opening through which they all might pass.

None of them knew much about medicine in industry except that it was part of the economic and social changes which had been taking place in American life since the beginning of the century.

Both Eichel and Gertz eagerly awaited Alan's return from his interview with the railroad company. The salary was generous, they all conceded. "It's our first break," said Eichel, "although I don't like the idea of doctors being put on a salary; but, of course, you mean it to be only temporary, don't you, Towne?"

"What I'd like to know," Gertz said, "is whether you represent the men as well as the employer."

"Isn't it the railroad that's paying the bill? Then the employer, of course," was Eichel's prompt rejoinder.

"As I understand it," said Alan, "it's both. The officer of the railroad I saw stressed the fact that it's a service voluntarily given to the men—a public-relations act. He was careful to emphasize, however, that it didn't extend to their families or to anything that happened to the men when they weren't working. Unavoidable accidents. I am to have the men fill out a questionnaire, I'd say to guard against claims being brought in for—well, for past injuries."

"How does the union feel about it?" Gertz asked.

"That I've yet to find out," Alan answered.

Just then the bell announcing patients tinkled, and a tall young man, quiet in bearing, with china-blue eyes and smoothly brushed light-brown hair, walked into the room. "I'm Powell from the Public Health Service," he said. "I've meant to come around before, but I've been busy."

"Have a seat, won't you?" Eichel pushed forward a chair. He was thinking, What's a young doctor doing in such a job? He knew the public-health work in this part of the country was highly developed and the salary paid to their doctors was very good, but, even so, no doctor with any ambition would go into it unless he had to. Caught, he supposed, like the rest of them. The button in Powell's lapel showed he was a veteran. The poor guy! thought Eichel.

"I've a proposition to put up to you. I'll tell you right off that the doctors in town I've tried to get to take it have turned me down," he began, taking the chair offered him.

"We're not in a position to be too choosy," said Alan.

"A few days ago I was doing a routine inspection of a small chemical plant just being put up," said Powell. "The manager asked me if I could get hold of a doctor who'd take care of their accident cases. Of necessity it would have to be on the basis of the fee schedule established by the state compensation act. The doctors I've talked to about taking it on say it isn't worth their while."

"If they can't make it pay, why do you think we can?" Eichel asked.

"My idea was, just starting here as you are, even small returns might seem worth your while. Contacts, I suppose, are what you're looking for."

Eichel shrugged his shoulders, suggesting annoyance—and he was annoyed. What nerve for a health officer to look down on them, for so he interpreted Powell's remark about small returns.

Aware that he had touched on a sensitive point, although he himself saw no reason why they should be sensitive over a situation any new doctor in a community had to meet, Powell hastened to say, "I thought it was possible, too, that you looked at medicine in a different way from the doctors I have so far talked to. One of them told me he wanted to make a hundred thousand dollars while he was young enough to enjoy it; then he was going to retire and go fishing. He wasn't looking for chicken feed. Another told me that, if a man sustained a fracture—you see, the floors in such a plant are slippery from frequent washings-down to avoid chemical poisoning, and such accidents are fairly common—the doctor would have to put on a new cast every few days to bring the compensation up to anything like what he considered a decent fee." Powell looked at Alan. "I believe your specialty is orthopedics.

It occurred to me you might be interested in the rehabilitation of handi-capped workers, and not just in the fee."

"Then you don't think the size of the compensation is the whole answer?" Alan asked. He liked this earnest, forthright man.

"Do you?" Powell countered and added before Alan could answer, "I probably wouldn't be in Public Health if I did."

Eichel was astonished. Could it be that Powell's job was no stopgap thing with him?

"How about thinking it over, giving me an answer by the end of the week?" said Powell, rising.

"I have an idea we can give an answer now." Alan turned to Eichel. "How about it? Fractures come under my specialty. You could do the follow-up work, Eichel."

"O.K. with me." Eichel crushed out his cigarette, saying with engaging frankness, "You guessed it, Powell. We are up against it just now."

"Good," said Powell. Then he turned to Gertz. "How about helping us out in our well-baby clinic? We have two doctors who are donating their services, but we could use another."

"I'm not a pediatrician," said Gertz.

"We have another general practitioner giving his services."

"All right," said Gertz.

"Thank you," said Powell, "but will one of you explain why on earth most doctors are willing to give time to a clinic and so against taking on moderately paid service like the chemical plant?"

"That's easy," said Eichel. "One's charity. The other's government inter-ference, and I don't like it. I'm for free enterprise. To limit fees is an infringement of our rights."

"Rot!" said the health officer. He took a step forward, and his china-blue eyes now looked black. "There are a hell of a lot of good doctors on fixed salaries in Public Health."

"I didn't mean to say anything against what you're doing." Eichel looked around for support from his partners, but neither of them gave him any. "Here, shake," he said, holding out his hand to Powell.

Alan studied Eichel. What manner of man was he? Alan wondered. Had he gone into the partnership simply to get a start? Would he ever feel any personal interest in patients?

Coming back from lunch that same day, Eichel ran into a crowd gathered at the junction of four highways some distance outside the town. Leaning out of the window of his car, he asked, "What's the trouble?"

"Collision."

"Anybody hurt?"

"Sure."

"Any doctors around?" Eichel was already getting out of his car.

"We're waiting for the cops and an ambulance."

"I'm a doctor." Using his stout strong body like a fulcrum, Eichel pushed through the crowd, repeating with automatic precision the words, "Let the doctor through!"

At his command the cohesive mass of men, women and children parted, making a path down which he walked to where two bodies were lying—a young girl, pretty in a cheap sort of way, with her skirt flung high exposing the white skin of her thighs above her stockings, and near her a young man. Eichel knelt first by the girl. He carefully turned her over, freeing her arm which was twisted under her and bleeding profusely. He clamped his strong finger about the wound. Instantly the spurting blood was stopped. Looking at an elderly capable-appearing woman standing near, he said, "Here, take my handkerchief out of my pocket and get me a stick." The tourniquet was soon in place. He moved over to her companion. The boy's shirt was torn, showing he was badly bruised around the abdomen. Internal injuries possibly. Might need to be operated on.

Just then an officer jumped off his motorcycle and strode up to Eichel. "Name," he asked. "Address. Business."

"I'm a surgeon," Eichel explained. "I happened to be passing."

As the ambulance drove off with the injured couple the crowd melted away, and Eichel squeezed his stout figure behind the wheel of his car, envying the doctor who had come in the ambulance and taken over the case from him. Like smoke to a war horse, he thought, expressing his driving desire to cut and repair in a cliché that cloaked the urgency of his desire to operate. Back at the office he went over his instruments, handling them lovingly. Only that evening when he was working in his garden did he lose the urgent need to cut into human flesh and repair it. Over and over until he was exhausted he drove his spade deep into the soil, cutting up the sod, turning it over. Cutting again, turning it over. Cutting, turning.

The next morning a well-dressed middle-aged man strode into the waiting room where Towne and Eichel were sitting. "My name's Whiteside, E. G. Whiteside. I'm looking for a Dr. Eichel."

Eichel rose. "I'm Dr. Eichel." Could it be this well-to-do man was to be his first patient?

"I've come to pay a debt," said Whiteside. "The intern at the hospital seems to think you saved that girl's life yesterday. Been a bad thing for my son if she'd died."

"Anybody, even a Boy Scout, could have done what I did," Eichel answered.

"Well, anyway you did it. Business is business, I always say." He thrust a check toward Eichel.

"I appreciate your feeling, but as a physician I simply did what my profession demands of its members." Eichel straightened himself as he spoke.

"You'd take money or send a whopping bill if I came to you as a patient, wouldn't you?" Whiteside was affronted and showed it. "You must have a hell of a big practice to be so lofty."

"In fact I haven't any," said Eichel. Without explanation he walked into his own office and closed the door.

At first Alan was annoyed. A quixotic performance . . . Not a very good way to build up a practice . . . Then he realized he liked Eichel better than he ever had before.

After Whiteside went out, the door of Eichel's office was suddenly opened. "Figure the guy meant to make it easy for his son if the case comes up in court." Again the door slammed shut.

∽ 20 ∾

On his first morning at the Railroad Center Alan was conscious that the men deeply resented him. Passing through the outer room where those with minor injuries were waiting, he caught remarks spoken in an undertone, but obviously meant for him. "What's the management after now?" . . . "I bet the doc sees that some of the boys lose their jobs."

These remarks coupled with the men's sullen acquiescence in filling out the questionnaire blanks challenged Alan. In the days that followed, seeking how to gain their co-operation, he realized that part of their antagonism was due to his own attitude. He had been regarding them as a gang who could make trouble for him if not properly handled, just as gangs other than his own could and did when he was a boy at school. When he began to think of them as individuals, members of families, fathers or sons or husbands with problems like his own, he found that their resentment covered anxiety. Constantly in their minds was the possibility that through accidents or sickness they might fail in their obligations to their families. It was this, he began to see, that made them resent him, fearing he played into the hands of management.

The first time he established a personal relationship which meant better understanding was when Jim Mulligan, a brakeman, came to see him about a minor disability which he had blown up in his mind into something serious. "I'm putting my cards on the table. Does it mean I lose my job?"

"You're strong and ought to live to be eighty if you take care of yourself," Alan told him. "What are you worrying about, anyway, with good health and a good job?"

"I've got six children and another on the way. What would happen to the missus and the kids if I got bumped off? With this here arthritis I have I don't know what the answer is."

"Well, perhaps you'd better stop with this child you say is on the way," Alan answered. "That would be a pretty good first move."

"I'm a Catholic," Jim answered. He rose to go.

Alan felt rebuked. He decided to give no more gratuitous advice. He couldn't jump off casually into a man's intimate perplexities and yet he couldn't let the man leave on that note. "It's not exactly my role to tell you what to do about your lame back, but I believe a carefully planned program of exercises would strengthen it."

"My doctor says there ain't anything to do about it."

Again Alan drew back, remembering his promise not to infringe on the practice of the private physicians. He was beginning to understand that his usefulness to the men was definitely limited.

A few mornings later Hugo Bockmeyer, an engineer, a burly fellow and a belligerent labor leader, came in from his run, threw himself down in a chair in Alan's office. "I've been after better seats for engineers for years," he snapped. "Do we get anywhere? No! Then they try to play Mama to us and put you in here to ask if we have a bellyache. Do we do what Ma told us, like good little boys, and go to the bathroom regular?" he mocked.

Ignoring the man's misinterpretation of his role as surgeon, Alan met the challenge, although he felt something of the old need to brace himself against a member of the rival gang. "Suppose I recommended a posture seat as part of a health-and-efficiency program, would you co-operate with me—as you are not doing now, by the way?"

"Sure, but you won't get 'em to do it," Bockmeyer answered.

"I'm going to try," said Alan.

Bockmeyer left, somewhat mollified.

He had hardly closed the door when it was opened again by a slim intellectual-looking conductor who, it turned out, had dropped in to discuss a book on economics he had recently read. Alan found a meeting of minds in talking to this serious young man. That day Alan felt he would be able in time to serve the men as well as management. Professionally the position wasn't yielding him much—a wrenched back, a sprained ankle, a broken toe. However, such minor accidents often did mean a better personal relationship with the men, he reflected.

As he finished taping the sprained ankle of a middle-aged porter the man said, standing stiffly by Alan's desk, "You called me Green just now, not George."

"According to the records it isn't George," replied Alan, smiling.

"You're right, it ain't. But most white men think we're all named George. I'd like to ask you something."

Alan motioned him to a chair.

"It's about my son. He's set his heart on being a doctor. He's fourteen. I dunno about the money. Suppose I get enough saved up, would a good school take him?"

"Isn't it pretty early to think about it? If he still wants to when he's a little older——" Alan wished to put off telling the father how small a Negro boy's chances were of being accepted by any of the noted medical colleges.

"He ain't ever changed his mind since he was a tiny fellow."

"I'll see what I can do when the time comes," said Alan. "Tell him that for me, and tell him he's got to have mighty high grades."

"I got to keep well if he gets his chance," were Green's parting words.

But what, Alan asked himself, did these small communications with the men mean after all? Anxiety was again piling up in him and his partners, for the contacts established at the Railroad Center, the chemical plant and the clinic had not netted them a single private patient. Although the men were beginning to bring their family problems to him, they did not seek him out at his office with the idea of consulting him about their families' ailments. Some had mentioned a family doctor in the questionnaire they filled out; more had not. Going back and forth to the Railroad Center, Alan detected in many women he passed, probably the wives of these men, symptoms of crippling diseases, slight in some, advanced in others. The neglect was in part an indifference to sickness until it became acute, which kept them from giving their families and themselves adequate medical care, but it was largely a financial matter, Alan was coming to believe.

♾ 21 ♾

THE FIRST week of July the temperature stood around a hundred; a dry wind blew from the west, a burning wind that scurried down the streets in little puffs. Windows and doors were shut against the heat and dust. Those who had cellars sought them to escape the airless, hot rooms of their homes. The nights when the wind went down seemed more unbearable than the days. Then air became a blanket of heat making sleep impossible.

In the morning the sun shone on the east side of the office building of the three doctors and in the afternoon on the west side. The windows were gleaming mirrors of heat and light. The flat above was even hotter than the first floor, for the galvanized-iron roof directly over it absorbed the sun's rays and sent the heat downward. Brenda Gertz, made half ill herself by the hot, suffocating days and nights, was constantly in attendance on her baby. In spite of all she or Nathan could do, the prickly-heat rash which at first had been only in the creases of his arms and legs spread over his body. His wailing cry was loud with anger at times; at other times soft and fretful. Brenda walked up and down, trying by the rhythm of movement to lull him to sleep.

It was the sixth day with the temperature around a hundred degrees. Eichel entered the office ahead of the others. Hearing Gertz come down the stairs, he placed himself at the foot. Teetering back on his feet, he demanded, "Why don't you do something about your kid's squalling? He'd stop it if I were his father."

Gertz, who had been up most of the night with his child, was in no mood to take anything from Eichel. "You can apologize for that or I get out."

The two facing each other in anger did not hear Towne enter. "Look here, Eichel," said Towne, purposely ignoring the obvious dissension between the two, "one of the men at the railroad telephoned me to ask if we'd see his wife. They're coming now. Offhand I'd say it's appendicitis. I'd like you to look her over."

After Eichel had made his examination he told Alan, "You're right: it is appendicitis. She must be operated on as soon as possible."

"Let me see what I can arrange at the hospital in the city where I am accredited," Alan answered.

"Look here," said Eichel, a note of desperation in his voice, "don't let them turn her over to anyone else. She's my patient."

Alan called his brother, explaining the situation while Eichel stood nervously by. "How's this?" asked Alan, his hand over the mouthpiece. "He says the best he can do is to let you assist an accredited surgeon according to the regulations. However, he thinks the man will simply supervise if he explains the situation to him. Will ten o'clock be soon enough?"

"Yes."

After the couple had left, into the silence that followed there came a thin, fretful wail. Gertz looked defensively at Eichel.

Eichel walked over, put his hand on his partner's shoulder. "I'm sorry. I shouldn't have spoken as I did this morning. It's this awful weather," he said. He acts like another man, thought Alan. He's no longer belligerent. Is operating absolutely essential to his well-being?

"Why don't you run your wife and child out to my diggings?" asked Eichel. "It's cooler out there. Gertrude would love to have another baby around. If she hasn't one, she's always saying, 'I'm out of babies.' You know —the way anyone would speak of being out of margarine, or some other household commodity? We're planning a large family."

"Thanks just as much," Gertz replied stiffly. "I think we'll stay where we are."

Eichel's offer gave Towne an idea. Why hadn't he thought of it before? He believed he'd talk it over right away with Esther. When he reached home he did not find her either in the kitchen or the living room. To his call there was no answer. He took the stairs two at a time. From behind the closed bedroom door he heard stifled sobs. Opening the door, he saw Esther lying across the bed crying with an abandonment entirely out of character.

"Darling"—he dropped on his knees beside the bed—"whatever is the matter?"

Immediately her sobs ceased as if shut off by some mechanical control. She sat up, smiling through her tears. "I didn't expect you at this hour. I— I——"

"Do you cry like this often when you don't expect me?" he asked gently. She kneaded the sodden handkerchief in her hand into a ball, pressed it down into the coverlet, her eyes lowered.

"Why did you, dear?" he urged, sitting down on the bed beside her. Pulling her into his arms, he murmured, "Esther, don't shut me out."

"I . . . my mother, my father. They are all I had."

"I thought our marriage, our love——"

"How do I know you love me?"

"How do you know!" he exclaimed.

"It's the heat," she said. "Of course you do."

At first Alan thought he'd better not burden her with his plan. Then, thinking that she was lonely and might welcome another woman in the house, he told her what had happened. "If we can just keep from getting in one another's hair until the hot weather's over, I think everything will be all right. We actually had a private patient this morning. If we could have the Gertz family here—say for two or three weeks—would it be too much for you?"

"I'd love to have them!" Esther exclaimed. "I'll drive back with you. I could do a few errands first, then go to see Mrs. Gertz. I could lead up to her coming out here—make it seem like my own idea!"

"We could give them our room," she murmured, moving about getting ready, carefully erasing the signs of her tears. "It's the coolest. It would be lovely for the baby. The crib could stand here." She seems to be talking half to herself, Alan thought, not to me. "Mrs. Gertz, if she sleeps on this side . . . she could reach out her right hand . . ." Esther's voice trailed away.

Studying her, Alan realized she hadn't been herself of late. She had been too gay, too bright, with a kind of brittle happiness not natural to her—and now to find her crying! Could it have anything to do with their decision that they'd wait to have a child? He was too good a doctor not to know that not having children often took its revenge on a woman. But it was she who, just a few days ago, had insisted that they wait, saying he should have no extra responsibilities until the three doctors were established. He dismissed the idea as entirely without foundation.

An hour later Esther knocked at the door of the Gertz flat. Brenda, holding the baby in her arms, opened it. "He's just fallen asleep," she whispered, standing aside for her guest to enter. But even as she spoke the child's fretful wailing began again.

Whatever have I been doing, thought Esther, not to have realized what it means to be cooped up in a place like this? She had met Brenda only once before, at a dinner which Alan had given at the Country Club for his associates and their wives after the partnership had been agreed on. She had liked, even admired, Mrs. Gertz, tall, almost majestic in carriage, but it had not occurred to her that Mrs. Gertz would ever need her. Now she exclaimed, "This is no place for a little child, or for you either while it's so hot! Please come and stay with us. It's cooler out where we are."

Brenda felt she should refuse the invitation, thinking it was asking too much of a stranger to take in a fretful baby. It might lead to some estrangement between Nathan and the man who was giving him his opportunity. She went over to the window, stood silently looking out, hushing her son and trying to think how to phrase her refusal so she would not sound ungracious. Almost no one was in sight; everyone who could had sought shelter from the merciless sun. A gust of wind sent a cloud of dust up in a small funneling cyclone. A newspaper danced frantically in the air, then fell to the pavement. Quite simply she asked, "Could I come this afternoon?" forgetting it was not for her to set the time.

"Right now," said Esther. "I'll help get what you need together."

Some three weeks after the Gertz family had come to stay with the Townes Alan was sitting with Nathan on the veranda one evening after dinner. They were comfortably silent. A very real friendship had been developing between them which often found silence the most satisfactory communication. But tonight Alan had a sudden impulse to lay before Nathan his bewilderment over Esther. Since the evening at Sam's house she had retreated into herself. He could not reach her. Ever since the morning he had found her crying she had maintained that bright, brittle happiness. Rather unwillingly he had come to the conclusion that her retreat from him was connected with Sam's remark about the Jews. He had hoped that Mrs. Gertz, belonging as she did to the same race as Esther's mother, might win Esther's confidence, something he had tried and failed to do. This evening he was beginning to doubt that Brenda Gertz could do it either.

Could Nathan help? Alan hesitated, fearful it was too delicate a subject, and it involved too many people. Looking up, he saw Mrs. Gertz and Esther standing in the doorway and was half relieved, half regretful that the opportunity to talk to Nathan had gone by. Light was thrown full on Brenda's face, emphasizing her fine high brow, her dark expressive eyes. A responsive human being, he was finding her. Surely in time Esther would confide in her. As he watched, Brenda seated herself on the veranda rail and Esther sat down on the steps.

It had become a custom for Brenda to sing each evening. So far she had chosen from operatic scores. Opera was almost a passion with her, and here in the house set apart from its neighbors by its large garden she could give full range to her deep and powerful contralto voice. Her singing was a personal affirmation of herself, a protest against the limitations of the flat over the doctors' offices. This evening it was different. The soft summer night, the goodness of this American couple who had given Nathan his chance, the goodness of America itself, moved her to an expression of gratitude, and she sang of America.

> O beautiful for pilgrim feet,
>   Whose stern, impassioned stress
> A thoroughfare for freedom beat
>   Across the wilderness! . . .

America!   America!
God shed His grace on thee
And crown thy good with brotherhood
From sea to shining sea!*

No one spoke when she had finished. She sang again, this time a simple lullaby. A slight wind swayed the branches of the maple at the foot of the steps, and the moon shone full on Esther's face. It was white and still. She is in deep trouble, thought Brenda with a shock, stranded somewhere beyond the ordinary avenues of communication. Brenda's intuition told her that the margin of privacy never surrendered by a very feminine woman like Esther had been extended, shutting her off from help gravely needed.

Once they were in their room, Brenda told Nathan the disturbing impression she had had of Esther and of which she could not rid herself. "Is it all my imagination?" she asked him.

"I think not," he answered. "I've been aware for several days that something is troubling her."

"Do you think Alan knows?" she asked.

"Yes and no," he answered. "He couldn't love her as he obviously does without being aware that something is wrong, but I doubt if he has suspected the real cause."

"And do you?"

"There's an expression in her eyes I know all too well. It's a fear that makes some women deny their deepest need. I see it often these days at the clinic. Memories of the last war, fear of another one, no place to live— uncertainty hangs in the air like a miasmic mist. For some reason Esther, I think, is denying her right to have a child."

"But why?" gasped Brenda.

"That's what I don't know, but I do know she loves children and passionately desires a child of her own." He went over to the crib and looked down on his son. Brenda came and stood beside her husband. "He's so beautiful, and so masculine!" murmured Nathan, bending down to smooth the soft baby hair with his hand. He parted it in boy fashion on the side. "Brenda," he said, "try to find out about Esther."

The next morning Brenda came into the dining room some time after the men had gone. "I'm sorry I'm late. Little Nathan wouldn't go to sleep. He is asleep now, probably for a couple of hours. He hasn't a bit of prickly heat any more. I'll never forget what being here is doing for him. It's been wonderful of you, never minding his crying when he first came. You must love children a great deal to have been so patient."

"Oh, it's nothing," said Esther in the tone of forced lightness Brenda as well as Alan was beginning to understand she used to ward off any intimacy.

Realizing she would have to go more than halfway if she broke through

*From *The Retinue and Other Poems* by Katharine Lee Bates (E. P. Dutton & Company, 1918). Reprinted by permission of the publisher.

the other's reserve, Brenda conquered her own reserve and said, "I suppose if we'd been sensible we would have waited to have children . . . certainly until after the war. It complicates things. But, you know, difficult as it's been, I'm glad we took the risk."

"I think it's lovely not waiting, even if it is safer. I mean—I guess I don't just know what I mean." Esther fingered the spoon in the sugar bowl, picked up a spoonful of sugar, dropped it back. If she could pour out the whole story, identify herself with her mother's people through Brenda! But she could not, for had not Alan sealed her lips against such a revelation? Alan didn't want anyone to know. His words of admiration for the Jews were empty of meaning. She would not subject a child of hers to such an inferior place in the family.

"Safer," she murmured. For a moment she lifted her eyes. Their mute appeal Brenda interpreted as meaning: it's safer never to have children.

Nathan's right, thought Brenda. She's frightened that she might have a child, but why should an English girl married into an established American family be frightened? Brenda reached over, put her hand on Esther's. She wanted to say, "Whatever it is you are troubled about, don't let it stand in the way of having children," but she saw that Esther had retreated into herself, raising a definite barrier between them.

Early that afternoon Nathan telephoned he had found a small house to rent. "Shall I take it?" he asked. Before Brenda could answer he went on to describe it. "There's a living room. At a pinch it will hold your piano—a screened-in porch at the side; a big maple shades it in the afternoon——"

"You don't have to sell me on it. By all means rent it," Brenda broke in.

"How nice!" cried Esther when she was told. "You won't ever have to take little Nath back to that awful flat. We must celebrate."

Together the two women prepared the dishes their husbands most enjoyed. The potatoes were creamed to suit Alan, and the onions French-fried for Nathan. The beefsteak which they had hurried down to the market to buy, they broiled with their admiring husbands looking on. Nathan with his son on his lap sat by the kitchen table.

When dinner was over they went to see the house. In the simple happenings of the evening and Esther's delight in everything Brenda wondered if she and Nathan had not exaggerated Esther's trouble. So did Alan.

22

THE NEXT morning Alan was up early with the idea of studying the records of the men at the Railroad Center before even the nurses arrived. Preparing his own breakfast, he moved quietly about the kitchen as he didn't wish to waken the others, his mind filled with the comfortable thought of the friendship developing between Esther and Brenda Gertz. He acknowledged to himself in this moment that there was a gulf between men and women which always existed, no matter how great their love. He believed Brenda would eventually fill this gap for Esther.

Coffeepot in hand, he walked across the kitchen to the table where he had already placed his bowl of breakfast food. The sun was shining into the bowl, picking out the separate grains of rice. The good smell of coffee was coming up to him from the pot in his hands.

Contentedly he ate. Drinking a first, a second, a third cup of coffee, he planned his morning. A couple of hours at the Railroad Center, an hour at the chemical plant, substituting for Eichel, who was at home caring for the children while his wife was at the hospital. The new baby was due any minute.

As he backed his car out of the drive into the tree-shaded street there was still a freshness to the air. But the moment he left the old part of the town he knew the day was to be very hot. Except where the apple trees of the old orchard had been left, there were no shade trees in the new town. The pavement, the roofs of the houses packed closely together, already gave off heat.

Grateful for the comparative coolness of his office, which was situated on the second floor of the railroad building, he had taken out some records from his filing cabinet and sat down at his desk preparatory to compiling the statistics he wanted when the bell rang, announcing one of the men.

"Come in," Alan called, ready for whatever kind of accident had brought a man in so early.

It was Hugo Bockmeyer who entered! "I suppose you're all set for bear," Alan said, thinking it was a pretty hot day for so strenuous an adversary. "I've had no luck in arranging for the seats."

Much to his surprise there was no spirited response from the militant union man. Instead Bockmeyer slumped down in the nearest chair and said, "The heat's got me, Doc. Had a dizzy spell just as I was coming off my run. Stomach. Got something to clean me out?"

Not just in my line, thought Alan. But every specialist was allowed a little leeway. He didn't like the man's color. He took his stethoscope out of the pocket of his doctor's coat.

"What you think you're doin'?" Hugo straightened up, his usual belligerence to the fore.

"Open your shirt!" Dr. Towne's voice carried a command which Hugo felt too sick to oppose.

Fate had dealt Alan the very worst possible hand. Hugo, of all men, with a bad heart! The management must be informed that Bockmeyer's condition made it unsafe for him to be driving an engine. He might black out any time under strain, even die at his post. But to send in such a report was to lose the confidence, little though it was, that Bockmeyer had felt in him. He must find some way to keep Hugo from thinking it was a frame-up to rid management of a troublesome union man.

"Hurry up with them pills, Doc. The missus will be callin' up the yards if I don't get along home."

Alan rose and went about preparing some medicine for Bockmeyer to take. "I want you to go home," he said, "and keep quiet. Stay in bed until I come to see you. I'll be round about noon." He wanted time to think. "I'll drive you home. It's too hot to be walking."

"Thanks, Doc." This small kindness for the moment broke down Bockmeyer's mounting suspicion.

While he was substituting for Eichel at the chemical plant Alan tried to figure out how best to handle the matter. He could go straight to the management, explain Hugo's condition, and let them take the necessary steps to remove Bockmeyer from his present job. This Hugo would deeply resent and rightly, Alan thought, yet he could not shift the responsibility entirely by advising Hugo to see his family physician. It was possible that Hugo would refuse to do so. It was also possible he might agree at the time and then, if he felt better, consider it unnecessary. Somehow Alan must know that the management was informed. It was ticklish business any way he looked at it.

On his way to the Bockmeyer house Alan thought of calling Sam to ask his advice. No, he'd stand on his own feet. But ought he to consult Eichel and Gertz? He decided against that, too. The reasonable thing to do was to let Bockmeyer handle the matter himself. There was plenty of time, since Bockmeyer's next run was not for two days. There was no use for Alan to bother his partners.

As he stopped his car in front of Hugo's house Alan noticed that the shade was drawn in a window on the south side. He hoped that meant his patient had obeyed him. Then he saw a big masculine hand reach out from under the shade. Good! Probably Hugo's own common sense told him that there was more the matter with him than a stomach-ache.

"Come on in. Missus out," shouted Bockmeyer as Alan stepped onto the porch.

Following the voice, he entered a bedroom just off the neat cottage parlor. The engineer drew his great body up on his pillows. "I done what you told me. Got into bed like a fool woman. But I ain't agoin' to stay here. I'm O.K."

Alan drew up a chair, sat down astride it, folded his arms on the back. "That being the case," he said, "let's get down to business."

"Yeah? What business?" the sick man demanded.

"I'm not going to mince matters with you, Bockmeyer. I think you're the kind of fellow that can stand up to the truth."

"Yeah." This time there was more than a little suspicion in the union leader's voice.

"I didn't tell you this morning. You weren't in condition then to hear the truth. I think you are now. That pain of yours has nothing to do with your stomach. It's your heart. With proper rest and an easier job you've nothing to fear."

"I get you!" Hugo shook his great forefinger in the young doctor's face. "You played it nice, didn't you? Sneaked over to the management and told 'em the fightin' union man's heart was bad. My God, I'd like to choke you!"

"Don't be a fool. Lie down!" Towne's voice crackled with command as he gently pushed the sick man back against his pillows. "Now let's talk this out. I've not been to your employers. You can check my movements, if you want to, since I left your door this morning. If you don't trust me, call your own doctor, let him examine you. If he agrees with me, I know you're enough of a railroad man not to endanger lives entrusted to you."

"Not on your life. There's nothing wrong with me except I want good seats to sit on!"

"Well, then the only other thing to do is to call some of your union members in. Let them decide whether to accept my diagnosis or get one from your doctor. I'll wait until tomorrow morning. Then if I haven't heard from you or your doctor, I'll have to inform management. It's not safe for you to take the train out."

Bockmeyer turned his back. Alan's only course was to leave him and give him a chance to cool off.

When Alan reached the office neither Eichel nor Gertz had come in and he had no chance to talk the matter over with them. He ought to have asked their advice this morning if he were going to ask it at all, he reflected. In time the three of them would probably work out a balance between each man's independence and the interdependence of the group, but for the present he'd have to play it all solo.

The afternoon dragged on. The telephone rang. He stiffened for combat, expecting to hear Bockmeyer's truculent voice. It was Eichel calling from the hospital to say he'd be late. "The baby has just arrived. A boy." His voice was full of pride. Again the telephone. This time it was Esther asking him to stop for a loaf of bread on his way home. Still no word as to what Bockmeyer intended to do.

Four o'clock and the telephone rang again.

"This is Dr. Corwin," the voice at the other end said. "I've been called in by one of my patients, an engineer on the railroad to verify a diagnosis I understand you made this morning. My diagnosis agrees with yours."

"I assume then that you are giving your report to the railroad," Alan answered, relieved to know that Bockmeyer wasn't going to play the fool.

"Yes," said Dr. Corwin. "But I want to say to you I object to your interference in the case. Your specialty is orthopedics, is it not? I had understood you were hired to handle accidents."

So Corwin was out to get them into trouble making it look as if he, Alan, an orthopedist, had taken over the prerogatives of another specialist by diagnosing and treating heart disease. If Corwin blew the incident up a trifle, he could give the railway officers the impression that the man they had engaged to look after accidents was deliberately encroaching on the territory of the physicians in private practice. A cad's trick, thought Alan, but he answered civilly enough, "I simply wanted to give Bockmeyer a little time to work things out for himself."

"I reiterate, you should have immediately turned him over to me."

"If you imagine that I was trying to take a patient away from you, you're mistaken. I have an obligation to the railroad."

"You're speaking then as an employee of the railroad—you, a physician!" snapped Corwin. There was ill-concealed scorn in his voice.

"What you mean is I work for a salary and you charge a fee. We're competitors. Why not say so?" Alan flung back.

"Frankly, I didn't go into medicine just to earn a bare living. I'm a good physician. I've put in years preparing myself. Now I expect my returns to be ample. I intend to give my family the best America has. Men like you forget your first obligation—your obligation to the profession." The scorn previously apparent in Corwin's voice was nothing to the anger expressed in it now.

"Let's leave the word profession out of it. Your large practice must be getting impatient. I'll not detain you. But I retain the right to know that the diagnosis on which we agree is reported by you to Bockmeyer's employers—and mine," Alan added. Once he had hung up the receiver, he regretted his angry words. He shouldn't have lost his temper. Corwin could make trouble for him.

He decided he must talk with Gertz when he reached home. Then the two of them could go out and see Eichel later in the evening and together decide what was the best course to take.

Nathan and Brenda, hurrying to get settled in the house they rented, did not come in until dinnertime. The four of them had hardly sat down around the big table in the kitchen when the telephone rang. It was Sam, asking Alan to come in that evening to see him. "I warned you, Alan, to watch your step over this railroad position."

"And you think I haven't?"

"It would seem not," Sam answered and rang off.

"It's surprising how fast the grapevine works," said Alan, coming back to the table. Then he recounted the day's happenings. "I should have consulted you and Eichel this morning, I suppose," he ended ruefully, turning to Nathan, "but it just didn't seem to be necessary."

"I don't know that you should have," Gertz answered. "After all, it's your work. Each of us ought to be as free as possible."

"I suppose what Corwin has done is to make it look as if I had gone out of my way to take a patient from him. Was I a fool to consider Bockmeyer's feelings?" Alan felt he needed support to face his brother.

"I think you stumbled into a trap," his friend replied. "I have an idea I would have, too, in like circumstances."

"I'll drive you in. That will give you a little chance to rest," said Esther. Alan felt bulwarked by the understanding of one of his partners and by Esther's ready response.

On the way into town husband and wife hardly spoke, each occupied with his own problem—the same one, had they known it. Esther was fearful that Sam's will might again control Alan; Alan was trying to brace himself against such pressure. He'd be darned if he'd let Sam decide what he should do. But as they turned into his brother's drive his confidence oozed away, for he remembered whose judgment in the past had proved more often correct.

Esther slipped her hand into her husband's. "You mustn't mind what Sam says. Promise me you won't. You can't let him decide for you. If you think you were right, stick to it whatever he says."

The house door opened and Sam stood revealed in the glare of the porch light, confident and commanding in appearance.

"Let the position with the railroad go if necessary," whispered Esther.

"You're wonderful!" was all Alan had time to murmur.

"I'm glad you brought Esther," were Sam's first words. "I think, as your wife, she should hear everything I have to say to you."

"Fine!" Alan answered, but he winced inwardly at the implication that he needed his wife for a guardian. You'd think I was ten years old, he thought savagely.

The house was filled with laughter and gaiety. A crowd of girls and boys were dancing. Sally waved as she was swung past the wide door into the hall by a very energetic youth. Jo was not in evidence. Esther doubted if she knew they were there.

"We won't be disturbed in here," said Sam, leading the way into the library. "Now," he demanded, sitting down at his desk, "I'd like to know what you're trying to do out at the Railroad Center, Alan."

"Do? I'm trying to do a good professional job. Why, has anybody told you differently?"

"I can't talk to you if you're going to have a chip on your shoulder. The trouble with you, Al, is you can't take criticism."

"I can take it if it's just. Suppose you tell me what I've done that you don't like."

"You're far too hasty in drawing conclusions." Sam's voice had its kind big-brother note. "I've simply been asked by the railroad official who is my friend to tell you they like what you've been doing in general, but they don't want you to interfere with the men's relationship with their own doctors."

"What a lot of words, Sam, to say Corwin's gone bellyaching to the railroad making a big issue out of my giving a union man time to get his bearings! Why doesn't the railroad stand by me in showing consideration to an employee who must of necessity lose his job?"

Sam said nothing, simply looked at his brother until Alan's eyes fell. Then the older man spoke. "Aren't you dodging the issue? Are you going to conform or are you not?"

"It depends on what you consider conforming," Alan answered. "I'm out to do a good job for both sides."

"Oh, nonsense!" Sam interrupted irritably. "For some reason you seem to enjoy being different. It's about time you grew up and thought about an assured place for your family."

"Why not let us decide that?" asked Esther.

With a shrug Sam dismissed her comment, addressed his next words directly to Alan. "I suppose I'll have to come right out with it. Either you set yourself right with Corwin or resign. The railroad official to whom you owe the position is giving you the chance to resign if you don't square yourself. For my sake he doesn't want to fire you."

"Suppose I choose to stand my ground?"

"I'd say you would be going out of your way to get into trouble. You had better think about your partners. Even if you want to ruin your own chances in the district, you haven't any right to ruin theirs. Don't play the fool, Alan. But there's no use my saying any more. I can see, with Esther to support you, you'll do just as you please."

Esther, watching, saw anger flare up first in one brother's blue eyes and then the other's. But something held between them, some deep brotherly affection in spite of their anger.

"You are right about my responsibility, Sam," Alan answered soberly. "I do have to consider my partners. I've already talked it over with Gertz. I intend to with Eichel in the morning. Probably I should have done it before I went to see Bockmeyer. However, Nathan was generous enough to say he thought I did the most natural thing in the circumstances."

Alan was always to remember how Esther on their way home had taken the sting out of what his brother had said to him. With love and tenderness she had taken his dreams so rudely attacked by Sam's stubborn insistence on expediency and given them back to him informed with feminine insight. His ideal of service was not an absurdity. It was the strong ferment that had been at work always to raise men above the animals.

The next morning, after an hour's talk with his partners in which he explained to them not only all that had happened between him and Bockmeyer but also everything that Corwin and Sam had said, Alan ended by saying, "This is what I really would like to do if you are willing. I'd like to go to the management and suggest they set up a committee composed of management and union to thrash out such situations as this. That would do away with suspicion among the men. We might work out something pretty good, do a bang-up job for both sides."

"Do you expect the railway executives would be willing to give labor that much say? What they want is to avoid an issue with Corwin over industrial medicine, isn't it?" Eichel was really alarmed. This was no time to pick a quarrel over anything. "I think you should make it right with Corwin."

"Where do you stand, Gertz? It's evident where Eichel does. Do I eat crow?"

Gertz hesitated. He felt he owed a great deal to Towne, but—a Jew could not afford to stick his neck out. "All things considered," he said, "I believe Eichel's right. It's no moment for us to become involved in an issue between ourselves and the local doctors over what technically might be regarded as unethical."

"I could resign," said Alan hopefully.

"We need the money. That's why you went into it in the beginning, wasn't it? We're just as much in need of money now as we were then, aren't we?" demanded Eichel.

"O.K.," said Alan. "Until we're out of the woods I'll avoid any personal relationship with the men that might put the management in an awkward position. In other words, I'm management's cat's-paw, which is what I might have foreseen. As far as I can I'll make it right with Corwin."

It's I who am the goat, not Eichel or Gertz, he thought. Then he faced it squarely. Financially the job was all but necessary if they were to survive. None of them was accredited at the hospital here. Gertz and Eichel were not members of the County Association.

That evening Esther was standing on the veranda when he drove up to the house. He waved his paper. "Hello, darling. Brenda get off all right this afternoon?"

He took the steps with a jaunty air, determined not to let Esther know how humiliating to him had been his interview with Corwin—no gracious acceptance of his apology; rather the established doctor who could afford to be generous had pressed the advantage he felt he had gained over Alan and indicated he meant to keep it. Then it was that Alan in self-defense had made use of his brother's name. The ambitious Corwin, not wishing to lose out with so prominent a member of the profession, had offered an armed truce which Alan had accepted, knowing that from now on Corwin would not come out openly against him, but would be a secret enemy.

Alan put his arm around Esther, drew her to him. "I guess it's all come out for the best. We decided on caution."

"You?" she asked. "You mean you've accepted Sam's judgment without even trying to get the railroad to see your side of it!"

"I had to. Please let me explain," answered Alan, but he saw by Esther's expression no explanation he could make would be satisfactory to her.

He walked away into the living room. She's disappointed in me. She thinks I didn't have the courage to stand by my guns. She thinks I'm Sam's tool.

He had sacrificed to necessity her faith of last evening. Disheartened, discouraged, he wished he'd never left Sam. He certainly wasn't getting much satisfaction out of his present life. Wasn't he just making himself one of the misfits?

Mechanically he answered the telephone, saying, "This is Dr. Towne."

"It's Pete, the night operator at the yards. There's been an accident down here. One of the men's kids has been hurt bad. Can you get here quick?"

"It's not my job to look after the men's families," Alan answered. "Call the man's regular physician."

"Hell!" Pete shouted into the phone. "Who do you think you are anyway? God Almighty! The kid's bad hurt. We can't get hold of Dr. Judd. I'll have you up for murder if you don't come on the double-quick."

"Cool off. I'll be down as soon as I can get there." Alan grabbed his bag, called out to Esther, "An emergency. Don't wait dinner for me!" He was out of the house into his car, enjoying the release from petty restrictions, enjoying the right to shoot through red lights on an emergency call which the emblem of the physician prominently displayed above his car plates gave him. He took the last miles at seventy. Drawing up at the station, he called out, "Where is he?"

"Over there!" The night operator pointed to a row of cars on a siding. "Looks like his belly's crushed. He was huntin' his dad and got caught between two cars."

"Have you sent for the ambulance?"

"No. I was waitin' for you."

"Well, get one and get one quick," commanded Towne, hurrying along the platform toward a hunched figure leaning over a smaller one on the ground.

The man looked up, and Alan saw it was Jim, the brakeman who had six children and another on the way. How'll he manage with a bill for an injury like this? thought Alan, leaning over the unconscious child.

Quickly, efficiently, he made his examination. Multiple fractures including the pelvis. He could prevent paralysis if, as he hoped, the spinal cord was not injured. Then suddenly remembrance of his promise came to him. He must turn the case over to the family physician.

He heard a siren in the distance growing louder and louder. Looking up, he saw the ambulance had backed up to the freight platform. The rear door was flung open, and two attendants stepped out. "Bring your stretcher over here," Alan called, adding, "I'm only the company physician. I happened to be around." Carefully they lifted the boy to the stretcher, slid it with its small burden back into place in the ambulance.

Just then a doctor's car drove up. "I came as fast as I could when I got your message, Jim." The man turned to Alan. "I'm Dr. Judd. And you?"

"Towne's my name, company physician," said Alan, thinking, So this is Dr. Judd. His name had appeared many times on the blanks made out by the men. He was a middle-aged, quiet-mannered man.

"You can tell me what you found on the way to the hospital," said Judd, standing aside for Alan to precede him into the ambulance.

The child was conscious now and moaning softly. Dr. Judd sat down by him, speaking gently to him, at the same time running his hands expertly over the little body. "Yes, I agree with you," he said. "We'll need the very best specialist we can get. Would you call Dr. Samuel Towne in the city when we get to the hospital? See if he will take the case. By the way, are you related?"

"Yes, he's my brother. I'll be glad to call him, although I understand he doesn't usually come out at night. In the circumstances he might, though. I'll get him for you on the phone."

"Thank you." Judd turned back to the boy.

"This is Dr. Towne."

From the tone Alan concluded he'd called his brother away from dinner. "This also is Dr. Towne, and I'm in a hurry, Sam. Dr. Judd out here wants to know if you will do an emergency for him—a boy with multiple fractures including the pelvis."

"Why don't you do it?" Sam's voice sounded a little impatient. "I'm entertaining guests."

"It's the child of a railroad man. I handle only the men, you know." Alan sounded smug even to himself.

"Get his physician on the phone. I'll speak to him personally about you. This is all nonsense."

Judd put down the receiver. "Your brother has referred me to you. He says you are as expert as he is."

Sam must have given me a great build-up, Alan thought with a warm sense of gratitude. Good old Sam! Out loud he said, "I am not accredited at the hospital here."

For a moment Judd looked puzzled. "When you're as good as Dr. Samuel Towne?" he asked. "We need a man like you on the staff. Is there any place where you can operate?"

Alan named the hospital where he had worked with Sam. "But the ride into town?"

"I'll give him a blood transfusion while you make the arrangements," snapped Judd.

Alan's sensitive fingers with delicate precision manipulated the bones into alignment and carefully adjusted the traction. For those hours he was the creator. The limitations set about him were gone. Like Eichel he was revitalized by the return to the work he had been trained to do.

It was very late in the evening when the two doctors felt justified in leaving. They were tired and hungry, for neither of them had had any dinner. Leaving the father at his son's bedside, they went out into the corridor. "How about some sandwiches and coffee?" asked Alan of one of the nurses.

While they were sitting in a quiet corner eating and drinking Judd said, "Make your charges as small as you can. I don't know how Jim will meet this extra expense."

"I'll have to consult my partners," Alan replied. "I'd like to make the charge purely nominal, but you see we're just starting in the neighborhood. The truth is, we're almost as up against it as Jim is."

"You're all specialists?" asked Judd.

"No," said Alan. "Gertz is a general practitioner."

"I do remember now," said Judd. "Their names were placed on the agenda for the next County Association meeting. I didn't give it much attention. My practice is with the laboring community and the run-down district by the railroad. We don't deal much in specialists. If it's not out of order, may I ask how you happened to choose the Southeast District?"

Alan knew he meant, Why aren't you with your brother? "I wanted a more personal touch than a busy city doctor gets with his patients. Does that answer you?"

"We're all too busy to get much of that," said Judd. "There's a doctor shortage."

"Really?" said Alan with lifted eyebrows.

23

In August, as mysteriously as the Black Death centuries ago had entered Europe, poliomyelitis entered the city of Athenia. Despite all that scientific research had learned of the causes of disease, when it came to what caused an outbreak of polio the modern doctor was as baffled as the doctors of medieval Europe had been over what caused plague. Only now such scourges were not laid to evil spirits. But as case after case was reported in Athenia and the neighboring towns, many were in panic, for the unknown still has power to haunt men's minds. Even members of the medical profession were not free from dread that this crippling disease might strike down someone in their own families.

Eichel looked at his healthy youngsters with little fear. To be sure, they were sturdy, robust and athletic and the toll was heavy among such children, but he congratulated himself that he had had the good sense to buy the country school. As there were no houses near, an automatic quarantine was established by not allowing the children to go into town so long as new cases of polio were being reported. He himself did the marketing, making it unnecessary for Gertrude to mingle with crowds.

Gertz felt thankful that he was no longer living above the office. His house was not isolated like Eichel's, but Brenda saw to it that their year-old son spent his days on the screened-in veranda adjoining the living room, and when the neighbors dropped in she closed the door leading to it. To make doubly sure, as his child was unusually active for his age and thus especially vulnerable to the disease, Nathan had decided to turn one of the unoccupied upper rooms of their office building into a bedroom for himself and to live there for the duration of the epidemic. Perhaps an unnecessary precaution, he told Brenda, but he was in close contact with the victims of the disease in its early stages.

As the cases in the Southeast District increased in number and the local hospital had no isolation ward, the village council, in conjunction with Dr. Powell of the Public Health Service, decided to rent an unoccupied two-story brick building and turn it into a temporary hospital where patients might be cared for during the acute stage. The local doctors volunteered to be at the Shelter, as the town people called it, at stated hours. At Dr. Powell's suggestion the committee asked Towne to take charge. Powell pointed out that Alan was amply qualified to do so because polio fell under his specialty. He also proposed Gertz as his assistant. Both of them, newly come to the community, could give their full time—a precious commodity with the disease reaching epidemic proportions.

Alan now gave up his position at the Railroad Center, and Eichel cheerfully took over the responsibility of maintaining their office hours, believing that the recognition thus given to Alan and Nathan would bring the firm, as he insisted on calling it, the publicity it needed. And, too, the contacts they would make at the Shelter would be valuable. Some of the patients the two doctors cared for during the acute stage of the disease would ultimately become their private patients, Eichel reasoned. The fitting of braces to paralyzed limbs, the operative work and general rehabilitation were slow processes which would extend over many months.

Another lucky break was that in the emergency all three of them were granted operating privileges at the local hospital. How it had come about against Corwin's opposition they did not learn until long afterward. Eichel took every opportunity to build good will for his partners by assuming all sorts of routine work at the hospital in order to relieve the doctors with large practices who were in attendance at the Shelter for certain hours every day. Corwin laughingly said to him one morning, "If you ever fall out with your partners, better look me up." Eichel didn't entertain the idea of taking Corwin up on that, although he did wish that Alan were a little more practical.

Once or twice of late Eichel had had an argument with Alan over some case either he or Gertz had taken which obviously never would be paid for—one in particular where three children in a small-income family had been stricken with polio. The local chapters of the Polio Foundation were unable to allot enough funds for daily supervision of the children after they went home. Knowing that weekly supervision by a therapist was insufficient, Alan and Nathan insisted on assuming the burden of daily visits. Eichel felt they were in no position to do so, but finally he gave in. He was finding Towne surer of himself of late, with a kind of new dignity which Eichel respected more than he cared to acknowledge.

Alan, going about his work, found the uncertainties of a few weeks ago disappearing. He felt a sense of direction now. His part in the community was becoming a reality to him.

During the worst of the epidemic nurses and technicians were brought in. On entering the local hospital late one afternoon Alan started when he saw a laboratory technician talking to the nurse at the desk. When he came nearer, he realized with a start that it was Martha Green. Surely this was no coincidence. She had come with a purpose. The usual thing when a woman felt she was injured was to go to the wife. Esther! At the very thought he felt as if a hand had tightened around his heart.

Just then Martha turned and, seeing him, held out her hand. "How are you, Dr. Towne?" she asked quite naturally. "I am to be here for only a few days," she added, "to help out during the emergency." Evidently she wished, as he did, to regard their former intimacy as definitely a thing of the past. In a day or two she had gone, and Alan, occupied with the growing demands of the stricken on his strength and time, forgot about Martha Green.

The Indian summer, usually so welcomed, this year seemed an unbearable prolongation of summer to a city full of people who looked to cold weather to end the toll of crippling and death. Long dreamy days followed one another, golden days which everyone hated, for they promised no end to a disease which flourished in such a benign atmosphere. Then, as mysteriously as it had started, the epidemic began to abate.

Early one morning Nathan called Brenda, saying, "I ought to be home in another week. We haven't had a new case in the Southeast District for several days. The city reports a slackening, too. How are you getting along?"

"Everything is going fine. Esther, as you know, has been doing the marketing for me."

"Yes. Is she less troubled?"

"I really don't know. She's here and gone so quickly."

"How do you look, Brenda? What are you wearing?"

"A dressing gown at the present moment," she answered.

"The red one?"

"No, I'm keeping that for you. Oh, Nath, I've missed you so! But you should see little Nath. He's growing up. He's a real boy. He's wearing a three-year-old suit Mother sent him."

"We'll have to think up another name for him when I get home. We can't have two Naths about."

"Listen—don't you hear him? He's hungry as usual."

"He has good lungs. 'By now, Brenda. Kiss him for me."

It was much like other morning conversations except for the exciting news that Nathan would soon be at home.

Brenda put down the receiver with a sigh which let go the accumulated suspense of weeks. She had felt so close to a precipice that, if once she looked over its edge, she might be hurled to disaster.

After small Nathan was fed, bathed and once more asleep, she went about the house putting everything in order. She sang softly to herself at first, then, joy mounting within her, she let her voice burst forth in full volume. Presently she remembered how near her neighbors were—she could look into their windows—and lowered her voice so as not to disturb them. How beautiful the day was, the soft Indian-summer haze, the golden light, a yellow leaf now and then drifting down from the soft maple tree standing sentinel over the house!

Earlier than usual she prepared her luncheon. She was hungry for the first time in weeks. Her body was rousing itself to share the joy of her spirit. Each mouthful tasted good; bread had its own flavor, the tang of cheese lingered on her tongue, the sweetness of cake was delicious after the long weeks when food had had no flavor. Motherhood, which in the anxiety of the past weeks had consumed every other emotion, receded into its rightful place. And as she sat there she again thought of Nathan with desire.

Long set to the rhythms of her son's needs, she rose at the regular time and fed him, but dreamily. Then she put him in his play pen. Today for the first time he tried to put the cover on a box, grew angry when he couldn't. She picked him up, comforting him for his failure. "Tomorrow, my darling. You mustn't be impatient." She rocked him and fingered his hands, capable even now. Did they indicate a potential musician? Or did the early desire to grasp objects mean that beautiful co-ordination between brain and hand which Nathan had? She had often felt Nathan should have been a surgeon, but Nathan disliked surgery.

The baby fell asleep in her arms. It was bliss to hold the soft warm body. What a fine head he had—beautifully shaped! She ran her hand gently over it. A cool wind was stirring. She felt its invigorating touch on her skin. The leaves came tumbling down outside the screened porch. She rose and laid her son in his crib, covered him warmly, gave one last look at him, half hidden under the covers. Just one cheek was visible, with his black eyelashes resting against it.

Quietly she closed the door and sat down at her desk to write some letters long overdue, hoping to fill the slow-moving hours before her husband's return. Her pen moved swiftly over the paper. "The weather has changed at last," she wrote her mother. "Evidently I've been under more of a strain than I realized. We have had an epidemic of polio, although the papers haven't said so. It's over now. Nath is coming home in a few days. I haven't told you before that he has been staying away on account of the baby. I thought it would only worry you." At the end she added, "Perhaps Nathan and I can come home for a couple of weeks during the opera season now that everything is going so well with him."

She sealed the letter, drew another sheet of paper toward her, wrote for a while. Finally conscious that little Nath was sleeping longer than usual today, she rose and softly opened the door, then as softly closed it, for he was sleeping quietly. She wouldn't waken him, would put him to bed a little later tonight. She looked at the clock. It was nearly four. She decided to make a cup of tea. As she started to go to the kitchen she heard a low whimpering cry. Hurriedly she opened the door and bent over the crib.

Little Nath was lying on his back. His face was flushed. I covered him too warmly, her mind tried to tell her, even as fear struck through to her heart. She put her hand on his forehead. Fever! That dry burning skin was not from overcovering. She started to lift him. He uttered a sharp cry. She forced herself to be quiet, to get the thermometer. Deftly thrusting it into his rectum, she soothed him as best she could, counting the three minutes, drew it forth—102°. She covered him again, went quickly to the telephone. Nath usually called her about this time from the office, but it was Alan who answered. "Is Nath there?" she asked.

"No. Anything I can do, Brenda?"

"The baby—his fever is 102. He's terribly restless. He cries when I touch him."

"Brenda, don't be frightened," said Alan; "it's probably nothing serious. I'll try to find Nath, and I'll come myself."

Alan turned from the telephone, went into the room where Eichel was examining a patient and beckoned him outside. "Look, get hold of Nathan, will you? Mrs. Gertz wants him. The baby is evidently pretty sick. I'm going out to see what I can do."

"Right," Eichel answered.

Nathan's car turned the corner just as Alan drove up to the house.

"I'll wait out here. If you need me, call me," Alan said, going over to his friend as he pulled up at the curb.

"Thanks." Nathan flung open the car door and ran up the steps, then with professional calm opened the door quietly, closed it quietly behind him. He found Brenda bending over the baby's crib, her back toward him. "It hurts him to be touched," she said in a strained voice.

"I'll be very careful." Gently he pushed her aside. It was hardly necessary to examine his son, so evident was it that he had polio. In spite of all his precautions the dread disease had slipped past his guard. Quickly he went to the door and called to Alan, "Telephone for the ambulance, will you?"

Brenda, hearing him, cried out in alarm, "What are you going to do?"

"The only way to save him is at the Shelter," Nathan answered.

"I'm going with him."

"You know the rule that during the acute stage——" A shudder passing through her was communicated to Nathan. At the door Alan stood looking on helplessly.

"Leave us for a moment," Nathan begged him.

Quietly Alan went into the dining room, closed the door. Again he picked up the telephone. This time he called Esther. "I'm at the Gertzes'. Little Nathan has polio. We're taking him to the Shelter."

"Poor Brenda!" cried Esther. "It will be terribly hard for her to give her baby to anyone else! I'll meet you there. I'll take her home with me." She rang off.

Esther was there as the ambulance drew up before the building. She watched Brenda walk by Nathan's side to the very door, stand there until they closed it, shutting her out. Blindly she groped her way down the steps. Brenda was making a futile effort to gather the straying fragments of her mind together. She shouldn't be alone, thought Esther, her intuitive knowledge of motherhood making her conscious, as even Nathan had not been, of what it meant to Brenda to be separated from her sick baby.

"Listen, Brenda—I'll see you are not out of touch with little Nath. You know the parents come, watch their children through the windows. We'll arrange it all for tomorrow. We'll get little Nath placed near the window so you'll be able to see him. Come home with me. As soon as Alan comes in, we'll see what can be done. He can telephone Nathan."

Now that there was something to do, the stricture around Brenda's heart lessened, and she gave quiet attention to Esther's plans.

The next morning the air was clear and sparkling, the kind of weather for which everyone had been praying. Faced with the unknown, even the cynical had implored God to end the heat. At the Shelter parents came and went, leaning against the broad window sills, smiling at their children. One young mother was stretched out on the ground just outside a basement window reading to her son. A man arrived with a ladder, gaily ascended it to the second story. His little boy was recovering; he wouldn't be crippled. Brenda took her stand at the window Nathan had designated. All day she stood there watching over her son.

In the afternoon rain clouds began drifting across the sky. The next morning a cold rain was falling, and Alan tried to dissuade Brenda from standing outside the Shelter.

"We'll put on warm clothes and rubbers," Esther assured him. Going with him into the hall, she whispered, "The rain won't hurt her as much as staying here just waiting."

"But you, Esther. I don't want you out on a day like this."

"It isn't going to harm me. I often walk in the rain."

"Do you?" With her words he sensed how alone she had been these weeks. Submerged in the immediacy of the demands of the sick on him, he realized she had moved through his days and nights as a mere background to his activities. "My dear, bear with me a little longer," he begged. "As soon as this is over I'll show you I can be a good husband."

For one brief moment they held each other close and looked into each other's eyes. He bent and kissed her.

Throughout the morning the rain fell steadily, at times running down the windowpane, forming a curtain through which Brenda could not see her child. Esther, standing beside her, begged her to come home, but Brenda shook her head, wiping away the rain from the windowpane. At noon Esther went home, changed into dry clothes, then hurried back with some hot soup. The window had been raised a little, and Brenda was singing, "Sleep, my little one. Mother is near."

Esther saw Nathan come out of the building, walk with a peculiar mechanical precision to his wife's side. He reached for her two hands, clasped his around hers. Esther could see by his face what he had come to say. This was between husband and wife. She turned away, sobs shaking her, the jar of soup still in her hands.

❧ 24 ❧

THE cold rain that foretold the approach of winter was still falling when Esther and Alan, after the baby's funeral, drove Nathan and Brenda home. Feeling that they must long to be alone, Alan gave his need to be at the Shelter as reason not to come in.

Once he had started his car, he noticed with concern that Esther seemed unable to sit erect. All the unflagging energy which she had used to sustain her friend during these days was suddenly gone. He reached for her hands. They were cold.

"It's too terrible," she murmured. "But little Nath, he won't ever know what it is to . . ." Her sentence trailed off, unfinished. Alan longed to see into her heart, but his concern at present was for her physical condition. Exhaustion was a bad symptom.

"I'm going to get you into bed, darling, the minute we're home." He left the car standing by the gate and helped her into the house. Once they were within the hall, he lifted her and carried her up the stairs. When she was in bed and he saw that the color had come back into her cheeks, chalky white in the car, his anxiety receded somewhat.

Quietly Alan left the room. First he called Judd to ask if he'd take over at the Shelter for the night. "I'll do your detail tomorrow, if you will," said Alan. "It's on account of my wife. I can't leave her while she's so exhausted." As he spoke his anxiety returned, but Judd's calm voice and his ready acceptance of the suggestion that Esther would naturally be worn out after the strain she had been under steadied Alan. He went into the kitchen and heated some milk. I doubt if she's eaten much today or yesterday either, he thought. No wonder she's exhausted. When he took the milk up to her he found her asleep. Sleep is better than food, he said to himself. After eating some supper he, too, went to bed. He'd get some rest while he could.

But he could not sleep, thinking of little Nath. It was perhaps better that he had not lived. He could never have recovered completely. Before Alan filed the victims of the epidemic. With all that science could do, many of those who had lived would be crippled for life. He thought with pity of Nathan and Brenda in their grief. He could not get them out of his mind. Even the death of his friend's baby a doctor shouldn't take as hard as this. It interfered with efficiency. Then his mind busied itself with the baffling question of what had caused this sudden new outbreak of polio, a question to which neither doctors nor research men in the laboratories had the answer. Since little Nathan had been stricken five more cases had been brought to the Shelter. The disease might again reach epidemic proportions. Had the change of weather been responsible?

Then back to Esther went his thoughts. It had been foolhardy of him to allow her to stand out in the rain—and Brenda, too. Grief and chilling, a bad combination, depleting the resistance of both women, but worse for Brenda. He was anxious about her. The shock of it all could not be so great for Esther. She would be all right in the morning. He heard a soft rustling as Esther turned first on one side, then the other. He whispered her name. There was no answer. There in the quiet house with the rain shut away the enemy of disease seemed shut away, too. Suddenly he was asleep.

Long afterward, so it seemed, he heard Esther speak his name. Pulling himself up from heavy sleep, he asked, "What is it, dear?" There was no answer. He sank again into sleep.

"Alan! Please wake up. My back—it aches so."

He was wide awake now. He turned on the light. She lay face up. He caught immediately the familiar rigidity characteristic of polio and the labored breathing.

"Only your back?" he asked.

"My neck—it's stiff. My back—it hurts me so."

He bent over her. "You've evidently taken cold. I'll get you some medicine." He tried to say the words in his most cheerful professional voice, knowing there was no medicine to help her. He took the blankets from her bed, covered her warmly, then hurried down the stairs to the telephone in the lower hall. He didn't want to use the phone in their room; it might frighten her. He called the Shelter. To his amazement Nathan answered.

"It's Esther," said Alan. "Send the ambulance."

At the Shelter Alan's and Nathan's hands met for a moment in a quick handclasp. Doctors, good doctors, both of them, and yet powerless before this disease which had now struck at the families of both. One had observed every precaution, and the disease had taken his son; one had insisted such isolation unnecessary, and the disease had struck down his wife.

"We'll have to use the improvised iron lung," said Nathan. "All the others are in use."

In the gray early morning Alan called Sam, moved by the instinctive need, when in trouble, to look to his older brother. In Sam there welled up all his protective love for his younger brother. "What can I do? I'm behind you, kid." That term, not used for years and always before resented by Alan, now gave him a sense of the goodness of family.

"Can you get hold of an iron lung? The only one we have left isn't too good."

"I'll get one somewhere," said Sam. "Don't worry. I'll bring it out."

Then a different voice on the phone—Jo's voice. "Is there anything I can do?"

"There's Brenda," said Alan. "If you'd go to see her. We're all so busy."

"What's wrong with Brenda?"

"Don't you know?" he asked in surprise. So deeply rooted had he been in the tragedy of little Nath's death, he felt he must have communicated it to his family. "Her little boy was buried yesterday." It was incredible they hadn't known.

"I'll be out immediately." Her voice was steady and strong.

Relieved and strengthened, Alan went back to Esther, who made no sign she recognized his presence. Laboriously under the action of the crude artificial lung her chest rose and fell.

Then, it seemed almost miraculously, there was Sam beside him. Slipping his arm through Alan's, Sam bent forward, watching Esther's minutest movements. Finally he drew Alan aside, saying, "I don't believe it's a hopeless case by any means. The paralysis of her chest is slight. I've a good lung coming. I'll stay and help you get her into it."

When Brenda opened the door Jo scarcely recognized the haggard, shrunken-looking woman as the tall and handsome Mrs. Gertz of a few weeks ago. Her dark eyes, then luminous, were now sunken and glazed, her cheeks hollow, her skin was dry. The afflicted spirit had penetrated the body and inflicted injury on it. Although it had been years since her baby died, Jo remembered how desperate had been her need to be alone. She believed it was so with Brenda. After sending a few telegrams and explaining to the neighbors who called out of curiosity or kindness that Mrs. Gertz was resting, Jo left.

Brenda was grateful for such understanding of her overwhelming necessity to be alone. It was this need that had made her insist on Nathan going back to the Shelter the evening before. All during the night in silence and alone she had experienced the throbbing sensation of separating herself from her baby, and now she must struggle to surmount the agony of that separation.

The days passed. The rain seemed interminable. The landscape was bleak and forbidding. The empty house, the unoccupied hours, the sudden overpowering sense that her son wandered alone somewhere, frightened and helpless, brought Brenda time after time into naked combat with her grief. A kind of paralysis of inactivity assailed her; only the desperate necessity to reach her baby was alive.

Gradually Nathan came to the conclusion that he was asking too much of Brenda to keep her in Athenia. He knew that work offered spiritual therapy. Each day new cases of polio were being brought into the Shelter, forcing him to work to the limit of his strength. Had it not been for this demand on him, he, too, might have been overpowered by the loss of his son. Brenda should be goaded to take up her music, work hard with a teacher who would call out every resource she had.

At his suggestion that she go to New York and take up the studies interrupted when they came to Athenia, Brenda wept. Some barrier between them was washed away with her tears. "I thought you didn't understand," she managed to say. She was in communication with him again. "Oh,

Nathan, I do love you, and I know what it will mean for you to live here alone! I won't stay in New York any longer than I have to—to find my way."

It was work, too, that held Alan up out of his anxiety over Esther. His only relief was to plunge into his not inconsiderable practice—a practice ironically growing out of his own and the community's calamity. As Sam had predicted, Esther was soon out of the iron lung, with a flexible bellows substituted to aid her in breathing. Before long, this, too, could be discarded. But her right arm and leg remained paralyzed. Each day Alan hoped her fever would subside, that the nervous exhaustion typical of the disease—so marked in Esther's case—would lessen and she would reach the point where they could begin the long, tedious training necessary if she were not to be permanently crippled.

❧ 25 ❧

ON THE twentieth of November the Shelter was closed. No new cases had occurred for several weeks, and all the original victims had passed the acute stage. Those still too sick to go to their homes were sent to the local hospital.

Alan took a private room for Esther. He hoped the privacy and quiet would help her to conquer the terrible lethargy, aggravated possibly by her nervous reaction to every noise. But day by day, he believed, by infinitesimal degrees the exhaustion increased. To the doctor in charge of her case Alan pointed out that to him this seemed an alarming sign.

"No two cases are ever the same. It has lasted longer than usual," was the answer. Alan went back to Esther. She was obviously weaker today. She neither opened her eyes nor spoke to him. The only sign that she gave of knowing he was there was a spasm which passed over her face, indicating that, quiet as he had been, the slightest vibration set up by his entrance had disturbed her. Watching her, he suddenly sensed there was no will in her to fight for life; she was slowly letting it slip away. With this realization came the remembrance of the young lieutenant who had died in China; he had faced a dilemma he could not solve.

Then the appalling thought came to Alan that Esther was faced with one too. He remembered how troubled she had been in the summer—no, there was nothing in that. It was morbid of him to see a connection between the two cases. But fear which he could not shake off gripped him. He must find out from another doctor whether there was any basis for such fear. He did not wish to talk with the doctor in charge, for he did not believe the man would understand. Nathan was the one to talk to.

As he entered Nathan's office Alan saw that Gertz had switched off the light on his desk preparatory to leaving. Feeling protected from his friend's scrutiny in the darkened room, he blurted out his errand. "I want to talk to you about Esther. Something's wrong."

Nathan knew the moment had come to speak of what he had first suspected when he was Alan's guest, what he had become certain of in the last weeks. But suppose he bungled his opportunity. He must take the risk. "If I ask you a few questions, could you forget for a little that you are Esther's husband and understand that I am not attempting to intrude on your privacy—that we are simply two doctors discussing a patient?"

"I hope I'm that much of a physician." The tone of voice indicated that Alan had already put up his guards.

A passing automobile threw a beam into the room. For an instant the light fell full on Alan's face. Gertz was startled to see how white and strained it was—the lines at the sides of the mouth had deepened; the eyes, usually alight with curiosity and hope, were frightened eyes.

Again the darkness shrouded them. "Is there anything troubling Esther?" Nathan asked. "Apprehension is one of the symptoms of polio, as you know. In her present condition such apprehension could be intensified into despair by something that had troubled her before her sickness."

"Nothing I know of," Alan answered.

"Nothing?" urged Nathan, wondering if it could be that Alan was entirely unaware how troubled Esther had been during the summer.

"You mean she's not happily married? You know us. You lived with us. Wasn't everything all right?" Alan demanded.

"Esther has a deep capacity for loving. She loves you as only highly imaginative women love," Nathan answered, accepting the challenge. "It has increased in her another capacity which, for some reason, she dares not satisfy." He paused, hoping Alan would make some response. As he did not, Nathan continued. "I believe she wants a child and for some reason she is denying her overwhelming desire to have one. Such denial sometimes takes a terrible revenge on a very maternal woman."

"You're crazy!" The words seemed ripped from Alan, but he did not rise and end the conversation, as for a moment Nathan feared he might.

"Is there any reason why she should fear to have children?" Gertz was determined to make his friend meet the issue.

"No," said Alan, stubbornly blocking off his remembrance of the evening they had returned from Sam's house when she asked him why he had failed to tell his family of her Jewish heritage. He had assured her that he was proud of the double heritage and ready to pass it on. Certainly she believed him. Nathan was on the wrong track. Like a lot of doctors he was riding his own hobby. Dealing with women as he was all the time, he had settled on certain theories to account for their difficulties.

"We are trying to save Esther," said Nathan gently.

With effort Alan began, "There may be one thing that troubles her, but it shouldn't. I decided for her sake not to tell my family that she was not all

English—it's not as if she were all Jewish. With an English father, it seemed unnecessary to mention it. As you know, it would avoid awkward situations, especially while I was overseas. I explained it all to her."

Emotions crowded in on Nathan: astonishment—he had never guessed that Esther's dilemma grew out of the problems of his own people; bitterness that the way for his people had been made so hard by Alan's people; anger at Esther for choosing to align herself with the dominant group. Then he was the physician again, thinking calmly and sanely. Esther's deep maternalism might, at the start, have been one factor in her love for a man who traced his lineage straight back to the Puritan beginnings in America. She would sense security for her children in such a marriage. And then that security had been shattered.

"Has anything happened recently, anything that made her feel that if"— he hesitated a moment—"that if her heritage were known neither she nor her child would be accepted by someone important to you?"

"Something like that, but there was no intention of hurting her. It was a general statement." Alan couldn't tell Nathan that his own brother—his beloved brother who had done so much for him, fought his battles for him, the distinguished specialist—had spoken out before Esther against Jews, against Gertz himself.

"If it was someone whose opinion she felt had influenced you to hide the fact, I can see it would not be easy just now when she is sick to rid her mind of such a shock." Nathan spoke with cold impersonality. Shock indeed it must have been for her to realize that the man she loved, who loved her and appreciated her rich heritage (at least so he said), denied publicly her Jewish ancestry. The very refinement of such racial prejudice in Alan was undoubtedly the subtle poison which was destroying Esther's will to live. "I'd like to think about what we can do," said Nathan.

By common consent the two doctors rose, thus ending the conversation so difficult for both.

Gertz watched Alan get into his car and drive toward the hospital; then he slipped into the driver's seat of his own car and drove to his desolate home, schooling himself as he did each night to endure its emptiness. Going about his kitchen preparing his solitary dinner of eggs, toast and coffee, he found his personal loneliness enhanced by the loneliness he felt as a Jew among Gentiles, brought home to him anew by Alan.

Without Brenda's once buoyant spirit to mitigate for him the dark memory of how members of his family had recently been persecuted in Germany, insecurity threatened to engulf him. Down through the centuries since the beginning of the Christian era persecution of his people had followed persecution. The final violence had now been administered in the very stronghold of European culture. Members of his family had died at Dachau. They had stood at the vortex of hate. He stood only on its periphery, but he could not help feeling bitterness over the many small discriminations which constantly drained away a man's dignity even here in America. There was his own exclusion from the medical building in the city—Alan's brother must have had a part in that. Undoubtedly it was he who had spoken before Esther against the Jews, and Alan had remained silent, letting his brother's prejudice communicate itself to him, racial prejudice in its most subtle form, not less ugly in its implications because Alan did not recognize it as such.

Nathan felt hate about to engulf him. The disease of the spirit which finds strength in hate—was it to become his strength? A battle waged for a man's soul in a suburban kitchen with a stack of unwashed dishes in the sink! he scoffed to himself, and laughed mirthlessly.

❧ 26 ❧

THE next afternoon Alan, again coming quietly into Esther's room, stood looking down on her. He had thought seeing Jo, whom she loved and trusted, might assure Esther of her place in the family. He hoped he was right.

"You are to be allowed to have a guest today, darling. Of course it is Jo." Esther smiled faintly. It gave Alan hope he had hit on the right solution. He stepped to the door. Jo had stood waiting outside until he prepared Esther for the visit.

"You're beautiful, Jo," Esther said a little above a whisper. Her next words indicated a very normal interest, further encouraging Alan. "Your furs—aren't they new?"

"They're my Christmas present from Sam. A little early. You must hurry and get well, Esther. We want you with us for Christmas. These are from Sam, as he couldn't come." As she spoke, she unwrapped a great bunch of long-stemmed red roses, held them up for Esther to see.

Esther's eyes fell shut. The rustling of the paper was a terrible violence outside herself, the mention of Sam a greater violence within. Exhaustion, which had lifted slightly, settled over her again.

Startled at the sudden change, Jo asked, "Esther, dear, am I tiring you?"

When the sick woman made no sign of having heard, Jo whispered to Alan, "Had I better go?"

"Yes, but wait for me. I'll join you in a moment," he whispered back.

Once they were outside the building, Jo asked, "What's wrong, Alan?"

A light snow which had begun falling at noon had made a white covering for the earth. The children were out with their sleds. Early Christmas crowds were moving up and down the street. People looked happy and gay. For an instant Alan thought Esther's weakness couldn't be dangerous. Then his fear clamped down again with greater intensity. "It was those roses! Why did Sam have to do that?" he demanded, his voice tense with feeling.

"What on earth have Sam's roses to do with Esther's condition? You didn't ask him to come to see her, only me, so he sent the flowers."

"That would have been worse!" muttered Alan.

"There's some misunderstanding. Do explain," said Jo more gently, realizing that Alan was under a great strain.

In terse clipped sentences Alan poured out his explanation.

At the end Jo said what the evening before Nathan had known but had not felt he could say. "You mustn't mind, Alan, since what we both want most is to help Esther, if I tell you what I honestly think. I believe fundamentally you are the one who is to blame."

"Me!" Alan was too astonished for the moment to be angry. Then he grew thoroughly indignant. "It evidently doesn't make any difference what happens to Esther so long as nobody touches your husband and your daughter. Always yours, yours. You shut your heart to the rest of us—even Esther."

"Now wait!" Jo laid her hand on his arm. "Don't make me your scapegoat —or Sam either. Sam would never have been guilty of that slip if you'd been frank about the matter. He's too much of a gentleman to strike out at anyone at his own table, least of all one of his own family. If you'd told him in the very beginning, the thing would have been resolved long ago. Why didn't you? You didn't want to do anything you thought would cost you Sam's good opinion! Isn't that true? A woman as finely tuned as Esther suspects such things."

"I did what I thought Esther wanted."

"You mean she did what you wanted." Feeling a little contrite over being hard on Alan when he was evidently in such desperate need of help, Jo added, "I do blame Sam, too. If he didn't have such prejudices, of course he wouldn't even unintentionally have hurt Esther."

"Exactly," said Alan. "He'll have to set things right, let her know that he really accepts her. I'll see him tomorrow."

"Let me talk to Sam," begged Jo. "I think maybe I can make him understand better than you. I know he'll do what he can to set things right. But, after all, no one but you can really do it. What the rest of us think would not matter greatly to Esther if she knew beyond a doubt that you have no slightest reservation in regard to her mother's people. If she knew that, I doubt if she, with her natural poise, would be greatly troubled over Sam's narrow views."

"It's snowing harder. You oughtn't to be driving without chains." Alan helped her into her car, closed the door, lifted his hat and was off down the street, his long legs carrying him forward in great strides.

Jo sighed. So like Sam when something she said was unacceptable to him! He repudiated not only the words, but the speaker, too.

Jo's always so sure of herself, jumping on me like that, thought Alan as he slipped into a near-by restaurant for dinner. His anger mounted. He must calm himself before going back to the hospital. But later when he was sitting by Esther, his anger surged up again. There was no one who would help him keep Esther from drifting farther and farther from him.

It was late when he reached his house. He was terribly tired. He took a shower, then got into bed and pulled the covers over his head, trying to shut out the click-clack of the chains on passing automobiles. At last he fell asleep. He started up, abruptly wide awake, thinking it was morning, only to see that the illumined dial on the face of the clock by his bed pointed to a few minutes after three. He closed his eyes, determined to go to sleep immediately as he had trained himself to do. But the usual relaxation of his body did not come. Into his mind poured an accumulation of events out of the past, seemingly unrelated yet all of them related to Jo's condemnation of him that afternoon. Slowly his defenses fell away—his effort to transfer the solution of Esther's trouble to Nathan, his anger against Jo, his self-righteous condemnation of Sam.

It was a shattering experience to strip himself of subterfuge and ask himself if his decision to keep Esther's heritage secret was a desire to avoid in Sam's eyes the responsibility of placing a stigma on the family. Slowly, unwillingly he faced it. Yes, he had stood by and let Esther go down into despair because, although he had not recognized it, he hadn't wanted to connect himself, his wife or his children with a race Sam felt inferior. Esther had sensed this. Yes, he had stood by and seen her initiated into that dark realm where the spirit in too great conflict takes upon itself to destroy the body.

Unable to accept blame for such a tragedy, Alan marshaled all the old subterfuges. Why, his marrying Esther was proof of his recognition of her as his equal, and certainly it was his own business whom he married. She was a very reserved and private person. She understood and welcomed his thoughtfulness in guarding her against embarrassment. She herself acknowledged that the loud and officious Jews made it hard for the others.

Esther was in no danger. The disease must run its course. His fears, his premonitions were fabrications of the night, Alan argued, as he sat up and swung his feet to the floor. But a voice within still challenged him. His defenses did not stand, not now when the very life of the woman he had glibly told himself he loved better than himself hung in the balance. He sank his head into his hands. He alone was responsible for Esther's despair; he alone could save her.

～♆ 27 ♆～

Jo, WORRIED about Esther, troubled over Alan's attitude, entered her house quietly, not wanting to encounter anyone until she had thought things out. Immediately she caught the aromatic scent of fresh pine.

"Is that you, Mother?" Sally called out. "You're not to come in here until dinnertime." Her voice was fresh and eager.

"In that case I'll rest awhile," Jo answered, relieved that she need not make an effort to be gay for Sally's sake. Halfway up the stairs she stopped. Sally had called to her. "I forgot, Mother. Dad phoned. He said he was bringing his new assistant home to dinner. I've told Anna. O.K.?"

Jo gave a fleeting thought to the dinner. These young men ususally had splendid appetites. There'd be plenty. She had ordered a roast and apple pie. No need to add anything extra. She went on into her own room where at Sam's wish the appointments had with the years grown luxurious. She herself would have liked this one spot in the house to be stripped almost to bareness. Too many material possessions often seemed to smother her; now was such a time.

She moved over to the window and looked out at the snow which swirled around an arc light at the corner, trying to sort out her thoughts about Esther, Alan and Sam. It was going to be a complicated, delicate matter to establish understanding among the three. And Esther was so very sick. That had been obvious to Jo's trained eyes.

A car turned the corner—Sam's. She must hurry. He would want her there to welcome his new assistant. Putting aside her concern over Esther, she slipped quickly out of her suit and into a dress Sam liked.

As she started down the stairs she saw the two men standing talking in the hall. Before she could join them, Sally pushed back the screen placed across the doorway to the living room, disclosing a scene Jo long remembered. Branches of evergreen outlined windows and fireplace, a bright fire burned on the hearth, holly wreaths hung in the windows, and Sally, her eyes alight, looking the normal girl Jo had determined long ago she should be, stood ready to greet them.

"Merton, you're really being given a reception," Sam said to his assistant. "My daughter—and, ah, here is my wife." This was the third time since Alan had left him that such introductions had been given by Sam. Jo hoped he had found the right man at last. Each time, as tonight, Sam had seemed sure of his choice; each time he had talked enthusiastically of the man he had selected; each time when the man knew his technique well enough to be of real use to him, Sam found him unsatisfactory. Was Sam unwilling to share his skill, or did these aspiring younger men become too aggressive? Jo wondered. Was this man a better choice than the others?

Evidently, if Sally were any judge, he was. The other men had been of no interest to her, but Dr. Merton obviously was. All at once she seemed to have lost her pride in the decorations. "Oh, it's nothing," she said in answer to her father's admiring glance around the room. "I just thought you and Mother did things like this so many years for my sake you'd miss it now I've grown up." She smiled at Merton as if he were in on this pampering of her parents.

Merton bowed his head slightly in order to look directly into her eyes, saying, "I like it." Jo thought what he wanted to say was "I like you."

Sally moved away, sat down by her father.

"You're from Boston, I believe, Dr. Merton," said Jo.

"Yes, but I took my training in the medical school Dr. Towne's grand-father founded."

During dinner Jo tried to evaluate him. I imagine this time Sam's found the right man, she decided as they rose from the table. He's self-assured enough to carry his share of the load, but at the same time he's modest enough to be willing to subordinate himself to Sam. And he's not so serious as Sam. His brown eyes are merry. He smiles easily. He'll be good for Sam was her final decision.

Just then the young surgeon asked a question she had not expected from him. "How do you feel about these consumer sponsored voluntary medical insurance plans that have sprung up all over the country?"

"I think the medical society believes they are not in line with our highest professional standards," Sam answered. "At least it has until lately, when there seemed no way to be rid of them."

"Why not in line?" Merton asked.

"I've read that some people here in America die because they can't afford to call a doctor when they're sick. Doesn't insurance help people like that?" Sally asked.

Sam looked at his daughter curiously. "Just when did you become in-terested in medicine—and the poor? Anyway, you've got things twisted. Here in America we've always taken care of the needy. Your old father spends at least a third of his time operating on poor patients who can't pay him."

Sally smiled at her father, and then in a clear, untroubled voice said, "I've decided to be a nurse."

"Aren't we getting pretty serious at seventeen? How about going over to the club for a little, Jo? Let Merton see what the city is like. I think it's stopped snowing."

At her father's words Sally flushed.

Too bad, thought Jo. Perhaps Sally was play-acting before Dr. Merton, but Sam shouldn't have let her down.

On the family's return from the club Sally abruptly announced she was going to bed, and, not stopping to kiss them as was her custom, she ran quickly up the stairs, calling out, "I'm off—good night!"

"What's wrong, Jo?" asked Sam, standing aside for her to enter the living room. "You're not worrying, are you, over what Sally said about being a nurse?"

"Mercy, no!"

"Of course it's absurd, just a childish notion, trying to seem grown-up before Merton probably," Sam went on.

"Even if she were, it was too bad to give her away. Besides, it's possible she wasn't putting on an act. She's old enough to be thinking about what she wants to do." Jo was a little indignant at the ease with which Sam dismissed what might well be a serious matter to Sally.

"Nonsense about my giving her away! She and I have always understood each other. Furthermore, she knows a girl brought up as she has been isn't supposed to work. I've worked hard so she shouldn't have to. But if that's not worrying you, Jo, what is?"

"Why do you ask?" she countered.

"Because you've been absent-minded all evening. Something's happened. You'd better tell me."

Jo wished she need not answer tonight, but she knew there was no use trying to evade Sam's questions. "I'm worried about Esther, and so is Alan."

"You mean she's not getting along well? Why hasn't Alan told me?" Sam was all attention now.

"It's not what you think. It's that there seems to be no will in Esther to get well."

"I never thought Esther a weakling," Sam answered in some surprise.

"She's not. It goes deeper. I'll try to explain." Jo watched the changing expression of his face, trying to judge the effect of her words as she told the story. "We're all to blame in one way or another as I see it," she ended.

"I fail to see that," he answered. "I certainly am not. How did I know she had Jewish blood? Besides, when I suggested Alan take no more Jews in with him I was only explaining that he would be apt to put himself behind the eight ball. I am no race hater. I pride myself, however, on being a realist. If what I said upset Esther, I would say she took my remarks too personally. Even if she did get upset, I hardly see how she can magnify that to the point of not wanting to get well. You don't die just because your feelings are hurt."

"Upset!" gasped Jo. "That's a good deal of an understatement, isn't it?"

"No. It was nothing personal. It's fantastic for her to feel injured by a little remark like that. I was simply stating facts. The truth is that in the medical profession certain attitudes exist whether rightly or wrongly. I was only recognizing them. Alan is always running straight into difficulties he might easily side-step. Medicine is a hard game, and if you're going to keep yourself on top, you've got to belong on top. I am a realist, Jo, as I said before, and Alan is not."

"But, Sam, I'm talking about Esther. How can we help her? There's no use saying she ought to be objective enough to apply your remark only to Dr. Gertz as Alan's partner and not to herself as Alan's wife. The fact is she's not that objective—if anybody ever is. I'm being realistic, too. If she feels rejected by the family, might it not get her down now she's sick?"

"I suppose you'll think me prejudiced if I say that what you've told me confirms my belief Alan doesn't have good judgment. He acts before he has thought out the consequences. Evidently neither he nor Esther is able to accept the situation their marriage has placed them in. As far as this business about her Jewish blood goes, the only smart thing they've done is to keep it secret. I don't see why they want to air it now. If Alan had come to me in the beginning, I'd have advised him against the marriage. And, as you see, I would have been right."

His wife looked at him in astonishment. "Sam," she cried out indignantly, "you are a hard man at times and to your own family!"

"A misunderstood one most of the time—and by my own family," he answered stiffly.

And a lonely one, she thought with sudden pity. If he could only let Alan go free to live his own life, he'd gain the confidence he so much wants his younger brother to have in him. "But you will . . . for instance, if you should go to see Esther . . . you would . . . well, you'd avoid hurting her," Jo ended a bit lamely.

Sam looked incredulous. "I'm not a fool, my dear. Nor am I cruel. Too, I happen to be a gentleman. I would not insult Esther, if that's what you are implying. Now about Sally. Don't let her get any crazy notions in her head."

Jo with some effort brought her mind back to Sally. "Sam, we've tried to keep her a child longer than we should have. She's growing up, and she'll probably have a lot of ideas that will upset us." She was trying to warn him. In the interplay of personalities within the family she saw that Sam would be the one, in the end, who might suffer the most.

Jo had a habit, when she had problems to solve, of waking in the night. Such periods she found good. With the family asleep, the house quiet, she did her best thinking. Accordingly, when she woke toward morning, her mind immediately took up its anxiety over Esther. It was indeed Alan who must solve her difficulty, and he would. For some reason Jo felt more confidence in him than she ever had before. Just how she had gained it she did not know. She certainly hadn't had it when she had left him in the afternoon. Here in the night she realized that maturity had been working in him like yeast ever since he had returned from the war. He was capable of facing blame in this matter, and she believed he would.

28

ALTHOUGH it was very early, as soon as Alan was dressed he went directly to the hospital. When the night nurse who had only a few minutes left before going off duty saw him walk along the corridor to his wife's room, she felt rightfully annoyed. Just because he was a doctor, he shouldn't upset the routine of the hospital. Then, seeing his haggard face and knowing how seriously ill Mrs. Towne was, she felt pity for him. "I'm glad you've come," she said.

Esther, roused by Alan's step out of a fitful sleep of nightmares peopled with shuffling shadowy figures with whom she had vainly struggled, lay weak and exhausted, bathed in perspiration.

Alan felt catastrophe very near. It was almost too late to open up the channel of communication between them.

"Oh, Esther," he whispered, "don't shut me out! Give me a chance to atone for what I have done to you. I asked you to deny the race you belong to—oh, Esther, not as I said, to protect you! I let you down. Yesterday I did what I should have done before we were married, told Jo. She's telling Sam. Can you forgive me?"

At first Esther found in his words no anchor to hold her drifting spirit. "I'm so tired," she pleaded. Her tie with him was the last thread holding her to life—almost frayed out now. Her eyes fell shut, hiding him from view. Then she felt the pressure of his lips against the palm of her hand. The locked doors of her spirit gave a little.

Esther's fight to gain even a small ascendancy over disease was a bitter one, but gradually the pain, the nightmarish dreams lessened. Still, often when dropping off to sleep she would be caught in a kind of overlapping of devastating sickness on returning health. The sense of rejection so long an integral part of her marriage threatened again to take shape as overwhelming catastrophe, and she would be bathed in perspiration and lie weak and exhausted to face hours of apprehension which robbed her of the will to fight.

One night she found she could hold herself up out of this apprehensive quicksand by recreating an experience of her childhood. Her father, in order to teach her the laws of gravity, used to take her on starry evenings to the garden that sloped away from their house in England. As they lay flat on the ground, side by side, he would picture for her the round earth swinging and turning in space, the two of them by the law of the universe held to it, cradled on the rounded surface, looking up at the other planets, safe and unafraid.

Now during darkness, the time so difficult for the sick and the troubled, she found safety in the presence of Him who directed the planets in their courses. From that safety she would step out cautiously on the thin ice of her new safety in Alan. At last dawn would come, bringing with it a stir of life—her breakfast tray, the arrival of the doctor and, climax of the day, Alan's visit.

Little by little she grew stronger, although her right side was heavy with its paralysis.

Warmed by the kindly atmosphere that friends and relatives, even Sam, created around her, she drifted in the backwater of convalescence, accepting at its face value her newly established position in the family expressed by Jo's and Sally's visits, and finally, one from Sam. One afternoon excitement swept along the corridor and into her room. The nurse entered, her manner not so coolly professional as it usually was. "Dr. Samuel Towne wants to know if you will see him," she asked, smoothing the bedcovers, then giving a quick tidying to the room. Esther's heart pounded in her weakened body as her brother-in-law walked toward her bed.

"It's good to see you," Sam said, sitting down beside her. "From all I can gather, you've been a foolish little girl. Now that you are getting better, we'll both forget it." Esther was quick to sense the condescension to the sick implied in his voice and words. "Little girl" indeed! Then relief claimed victory over her resentment. Sam was offering her a place in the family even if on his terms, not hers.

But the paralysis of her right side remained. No effort made by doctor or therapist brought to her mind the function of the useless muscles. Nathan, watching her closely, thought he understood why. He bided the time when he would be alone with her. Then he hoped to make her face it.

One evening when Alan was busy Nathan suggested that he go to see Esther in Alan's place. The two men had grown close together since that afternoon when Alan had called on Nathan to help him. Each had come to have great confidence in the other—Nathan in Alan for acknowledging he had held prejudice; Alan in Nathan for not holding it against him.

Esther, seeing Nathan enter the room alone, immediately became aloof, answering questions in monosyllables. Then abruptly she cried out, "I suppose you despise me! You think you wouldn't have kept it secret."

"You're wrong, Esther. Quite the contrary. I think you were wise to identify yourself completely with Alan's people. That is, it was a rational decision, good if you could do it without injury to yourself."

"You're saying the same thing, aren't you?" she demanded defiantly.

"Let me explain what I mean," said Nathan. "My family is orthodox. As you know, Brenda and I are not. In the eyes of our parents we are betraying our heritage. Everyone, whether Gentile or Jew, breaks with the past generation in some way, but for a Jew it is especially difficult. He does it often at a very high price. Most of us manage to pay that price without injury to ourselves."

Even in the subdued light cast by the shaded lamp at the side of her bed Esther's pallor was startling. Her eyes burned, her lips set in a thin line.

"What is it you are hiding from, Esther? Tell me. I, a Jew, shall not condemn you."

Tears unheeded ran down Esther's face. "I was a little girl. We were in Poland for the summer. My mother was running to get in. I hid. I didn't help her. I'd almost forgotten about it—until I was sick."

Nathan was filled with compassion. So often the maladjustments of his people were due to some scar received before they were mature enough to bear persecution, undetected until they themselves were discriminated against. "You know," he said very gently, "you couldn't have helped her." He waited, then urged, "You know that."

"My silence. You know, not even telling you and Brenda. Don't you see? My mother was right in thinking I had no courage."

"So you are going to punish yourself and Alan for what you interpret as disloyalty on your part?"

"You mean——"

"I mean by not having children. You're holding back from full recovery right now, using your sickness to justify such a decision."

"Of course I'm not!"

"Remember I am a Jew, and I know how we punish ourselves. Giving up children isn't going to atone to your mother."

In her stubborn silence Nathan recognized Esther was not yet ready to give up invalidism and the protection it afforded her. But from then on she did welcome his visits. It seemed to be a relief to her to talk of her childhood. To his surprise he found it was the story of a happy one. But when she told of her later girlhood it was different. One evening she gave an elaborate explanation of why she had wanted to be confirmed in the Church of England. "I'd always attended with both Father and Mother. I was at the adolescent age when a girl seeks religious experience, my father said. Mother was different after that. I'm sure she thought I was using the Christian religion to protect myself. I think even Father didn't grasp how troubled Mother was. Her eyes were on Europe even then."

What a cruel coincidence, thought Nathan, that the strains daughter and mother were under—one caught in the dark war between child and woman, the other in the equally dark war a woman enters when she is about to give up her unique value to society—should be complicated by the loyalties to race.

Nathan knew that somehow Esther's link with the past must be broken, and so did Alan. Reluctantly, with Nathan's help, he came to the conclusion that she must take a more active step out of her sickness, and that she could take it only if she were away from the solicitude of the family on which she now leaned, away even from him. She must make the hard struggle to get well among others who were making it.

Throughout the country there were many rehabilitation centers for victims of paralysis of all kinds, although none in Athenia. Gradually Alan sifted them out until only two remained on his list of possibilities. In the others either the treatment, he felt, was not scientific or patient-doctor relationship was not what he desired for Esther.

Then, quite by accident, he read in a magazine article of an institution in Nevada established by a Dr. Carothers, where new and surprisingly effective methods had been introduced. It was a popular article without the scientific data that he, as a specialist, needed to evaluate the methods and the man. He began asking other orthopedists about Carothers. One or two had heard of him, among them Sam, but not favorably. "Too much of an innovator" was the criticism. Alan, remembering his grandfather's experience when he had introduced new ideas, decided he would investigate for himself.

Leaving his practice in the hands of his partners and with the promise that Nathan would go to see Esther every day, Alan took a plane for Nevada. Arriving early in the morning, he went directly to the Carothers Institute, as it was called. While he sat in the doctor's private office waiting for him to come in, he began to fear that he had followed a false lead. The building was not large; the lobby was shabby; there was none of the almost military precision deemed by the profession so necessary in hospitals. There was more the atmosphere of a comfortable European pension.

Alan heard voices in the hall. One caught his attention, soft, musical, strangely compelling. Then the door opened, and the man who entered said in a soft musical voice, "I am Dr. Carothers." One might have taken him for an Italian because of his luminous brown eyes and olive skin. However, Alan's guess was that he came from one of the Balkan States. Both as physician and husband, Alan tried to gauge the quality of the man. Of his humanity there seemed little doubt. Also he seemed to have a kind of basic patience which Alan knew was invaluable in rehabilitation work. Looking into the man's soft brown eyes you were conscious of it; you felt it in his quiet manner. A man who did not have both patience and humanity would never have thought up a process so delicate and so tedious, Alan realized as Dr. Carothers explained his theories of rehabilitation. Also in his lucid explanation there was continual evidence of the well-trained physician. His stocky, well-built body indicated strength and vigor not usually found in so gentle a man. These, too, Alan saw were definitely needed qualities in the techniques Carothers used.

After a half hour spent explaining his theories Carothers said, "Let me show you what we are doing." They entered a large room filled with men, women and children, all intent on trying to sit up, stand, or walk. Under Carothers' guidance Alan, moving among the victims of polio and arthritis, the spastics, the paralytics, and those with multiple sclerosis especially doomed, felt a kind of aggregate will to get well dominate the room.

"Surely you don't expect they'll all recover, do you?" he asked.

"Why else would they be here? I can help them to lead useful lives. Even those afflicted with multiple sclerosis can often keep ahead of the disease by learning to use uninjured parts of the brain to do the work of the injured part, make new pathways, detours around the brain devastation. Is that not enough? Where do sickness and health begin?"

Alan answered his question by asking, "How long do you think it will be before your ideas are generally accepted?"

"Years, I imagine," Carothers answered. "Ideas take a long time to penetrate. By the way, did another doctor recommend me to you?"

"No," said Alan. "I saw a magazine article. I began making inquiries."

"And you didn't get very far with the men of your specialty. That's what I mean when I say ideas penetrate slowly." His words held no bitterness, rather the patience Alan had been conscious of ever since he had met the man.

"I want to show you the resistance treatment we use so much," Dr. Carothers said, stopping beside a heavy-set man who lay on a table. The patient's feeble efforts to sit up were pitted against Dr. Carothers' carefully calculated resistance. Over and over it was repeated. As the patient was able to increase his effort so did the resistance of the doctor increase. This, thought Alan, is a physician in the Hippocratic tradition, using his own strength literally to augment the inferior strength of his patient. It is his hope, his will, his courage that dominate the group. That tremendous concentrated will Alan had felt on entering the room had its dynamic center in Dr. Carothers.

Later, in his office, the doctor went over with Alan what he thought could be done for Esther. "Only if your wife is determined to recover can we teach her to remember the original function of the now useless muscles."

"Even her desire to live is a recent triumph," Alan answered. "The idea that she can ever walk again flickers up, then seems to die down again."

"If the flicker is there, we've every chance of increasing it until it's a constant flame." In Dr. Carothers' eyes as he spoke was a look of compassion. Now Alan was certain that this was the place for Esther. He was a little taken aback when he learned how expensive it would be to send her to the Institute, but of course treatment like this couldn't be cheap. Such individual help meant many trained therapists. But for the inheritance from his grandfather Alan could not have sent Esther here.

Gradually Alan prepared Esther for the undertaking. At last he was able to arouse her to consent to the adventure, a consent easier for her to give because the adventure was still in the future. But on the day he told her he had received word there was room for her at the Institute she drew back. Emotions over which she seemed to have no control crowded in on her. Fright, fed from mysterious inner sources, threatened to engulf her. Seeing the look of terror in her eyes, Alan reached out to pull her back. "You can do it, Esther. I'm going with you. I'll stay for a day or two, and I'll come often to see you. Sam is chartering a plane for us."

Sitting in the plane beside his wife, Alan felt gratitude to Sam, who had made it possible for them to travel in the privacy which shielded her from the stares so wounding to a crippled person. More than once in the course of the flight, he said, "It was nice of Sam, wasn't it?"

"I'm glad for your sake," Esther said finally toward the end of their journey.

"Only for mine?"

"Yes, I know what your family means to you. If they've accepted me for your sake, I'm glad."

"It's for yourself. Really, Esther, it is."

She looked out past the wing of the plane at the green winter hills of Nevada over which they were passing. "I don't know how to say it, Alan. I'm still confused. It's not clear to me yet what my place in the family is— my responsibility to it. I must wait to know." . . .

The plane was flying lower now, circling for its landing. There was the jolt of its wheels as it bounced along on the ground.

Esther listened to Alan's step growing fainter as he went down the hall of the Institute. To be without him seemed a new crippling, for the separation left her with the sensation of actual physical impairment, as if a part of her essential self had been torn away. For a few days she lay helpless, no will driving her to effort. Then came a morning when the vitality of Dr. Carothers' mind seemed to vitalize hers, a rapport mysteriously achieved by which his mind conveyed to hers its belief in recovery. There was a stirring of her imagination to the idea of recovery and then a stirring of her will.

And then Bridie came into Esther's life—the Irish therapist who had been with Dr. Carothers from the beginning of his work, a tall compact woman with a deep compassion for suffering who could take a strong man or the frailest child and fit her strength in powerful or tiny resistance. Patiently day after day she put her strength at Esther's service. Slowly Esther's paralyzed arm and leg began to show signs of life. She was fascinated with herself. It was as if she gazed into a mirror which gave back to her only her own marvelous recovery.

Then, bit by bit, she awoke to the world around her, a world of others struggling as she was. At first the members of that world seemed unrelated to one another or to her. Some had every evidence of coming from luxurious homes. Some were miners injured in the mines, sent here by their union. There were others who were supported by charitable organizations. There were those who were here by benefit of the sacrifice of their families. There were the educated, the illiterate. Polio was no respecter of persons, nor was arthritis, nor multiple sclerosis. This was a motley crowd but united in a fight to conquer the enemy of them all—disease. Esther learned she could be one of them if she made the demands on the spirit Dr. Carothers had taught the others to tap.

Among the group was an eager handsome young man with whom Esther liked to talk. "I have a chance to keep ahead of multiple sclerosis," he explained, leaning on his crutches. "I am making new connections to my muscles, going around the brain damage," he said earnestly. "I hope to go back to my work pretty soon. I'm a minister. Dr. Carothers' first patient with this disease now does a full day's work in his father's office." Each day the young man showed Esther how much he had progressed. To all he was like some knight in bright armor on crutches enlisting them in battle.

One day he was not among them. Soon they learned he never would be. Their common enemy, disease, had struck with all his force, and their knight was dead. Hope seemed to go with him, and their aggregate will became a dangerous and profound aggregate discouragement. Death they envisioned stalking the corridors, the great gymnasium, and, worst of all, entering their private rooms. Then it was they came to understand that they could lean on no knight. It was a grim battle captained by Dr. Carothers. He moved among them now, giving this one a new exercise, helping that one to take his first uncertain steps. To Esther he brought crutches. "It's in your power to use them." So did he quicken to life the dying will of the group.

29

By THE END of the year the struggle of the three doctors to establish a practice was behind them. The polio epidemic had, as Eichel had foreseen, given them the contacts they needed. But Alan was not satisfied. As he saw it he had simply duplicated the struggle Sam had made; in the end he would come to the same busy and highly remunerative position his brother held. Alan was honest enough with himself to grant that he had a good deal of satisfaction in making the grade without Sam's help. However, he recognized that this was a passing gratification, that his fundamental purpose in leaving his brother was as far as ever from being realized. During the evenings, terribly long without Esther, he sought a way to implement his desire to make a doctor's role a deeply social one. He had to acknowledge that as the practice of the three doctors had increased, in direct ratio the shared interest in their patients had decreased. He saw that more and more what the three of them shared was their financial situation—the disbursement of funds, decisions to buy new equipment, the hiring of a nurse, the possibility of taking on a secretary—all indications of their success.

If his original idea that together they would try to integrate the patient with his environment was to be realized, some way must be found for the three to focus their attention on the background of disease. This meant a closer relationship with their patients. Alan was coming to believe that the ideal patient-doctor relationship would never be established as long as the question of fees stood between them. Anxiety on the part of the patient that he could not afford the treatment he needed, even suspicion at times that the physician was prolonging the relationship in order to collect more money, negated to a large extent the rapport which Alan sought. He had come to understand while he was at the Army hospital how delicate and intricate was the process of healing.

He knew he was not the only doctor thinking along these lines. Voluntary medical-insurance plans and co-operative schemes had been burgeoning all over the country for years in response to what forward-looking doctors felt to be a public demand. He knew also that because these plans constituted a departure from medical tradition they had in the beginning represented radicalism to the rank and file of the profession. What he was after he saw all too clearly would be considered even more radical. None of these insurance plans as he saw it would bring him to the relationship he was after. He wanted families to come freely before disease reached the proportions which the medical-insurance groups recognized as worthy to be paid for. To accomplish this, his idea would be that the three doctors set up a yearly fee for their services to a family and study its medical needs. Esther's sickness had shown him that the unit of illness was the family. Alan was not at all certain that his partners would go along with such a plan. He would, of course, have to abide by their decision.

He was trying to think how to present his thinking to them when unexpectedly the opportunity to do so offered itself. They all had stayed at the office one evening to straighten out their finances. It was a very satisfactory situation in which they found themselves. The group was making enough so that each could look forward to a comfortable living. Furthermore, out of the combined take Eichel proposed a certain amount be put aside each month from now on to repay Alan for what he had advanced during the summer.

"We're pretty smart hombres, if I do say it." Eichel looked enormously pleased with himself.

"Actually it was the epidemic that set us on our feet, wasn't it?" asked Alan.

"You act as if we'd gone out to profit by the people's misfortune. It was damned lucky for the community we were here," Eichel flung back.

"Sure," said Alan, "but I believe the community could be a lot luckier than it is now. You know as well as I do that many of the polio victims we saw through the first stages we ought to be looking after now, and we're not because they can't pay for the close supervision of daily visits."

"How do you know they can't pay?" Eichel demanded, a little uneasy over the turn the conversation had taken. "If grown men and women haven't sense enough to take care of their families, there isn't much we can do about it. I'd be willing to bet they'll find the money to buy new cars or radios."

"Some of the families in this district are pretty hard hit," Nathan put in, thinking of the signs of economy he had seen in a family where two children had been stricken with polio. Both mother and father were working now, leaving the five-year-old child, who only under daily expert supervision could escape major crippling, to the inadequate care the grandmother gave him. Often when Nathan called he would find the old lady holding the little boy when he should have been lying in his crib with the soles of his feet pressed against a board at the foot.

"What I've been wondering is, if we worked out what we considered a reasonable income for each of us and then hired ourselves out, so to speak, to the members of the community to keep them well as far as it's possible—check disease in its early stages—if we didn't want too big an income—well, couldn't we put ourselves within reach of most of the families?" said Alan.

Gertz's face showed astonishment at such a radical proposal.

"Don't look so surprised," said Alan. "It's not a very original idea. There are doctor co-operatives in the country, run just the way other co-operatives are."

"My God!" exclaimed Eichel. "I for one am not for hire like a grocery clerk. Besides, that Southwestern co-operative is in all sorts of trouble.

Doctors fighting it. Let's give our services to those who can't pay. The clinics are open to anyone who needs them."

"First time I've heard of it. Didn't you ever hear of the means test? It's mean all right," Alan answered. "Before you get help they turn you inside out to find out if you've anything you could cash in on to pay the hospital charges. From accident or major sickness a family often emerges stripped of its tiny backlog. I'm talking about a plan for the Southeast District in Athenia—middle class. These people aren't eligible for the free clinics, and they wouldn't use them if they were. They hate charity as the devil hates holy water."

"Give us a chance to think this over," Nathan pleaded. "You've evidently worked it out in your own mind. What you propose is pretty startling, and we need time to think about it."

"It's not so different from what the pediatricians have done," said Alan. "They charge so much monthly for keeping a child well."

"It sounds more reasonable put that way," said Gertz with a smile.

Eichel was alarmed at the possibility that Gertz would join with Towne in what he considered a highly unprofessional scheme. It was he who had carried the responsibility of the office during the epidemic. Were they going to push aside his judgment now? He had seen their growing friendship and resented it. He closed his heart to the fact that they had been drawn together by the experience of sickness and death which he mercifully had been spared; he closed his mind to the fact that he did not wish to recognize Gertz's response to what Alan proposed because it threatened his own ambitions. Nor did he wish to acknowledge that the cleavage which seemed to be developing between him and his two associates lay deep in the difference in their personalities. "When did you two cook this up?" he demanded.

"It's as new to me as to you," Gertz answered, "and frankly, although I see the value of Towne's plan, I don't believe that we're in a position to gamble on it—because it definitely would be a gamble."

Eichel felt less threatened now. If it was a gamble, naturally it was out.

"Don't condemn my idea until you've studied the plan as I've set it up," Alan pleaded. "I haven't thought we'd do anything drastic. Put it up first to a few of our patients, let them try it out, see how it works. Establish a control. Keep records."

"You think we could get well people to pay us money! The women would rather buy cosmetics," Eichel scoffed, glancing out the window at a woman passing. "How much do you suppose that woman pays for lipstick and powder, let alone perfume?"

"But we could build toward it, and in the meantime our regular practice would go on just the same," said Alan, ignoring Eichel's cynical remark.

"How many hours do you mean to put in each day?" asked Gertz.

"Not more than Dr. Judd puts in. Not more than most general practitioners do, even specialists unless they've reached the place the big fellows have, where they take no night calls. Let me just explain what I've been trying to work out. Isn't it possible doctors are attacking their problem backward? People come to us only when they're actually sick. By that time very likely they need an operation—at least in Eichel's field and mine. I'd like to prevent such an emotional and financial catastrophe to the family, if possible."

Eichel got up, walked around the room, his lower lip thrust out. How often would he have a chance to operate, he thought, with all the emphasis on preventative medicine? "We couldn't insure them against a major operation or a bad accident. We couldn't afford to include their hospital bills. I don't think they'd feel they were getting much out of it," he argued.

"I guess they'd have to do a bit of gambling too," said Alan. "They might be caught with a big hospital bill, but if we are good diagnosticians, we'll save them many a potential operation by discovering, say, cancer in its early stages and recommending treatment in time. I've lined up a good X-ray machine. We all have training in reading X rays."

"Why try to do the work of one of the well-established insurances?" Eichel demanded.

"They cover only actual sickness. I want to prevent it," Alan answered.

"Wouldn't we run the risk, Towne, of losing our standing as specialists? We'd be dabbling in diagnosing a lot of diseases we're no longer supposed to know anything about. It looks dangerous to me."

Alan felt he was losing the argument, but, to his astonishment Gertz said, "I don't see there'd be a chance of that, Eichel. As general practitioner I'm in a position to recommend other specialists if the diagnosis calls for it. Besides, I don't understand that a specialist is barred from the occasional practice of general medicine, but you have to watch your step. You know what Corwin did."

"Aren't you going to infringe on the Public Health field?" Eichel was bringing up every argument he could think of, fighting desperately to do away with the threat, as he saw it, to the good living he had until now believed was in sight for his family.

"It's not that kind of prevention I'm talking about," Alan answered. "It isn't in the province of Public Health to take care of individuals. Their preventive work is community-wide. For instance, chest X rays for tuberculosis."

"I'm not going to sacrifice my professional standing or my family for any such harebrained scheme," Eichel retorted. "I've four children to think of, one a baby." He caught himself up just in time. He had almost said, "You have no children to look out for," forgetting for the moment how recently Gertz had lost his only son. "I've worked hard to make myself a good surgeon. It's time for that investment to pay off. I didn't have much when I was a child. I mean my children shall have the best. I'm getting out if that's your plan."

"Don't say that," Alan pleaded. "I'm not forcing you to a decision now. It's just something to think about. We owe you a lot, Eichel; you looked after our interests during the epidemic. We need you. Let's drop my plan for now at least."

"Wait a minute," Nathan put in. "Don't let's give an answer now, Eichel. I'd like to think it over. We owe you a lot, just as Towne says, but we also owe Towne a lot, and we owe him money."

"Don't worry. Towne will get his money. You'd better pay Towne up and get out, too. You'll find out what the profession thinks of you soon enough, if you don't." Frightened over the possibility of being classed with the unorthodox, his face red, his hands trembling, Eichel made straight for his office and shut the door. He was in a panic that ruled out calm thinking.

Alan said, "I didn't mean to stir up a mess like this, Nathan. I shouldn't have sprung my idea so suddenly. I just thought it was something we could mull over. Couldn't you talk to Eichel and make him understand I'm not hell-bent on it?"

"Let him have a chance to come to his own conclusions. He needs time. He can't be hurried. Your mind jumps at new ideas; Eichel's plods slowly toward them," Nathan answered.

Now Alan was not a little appalled at what he had set under way. This was the kind of precipitate action Sam had always cautioned him against. "Maybe I'm the fool Eichel implied I was," he said.

"Oh, I don't consider you a fool. But I'm not sure most of the profession won't agree with Eichel about this scheme of yours." Nathan smiled.

"Where do we go from here then?" asked Alan. "If we tried it without him, it would be a blow for us to assume Eichel's part of the overhead. Suppose Eichel does leave—he'll give the reason, spread my idea around town, even if we don't go ahead with it."

"I doubt it. No, you're misjudging Eichel, Alan. He has his own ideas of loyalty and he'll live up to them. They just aren't yours."

"Of course I won't press my plan, Nathan."

"I don't know that I'm for giving it up. I don't know that Eichel will be in the end," Nathan answered. "I want time to think it over. We could begin as you say in a very small way, ask a few of our patients to try it out. Keep records and study the results. It might be several years before we gave up entirely practice on a fee basis."

But Alan had turned cautious. "Perhaps this isn't the time to try anything so new," he said.

Nathan smiled. Maybe trying out something new is like having a baby. The women tell me there's never a convenient time. With overwhelming force it came over him how he and Brenda had so longed for little Nathan that they had not let anything stand in the way and now—he must get away, somewhere by himself, fight this aching longing for his son.

Nathan began his evening not with the question whether he would accept Alan's idea, but with the larger question where his partnership with Alan might lead him. If he continued in association with a man who had so restless and inquiring a mind would there not always be some controversial issue? Would not Alan always attempt to break any mold that he felt

134

crystallizing around him? In the end men like Alan were always crucified. Should he cast in his lot with him?

As the evening wore on, Nathan found himself surveying such a future less negatively. He recognized the imaginative quality of Alan's thinking and its essential soundness. Preventive medicine was a growing idea in the profession, and he knew also that he had chosen to be a general practitioner because it brought him in touch with families. He, like Alan, did not believe disease could be isolated. Finally the experiment, and experiment it certainly was, roused in him his own creative powers, bringing him his first real relief from the deadening grief of the last weeks.

Eichel, too, spent the evening thinking over what to do. He was caught between two fears. There was the fear of whether he could make a go of it alone. He'd have heavy expenses and, in spite of his promise to Towne that he'd pay him back what he owed him, he did not know where he'd get the money. On the other hand, there was the fear of losing the respect of other doctors if he remained Towne's partner. What a lemon Towne had handed him when he offered him partnership! He was a sap to have accepted, but he hadn't known then what a visionary chap Towne was. He should have if he'd stopped to think, for certainly something was screwy in a doctor who left a well-established practice with a brother prominent in the profession to come out to this Godforsaken part of the city and start in on his own. Eichel's anger grew as he thought how Alan had trapped him.

Finally he took his bewilderment to Gertrude, practical Gertrude. She reminded him of all the expenses they had to meet in the next few months. "On your own you couldn't expect to have more patients than you have now, and you'd have a lot more bills to meet."

"So you don't think I'm smart enough to go it alone?"

Gertrude did not answer him at once, simply rocked back and forth in the old rocker which had once belonged to her mother, looking at him much as she looked at her children when they were cantankerous, waiting for his reason to re-establish itself. Seeing no sign of it, she said, "There's another baby on the way."

The shock of this announcement had the effect Gertrude felt necessary to bring him to his senses. He could not throw over a comfortable livelihood for an uncomfortable one just because Dr. Towne wanted to experiment. He was that kind of man. She had shrewdly evaluated him in the beginning. "You have to take the bad with the good," she reminded her husband. "Towne has initiative and he has courage." These were qualities Gertrude knew her husband lacked.

~ 30 ~

ALAN could scarcely believe his good luck when the following morning
both of his partners consented to try out his plan. In a very small way, both
of them insisted, and Alan readily agreed. Each chose from the list of his
patients the ones they thought would best understand the experiment. It
was discouraging to Alan to find the response all but nil. Some were on
guard, evidently fearing a trick in the scheme; others, as Eichel had predicted, preferred to take a risk on sickness and spend their money for more
immediate needs or pleasures. A few, a very few, consented to accept the
offer. Most of them were the heads of big families where the advantage was
all on their side. A number of hypochrondriacs eagerly grasped at the opportunity for endless consultation over endless ills.

One clear cold afternoon when the snow crunched cheerfully under
people's feet as they passed and sickness seemed to be held in abeyance, the
three doctors met after office hours to decide whether to attempt even a
"pilot plant" as they had dubbed the experiment.

"I'm forced to accept the fact that the group isn't representative enough
to warrant our going on with it," Alan acknowledged ruefully.

Eichel said, "Then we call it off, do we?"

There was no answer. They sat for a while in silence, Eichel secretly
elated, Alan glum, searching his mind for possible last resorts and finding
none. He would start to say something and think better.

The sound of the outer door shutting broke the long and awkward silence. In a moment the door to the room where they were sitting opened,
and in strode a woman who was known to everybody in the community for
her participation in civic affairs and for her sharp tongue. After every meeting of the school board or the hospital board, of both of which she was a
member, her cogent sayings were passed from mouth to mouth. Her short,
ill-proportioned figure was clad in a sport skirt and a plaid mackinaw. She
wore no hat, and her yellowed white hair was cut short and brushed
severely back. Not by the wildest stretch of imagination could she be called
even passably good-looking, but she instantly commanded the three doctors'
respect and their gratitude, for, although they had never met her, they had
recently learned that it was she who had fought down Corwin's opposition
to giving them hospital privileges.

"Good afternoon, gentlemen. I'm Miss Benninger, pronounced with a
soft 'g,'" she said. She pulled off a pair of heavy woolen gloves, stuffed
them into the right-hand pocket of her mackinaw; then she took off the
woolen scarf around her neck, stuffed it into the left-hand pocket. "This

Southeast District, as you probably know, was once a part of the Benninger farm. I've appointed myself a guardian of the people who've settled here. Little thanks I get for it. I've come to discuss this scheme of yours. I've been hearing about it from one or two of your patients. Pretty ambitious, isn't it?" She seated herself, crossed her short legs, and waited for them to speak.

"That's what we've been trying to decide this afternoon," said Alan. "The response hasn't been very encouraging."

"Umph!" she scoffed. "I thought you really meant to attempt something. Scared out already, are you?"

"Well, we do have to find out what we're getting into," Alan answered. "If we go into anything of this sort, we've got to know whether it will work —for our own sakes as well as for the community."

"You are not very certain it will, then? I don't want you to take people's money and then fold up and leave town somewhere in the middle of the year."

"What kind of doctors do you think we are—charlatans? If you're the custodian of the town's interests, as you represent yourself to be, you should know of our record during this summer's epidemic," Alan told her.

"Good!" she cried. "I see you can defend yourself. That's what I wanted to find out. There's no use of a set of starry-eyed philanthropists going into this sort of thing." She threw open her mackinaw.

Alan rose. "May I help you? It's pretty hot in here."

"I'm used to deciding when I want to take off my coat, young man."

Alan sat down.

Miss Benninger, pulling her mackinaw more tightly around her, said, "I suppose you realize you'll have to have guts to see this through. The doctors around here won't take this lying down. They'll fight you. And you'll get a lot of fools and chiselers to care for."

"Perhaps you overlook the fact that we went into all these problems before we approached our patients," said Alan, determined to take her down a little if he could after the mackinaw episode, but it didn't work.

"Idealists," she added, ignoring his remark, "are considered notoriously bad businessmen."

"And you place us among them?" Alan asked.

"I hope not. But you'll be competing with experts. Most of the doctors around here believe they've earned the right to a big income." She rose. "Understand, I didn't come to accept your offer. I can afford to pay for a doctor like Corwin. What I am going to do is tell the teachers around here about the service you're offering. A lot of 'em never go near a doctor until they're half dead. Can't afford it on the salaries we pay. But, mind you, don't you take any patients away from Corwin. He'll fight you if you do. He may, anyway. I've been going to him for ten years. I know him."

The door closed behind her. The men looked at one another. "Is she going to help us?"

"Whew!" gasped Alan. "I feel as if a truck had driven over me."

Eichel inwardly cursed her for bringing to life a crazy idea that a few minutes before had given every indication of dying.

It wasn't many days before a group of teachers came to see them. Some were young, some middle-aged, a few near retirement, most of them single. Their spokesman stated they were prepared to try out the plan.

"May we ask where you heard what we're up to?" Alan said.

The teachers laughed. "Who else but from Miss Benninger?"

Alan told them, "Frankly, we haven't a representative enough group even yet to warrant our trying the experiment, although you would help to balance up the expense of taking care of the large families. We'll let you know a little later."

When this word reached Miss Benninger, she took matters in her own hands. All this region had been her grandfather's farm in old days, one of the most productive in the state. She did not intend that its rich black earth should now produce a feeble, impoverished crop of human beings. Despite a sudden thaw which had turned the roads into a mixture of mud and water, she drove into town. Often walking tiptoe, for she hated getting wet as much as a cat does, she entered shops and houses, shrewdly choosing small families or the unmarried, those who would be the least risk to the plan. She pleaded, scolded and coaxed until she roused considerable interest in its novelty. Then suddenly enthusiasm for it began to spread almost like an epidemic.

The result was that a project which had seemed to be dying from lack of interest looked as if it were going to run away with itself. The three doctors had wanted to try out their experiment quietly. Now they knew they were in for unsought publicity, which as good physicians they deplored. People came during office hours to have the plan explained to them. The three doctors' telephones rang incessantly in the evenings. Finally a minister came to see them and asked if they would be willing to meet with a group in the basement of his church and answer questions.

Eichel was growing more and more alarmed. "Let's pick a few of the most desirable for our 'pilot plant' and stop at that before the other doctors decide this is unethical and take away our hospital privileges," he begged.

"There's no danger of that with Miss Benninger behind it," said Alan.

"You'll have to do the talking, Alan, if we accept the minister's invitation. It's your baby," said Nathan, and laughed at the consternation in Alan's face.

"You can count me out on any such display," said Eichel.

The night of the meeting Nathan sat in the back of the room, taking note of the people as they came in. Most of them were young, about to found families, he imagined. There was a sprinkling of older people, some probably retired on fixed pensions or annuities.

At the invitation of the minister Alan stepped forward. Gertz had a sudden feeling of affection for this tall angular man. The lines in his face had deepened in the last months. Nathan knew only part of the struggle and part of the victory. He knew that together Alan and Esther were fighting a battle and he suspected that they would win it solely because of their growing faith in each other. His thoughts jumped to Brenda. The wall between them seemed to be growing higher and thicker. Once it was he and Brenda who were united. Now it was Alan and Esther. Was marriage a shifting thing, whole and beautiful at one moment, fraught with pain and division the next?

Pushing to the back of his mind such thoughts, he brought his attention to bear on what Alan was saying. His approach seemed awkward at first. Then all at once he established communication with his audience. He was no longer the doctor and they the laymen. "We are a community," he said, "facing our common enemy, disease. It has no favorites. It may strike down a member of your family, as it undoubtedly did during the epidemic this summer. It struck down also a member of mine."

A sigh, almost a sob passed over the roomful of people. Gertz felt his throat tightening. Alan cleared his, then went steadily on.

"You and we—my associates and I—are all medium-income people—in other words, like the majority of Americans, neither rich nor poor. Most of you are on salaries. Our income is definitely tied to your prosperity. When you can afford it you come to us. When you can't, you stay away, except when an emergency hits you, such as an operation or an epidemic like the one this summer. This means that the medical profession must focus its attention on disease in its advanced stage. Isn't it possible that we are attacking our problem backward?

"Medical men who hold this idea, and there are a good many of them, think in terms of health. My partners and I want to have well people for patients. It's less spectacular. Doctors would not be able to say, 'That man was on his deathbed and now look at him—as spry as a cricket!' We'd like to check disease before it reaches such a stage. Preventive medicine is what I'm talking about."

"How we going to get it, Doctor," someone in the back of the room asked. "Isn't it a good deal of a pipe dream?"

"Yes, quite frankly, it is," said Towne, accepting the challenge. "Our idea is this. We'll be responsible, so far as it's possible, for keeping you well. For this service you will pay a stated amount for the year. We'll have to discuss later what the amount will be. You will be free to come to us whenever you need us, or think you need us. In short, it's health insurance. We eliminate one major cause of disease—financial anxiety, and its attendant tardiness in reporting the enemy. And really it's not so revolutionary as you might be led to believe. Those of you who have put your children in the hands of pediatricians know that."

Alan took a paper out of his pocket. "This is what we can offer: a preliminary examination, treatment for any ailments we find within our specialties, services in case of accident or sudden illness—not hospital expenses. We do include operations that in the eyes of the profession we are considered competent to perform. If you need specialists other than ourselves, we'll try to get the best rates possible for you. And we'll care for you during your convalescence."

It was a long session lasting until midnight. Some were skeptical; some were enthusiastic.

Alan ended by saying, "You aren't getting full security by any means. You still have to take a chance on illnesses we can't handle, which, in all honesty, I'll have to say might cripple you financially. But we, too, are taking a chance. Some of you will need a lot of attention. Some of you will think you do. You can overburden us to the point where we break down and then the plan breaks down. That's the chance we are taking."

As the meeting broke up Nathan and Alan saw a familiar figure in a bright mackinaw edge forward, blocking the way of a young man whom Alan recognized as a representative of the suburban paper. "What are you doing here?" she was demanding.

∽ 31 ∾

WHEN Nathan picked up the suburban paper from his doorstep the next morning, he was not too surprised to see a conspicuous editorial on the meeting. The final paragraph read: "Some in the community are asking, are there doctors among us so hard up that in order to get patients they need to stoop to bargain with well people? Why do our citizens turn to them when there are doctors in the community who are reliable and have proved their ability? In the final analysis, is not what these doctors offer essentially a lower grade of medicine?"

Eichel did not stop for a paper on his way into town as was his custom. His mind was on the operation he was to perform on a patient of Corwin's. Corwin had thrown several operations in his way of late, much to Eichel's gratification.

As he entered the hospital he saw Corwin standing by a window, deeply engrossed in the morning paper.

"Am I too early?" Eichel asked in a tone of deference.

Corwin swung around, frowning. "How much did you have to do with this?" he demanded, tapping the editorial page with his finger. Eichel, quickly taking in the threat to himself not only in the writer's interpretation of last night's meeting, but also in Corwin's attitude, hastened to clear himself of all responsibility. "I'm not in it at all. I refused to have a part in such a gathering."

"Well, I'm glad to hear it," said Corwin, slightly mollified. "You can see how the community regards such an attempt to get money out of well-meaning people. Although, of course, being a partner of Towne's does implicate you."

"I fear it does," Eichel acknowledged.

While they were scrubbing up, preparatory to performing the operation, he made a bold decision. He'd hint to Corwin that he was thinking of leaving his partners. Then to his enormous relief, when for a moment they were out of earshot of the nurses, Corwin made the suggestion himself. "I've been watching you for a long time," he said. "I like your technique. Would you care to join me?"

Before Eichel left the hospital they had made a tentative agreement dependent on Eichel arranging matters satisfactorily with his partners. All day he put off taking the final step.

Their office hours were over. Now or never, thought Eichel, as he walked over to Alan's desk and picked up the paper lying on it. Blusteringly he began, "This is just the sort of thing I've been telling you you'd bring down on our heads." He flung the paper down with a show of disgust.

"Oh, that," said Alan. "That doesn't mean anything. We expected some kind of opposition, didn't we?"

"I can't stomach it any longer," said Eichel. "You'll have to leave me out of this."

Nathan was alarmed. Alan was angry. "This is a pretty time to be backing out. The families that have promised to sign up if terms could be agreed upon did it with the understanding that they were getting your services in the contract. Where does that leave us?" Alan demanded.

"I . . . I . . . I hadn't thought of it in that light," stammered Eichel. "I . . . I . . ." What was he to do? He was in a jam certainly. Suddenly he saw his way out. "I just can't go along with you. It wouldn't be honest for me thinking as I do. You went farther last night than I had any idea you'd go. You hadn't any business to go that far without consulting me," he blustered again, feeling a little surer of himself.

"You had your chance. You dodged the meeting," said Alan.

"I won't perform operations on a contract basis," said Eichel, squirming in his fear that he couldn't free himself. But he must! "I'm an honest man. I'll do what I promised. I'll perform any operation in my specialty that your contract patients need—for nothing. It will be my charity." Suddenly he saw himself confronting Gertrude and telling her that he had delegated a large part of their income to charity!

"That's just what we're trying to avoid," said Alan. "Charity is out."

Now Eichel had what he considered a real inspiration. "Suppose then I do the operations and you figure what my percentage from them would be if I had gone in with you—and apply this to what I owe Towne on last summer's expenses until it's cleared. After that I'm free of the whole business."

"Isn't that rather sharp practice on your part?" Nathan asked. "You're getting a benefit and taking no risk."

Alan said nothing.

"You can take or leave it," said Eichel.

After he had gone Nathan and Alan set about repairing the havoc Eichel had wrought. They'd hold him to his promise about operations. That would mean they would be fulfilling their moral obligation to those who were planning to take out insurance with them. But the hazards of their success were much greater: more work and more overhead expense. Hour after hour, forgetting they had had no dinner, the two planned and schemed how to carry the extra load.

About midnight they believed they had a working program. "If it hadn't been for that damned reporter who got in last night," said Alan, "Eichel wouldn't have run out on us!"

"I think it would have come anyway," said Nathan. "Something would have happened to scare him." Gertz did not add that the temperaments of the two men were, as he saw it, irreconcilably different—the less imaginative Eichel would be always uneasy under Towne's sudden flashes of original thinking.

When later they learned that Eichel was going in with Corwin they both feared the worst. If the other doctors of the region joined with those two they might be in real difficulty. There might be a move to drop Alan from the County Association. Thus automatically he would lose his hospital privilege. Both of them were definitely relieved when no further opposition developed among the town doctors. Dr. Judd even dropped in to see them, ostensibly to ask Alan to operate on a patient of his, but in reality, the two doctors felt, to express openly his approval. "I couldn't float such a plan in my district. No one there has enough money at one time to pay for insurance," he said. Alan and Nathan knew that this was true. Dr. Judd's office was situated in the no man's land of half poverty between the moderate-income district of labor and the white-collar district. That many of Dr. Judd's patients never paid for his services Alan and Nathan were reasonably sure.

Powell of the Health Service was heartily in favor of what they were doing. "Someday," he prophesied, "the emphasis in the profession will be shifted to prevention."

When Esther received Alan's letter telling her of the venture on which he and Nathan had embarked, she felt utterly deserted. It would be almost impossible, as she saw it, for Alan to leave his practice long enough to come to see her. It was on his promise to do so that she had been relying. When he had first proposed leaving Sam, she had given lip service to the idea that his profession rightly took first place in his life. Now when she was confronted with the personal sacrifice entailed, she drew back. Her handicapped body shouted its protest against struggling for recovery without the help his visits would be to her. She started to write a letter accusing him of leaving her to fight alone a battle to which in her weakness she was unequal. Half-consciously, half-unconsciously she exaggerated the clumsy writing with her left hand. She knew that she should give him the freedom to fulfill himself by relieving him of all anxiety concerning her and so releasing his creative powers. Yet such was her desire for his presence that she yielded to the temptation to limit his freedom and his usefulness through her weakness. . . . But she did not send her letter.

It still lay on her table when, a few days before his promised visit, she received a telegram explaining how impossible it was for him to get away; without Eichel to help stagger the examinations, they were 'way behind their schedule. Alone there in her own room she stared down at what in her first disappointment she had written him. She tore the letter to bits using her teeth and her left hand. She would make no such unfair use of her sickness as she had contemplated. Slowly, carefully she wrote to him.

That night she woke conscious of a securer relationship with herself. All her life her effort had been to maintain her place in a family—first in her own, then in Alan's. Now she sensed the fundamental relationship must be with herself. In freeing Alan she had freed herself, and in so doing she had strengthened their union.

Her letter reached Alan on the day Sam learned of his brother's undertaking. An enterprising reporter had written up the experiment for her woman's column in the city's leading paper, playing up the family angle. In turning the page to get to the financial news Sam caught the name Towne. His anger over this new indiscretion of his brother's carried him straight to the telephone. Getting no response at Alan's house, he dialed the office only to find that Alan was already out making calls. He left word with Nathan to have Alan get in touch with him as soon as possible. The delay increased Sam's anger, intensifying his feeling that Alan was completely out of his control.

When late in the afternoon he at last heard his brother's voice over the telephone, Sam forgot he was talking to the man Alan and addressed his caustic remarks to the boy Alan, the nuisance factor of his youth. "So you thought you'd destroy my reputation along with your own!" he shouted.

Alan, not having seen the story, was at a loss for a moment. Then he knew that Sam in some way had heard of what he was doing. What business was it of Sam's! "If that's why you wanted to get in touch with me, you'd better ring off," he said. "I'm not hurting your reputation or my own either. Don't be a fool, Sam."

A fool! That Alan should call him a fool! In a cold hard voice Sam replied, "So this is the thanks I get for all I've done for you. You get our name in the paper, make us look like crackpots. Do you want to pull the whole family down to that level?"

The oral battle went on and on, each giving as good as he received. But when it was all over Alan felt the old uncertainty returning. After a solitary dinner at a near-by restaurant he went home with the familiar sense of inadequacy. He was a bad brother—a bad husband, too, he thought as he took Esther's letter out of his mailbox. He had failed in his promise to her, carried away by an experiment that would undoubtedly fail. Disheartened, he opened the letter. There, in the careful writing of Esther's left hand, was the faith he needed to bulwark him for his struggle.

❧ 32 ❧

In the days that followed Alan found that Sam was not a fool but a prophet. Suspicion of him grew among the doctors. Gradually there passed to the community the distrust doctors like Sam felt for doctors like Alan and Nathan who set aside established custom and honored tradition. Even among their own patients the two innovators began to detect a certain amount of this distrust. Why would any man who was good for anything voluntarily give up his opportunity to make money? There must be some ulterior motive. Doggedly Alan and Nathan went about their work, believing that in time the quality of their services would outweigh the distrust.

Then all at once the suspicion crystallized around Alan. Nathan heard it first from a neighbor who came to borrow his shovel during a heavy snowfall. "Just as a friendly act, I thought I ought to put you on your guard, Gertz. You'd be the last to learn that your partner isn't just what he represents himself to be," the man volunteered as he shouldered the shovel preparatory to leaving.

"At least I'd be the last to accept it," Nathan answered dryly.

"Don't be so highty-tighty. Take my advice," the man went on despite Nathan's lack of encouragement. "You'd better investigate. Something very fishy about Towne being sent home from a hospital in India during the war. Dropped from the service very soon afterward, I understand."

"What a cock-and-bull story!" exclaimed Nathan. "He left the service with an honorable discharge—a medical one."

"Cock-and-bull nothing!" the neighbor retorted. "I was told it by someone who knew someone who was intimately associated with Towne overseas."

"I can give you more direct information than that. I was partially responsible for Dr. Towne's sudden return to America," Nathan answered with considerable satisfaction. "It was my medical report that if he remained in the Indian climate he'd never recover from the very serious case of malaria he'd contracted. You see, I am one jump closer to the facts than your informant. It's no hearsay report I'm giving you."

"You might have had two reasons. You're sure you didn't make it an excuse?"

Nathan wished with all his soul he dared kick the man. The beastly ferret! He'd smell evil in a rose garden. "Why do you want to injure a man like Dr. Towne?" Nathan asked in a cold cutting tone.

"So you don't wish to answer whether you had another reason."

"Of course I wish to answer. As I've told you, Dr. Towne was a very sick man. When he left we lost one of the most skilled surgeons in the unit. Besides, would I deliberately associate myself with Dr. Towne if I didn't trust him, or are you implying I'm in on it, too?"

"Of course I wouldn't expect a man like you to be involved. It's possible, isn't it, that you weren't informed of the real reason why your report was accepted? They're saying the Army knew he's a deep-dyed Red. Oh, I know Russia was an ally, but the Army didn't like to have subversives around. That's common knowledge."

"Bunk! He's no more a Commie than you or I."

"Maybe you don't know. He was accused of insubordination, too. That's what they say. And India is pretty close to Russia, isn't it?"

"What's that got to do with it?" snapped Nathan.

"Plenty." Shaking his head, the man went off.

Nathan watched him, realizing he had not stopped the story; perhaps in trying so hotly to defend Alan he had strengthened it and furthermore brought suspicion on himself, too. Words could be twisted to mean almost anything. A witch hunt would be started against anybody, it seemed nowadays. On anybody you wanted to hurt you had only to fasten the name Communist. Just because a man had been on the other side of the Himalaya Mountains from Russia he was now accused of being an enemy to his own country! Preposterous!

"So that's what they're trying. I guess that's the way to work it if you want to get rid of a man for any reason," said Alan, when Nathan had finished telling him the gossip that was going around.

"If I weren't your partner, I could refute it, but, as I am, my word won't bear much weight. Perhaps the best way is to run the slander down and stop it, if we can, at its source. My guess is that somebody is behind this who has a personal knowledge of your life overseas."

"Do you remember a woman who used to come to see me in the hospital?"

"Yes. I didn't like her."

"Perhaps you remember she was a highly trained technician. During the epidemic here when so much outside help was needed she was brought into the hospital. You didn't see her?"

"I wouldn't have recognized her if I had, probably. You're certain you weren't mistaken?"

"Hardly. She came up and spoke to me. She left as soon as the emergency was over. She's the only one I can think of who would have details such as you speak of." Alan had had a sudden sickening sense that Martha Green was behind this. And yet how foolish of him! If Martha wanted revenge, she would naturally have gone to Esther; she would not have waited to act until Esther was out of town. If she was the originator of the story, she must be trying to ruin him professionally, but what good would that do her? Besides, in the one brief meeting with her at the hospital he had thought that she, like himself, wanted to treat their former relationship as something belonging to the past which had no validity for the present.

He heard Nathan saying, "Don't worry. We can ride out this kind of attack. After all, you're the brother of the Dr. Towne. His word, I'd think, would stop the gossip."

"I don't want to lean on him," Alan answered. "He's dead set against this plan of ours, and I don't want to go running to him the first minute it's got me into trouble."

"Suppose then we do nothing right now. Perhaps it's better just to ignore it."

The next morning, as Nathan entered the hospital, Dr. Corwin met him in the hall. "You're just the man I want to see. I've something of importance to talk over with you. We can be quiet in here," he said, leading the way into one of the smaller reception rooms.

"It has been called to my attention," Corwin said as soon as the door was closed, "by a technician we had here this summer that Dr. Towne was shipped home from India during the war under suspicious circumstances. We have sometimes wondered why Towne left his brother's office. We like your work here, Dr. Gertz, and we don't want you to get into trouble over this matter. I thought you ought to know that, if we find it's true, I'll have to bring it to the attention of the County Medical Association. I'm president, you know. If Towne is dropped, of course he's automatically out of this hospital. And eventually he might even lose his state license."

Nathan saw the whole design now. Corwin and his satellites intended to get rid of what they considered the threat to the profession in Alan's plan, but they did not want to come out openly against it. How they had enlisted Martha Green's services he could not guess. But he did see what part Corwin hoped to get him to play. If, on top of Eichel's leaving Alan, he left him too, it would be easy to make the public believe that Towne was guilty of the charges they were bringing against him. With his flair for new and different approaches to the profession Alan not only threatened them financially but threatened also their established thinking. They were after him. That was certain.

Realizing the importance of his answer, Nathan knew he must make no heated defense of Towne if what he had to say was to carry weight. "I can understand," he said to Corwin, "that you must go to the bottom of such an accusation. Fortunately I'm in a position to give you firsthand information. Dr. Towne was sent home from India because he had a serious case of malaria which might well have proved fatal in that climate. In fact, I was the physician who attended him at the military hospital. I can give you the names of the officers there at the time. You can verify what I say through their records."

"Umph, this puts a different light on the matter," said Corwin, "and of course I'll get in touch with Washington. But that won't entirely satisfy us. Apart from his recall, this technician I was speaking of may have evidence about him the military doesn't have. Often that's the case. She must be reliable, for Dr. Samuel Towne has engaged her as his technician. I hardly think a man as respected as he would engage a woman who is speaking against his own brother, if he had not broken with him. Might not the eminent Dr. Towne wish to undo the harm the black sheep of his family is doing? Professional ethics would demand that of him, wouldn't it?"

"There has been no break between the brothers that I know of," Nathan answered.

"Are you sure?"

"And are you sure," asked Nathan, "that Dr. Samuel Towne knows anything about what's being said out here?" He was about to add, "Why don't you call him up?" when he stopped himself. Samuel Towne was against Alan's experiment—that Nathan knew. If Corwin got hold of Sam first, he might convince him that Alan had committed professional irregularities. Decidedly Nathan did not trust Dr. Corwin. "Suppose I ask Alan Towne to come to see you. I think we should give him a chance to clear himself before we go any farther," said Nathan.

"I suppose that would be the thing to do," Corwin conceded—reluctantly, it seemed to Nathan. "In the meantime I hope you'll treat what I've said as confidential."

Nathan left with no such intention. His first task was to get hold of Alan. As soon as he could leave the hospital Nathan went to the office. It was Alan's turn to take the calls their patients were instructed to make at this hour. Good! He was already there.

"I think I've run down this story about you," Nathan began, dreading to tell Alan what he had learned. "I'm sure you can kill it, but there are some rather complicated angles and you'll have to act quickly."

Just then the telephone rang. "Can it wait until I get through here?" asked Alan.

"Yes, but don't promise to make any appointments for yourself this afternoon. You'll need the time."

"O.K.," said Alan.

Nathan waited. He didn't believe Sam was giving his support to a despicable effort to destroy his own brother; he just couldn't be! Difference of opinions, yes, sometimes leading to bitterness between the two, but there was great loyalty to each other. Of this Nathan felt sure. If he could only make Alan see that Sam was the victim of a well-laid plot just as he himself was! But when Nathan finished telling what he had learned, he knew he had failed to clear Sam.

"Thank you," was all Alan said. He made no outburst against his brother, but he looked like a man who had received a mortal wound.

"You mustn't doubt your brother," Nathan urged. "I don't believe he knows what's going on, and you have no right to condemn him before you give him a chance to clear himself."

Alan's only answer was to dial Sam's number and make an appointment. "He can't see me until after his office hours," he said, adding bitterly, "Nothing of mine is important enough to delay such a busy specialist."

The ugly suspicion that Sam had publicly broken with him in order to see him ruined held Alan in its clutches. Everything fell into a pattern now.

Sam intended to break him in order to protect his own precious reputation. Sam then would play a magnanimous part—take back the erring brother. With fury Alan flung shut the doors of his mind, barring Sam out. The bitterness which can develop only between two people who have been close to each other wiped out the memory of all the many good things Sam had done for him. I'll have it out with him if it's the last thing I do, Alan kept telling himself during the ride into town. I'll confront him with his part in this whole miserable business.

When he entered the famous specialist's reception room the secretary said, "Go right in, Dr. Towne is in his private office."

As Alan entered Sam rose from the couch where he was lying. So at last Alan was seeking him out. His ill-advised experiment was evidently going on the rocks. Sam's patience was to be rewarded. "I'm glad you've come, Alan. I've missed you."

For a fleeting moment Alan wondered if he were accusing Sam falsely. Then bitterness once more claimed him. "I haven't come to shake your hand. I've come to find out what your object is in trying to destroy me." The two brothers were standing only a few feet apart. Alan looked straight into Sam's puzzled eyes.

"Destroy you! You're talking rot. I do not destroy the members of my own family. Why should I?" A look of fastidious displeasure crossed Sam's face.

Alan was taken aback. For a moment he wondered if he had fallen into the trap set for the man who looks at life from a different angle from that of his associates. Feeling he is set apart, such a man begins to think there is opposition, even persecution, where there is none. Then there flooded over Alan again the reason for his coming. "That sounds O.K., but, if you're so lily-white, why do you have Martha Green here?"

"What has she to do with us? She certainly means nothing to me other than that she's an extremely good technician. I hope she means nothing to you."

"Don't try to be funny," Alan flung back.

Suddenly all Sam's anger against his brother fell away. Alan was in trouble. Alan needed him. "What's this all about?" he asked. "You'd better sit down and tell me."

"I suppose you've heard what's being circulated about my record overseas—how I was sent home because I was tied up with Russia."

"What a phony story!" Sam exclaimed. "But you exaggerate its importance. If it amounted to anything, I'd certainly have heard it."

"You haven't heard it! The person who started the story is your technician. She was in the same sector in India that I was, and she has used a lot of little facts she knew to make the yarn sound circumstantial."

"Has she any reason to want to hurt you, Alan?" Sam's tone, his look, were familiar, part of Alan's childhood memories.

"You might ask her," answered Alan wearily. He supposed the sordid relationship with Martha would have to come out. He knew already how it would look to Sam—another one of little brother's indiscretions.

Using the interoffice system Sam asked his secretary to send Miss Green in. Silently the two brothers waited.

The door opened, and Martha entered. For an instant she appeared to be caught off guard. She glanced uncertainly from one brother to the other. Then she had herself in control. She stood like a soldier before his officer, observing the code of the medical profession which was much like the military; nurses and technicians did not sit in the presence of their superiors. She wore over her dress the long white coat, the garb of the technician. Her small neat features had the tight indrawn expression of the self-righteous. Looking at her as she stood there waiting for Sam to speak, Alan wondered that she had ever evoked in him the passion which had driven him to what now seemed an insane rebellion against all that was good in his life.

"You sent for me, Dr. Towne? I've brought the report you asked for this morning." She stepped forward and laid a folder on his desk.

"Thank you. I'd like to ask you a few questions before you go." Suddenly Sam swung his chair around and faced her. "I understand from my brother here that you were in the same theater as he during the war. He has evidence that you've made certain accusations against him, namely, that he was in touch with the Communists during that time."

"I've heard there's such a story going around," she answered. "I see no reason to credit it to me. However, I am not surprised. A man who——" She paused. Alan set his teeth, prepared for the revelation of their intimacy.

"Go on," said Sam.

"A man who marries a Jewess and then tries to cover it up—why wouldn't he be a Communist?"

All at once Alan realized Martha would rather cut off her right hand than tell of her part in his life. In fact, she had undoubtedly made herself believe she, the good woman, had been trapped and defiled with no consent of her own. Through the years since he had seen her she had, in seeking to rid herself of a sense of guilt, turned his betrayal of her into a betrayal of his country!

He saw, too, that had it not been for him, Martha probably would have lived out her life in narrow goodness. Now she was a tormented woman who must convict him if possible to preserve her own righteousness. It was no coincidence that she was the technician in his brother's office. She had maneuvered herself into the position with the full intention of making real to herself the fabrication of her innocence. She had come to the region for the purpose of destroying him. It struck him suddenly that a doctor who broke tradition in professional matters had better have no irregularities in his personal life.

He heard Sam speaking. "Miss Green, you will either correct the false statements you have made, or I will correct them for you. With the doctors to whom you have made derogatory remarks about my brother I think my word will carry more weight than yours. I think, too, that in the circumstances it would be better if you settled in another city. When you have arranged matters satisfactorily here, I believe I can place you to advantage. That is all."

When the door closed on her there was a short silence which Sam ended by saying, "Well, I guess that'll about fix things." He made the gesture of dusting dirt off his hands. "Suppose we have a cup of coffee."

So Sam wasn't going to ask him to explain about Martha. He had dismissed the whole miserable incident when he dismissed her. Alan rose, went over and swung back the panel that hid the stove and small refrigerator, and took up his onetime duty of coffee making. He was glad to be occupied while he sorted out his conflicting emotions: relief that the menace Martha had been both to his home and his career was ended; realization that it was Sam, because he was so orthodox that no suspicion could ever attach to him, who had the power to bring it about, and also who was ruthless enough to use that power against anyone who threatened the reputation of his family. There was gratitude to his brother, too, for not, when he held the advantage, forcing a confession from him. Sam had respected his privacy. It gave Alan a sense of security in his brother which he had not felt for years. Mingled with these emotions was remorse over what he had done to Martha. He could see her as she had looked standing by Sam's desk, a woman just entering middle age, her mouth drooping at the corners, her eyes hard and sullen.

"Jo tells me Esther is beginning to gain," Sam said, stretching out in his easy chair, his long legs twisted about each other in odd angles.

"Yes, she is, but she has a long way to go," Alan answered. His reeling world was settling into stability.

"I wonder at your willingness to experiment on her. However, that's water over the dam." Sam sipped his coffee leisurely.

"Carothers is certainly on a new track. He's getting impressive results," Alan said.

"Yes," said his brother dryly.

"Jo wrote Esther you had taken a new assistant from the East. How is he working out?" Alan asked, shifting the conversation to safer ground. He didn't want any argument to spoil the recently attained harmony with Sam, and Sam obviously would never accept Dr. Carothers' ideas.

"Yes, he's pliable enough for me to mold. The other men I've tried had too many preconceived ideas of their own. Perfectly good ones, of course," Sam hastened to add, for he, too, did not wish to break the harmony, "but they don't fit in with mine, as you've discovered. I want somebody I can teach all I know. I'd like you to meet Merton. He should be in very soon now. We planned to talk over an operation scheduled for tomorrow morning. I gave him a few hours off for golf. It's important for him to make the right connections."

Sam launched out on a recital of office and personal affairs. "It might be we'll move to Chicago in the not too distant future. This is in strictest confidence, but I've been offered a position in the National Medical Association. I might take it."

"Give up your practice! I don't believe it, Sam. You're too good a surgeon."

Sam beamed benignly. "Probably just flirting with the idea. Of course the offer is flattering. I've one anxiety, Alan. I'm worried about Sally."

"What's the matter with Sally?"

"She's headstrong, and she's got an idea into her noddle that she wants to be a nurse."

"What's wrong with that? After all you might expect it with doctors on both sides of her family."

"Nonsense! Why should that have anything to do with it? It's out of the question. I want no daughter of mine standing at attention before some mediocre man just because he has a doctor's diploma."

"We might change the custom," Alan answered, his eyes lighting up over the prospect. Then, realizing he was again on controversial ground he added, "She'll probably get over it. It's a strenuous life, and Sally has had a pretty easy one."

"Exactly," said Sam. "I've given her everything a girl could possibly desire. You know, if I do stay on here, I'm thinking of buying a week-end place in the country. You know the call back to the land—it's strong in us. It might interest Sally and give Jo something to do."

Rarely had Alan known Sam to be so expansive. He doesn't want our differences to divide us. A comforting thought.

They were loath to part. It was good to sit here in friendly conversation, each seeing in the other a physical replica of himself, a tall, lean American directly sprung from New England stock, each relying on his affection for the other and the ties of blood and childhood association to bridge the widening chasm in their thinking.

Finally Alan rose, saying, "I must get back. I've left everything to Gertz, and he'll be anxious to know how things came out. Thanks a lot, Sam, and look here—I owe you an apology. I should have known you wouldn't let me down."

"Forget it. Glad if I've been of any help. And don't worry. I'll see the story is scotched." Sam let his hand rest on Alan's shoulder in parting.

Hurrying through the lobby, Alan almost ran into Sally. "Hello, what are you doing here?" he asked.

"I've been teaching golf to Dad's assistant. Here he is." She introduced Dr. Merton.

"You both look as if you'd enjoyed it," Alan answered, thinking, Young Merton, if I'm any judge, will do his best to keep Sally from going into nursing.

"We forgot the time," said Sally. "We're late and Dad doesn't like to be kept waiting. 'By."

But for once Sam was thankful that an assistant had failed to arrive on the appointed moment. With Alan's going the pleasure in the afternoon's companionship was quickly replaced by anxiety over Alan's persistence in doing things that made other doctors suspicious of him and for which the older brother had to hold the bag. He'd have to think up some way of smoothing Corwin down. He couldn't just call him up and say, "Don't discriminate against my brother or else——" That would be a form of black-mail. What could he offer Corwin in exchange for giving up the fight against Alan? Corwin didn't need to worry. Alan's experiment was too un-realistic; it would never succeed. Several times during the afternoon Sam had been tempted to tell Alan so. Then he had decided this was not the moment. Alan was in no condition today to take advice. There was nothing to do but wait.

Sam rose, went to the window and looked down on the city he delighted now to call his own. A thick fog compounded of mist and smoke had settled over it. The street lights shone dimly. If only he could make his brother a part of the distinguished circle of doctors in which he himself now moved!

"Here we are, Dad!" Sam turned to face his daughter, his love for her lifting him out of his sense of frustration over Alan. "You mustn't blame Dr. Merton for being late. It's my fault. I was so interested in his golf lesson we forgot the time. You wanted him to learn the game, didn't you, Dad? You didn't mind waiting?" A slight note of anxiety crept into Sally's voice.

"Not in the least." Her father gave her a lingering glance as she curled herself up in the corner of the couch, took off her hat and ran her hands through her softly waved hair. Artificial, but very effective, he thought. She's getting to be a very good-looking girl and a perfectly groomed one. Then he turned to Merton. Soon they were deep in discussion.

Alan, absorbed in his thought, did not notice he had passed the junction where he should have turned south. When he discovered his mistake he was several miles out of his way. He was annoyed. He was late enough without this extra delay. As he was on a divided highway, he'd have to go on until he came to a turn-off. By the time he reached one and had made the turn he could see ahead only a short distance in the murky atmosphere of fog and smoke growing thicker every minute. He stopped and lowered the window at his right, intending to ask a passer-by the quickest way to the Southeast District. Instead he stared silently at the house before which he had stopped. It was his childhood home! Why, Sam had told him it had been torn down when they widened the street.

The street had indeed been widened, but the house, shorn of its garden, stood there flush with the sidewalk. The elm tree which once had half hidden the front windows from view had been cut down, leaving his old home starkly revealed. The house, the street seemed to have been caught in a kind of creeping decay of mediocrity. Except for a dim light shining through the colored-glass panels at the side of the front door, the lower floor was dark, but the light from the naked electric bulb shone harshly in the front bedroom upstairs which had been his mother's room.

A rush of memories held Alan motionless—the sense of utter defenselessness which had come upon him after his mother's death, the threat held over him by the woman who had taken her place, the grim unsuccessful battle he had waged against her until Sam came to his rescue. And then into his mind came a vivid memory of his father, "the good gray Francis," as his mother had called him. After her death his father had become more and more withdrawn, seeking anonymity in this neighborhood as yearly it had become more drab, a drab obscurity Sam had passionately fought to escape, pulling Alan with him. If Mother had only lived, Father would have been different, thought Alan with sudden understanding. "Oh, Esther," his heart cried out, remembering his own great need, "do get well!"

Then again he was back in the past, just entering adolescence. Hunting in his father's library one day, he had come upon a history of his family with all the details of the Salem witchcraft. It seemed there had been another Francis, long since dead. With his three brothers, Samuel, Benjamin and Nathaniel, he had gone under cover of darkness to the pit where the body of their mother had been cast, gently lifted her and carried her to their boat. Vividly Alan had seen their black-clad figures moving in the darkness, heard their muffled oars as they rowed down North River, up the brook to their farm, the sucking sound of their feet in the shore mud, the sighing of the pines over the grave into which they lowered her. He could hear them shoveling earth, softly patting down old sod so none would know where she was buried.

He had closed the book, his hands cold, his eyes burning, the burial of his own mother poignantly vivid in his mind. Then the inadequacy of his father and the other Francis to avert such tragedies had taken hold of him. Only in Sam had he found the strength he needed. Sam was going to be a doctor; he would be one, too. He would take care of women like his mother. It was later when Sam decided to be a surgeon that Alan made up his mind to follow his example.

Wrenching himself free of his childhood, Alan started his car. How good the Southeast District looked to him when he reached it! There was no fog here, and the lights in the houses were shaded and shone softly. In many of them the curtains were not drawn, and he could see families at dinner. The women were young. The children looked rosy and well. In one house they were evidently having a party. Some of the women had flowers tucked in their hair. A great contrast, this Southeast District, to the Northeast into which he had gone by accident—or had it been an accident? Had his talk with Sam unconsciously drawn him back to his old home?

It hurt him to think how hopeless this region, once a district of gracious homes, had become with its rundown boardinghouses, its cheap eating places, the breeding ground of delinquency, crime and disease. He was coming to understand more and more clearly that disease and poverty were handmaidens, each bringing the other. Prevent poverty, prevent sickness;

prevent sickness, prevent poverty. His effort to bring medicine within reach of the families of the Southeast District leaped to life in his mind. That district, carved so recently out of farms which had once bordered Athenia, should never become like the Northeast District if he could prevent it. Even though he had followed Sam and become a surgeon he was now, in caring for families, fulfilling that early promise to the memory of his mother —that he would take care of women.

Alan found the office dark and drove directly to his partner's house. Nathan, who had been anxiously waiting for Alan's return, heard footsteps on his porch and opened the door before Alan had time to ring the bell. Together they entered the living room. "I hope you'll excuse the mess. The woman didn't come to clean today," said Nathan.

"Looks about like my place," Alan answered, seating himself. Then, going straight to the point, he said, "You were right. Sam hadn't heard the story. He's going to get in touch with Corwin. He says we needn't worry." Alan couldn't bring himself to tell Nathan about Martha except to say, "He isn't keeping Miss Green."

Nathan was content with the meager explanation. Both men felt they could afford to forget the whole unpleasant affair now that Sam was going to back them with his unchallengeable reputation.

33

WITH nothing to feed on, little by little the gossip died down, and as their undertaking lost its novelty it became less and less a topic of interest to the community. Like a seed covered and forgotten, their idea of the social role of the physician had a chance to germinate in the oblivion which now protected it.

Gradually an atmosphere of confidence grew up between the two doctors and their insured patients. At first there seemed a persistent undercurrent of doubt about a doctor who wanted to take care of healthy persons. Surely just doing that wasn't a practice large enough to bring him the income he desired. Was he really after the chance to operate? There was a tendency to trust Nathan before they trusted Alan, first because Nathan as general practitioner did not operate; second because the mothers who made up a large percentage of Nathan's patients had been trained during their pregnancy and in the care of their children after birth to the idea of forestalling sickness. But even they were inclined to doubt the concept of preventive medicine, when it came to seemingly healthy adolescents or adults.

Alan and Nathan had never realized before how deep-rooted was the suspicion of the doctor's motive. It took patience and much understanding on their part to break down that mistrust and establish a relationship of mutual confidence. It was a definite help to have no question of fees complicate this effort; no occasion to ask, in a case of prolonged treatment or an operation—that is, if it came under the specifications of the insurance—what the patient could afford to pay; no reason to see the patient's eyes glaze over, indicating that he must play for position to guard against too great an encroachment on the family resources.

An important thing happened to Alan. He began to drop a not uncommon notion in the medical profession, one that Sam held—that patients were enemies out to gouge doctors if they could: the old conception of the opposing gang. As Alan let down his defenses he found a lessening of tension in himself which, as at the Railroad Center, helped to open up the channels of communication. In his first enthusiasm over the rapport thus attained he gave of his time and his strength with a prodigality that alarmed Nathan. But after a little Alan began to learn that he must conserve his resources, not expend them indiscriminately. Not every patient needed or wanted such a personal relationship; some wanted it who didn't need it. He saw that a nice balance of precious time and personal relationship must be attained, requiring a sensitivity to human needs as fine as a violinist's sensitivity to sound. It seemed to him that Nathan had been endowed with such sensitivity while he had to develop it. He was often uncertain how far to press for a more intimate knowledge of a patient's problems.

The defensive attitude of one of their insured patients baffled them both. Miss Prentiss, a middle-aged schoolteacher, had resisted every effort on the part of the nurse to get her to make an appointment for X rays. Neither Nathan nor Alan could understand it, for she had been one of the first to take advantage of the plan and she had driven a sharp bargain, claiming that the one insurance should cover both herself and her sister who lived with her—family rates or nothing. Her opposition was a challenge to Alan. He decided to telephone her himself. In a tone of opposition that implied Alan had some ulterior motive she asked, "Is it necessary?"

"You're entitled to it under your insurance," he answered.

"I find myself annoyed by the persistence of your office. It's like a canvasser's foot in the door," she answered crisply.

Remembering how much she had desired the contract, Alan wondered if she feared some emergency later on either for herself or her sister, some disease of which she had not spoken but for which she was trying to provide. "We can't agree to take care of you later if you don't fulfill this part of the arrangement," he told her, with the idea of testing this explanation of her curious behavior.

Then quickly though still reluctantly she made an appointment. After the X rays were taken she said, "You can file them. I don't want to know what you find."

"And why not?" he asked.

"There's nothing but my salary to keep my sister and me from the poorhouse. I can't afford to have a long sickness."

"You fear something is wrong then," he said, thinking, This case demands all I can give.

"I know what I face," she retorted tartly. "Cancer is in the family. But it's not yet time for it to hamper me."

"It is not a hereditary disease."

"It may not be, but I know the symptoms. I took care of my mother," she replied.

This might well be fear assuming the aspect of disease, but Alan was aware that even to suggest such an idea would be to kindle within her further resentment.

"I want you to come in tomorrow afternoon without fail," he said, dismissing her somewhat peremptorily before she could argue further with him.

When she did not come, he telephoned her. "I insist you follow my instruction or I must refund your insurance money." When she came in the next day he announced without preamble, "As far as our study goes, including the X rays, you haven't cancer."

"Why didn't you tell me so on the phone instead of wasting my——"

"—time, not money," he supplied the end of her sentence. "You haven't even a stomach ulcer, but you may have if you don't let up on yourself. If we can lessen the strain——"

"How are you going to do it?" she asked. "I must see that my sister has enough to manage on without me."

He ignored this indication that she did not accept his diagnosis. "I certainly can relieve your pain if you're willing to let me try, and if you'll stop driving yourself so hard."

"It's impossible for me to do so," she answered. "It's necessary for me to tutor pupils outside of school hours. I have an invalid sister to care for. There's nothing you can do about that."

"Your sister is included in your contract. Why did you want her included if you feel that way?" Alan asked.

"I simply wanted to make certain that if she had flu, as she did last year, she'd be cared for without extra expense," Miss Prentiss answered.

"From the form you filled out I see she has arthritis."

"That's why I say there's nothing one can do to help her. We've tried everything. She's a chronic. We have ample testimony to that. We have invested heavily in opinions." She rose and put on her gloves.

Conscious of the growing demands on his time, Alan considered whether or not to let the matter drop there. Although arthritis was a chronic disease, it did not of necessity mean invalidism. There were his grandfather's findings and those of Carothers. Neither took such a defeatist attitude. And, too, with his growing concept of the family as a unit of disease, Alan realized if he were to help one sister he must consider the other sister too. Knowing he was taking on a good deal, he said, "I'd like to call and see your sister. She's entitled to my services, and my specialty is orthopedics. It might just be that something could be done for her."

A flicker of hope came into the middle-aged woman's eyes and then died out. "At her age! The doctors have all told us nothing can be done."

"My grandfather before me devoted his life to chronic cases. I've been conditioned by him to believe that a fair degree of health can be restored, even after fifty—where certain conditions exist," he added, not wanting to give false hope. "May I call on her today after my office hours?" He named the time.

Late that afternoon Alan rang the bell of the small white house where the sisters lived. Miss Prentiss opened the door and led him from the diminutive front hall into a diminutive front room. In it was a minimum of furniture; two wing chairs, one on either side of the front window, a low table between; opposite them a bookcase, flanked by two straight chairs; three good engravings, well hung, on the wall above. Before him an archway led to a dining alcove evidently used as a bedroom, for he could see it was almost filled with a hospital bed.

Rather grimly Miss Prentiss said, "Mrs. Watkins will see you now, although it's one of her bad days."

After an exchange of greetings he said to the frail-looking occupant of the bed, "I'd like to examine you."

"It's been done so many times, Doctor." She smiled, and the left corner of her mouth went up in a wholly unexpected way, lending humor to her thin face. Glancing slyly at her sister, she added, "I've been examined so often I instinctively begin to undress when a doctor enters the room. This time I didn't wait that long."

Alan laughed as much at Miss Prentiss' shocked expression as at the remark. He saw that it had been made to cover an almost unbearable hope that after all there might be some reprieve from the verdict of invalidism which had been passed on her.

Already he had noted that the fingers of her hands lying on the coverlet were long and slender, not spindle-shaped. There was no deformity of the joints. So the symptoms were lacking which indicated the sort of arthritic condition his own grandmother had suffered from. Neither were her knees drawn up, nor was there any other deformity—the manifestation of a profound failure of the body to do its work. Deftly he went about his examination, his hands feeling out the sunken chest, the narrow trunk, the down-drooping ribs—a body posture which, if corrected, he believed would ease the pain and do away with invalidism. Years ago his grandfather had found that if he brought the human structure back into alignment, the whole system would be permitted to function more normally. Better body mechanics would relieve the strain on joints and muscles which produced pain and difficulty in moving, and would strengthen a weak back. It was to help all arthritics in this way, but especially arthritics with the symptoms of this woman, that his grandfather for years had endured the ridicule and ostracism meted out to him by the profession.

When Alan had finished his examination he looked for a long moment into Mrs. Watkins' eyes, measuring her spiritual stature. It would be a long, tedious struggle. More would depend on her than on him. Then he spoke. "Your condition is serious. There's no use to minimize it. However, I believe I can make you reasonably well. You're like a house that's out of plumb. We've got to jack up the structure."

"When it's old and been out of plumb for years? Bones are not like beams and rafters," she countered.

"You'd be surprised how quickly the body responds to a chance to re-habilitate itself—at sixty, even seventy," he answered. "And you're not that by a long shot. If you'll co-operate with me, and I believe you will, together we can do it. You are an intelligent woman. You can handle this."

So far she had maintained the half-humorous attitude of her first remark. Suddenly she dropped it. Timidly at first she asked questions. He answered, treating her almost as if she were another doctor, only omitting the technical phraseology. Slowly she reached out, recapturing the self-respect she had lost in the long years of her sickness. How often she had apologized for being sick! How often she had swallowed her pride, maintaining the un-questioning and deferential attitude she believed would please the specialist and make him try to find some way to help her! Now here was a doctor who not only believed in what he could do for her; he believed in her. Neverthe-less this hope he held out to her she would have refused had money been involved. She would try nothing which would further drain her sister's slender income. After all it was a chance whether he could help her. On long chances she had gambled away her own resources and impaired her sister's. Since no extra money was involved in the experiment, she was free to make this last desperate effort to get well. "What do I do first?" she asked eagerly.

"X rays," Alan answered. "Then you get to work." He outlined the treat-ment. Positions, exercises. "The small amount of nursing involved your sister can do, and I'll do the directing."

When the door closed behind him Miss Prentiss turned to face her sister. Her eyes said what she dared not express in words—the richness of life opening before them. "Dr. Towne may fail, just as all the others have. It's too early for us to plan a trip to Europe." She went into the kitchen to pre-pare their simple dinner.

Alan, getting into his car, felt he understood, as he never had before, why his grandfather, even with the honors which both England and America had eventually bestowed on him, had died a frustrated man. He had spent a lifetime trying to get an idea across, and yet he'd known that much he'd taught would be lost with his death because the profession as a whole re-fused his findings. Of late when Alan came in from his last call he had taken to reading his grandfather's journal, finding much of human wis-dom in it besides the minute recording of his work with chronics. Some-times Alan wondered if his grandfather had not put down his notes with such minuteness in the hope that someday his grandson, to whom he had left the record, would carry on his work—a last effort to rescue from oblivion precious knowledge acquired through years of study and careful observation.

Here was a woman that had expended her own and her sister's financial safety in consultation with specialists who had access to his grandfather's findings and yet had not used them. That operation on her spine performed by one of them old Dr. Towne would never have performed—a short cut to health that was not health, for it had weakened the structure.

What was the block in the medical mind that refused such evidence as Dr. Towne could present of people rescued from invalidness and suffering? Alan thought with shame how he himself had ignored until lately his grandfather's contribution. All through the history of medicine there were tragic examples of new ideas obstinately refused. There was Semmelweis, the Hungarian doctor who proved that childbed fever could be eradicated from the hospitals by simple cleanliness. He had been ridiculed, even persecuted. For fifty years after his death thousands of women had died needlessly because doctors held to their theory that a miasma in the air was lethal. It was so, too, with Sister Kenny's findings on poliomyelitis. Doctors continued to put their patients in casts long after she had emphasized that it only made the initial paralysis permanent. Alan had tried once or twice to tell the hospital doctors of the advancement Esther was making under the heavy-resistance treatment Carothers used, but they all appeared skeptical. Skepticism, as his grandfather had said in his last address to graduates, was an essential quality in the profession. Every new idea, every new medicine must be proved before it was accepted. Where should skepticism cease and acceptance begin?

Slowly Mrs. Watkins began to improve. Sleep was the first sign of returning health. There were setbacks. At such times she would look anxiously at Alan, fearful lest, like all doctors who had treated her before, he would now lose interest. But as the weeks passed and the intervals between setbacks grew longer she won confidence from his continued interest and gained more rapidly.

Miss Prentiss also came to trust him—he had indeed relieved her pain by helping her sister. A good and solid friendship soon grew up between Alan and the two women.

Watching the valiant struggle Mariana Watkins made to slough off the resignation and the fears of the chronic, he understood better the fight Esther was putting up. Sometimes when he left the little house he was not certain whether he or Mariana had been the strong one, for it was often her subtle understanding that sent him away with new hope for Esther's complete recovery.

Time after time he had had to put off his visit to her. Some crisis always occurred to keep him in Athenia. He felt gratitude that Esther always seemed to understand, but he was uneasy, realizing that while he was giving of himself to help others he was giving none of his strength to his wife.

34

EACH afternoon now there filed through Alan's and Nathan's waiting room America's middle class, no rich, no very poor—white-collar men and women, teachers, clerks, owners of small stores, young men on the bottom rung of the banking ladder, local managers of gas stations, hairdressers. Some showed signs of sickness, some were there to avoid sickness later on. The tall growing boy who stooped ever so slightly was given special attention by Alan. Now was the time to guard him against the inroads of the age-old disease of arthritis. Girls entering puberty were watched by Nathan to see that they developed into healthy, happy women.

One day at the beginning of their office hours a woman and a boy about twelve entered. Their expensive clothes indicated they did not come from the neighborhood. There was a faintly perceptible stiffening of the other occupants of the room, as if they felt the woman an intruder and would defend their prior rights to attention. Then, as they looked at the boy, their defenses went down. He wore a brace that showed above the collar of his coat. In his eyes was the knowledge of pain. The woman spoke in a low voice to the nurse who was seated at the desk looking over the day's appointments. There was some discussion, and then the others in the room heard the nurse say, "We'll try to fit you in, although we usually see patients only on appointment."

With some impatience the woman waited, glancing often at her watch. Each time the door into one of the consulting rooms opened she half rose and then with a sigh settled back when the nurse called the name of someone else. Finally the nurse came to her saying, "Dr. Gertz will see you now."

"But I told you I wanted to see Dr. Towne," the woman protested.

"Dr. Towne is busy," the nurse replied. "Dr. Gertz will see you first. It will save time."

Alan and Nathan often helped each other out in this way. As the load on them had increased they had learned to supplement and complement each other.

"I came to see Dr. Towne," the woman reiterated when Nathan entered the room into which she was ushered.

"I understand," answered Nathan. "He'll see you directly."

"It's curvature of the spine," the mother said, diagnosing the case for Dr. Gertz. "He's had all kinds of treatment. One doctor suspended him. He said he could get him straight by stretching him. Roger couldn't stand it. I couldn't either." Something close to a sob escaped her. "We got a new doctor. He put this brace on him. If it doesn't work, he said we'd have to fuse the whole spine. But I refuse to accept such a verdict. I'm not used to giving up while there's still a chance. Money is not a question with us. I am Mrs. Gunsaulus," she added, as if that settled everything. When she saw this made no impression on the doctor she added, "Mrs. W. L. Gunsaulus. You probably read about my husband during the war."

"I was overseas at that time," Nathan answered. Like the patients in the waiting room, he felt himself warding off the appeal to privilege she was obviously making. They did not deal in that commodity. "We do what we can for all our patients," he said.

Hearing Alan's voice in the hall, Nathan excused himself and went out. He quickly briefed Alan on the general nature of the case. "I haven't learned yet why she brought her son to us."

"I'd like you to be in on the examination, Nathan," was Alan's reply. "When I've examined him I'll want to talk the case over with you." When he saw the boy he felt the same pity that had moved Nathan. The viselike contraption at the back of the child's head was held in place by means of a leather chin strap. His arms hung inert, indicating the iron grip of the brace around them. His eyes were dark and brooding; his mouth was drawn down.

"How did you happen to come to me?" asked Alan, turning to Mrs. Gunsaulus.

"A Miss Prentiss is tutoring Roger. She's been telling me what you have done for her sister. She said if anyone can do anything for Roger, it's you."

Since it was obvious Roger was afraid he would be hurt, Alan asked Nathan to remove the brace. Nathan had a special way of helping children over those first terrible moments when their mothers so often told them the kind doctor wasn't going to hurt them—and they learned otherwise. He offered no such subterfuge. He spoke to the boy as an equal. "I imagine you've had rough going sometimes. Getting well is a man's job, isn't it?" While he spoke, Nathan's deft fingers loosened the buckles which held a leather girdle around the waist.

Roger, shivering under Nathan's touch, said in a high-pitched voice with a pitiful effort at bragging, "I . . . yes . . . I can stand up to anything."

"I think you can take it from me that Dr. Towne isn't going to hurt you. If he were, I'd tell you. Maybe later he will have to, but not today."

The nervous shivering stopped. The boy lay quietly now on the X-ray table while Alan made his examination, with expert fingers feeling out the muscles of the boy's back, and then took the X rays he wanted.

When it was over, with gentle hands Nathan helped Roger into his brace, and then into his clothes. Alan went back to Mrs. Gunsaulus.

"What's the answer?" she demanded.

"I'll have to study the X rays before I give my opinion. May I ask you a question? Do you remember any sickness that Roger had before this curvature occurred?"

"Nothing that wasn't tended to," she answered.

"A small illness, a fever for a day or two that you didn't think was important?"

"We've never neglected anything, no matter how small," she answered defensively.

"I'm not questioning your care of him," Alan answered. "I'm trying to trace the cause of the curvature." The mind of the specialist was at work. He was already reasonably sure that the case had never been properly diagnosed. Here was an instance of undetected polio, he believed.

When Mrs. Gunsaulus came the next day, on appointment this time, he told her, "I'm going to be honest with you. It's late to try to correct the condition, which I think is the result of a light case of polio, so slight it wasn't detected at the time. My opinion is that the Sister Kenny treatment even yet might help your son, at least to the extent of arresting the curvature. Possibly if the muscle spasm can be lessened the spine will straighten —how much I can't predict. It means several months of patient effort."

At the mention of Sister Kenny, Mrs. Gunsaulus showed considerable skepticism. "Sister Kenny was just a nurse. How'd she know more than the doctors we've been to?"

"Such things have happened in the world many times. You know, the simple carpenter's son once confounded the learned," Alan answered.

"That's different," Mrs. Gunsaulus answered.

"I'd recommend you take Roger to one of the places where such treatment is given."

"Couldn't we do it at home?" she pleaded. "You care for him. Money means nothing to us." Again she seemed to be thinking it was all a matter of money. "My husband made a lot in the war, and yet it's not done anything to make Roger well." She seemed puzzled over money's failure. There was bewilderment in her face and voice. Money, which she relied on, had failed to give her the greatest gift of all—her only child's return to health.

Thinking how Roger had shrunk from Nathan's touch when he loosened the buckles and remembering the torturous suspension treatment recently inflicted on the boy, Alan had some doubt himself as to the advisability of subjecting him to a strange environment. The demand on his morale might prove too great. Then an incident out of Alan's childhood came back to him. His grandfather had sometimes taken patients into his own home. One summer when Alan was there he had brought home a boy of Alan's age, crippled with arthritis.

Alan's house was empty, terribly empty. Why not install Roger there? The treatment he was going to try was to wrap him hour after hour, day after day, in warm moist blankets, then, after a little, begin very carefully, under a therapist, exercises to strengthen the back muscles. Alan could watch the case thoroughly, something he longed to do, learn for himself whether the muscles so long in spasm could still be relaxed. A sense of excitement took possession of him. For once he'd be able to let himself go. Expense would be no item as it was with the polio patients of the Southeast District. Nurses, therapists, the most skilled, would be his to command.

"I'd like to talk to your husband," said Alan. "If he accepts my diagnosis, we could talk over what would be best for Roger."

At noon the next day, during the hour Alan was at the telephone desk while the nurses and Nathan were out for lunch, there was a call from Mr. Gunsaulus' office.

"Just a moment, please," said a feminine voice. "Mr. Gunsaulus wishes to speak to you." A pause. "Just a minute more. He's been detained."

I suppose he thinks his time is more valuable than mine, thought Alan, drumming on the blotter in front of him as he waited.

"I suggest he call me later. I'm expecting a number of incoming calls from patients," Alan replied. He was lowering the receiver when he heard the girl say, "Here is Mr. Gunsaulus."

Immediately deep masculine tones came over the wire. "Gunsaulus speaking. I'd like to come to see you this afternoon, say around four."

"Make it five," Alan answered. "I have appointments until then."

"I'm a busy man. Couldn't you put me through? A special entrance maybe to your office?"

Alan felt his blood pressure rising. "No preferential treatment" was the principle on which he and Gertz had built their reputation. "We've made a rule that patients wait their turn. We try not to delay anyone if we can help it."

There was no immediate answer. Towne felt certain that in most circumstances Gunsaulus would have hung up the telephone immediately without answering or after saying, "We'll let it ride then." But Alan was also certain that Mrs. Gunsaulus was one person her husband could not browbeat. She meant to make one more effort on Roger's behalf, and Gunsaulus could not afford to be highhanded with the doctor who had offered her encouragement. Alan was right. Gunsaulus did not ring off.

"About five then," he said. His voice had a dry note which, if Alan had known the industrialist as well as his competitors knew him, would have been a warning that the man had marshaled all his forces for combat.

At five o'clock Alan was ushering out his last patient when she stopped and said, "Oh, Doctor, I promised to make an appointment for my husband." He took a pad from his pocket, jotted down the hour. As the woman lingered garrulously explaining why she had forgotten to speak of the matter earlier, Gunsaulus entered. Ignoring the woman, he said, "I believe my appointment is for five."

Alan was surprised to see that the industrialist was a much shorter man than his pictures in the newspapers indicated. He had a full chest, powerful shoulders and arms and a big head, but from the waist down he was shorter than the average man. Towne, who, except that he was smooth-shaven, could have posed for a statue of Uncle Sam, would have towered above him if they had been standing nearer together, but Gunsaulus stayed far enough away not to have to look up to the man he had come to see. Sensing that his caller was sensitive about his height, Alan motioned him to a chair by his desk, then sat down behind it. They were more evenly matched now.

"I want you to know," Gunsaulus began immediately, "I'm not sold on the almost unreasonable hope you gave my wife yesterday. She's convinced, but before I accept your diagnosis you've got to convince me you can produce the goods."

"I'd like to make it plain I'm not out to sell you a bill of goods," Alan answered. "I gave your wife my diagnosis of the case because she asked for it. I think there's a good chance not only to arrest the curvature of your son's spine, but to straighten it. It's a gamble, one worth taking, I'd say. It's entirely up to you whether or not you wish to take it."

"My gamble, but not yours."

"Just what do you mean by that?" Alan demanded.

"Let's not beat around the bush, Dr. Towne. You will expect to be paid whether you succeed or not. And the charges are never small for a man like me. Your profession believes in making the rich patient carry the poor one. With a specialist I consider it justified. With you—" Gunsaulus glanced around the office—"I'd hardly consider it so."

"I am not trying to induce you to take me on as your doctor," said Alan quietly. "I have advised your wife and I now advise you to take your son to one of the institutions qualified to give the treatment I have suggested."

Gunsaulus weighed Alan's statement, not knowing just how to classify this man. Was he extremely shrewd, pretending he didn't want the case, or just a plain fool, letting a rich man slip out of his hands? Was he going to have to urge him to take Roger? Amanda wanted this doctor. That meant they'd have to have him, he supposed.

Part of the father's obstinacy was a determination not to go through again the cycle of hope and despair repeated too often in the last three years—hope rising and with it reconciliation with Amanda; hope dying and the bickering between them beginning again, he angry with her as there rose in her resentment toward him, who in the first flush of their good fortune had made her believe money would buy happiness. It was unreasonable of her to hold him responsible for her heartache. There were times, too, when Roger's acceptance of his suffering had made Gunsaulus angry. Why didn't he raise the devil about it? Maybe if he did, he'd get well somehow. Should they go through it all over again? He found himself hoping in spite of himself.

"I suppose," said the somewhat puzzled man, used to commanding, not begging, "it won't hurt to try your idea out. We'll just be where we are now if you fail. The wife is unwilling to have the boy leave home. That means you'll have to take care of him here."

"I can't do that," said Alan. "I should want to see him every day, and that is impossible with my other practice. You live too far away."

Gunsaulus narrowed his gaze, ready for bargaining. So the man wanted a big fee. Now that he knew what Towne was after, Gunsaulus could go ahead. He knew how to bargain. "An extraordinary situation would mean an extraordinary price, wouldn't it? I'm prepared to buy as much of your time as is needed."

"You don't understand," Alan answered. "I'm not after your money. It's time I can't give you. I haven't enough of it as it is. I can't take time to drive over into your section of the city every day."

"Well, then, I'll take Roger to a hospital where you have patients. Certainly you can arrange that."

"I'm sorry," Alan replied. "The local hospital accepts no chronics. Your son comes under that heading."

"You'd have me build a wing onto the hospital? Nothing, of course, costs too much if a man wants his son cured." Gunsaulus' sarcasm was tinged with bitterness.

Alan, studying the resentful little man, said, "I've one solution to offer, but I don't know how you'll receive it."

"Make it anyway." So the man did have a plan up his sleeve. Again Gunsaulus girded himself for combat.

"My wife was one of the victims of the poliomyelitis epidemic last summer. For many months she will be at one of the institutions I mentioned. If you wish to rent the extra rooms in my house and install your son and a full-time nurse, my partner and I will take your son's case. Mrs. Gunsaulus could spend the day with him, and you, I imagine, could get in occasionally."

The plan was so novel, so out of the ordinary, that Gunsaulus for a moment had no comeback. What was this fellow after? "Let's see," he said finally. "Rental as under the law and your services at a reasonable price?"

The issue might as well be fought out right now, Alan decided. Gunsaulus had to respect him or he could not succeed in helping Roger. Undoubtedly Gunsaulus was a strong, willful man. Anyone who had risen as he had in less than a decade from a small contractor to a leading industrialist would look down on men he considered failures. He had competed single-handed with powerful corporations which had a network of banking connections and astute lobbyists in Washington to bulwark them. Successful without these aids, he must have come to think of himself as uniquely endowed. In fact, it did take unusual attributes to crash the gates of entrenched interests. Once within these gates, tolerated if not accepted, Gunsaulus would have come to believe that money and bigness were the hallmarks of his equals. He had left behind the little men; he lived among titans. Alan was not ignorant of this group. When he was associated with his brother, he had met them socially at their clubs and in their homes. A doctor who did not have his office in the chromium-outfitted building in the city would be estimated by Gunsaulus as a little man, a man not quite up to his job.

If Alan took the case, Gunsaulus must believe in him. Otherwise there would be conflict and friction between them which would react on the boy. Only if Gunsaulus respected his professional ability would Alan be able to create the atmosphere of confidence necessary for the boy's recovery. These thoughts passed quickly through his mind before he answered.

"My partner and I are attempting to bring medicine within the reach of this community. To do this we are trying out an experiment in insurance on a limited scale. I gave up an office in the medical building in the city to do this. I am an orthopedist in good standing. Poliomyelitis is one branch of my specialty. My fee is the one generally accepted by specialists. If you accept my offer, I'll see your son twice a day as long as it's necessary, and my partner will look after Roger's general health. I neglected to mention that I'm renting you my house with the proviso that I keep my own room and get my breakfast in the kitchen each morning. I'm addicted to early-morning coffee."

"Under such conditions this won't be an outside call. I'd say your fee should be the same as you charge at your office." Gunsaulus felt he must not surrender too easily.

"I'm of Yankee descent, Mr. Gunsaulus. I understand horse swapping. It's all right up to a point. I consider we've reached that point." Alan rose, indicating the conference was over.

"I'll arrange for a lease on your house that I will sign. I'm a businessman." The implied insinuation that the doctor he was hiring was not gave Gunsaulus the feeling of superiority he needed just then. The fool! he thought. I suppose he'd have let me rent his house without protecting himself with a written agreement.

In the first turmoil of the arrival of the Gunsaulus family in his house—for turmoil it proved to be—Alan almost regretted his offer. His masculine mind had conceived of the boy's installation there as a simple matter—a bedroom equipped with some hospital appurtenances and a second bedroom for the nurse. Mrs. Gunsaulus had no such conception. The house must be in accord with their moneyed position. She took it over as a general would his headquarters. Alan came home one day to see the hall cluttered with extra equipment for the kitchen, furniture for the living room which she had explained she would use during the day. The next afternoon when he arrived with Roger, whom he had taken to his office for another series of X rays, he found Mrs. Gunsaulus busy unwrapping a bundle of heavy silk curtains. Immediately she introduced him to a slender little man who was just coming down the stairs. "This is Mr. Whimple of the decorating firm of Whimple and Whimple from the city."

"You know, Mrs. Gunsaulus, this arrangement is for only six months," Alan said. He deeply resented having his home invaded like this. Now, indeed, he was thankful for the written agreement. "Bring in what you wish, but no basic changes are to be made, and Roger's room I insist be kept plain. He's here for treatment."

And yet when all was done and the commotion was over Alan found Mrs. Gunsaulus a help. She and Miss Reich, the nurse, obviously understood each other. Hours were arranged between them. The two gave the co-operation needed by a busy doctor. He would come in each morning before leaving for his rounds to find Roger wrapped in the steaming blankets, Miss Reich in charge. When he returned later in the day Mrs. Gunsaulus would be on duty and Miss Reich taking needed rest. Sometimes when he arrived at nine or ten in the evening from an emergency call, again he would find Mrs. Gunsaulus there. "We owe Miss Reich a little fun," she would say half apologetically. In spite of her position as the wife of the great industrialist, Alan discovered that she found herself more and more enjoying the old relationship she had had with those who worked for a living.

Strangely enough, the only person who did not appear to be co-operating in Roger's recovery was Mr. Gunsaulus. He seldom came to see his son.

Slowly Roger's spine was straightening. But such waste! In an institution the time and effort expended on one youngster could be distributed over a number of patients and Roger would be the better for being in a group. This was a lonely life for a boy. I'm curing his body, Alan thought, but what about his mind? At times Roger was difficult out of all reason.

❧ 35 ❧

THE dull gray winter compounded of fog, smoke and rain was giving way to an occasional springlike day. The three months Alan and Nathan had carried on their experiment had proved to their own satisfaction its value to the community, but they had to face the fact they had not proved it was practical financially because it was partially supported by the patients who did not belong to it. If they were to depend wholly on insured patients for a livelihood, they must either raise the rates, thus putting themselves out of the reach of many, or they must enroll such a large number there would be little time for that personal attention to the individual which was the very core of their idea.

There were other flaws: Too much of their time was consumed by those coming to consult them about every little ache and pain. This was particularly true with Nathan. As general practitioner he was consulted on many a vague or imagined disorder. However, both doctors found such visits were lessening as the novelty wore off. The community was a busy, hard-working one, and time was valuable to the patient as well as the doctor. The amount of disease resulting from previous neglect had proved to be much greater than they had bargained on. But if their idea of preventive medicine were correct, this was a load on them that also would lessen as time passed. They found, too, a certain amount of dissatisfaction to cope with in those who had to incur expensive hospital and specialist bills not covered by their insurance. This was true of all insurance plans; they never seemed to cover enough. They agreed that three months was too short a period to come to any conclusion.

"Of course, what we need more than anything else is a general surgeon to take Eichel's place," Alan said at the end of their discussion.

They had been handicapped from the beginning by the loss of Eichel. Although he had stuck to his promise and performed operations for them, they had lacked his help in other ways. The three together could have given a fairly comprehensive service; two of them couldn't compass it. They had tried to fill Eichel's place, but as they could not guarantee hospital privileges they had not been able to secure a well-qualified man.

"Rather, we need specialists in every field, including a psychiatrist," Nathan said. "I could turn over to him the people with psychosomatic complaints."

Nathan had looked very tired of late. Alan was beginning to fear that the constant demand on Nathan day and night was taking its toll of him. He wasn't too strong, and as general practitioner he carried most of the burden of the night calls.

Nathan's eyes looked tired even at the beginning of the day. By evening there were dark pouches under them, so dark that they looked like bruises. Alan tried to convince himself it wasn't the work but worry over Brenda that was responsible. Was something wrong between them? Delicacy forbade his asking. He could not invade Nathan's privacy, good friends though they were.

For a few days his concern over Nathan was pushed to the back of his mind. On a rainy morning Miss Prentiss while going up the steps of the school fell and broke her hip. It meant she would be out of school for the rest of the term, and Alan could see no way to avoid her incurring a heavy hospital bill. The umbrella of security collapsed which the Towne-Gertz insurance until now had held over her head. The only redeeming feature, as he saw it, was that her sister was now well enough to take care of herself. In fact, it would be good for her to be thrown on her own resources.

What concerned him was Miss Prentiss' unhappy state of mind, due, no doubt, to worry over the extra expenses. She had scarcely spoken since, en route to the hospital in the ambulance, she had told him she wished to be placed in the ward. The third day after the accident, when he stopped beside her bed, she waved away the nurse and asked him, "How long is it going to be before I can get around?"

"I can't tell just yet. Some time, I fear."

"You're trying to put me off, aren't you? I suppose I am a child to you now that I'm sick."

"Have I ever regarded your sister in such a light?" he asked, marveling how quickly understanding between patient and doctor could be lost.

She shrugged. "Mariana has been protected by my earning power, still is. You know this is going to be a long business, but you're trying to put off telling me so. Divert the patient! I just wanted to take this opportunity to say I've been carrying hospital insurance."

"Grand, Miss Prentiss! I would have expected such foresight on your part. I repeat that I'll tell you just as soon as I can how long it will be."

So far Alan had found time to talk to Mrs. Watkins only by telephone. He had been too busy to go and see her. The cold rain turning into sleet had brought him several accident cases; the most serious and time-consuming were the injuries to a family of four whose car had skidded and gone over an embankment. Feeling he must take the time to call on Mrs. Watkins, he went over after dinner. To his surprise she did not open the door at his ring. Instead, as in the beginning days when he had attended her, she called out for him to come in. He entered to find her in bed. Here was the retrogression he had known might come. The long fight back to health was never a continuous march forward, but certainly now was an inconvenient time for a setback.

"Why, Doctor, just when Agatha needs me do I have to have a setback like this?" she demanded. "Promise me you won't tell her. How is she really?"

From the tension in her voice and the nervous clasping and unclasping of her hands, he recognized that here was a crisis he must meet. Unless he could restore Mrs. Watkins' serenity, arthritis might reassert itself. It was recognized that worry had a very definite effect on the disease. Odd that she could have met her own struggle so valiantly but could not face her sister's. He must show her that in reality it was one and the same struggle.

"You must take my word that your sister is not suffering unduly. In fact, she's getting a very much needed rest."

"Dr. Towne, you know just lying in bed is no rest unless you have nothing to worry about. It will be torment for Agatha with her responsibilities."

"But aren't you exaggerating? What need is there for your sister to worry as long as she knows she'll fully recover, and I've assured her that she will. She retires in June, doesn't she? She's losing only two months of the term. The school board pays for absences of that length. Her insurance with us and her hospital insurance——"

"Hospital insurance!" exclaimed Mrs. Watkins.

"You didn't know?" he asked in surprise.

"No, but it's like Agatha not to tell me. She may never tell me, and, of course, I shan't mention it to her." The change in Mrs. Watkins was startling. "You've done me so much good! You always make me feel I'll get well."

"We have a special goal now," he said.

"Yes?"

"For you to visit your sister. It would be the best medicine she could have for you to walk in on her."

"And you think I can!"

"If there are no more setbacks, yes."

"Let's make it a surprise," she said, her eyes alight.

A mysterious thing had happened. Mysterious always to him, though he had often seen it happen before. Mrs. Watkins knew now she would be well and active again. Before, she had simply trusted in his promise that she would. Somewhere in their conversation this afternoon she had jumped over a mental hurdle. Her progress from now on he believed would be rapid.

One morning before making his rounds Alan dropped in at the office to find a haggard and irascible Nathan. "You look as if you hadn't been to bed. Too many babies last night?"

"Too many!" Nathan fairly spat the words out.

"Perhaps it's the lambing season." Alan grinned. He was feeling as if he could cope with anything this morning. He had had a letter from Esther saying she now could use her right arm.

"Lambing season nothing!" Nathan refused to be amused. "You know Mrs. Jessup. She's gone and had triplets."

"It would happen to us, wouldn't it? You get four to care for, not two. And I suppose they're premature."

"Certainly. It means an incubator for weeks. Something like thirty dollars a day extra for the couple. He's just starting out in the research department over at the oil company's refinery. I had prepared them for twins. But triplets! Once out of thousands of births—and it had to happen to an insured patient of ours!"

"I bet they get along all right," Alan consoled him. "The community will be proud of such productivity. I bet a fund will be raised, and there'll be diapers enough sent in to garb the whole infant population of the town."

He proved right. The evening paper carried the story, and by noon the next day contributions were coming in to pay hospital bills. A baby-food company was providing food for a year.

"But nobody's helping us out," Nathan lamented.

"We're like two old bachelors with the grumps," Alan answered, trying to shake off the feeling that, in the end, the odds were against them. His apprehension that Nathan was breaking under the strain returned.

"To all intents and purposes we are bachelors," Nathan replied. "We're leading unnatural lives. Suppose Esther and Brenda were here—what kind of life would they be having?"

"If we could get even one more doctor to go in with us!" said Alan.

"And why can't we?" Nathan demanded. "You know the reason. It's too uncertain a livelihood. The medical schools don't train doctors to accept a vocation of poverty and celibacy."

"Why celibacy?" Alan exclaimed.

"A man wouldn't think he had much to offer a wife."

"Oh, come on, Nathan, you're carrying your grouch pretty far, aren't you?"

"It's not a grouch. It's not only that we're working too hard. Let's face it. We'll never be able to give sufficient financial protection without a hospital, and a hell of a chance we've got of getting a hospital! Even Miss Benninger can't help us to that extent."

"We've never asked her," Alan replied. "She's done things almost as impossible for us—like getting you special privileges, even if you are a general practitioner, to handle operative births."

"But that was because Corwin had the privilege."

Alan's jaw set, thinking of his hospital of one patient in his own house because the local hospital had no room for chronics. There were a number of other chronics he was treating at their homes. "I'd be tempted to ask Miss Benninger," he said aloud, "but I never see her around any more."

"We're talking pipe dreams." Nathan rose. "Let's go and get some dinner."

While they walked down the street to the nearest restaurant neither was conscious of the sudden burst of spring and the evening's beauty. Both had come to dread this hour of the day. They were family men by preference; the long-continued eating in public places was getting them down. They knew every dish on the menu; they knew the special taste of restaurant coffee; they knew the peculiar smell of mingled food and air conditioning.

As on previous nights they ordered, then lighted their cigarettes to put in the time until their dinners were served. Suddenly Nathan crushed out his cigarette. Alan noticed how white his fingers looked against the red pottery ash receiver, standard equipment of the restaurant. I'm never going to have anything red in my house, Alan was thinking, when Nathan startled him by saying, "I've something I want to tell you, Alan. I've been trying for a week to get up my courage. Brenda isn't coming back."

To Alan it seemed incredible. Surely things could be set right between them! They had been separated too long. How stupid of him not to have arranged for Nathan to pay his wife an occasional visit. "Look, Nathan. I can manage over this week end. Go to New York, talk to Brenda. Quarrels aren't fatal."

"It's not that," answered Nathan, pushing aside the plate the waitress had brought. How could he explain to Alan? In his pocket was a letter from Brenda received a week ago. He had been hurt by its contents at first, but little by little he had come to see that there was much truth in what she had to say and much wisdom. Her words came back to him now.

You've been wonderful, Nathan, my dear [the letter read—he knew it by heart], never urging me in all these months to come home, giving me time to get hold of myself. I've been grateful for your patience—do understand, Nathan—but resentful too because you have thus put the burden of decision on me, and I do not want to take the responsibility of making a decision involving both of us. But now that I've conquered my grief to the point where it does not overpower me, throwing me into hours of despair, I've begun to see the reason why I have recovered as much as I have. There has been therapeutic value (I'm trying to use your terms) in studying under a teacher who drives me to hours and hours of practice. Music is doing for me what medicine has done for you.

I could have gone on in Athenia as we were if I had not lost my baby. But whenever I think of leaving the daily study here I draw back in panic. We should have other children. I know you want them. But I can't rid myself of the feeling that something terrible will happen to them if we do. In time I'll get over this surely, but I can't do it in Athenia where I won't be driven to work hard as I am here. I can't do it alone just now.

If there were no other place than Athenia for you to practice the kind of medicine you are interested in, that would be different. The sacrifice on my part would then have its own therapeutic value. As it is now, I can't seem to make it. Nathan, dear, please understand. Here in New York we could have the kind of life that would heal us both, neither of us asking too much of the other. As you know, there's a group-insurance plan here on the order of what you and Alan are trying to work out. I've met some of the doctors. You'd have a bigger opportunity if you joined them. I'm certain they'd take you in. In fact, they said as much to me.

It was all just as Brenda had stated it except for one thing. She had not considered his obligation to Alan. But Nathan could not dismiss that duty so easily. He had come up against the problem of conflicting loyalties. How great was his responsibility to the man who had given him a start? He could not rid himself of the sense, not only of personal obligation to Alan, but of obligation to the plan they had together undertaken. He had entered into a contract with the community to try Alan's experiment for a year. If he backed out now, it would fail. Well, it probably would fail anyway.

Then there was Brenda. Was not his responsibility to her the greater one? She was using the will of her teacher to strengthen her own will in order to surmount a personal disaster. This aid he himself had seen was necessary. That it was taking her longer to win out than he had expected was nothing against her. He trusted Brenda. If she felt she was still unable to get on without her teacher's help, had he any right to deny her that help? . . . But how could he explain all this to Alan?

"It's not what you think, Alan," he said at last. "Brenda and I haven't quarreled. It's pretty complicated. I'm not certain I can make it clear. Brenda's up against something in herself that just won't let her come back here. No, that isn't it exactly. It's the need for something to take the place of little Nath. She says music is to her what medicine is to me. It's as if she were drowning and had caught at music to save her."

"I see," said Alan at last. "Of course we've taken on an obligation. It's yours as well as mine."

"Yes, that's what is troubling me. Surely you know, Alan, I don't want to let you down."

"And you don't want to let Brenda down either." Alan smiled a little grimly, trying to lessen the tension between them. "If we could carry on to the end of our year—fulfill what we promised——"

"Perhaps that's the solution," said Nathan. But six months more with the inexorable forces of time working to divide him and Brenda! He had a premonition what that would lead to. No, it wasn't a solution; it was a sacrifice.

And so, too, in his heart Alan regarded it. But hang it all, was Brenda the only one to be considered? "Suppose we sleep on it," he said aloud.

The two rose, leaving their dinners all but untouched.

"Anything wrong with the food?" the waitress asked.

"No, nothing."

"Or the service?"

Seeing her anxiety, each reached in his pocket for change to add to his regular tip.

As they stepped outside Alan looked at his watch. "I'm late," he said. "I promised to get Roger up this evening for his father's visit. We're going to show Gunsaulus those last X rays." He was glad for an excuse to get away. He wanted time to think. All that he had tried to do since he left Sam he saw destroyed. Some solid core within him seemed to be giving away. He strode quickly to his car.

He slid his long legs in behind the wheel and drove as fast as if he were out on an emergency call. The police along the way smiled indulgently. They had put him down in their minds for a pretty good guy, even if he might exceed speed limits now and then when he didn't have a professional excuse.

❧ 36 ❧

WHEN he drove up in front of his own house Alan saw the nurse standing in the window. He envisioned the scene in the sick boy's room, Roger's growing anxiety as the time for Alan's arrival passed and the time for his father's arrival drew nearer. It was Nathan who had guessed the boy's secret distress. How Roger had learned that he was a disappointment to his father was a mystery. Gunsaulus bore himself well. By every outward sign he displayed pride in his son, a pride which was genuine so far as Roger's mind was concerned. Miss Prentiss, knowing her pupil had a good brain, had not allowed him the easy excuse of a weakened body. His grades were above average.

"He can beat me every time. He'll take over my business someday," Gunsaulus had bragged one evening when Alan came in for a last look at his patient and found father and son playing chess together. It was one of the rare occasions when Gunsaulus found time to come to see Roger. As always, he explained in elaborate detail the many reasons why he did not get around oftener. Was it those painstaking explanations that had given Roger the clue to his father's disappointment? However he had learned it, Roger understood that in his heart the successful industrialist could not take real pride in a son who was deformed, and so avoided seeing him.

Tonight was designed to change this image, so deeply seated in the father's mind. There was an imaginative quality in Gunsaulus, Alan believed. It was this response he wanted to arouse in Roger's behalf. In place of the image of the crippled boy with his patient, submissive expression which now occupied Gunsaulus' mind, he would put a glimpse of the stalwart individual his son really was. For Roger was fighting as stubbornly as ever his father had fought his adversaries, to win victory over his deformity. If Alan could accomplish this substitution he believed the father would no longer suffer the humiliation which unconsciously he now attributed to his son.

Alan had drilled Roger in his part of tonight's venture. The boy was to explain the X rays to his father, show him how the column of his spine was straightening.

Alan parked his car, hurried up the stairs with the package of X rays. "I thought you'd never come!" Roger exclaimed fretfully when Alan entered the room.

"Steady there!" Miss Reich admonished him. "We've only to unwrap them."

Everything was soon in readiness. The hour for Mr. Gunsaulus' arrival came. Ten minutes, twenty, and still no sound of his car. Tension grew in the room.

"Of course my father is a very busy man, one of the busiest in the city and one of the richest," Roger bragged.

It grew dark. The street lights came on. Roger's voice again broke the silence which seemed to hang like a pall over the house. "He could buy the whole town out if he wanted to!"

Miss Reich turned from the window. "Roger, stop it! Stop telling us how important your father is. Any little sparrow is just as important."

"Oh, yeah! Tell it to the marines," Roger shouted.

The telephone rang. "You answer it, Nurse," Roger commanded. Whenever Miss Reich said anything against his father he refused to use her name.

"It's for you, Dr. Towne," she called. Lingering outside the door she whispered, "It's his father. He's not coming. Tell him he's got to." Entering Roger's room, she commanded, "Young man, you pipe down or I'll have to cut you down to size."

"Your father is on his way; he's been delayed. He'll be here, at the latest in half an hour," Alan reported. If only the boy didn't guess his father had not meant to come!

It seemed he didn't, for in his politest tone Roger asked, "Couldn't we go over the X rays again, Dr. Towne?"

They went through them. Again they waited. Finally there was the sound of a car stopping before the house, the opening of the front door. Miss Reich rose from the chair beside the bed. "I'll go down and meet him."

"No, you don't!" Roger caught her by the hand. "No first talks." Miss Reich pretended to struggle with him. He laughed hysterically.

"You all seem pretty gay in here." Short, thickset Gunsaulus strode into the room. "Thought maybe I'd see you walking around this evening." This was his regular salutation, the challenge which, up to this time, Roger had been unable to meet. Although out of bed now for a part of every day, he refused to get up if he thought his father was coming. For several days Miss Reich had been suggesting that he sit by his father when the X rays were exhibited, but each time he had said, "I guess I'd better wait a little longer." They had not urged him, wanting him to make the decision himself. To the surprise of nurse and doctor, at his father's words Roger threw back the blanket that covered him, slid his legs over the side of the bed and got unsteadily to his feet.

"Good enough, Son! That's great! You're doing fine." Gunsaulus patted Roger on the head. "And no brace."

"Never any brace!" cried Roger.

"Roger thought you'd like to see what's been happening to him." Alan picked up the X rays. "If you'll both sit here . . ." Miss Reich pushed chairs behind the two. She could see the perspiration standing out on Roger's forehead, but he motioned her away and took his seat beside his father.

"You see, Dad," Roger began a little uncertainly, "nothing's wrong with me really. This is me"—he pointed to the plate Alan held up—"when I came here." The plate showed the column of his spine with its double curve. "And now here's what we've been doing. Plate II, please." Alan displayed it. "Plate III, please . . . IV . . . V . . . Plate VI." Roger's voice grew stronger. He was going too fast, and he was giving none of the details so carefully rehearsed. Alan feared that Gunsaulus would not see the slight differences in the plates. Roger looked anxiously at his father for some comment, but there was none. "Back to Number I!" he cried. "Hold it up against VI." It was a command not rehearsed, but Alan obeyed it. "See, Dad," he shouted, "it's lots straighter."

And Gunsaulus did see. He saw more than the straightening spine. He saw his son in a new dimension—a fighter like himself. Why, he'd be the superior of any business rival when he grew up! For once he looked beyond the boy's deformity. "I take my hat off to you," he said, and with a humility new to him he added, "I don't know that I could have done as well myself, partner." He shook his son's hand and then hurried toward the door.

Without protest Roger let Miss Reich help him back into bed. "Partner! Did you get that, Miss Reich? Partner to an important man." This time Miss Reich did not attempt to cut him down to size.

Alan followed the boy's father downstairs. Not until they reached the hall below did Gunsaulus speak. "Will his spine be straight in time?" he asked, his mind slipping back into the old groove of estimating his son on his physical fitness.

"That I can't say yet. The human body has marvelous recuperative powers. It's on them and on your son's ability to keep up the fight that everything depends."

"You mean maybe he can't keep it up?"

Alan realized he'd said the wrong thing. "What I meant was, it's a man's job, and we're asking it of a boy. He's put up a superb fight. Your admiration meant a great deal to him tonight."

"He's done well enough as far as it goes," replied Gunsaulus. "See that he keeps it up."

Alan stood with his hand on the doorknob, but he did not turn it. They couldn't put on a show like this for Gunsaulus every time. If he again lost interest in the slow process of rehabilitation—and he probably would, conditioned to action as he was—Roger might stop fighting, refuse to endure the tedious boring hours when he lay wrapped in the moist blankets. How could they further dramatize the inch-by-inch struggle still ahead?

All at once Alan's problems seemed to be related. If he could interest Gunsaulus in establishing for the community a well-staffed hospital run on the insurance plan, not only would his project be saved and Nathan be free to join Brenda, but Gunsaulus could share with his son the new undertaking. Alan would see that the boy took part. If he could get father and son working together, both of them might siphon off their personal anxieties into creative planning.

It is the hunch of all hunches, thought Alan. A dangerous hunch in some ways. It might arouse Gunsaulus' suspicion that I've been after money all along. With lightning speed the possibilities and the hazards passed through Alan's mind.

"Well," said Gunsaulus, "you seem to be on the verge of saying something. Either say it or open the door. It's late."

"What I was thinking would take time to explain. Would you let me come to see you some evening soon?"

"Do you think you could spare the time to come so far?"

Alan detected a twinkle in Gunsaulus' eye. "I might manage it for once."

"Tomorrow night then. Promptly at seven." Gunsaulus walked with light tread for such a heavy man across the veranda and down the steps to his car.

What have I let myself in for? thought Alan, closing the door behind the industrialist.

37

Working almost with Sam's precision technique, Alan cleared his office of patients a little early the next afternoon. He must run no risk of being late for his appointment with Gunsaulus. The shortest route to his destination was by way of a diagonal cut south across the Southeast District and the wedge-shaped rundown area, once a part of the old town. From there he could strike into the main thoroughfare. It would take him through the factory section beyond which lay the very exclusive suburb where Gunsaulus had his home. As the rows of inexpensive houses with which he was so familiar gave place to old dwellings fast slipping into decay, he increased his speed, anxious to put behind him a region which always depressed him on its own account and because it brought back the memory of the Northeast District. In ten minutes he had left the drab streets behind and entered the wide belt of factories which had taken over much of the original no man's land of half-poverty. Only occasionally did one of the old houses still stand between factory buildings.

Cars passing his threw against his windshield the slush compounded of recent rain and dirt, blinding his vision for a moment. He put on his windshield wiper. In the cleared space he saw the tall smokestacks of factories, noble and imposing columns against the piled-up rain clouds along the horizon, touched with the rosy afterglow of the sun.

All at once the pavements were cleaner. The streets freshly washed down were bordered by moderate-priced cottages. Quite suddenly they gave way to the closely mowed acres of a golf course. Soon he was driving down the wide streets of the residential district he sought. Here the new-rich of the city lived. These were the dwellings of men who, boasting that they alone possessed the pioneer spirit of America, had, during the war, built planes and tanks with fine disregard for the caution of the old industrialists of Athenia. In the midst of the wide lawns stood beautiful modern houses. Their owners had been as adventurous in choosing new forms of architecture as in choosing new industrial processes. Some of the houses were good, some atrocious, all daring and, yes, grandiose. Alan, looking at them, thought he preferred the restrained lines of colonial architecture, and then it crossed his mind that his own grandiose idea of a hospital ought to mean he'd be understood here.

He was driving slowly now. In the gathering darkness it was hard to see the street numbers painted on the curbs in front of the houses. He didn't want to lose his way. It was important he should not be late for the appointment. This was the time when he would either sink or swim. He was up to his neck in a daring enterprise. He had to succeed with Gunsaulus.

He stopped. Leaning out of his car, he hunted with his flashlight for 6057 Buckminster Drive. There was the number just ahead. No flashlight was needed to see it, for it was done in large illuminated figures. A floodlight played on the long drive leading up to the brilliantly lighted mansion. Although it was a stone house, the windows were so wide and so many they gave the impression that it was built of glass.

He rang the bell. A man in livery opened the door. When Alan gave his name the polite masked expression of the perfect servant gave way to a broad smile. "Come in, Dr. Towne. And how is the lad?" he asked with affectionate concern. "We miss him here."

"He'll be coming back to you strong and straight, I hope, someday."

"Mrs. Gunsaulus is with the boy tonight, but the master left word he'd get home at seven-thirty," said the butler, ushering Alan into a room at the end of the wide hall. "Make yourself comfortable until he comes."

Seven was the hour Gunsaulus had named the evening before. So that's his game, Alan thought. He hasn't forgotten one detail of our first meeting when I made him fit into my program. Waiting there in the great empty house, Alan found it hard to remember how invulnerable he had felt last evening when he had decided to play his hunch. The sudden idea had been like a rocket, exploding in his mind, lifting him up out of himself into a region where he was free of inhibitions.

But in the night he had wakened, and in that first moment of waking he had felt himself a small insignificant creature in a postwar world which grew daily more threatening with man's exploitation of his knowledge of the universe. Then the larger anxiety had given place to his own special anxiety—how not to go under in his own little world. Sam's oft-repeated advice leaped up in his mind: Watch your impulses, don't get yourself out on a limb. This he very possibly had now done. Gunsaulus might ascribe all sorts of ulterior motives to his taking Roger on as a patient, might even take Roger away, expose Alan as an experimenter.

With daylight and work Alan had regained confidence in himself. But this wait—he had not counted on it. He stood leaning against the mantel, looking down the vista of the rooms through the open doorway. The inadequacies of his life—his frightened childhood, his present incomplete marriage, his sense of Sam's disapproval, the inevitable loss of Nathan on whose friendship and understanding he had come to rely—seeped away his self-reliance. Who was he to think he could carry his dream through? Then he saw Gunsaulus coming down the hall, and such phantoms slipped away like discredited ghosts. After all, his Goliath was a short man.

"Sorry to have kept you waiting, Towne. Sit down, won't you?" Not until Alan was seated did the shorter man pass to his tall guest a fine leather-embossed box filled with cigars and cigarettes. He held a lighter to the cigarette Alan selected. Then he took a cigar, slipped off its gold band and sat down opposite his caller. "Let's get to the point. What do you want to talk to me about?" He crossed his short legs and, tipping back his head, looked up at the perfect smoke rings he blew ceilingward.

Alan plunged. "You and I, as I see it, Mr. Gunsaulus, have been running a kind of horse-and-buggy hospital. I had the idea that we might co-operate on a streamlined affair worthy of our abilities. I had to take my wife to Nevada to get the treatment she needs. We had to figure out this makeshift arrangement for your son because you didn't wish to take him so far away. Such things seem out of keeping with the industrial advancement of this city—I might say our city."

"You certainly aren't hampered with small ideas. Whether they're practical or not is something else again." Gunsaulus brought his feet down, placed them close together, signifying he was ready for combat.

"You could make such a hospital a monument to Roger's splendid recovery." Alan met the challenge.

"Isn't it a little early to memorialize your success with Roger?" asked Gunsaulus dryly.

Alan felt his mind sharpening under the thrust. No more sparring, he decided. "We need a hospital around here run on what I consider modern ideas, owned really by the people, supported by their insurance, a nonprofit hospital. I'm putting it up to you as a business proposition. In the beginning it may not meet with your ideas of a good investment. In time I think it will. You'd have to gamble on it at first. I judge you gambled when you decided to make yourself a big operator."

"You flatter me, both as to my abilities and the size of my pocketbook."

"I think not," Alan answered quietly. "Let me lay all my cards on the table."

As Alan in a few words told what he and Nathan had set themselves to do and what they had accomplished Gunsaulus grew interested in spite of himself. His mind quickly grasped that Alan respected the man of moderate income and understood that charity was an affront to sturdy independence. For a moment Gunsaulus laid aside the mental trappings of his wealth and remembered himself as he used to be, a small dealer who, had he then been confronted with Roger's sickness, would either have gone broke or have had to ask for charity—something he would have loathed. He saw that this young doctor was devoting his talents to remove such humiliation to working people. He liked that, for he really belonged with them.

But aloud he said, "It sounds crazy. You don't build a hospital like that in a day, even a year, or maybe ten years. What about a building? What about doctors? We're short of them all over the country. What about nurses? We're shorter of them."

"Take the building first," said Alan. "I've had my eye for some time on a private school the Army used as a hospital during the war. They've abandoned it. I understand it's up for lease. Why not lease it? Build later if we want to!"

"You could manage the drive each day?"

"It's not far out of my present beat." Alan marveled that Gunsaulus so long nursed resentment for the concessions he'd had to make the first day.

"How about doctors?" snapped Gunsaulus.

"I think we could get them. It's difficult for young doctors to secure hospital privileges. I believe there are plenty of doctors who'd grab at the chance of an immediate place on a hospital staff."

"You mean we'd have to take inexperienced men?"

"Not at all. The two men who originally joined me here in the Southeast District had been operating overseas for three years."

"But you had no hospital. How did it help them to join you?" barked Gunsaulus.

"Well, I had hospital privileges in the city and believed I could get them into the same hospital as my partners. But that's off the point." He didn't intend to tell Gunsaulus about Sam. He was going to win the industrialist to his scheme without his brother's influence or not at all. "It's not that the doctors who are trying to get a foothold aren't good. It's that, in a lot of communities, they run up against what amounts to a medical monopoly. Often the old doctors don't want competition."

"Umph!" Gunsaulus' eyes narrowed. "So the entrenched interests are in medicine too. By Gad, we'll give them a run for their money! I believe some of the other men I'm associated with would go in on a scheme like this.

Among us we could put up the capital needed. We'd get hold of some of the bright young doctors who've been pushed around . . . show these highjackers where to get off."

Things were moving too fast for Alan. He seemed to have accidentally touched a spring that set off all Gunsaulus' resentments against the men who individually he felt had tried to exclude him from the industrial world. It was naïve and it was disturbing. If Gunsaulus made promises in that mood, he might repudiate them later. He should not go into the scheme for emotional reasons. "I'd like you to see just what's involved," said Alan.

A shrewd look came into the little man's eyes. "You didn't think I'd play it blind, did you?"

"No, not exactly." Alan was slightly discomfited. Recovering, he said, "Certainly I didn't. I've brought you statistics of hospitals of this kind which have been in existence for several years. I knew a businessman like you would want something of the sort." Alan took out of his pocket condensed statements of two such undertakings, handed the papers to Gunsaulus, and watched with interest the businessman's quick grasp of details.

He fired question after question at Alan.

When he came to the salaries paid doctors he barked, "Do you think any doctor with spunk is going to agree to his income being limited? Poor stuff he'd be, wouldn't he?"

"Lots of doctors already have accepted a limitation. Men are on salary at some of our biggest clinics."

They talked for an hour. Alan presented figures showing what he believed the initial investment would be, what return could probably be made on that investment. Gunsaulus questioned every estimate.

"It sounds pretty good," he said at the end. "If the investment is as good as you make it out to be, I'll see what I can do about getting a board together."

"I'd like to mention this," said Alan. "Many of the brightest doctors pushed around are Jews. Many hospitals limit Jews to a quota. If we go into this, I want no race distinctions in choosing the staff."

"You can't take on all the fights at once. Besides, this brings me to your place in the hospital. If a group of us put up the money, we're certainly going to have our say about the way the place is run. The board would have to pass finally on any men you select." Gunsaulus rose, went over to his desk, sat down behind it.

Alan gathered that the man's change of position signified he was ready for battle, and that with him a battle meant a victory, but Alan could not afford to relinquish all authority. Certain issues must be decided by the doctor in charge.

"Medical matters cannot be turned over to men who know nothing about medicine. You wouldn't run a factory that way," Alan said. "This has got to be understood between us in the very beginning." He seated himself on a corner of the desk. "I must have the right to choose doctors on their professional know-how."

Gunsaulus stuck out his under lip. It gave him a pugnacious look. "I'll accept Jews."

"The best therapist I know is colored." Alan waited.

"I'm not going to be called a crackpot. I've got a reputation among businessmen," Gunsaulus said in a loud voice.

His words were like a bell ringing an alarm in Alan's mind. Crackpot—that's what Sam would think him, if he insisted on such terms when he had a gilt-edged chance to get a hospital run on his own plan. For a moment he hesitated. Then he remembered how close he and Esther had come to disaster because of his unwillingness to meet prejudice.

He leaned over the desk. "Crackpot, nothing! You're too smart to be put in that category, and so am I."

Gunsaulus gave a short hard laugh. "I guess you're right, Towne. Now as to the staff. You know the professional angle better than I do, but I know men. I must have a look at them, and I won't have one of those mind doctors around."

"No need to worry about that for a long time. We can't afford it. We must trim our requirements down to the minimum until we're on our feet."

It was eleven o'clock when Alan left. All the controversial points had been threshed out between them and Gunsaulus seemed reasonably certain he could get men to invest in the undertaking. "If not, I'll do it all myself."

That he was to have a hospital was not yet real to Alan. The sudden assurance of success after the months of struggle and uncertainty was a strong potion which made him feel lightheaded, but which also washed out of him the accumulated weariness of months of hard, unrelieved work. As he drove his car along the familiar streets of the Southeast District nothing looked too difficult. The houses were dark, shrouded in sleep—and the families defenseless in sleep were his to care for.

He hoped he'd catch Nathan at the office so he could explain why he had left everything to him this evening. All day he had avoided his friend. He hadn't wanted to bring up last evening's conversation until he had seen Gunsaulus. When he came in sight of their office he saw a light in the upstairs room which they now used for their laboratory. He slipped his key into the lock of the front door, ran up the stairs and into the lighted room. He was shocked at how weary Nathan looked as he glanced up from the records he was going over.

"Guess you thought I'd run out on you. After what you told me last night I had to work something out."

"Evidently you've done it. You look as if you owned the world." Nathan felt his own weariness the greater for the contrast.

"Almost. I've got a hospital in my pocket."

"You've got what!"

"A hospital financed by Gunsaulus and Company, managed by—well, who do you think?"

"No other than you."

"It could be us, of course, if—but I know it can't in the circumstances."

Both of them were silent. Nathan had not realized until now how good their partnership was—something that might never come to him again. Last night he had felt Alan was trying to make the obligation to him greater than the obligation to Brenda. He saw now he had been unjust.

Alan realized that a relationship delicate and uncharted was going out of his life, and he would be the poorer for it. "Together I believe we make a whole man," he said and then added, lest Nathan should think he was trying to hold him, "Do you think you could stay on until I've found someone to help me out while we're getting the new setup going—perhaps two months?"

"Yes, but can you spare me for a few days in New York?" As Nathan spoke his life here in this city, his friendship with Alan, the success of which he was not to partake, all fell away into nothingness, out of which his love for Brenda rose like a plume of light.

"Of course I can. . . . Well, I guess I'll be getting along." Alan rose. Of a sudden he was inexplicably lonely. If only he had Esther to go home to! What were the skills he would be gathering together worth to him if Esther was to be crippled for life? He still dared not hope that she would ever walk without a brace. If she did not, what did his puny undertaking amount to after all? But when he sat down to write Esther that evening the splendor of the enterprise came back to him. He filled page after page with all that he meant to do.

Esther had been watching summer come to Nevada, a strange summer made up of tawny brown hills, parched valleys and unchanging blue sky. Today excitement hung over the little community of the handicapped. Some were going home to stay, some for a vacation. There was an air of departure about the place. Esther was sitting in the courtyard. Alan's letter telling of plans for his hospital was lying in her lap. She was between laughter and tears. This husband of hers was always reaching out to new undertakings, prodigal of his time and strength. She doubted if he'd get to Nevada until he came to take her home. Tears were winning out. Was she always to be sacrificed to his work? It had been so long since she had felt his strong arms around her. This daily, hourly struggle—how could she keep it up? Doubt assailed her. Surely Alan couldn't love her or he would realize how much he was asking of her. All at once she thought of Grandfather Towne. He must have been like Alan when he was young. She wished she might have known Sarah Towne. The older woman—did she ever resent the absorption of her husband in his work?

Looking up, Esther saw Dr. Carothers leaning against the jamb of the door that led into the building. He was regarding her intently. After a little he came and pulled a stool up beside her and sat down. "I had a letter from your husband today. I see you did, too." He pointed to the letter in her lap. "A wonderful opportunity, isn't it? He'll have plenty of problems. I know what it's like." Then he began telling her of his own beginnings—the patients coming to his home, how he had filled the house with them, how his wife had to move the babies out into the hall in the daytime. He told her story after story of those days. In each he paid some tribute to his wife.

"I couldn't have done it without her," he ended, fixing his brown eyes thoughtfully on Esther. "Two months more and you'll be ready to go home. It means hard work. How about it?" he asked.

Esther was silent, making the long spiritual journey out of her protected life into the life of well people.

"It would help your husband through the summer if he could look forward to your coming." Dr. Carothers rose and left her.

That night, lying in her bed in the small cubicle allotted to her, looking out at the stars so brilliant in the Nevada sky, Esther felt a crisis was upon her. She had come to the edge of a dark and bewildering land in which all her life she had wandered, fearful of the results of independent action. Either she went back into that wilderness alone, or she went forward on an ascending road, traveling in a goodly company of people like Alan and Dr. Carothers who lived courageously. She was beginning to see that she could become of the stalwart of heart who make the demands on the spirit that Dr. Carothers had tried to tap this afternoon. Suddenly she could face what Nathan had called on her to face when he had talked to her in the hospital. She reached out to grasp the common dream of women—the wonder, the delight, the danger in bearing a child.

38

July came and still the final business arrangements for the hospital were not completed. Although Gunsaulus that first evening had seemed almost precipitate in making promises, when it came to putting his name on paper he was both cautious and canny. He had his lawyers go over the smallest details, and so did the other men whom Gunsaulus had succeeded in getting to participate in the financing. Already scattering cases of polio had been reported in some sections of the city. It had been decided to add to the girls' school a wing for polio patients in the acute stage, thus avoiding the makeshift arrangements of last summer when the inconvenient office building had had to be used. To Alan it seemed stupid to hold up the final arrangements when another epidemic might break out any day. He was often impatient, sometimes close to anger, over delay which seemed unnecessary to him.

Finally on August first the last detail was settled. He was asked to attend an organization meeting where the articles of incorporation were to be signed, after which he was to be formally authorized head of the hospital. Alan, a bystander, looked on with interest at the gathering of the ten-man board and their lawyers. Most of the members were much like Gunsaulus, shrewd, adventurous businessmen. The group hospital appealed to them as a practical venture. They knew the value of keeping overhead down. The one-man outfit, whether in business or medicine, they believed outmoded.

It was midafternoon when the meeting was finally over. Alan immediately telephoned Sam's house. An announcement of the new hospital was to come out in the morning papers and Alan wanted Sam to hear about it first from him. The maid answered his call, saying the family had gone to the country for the week end. So Sam has his farm, thought Alan, realizing how many months he and his brother had been out of touch with each other.

When he rang the rural number the maid had given him Jo answered. "Alan! How nice to hear your voice!" she exclaimed. "Can't you come out for dinner? We're still eating picnic-style. Everything's in a mess, but if you don't mind that——"

"Mind!" said Alan. "After a steady restaurant diet?"

With keen anticipation he started out. He wanted to see what kind of country place Sam had chosen. And there was his great surprise, his own hospital, to tell Sam about.

The long straight highway going west across America's central plain stretched out before him. Side roads marked the half and quarter sections, setting off the richly productive farm land familiar to him from early childhood. The corn stood high on either side of the road. Above it rose farmhouses, barns and silos. The introduction of hybrid corn and the recent war had brought a prosperity to the Middle West beyond anything the farmers had dreamed of before.

At the end of an hour he turned off the main road, following the directions Jo had given him. At the top of a slight rise he stopped his car to look out over the great plain stretching away to the horizon: vast fields of corn, rank upon rank of sturdy stalks, with green sword-shaped leaves, bright blades in the intense light, huge squares of Kaffir corn low-growing and lush, stubbled fields from which the spring wheat and barley had been harvested, golden where they were touched with the sun, brown where an occasional summer cloud empty of rain floated white and billowy across the blue sky, throwing shadows down on the fields—the earth brought to fruition, the wondrous fruition of the fertile new earth of America. Alan, a product of this three-hundred-year-old country, was filled with the hope all its children had.

He started his car, and in another ten minutes he came to a gate with Sam's name on the post. Up the long private road he drove. Fields of corn, native and Kaffir, were laid out in the squares he had seen along the way. So Sam had not bought a fancy play place but a real farm. He was following the tradition of his Massachusetts forebears.

The unpretentious road ended at the edge of a grassplot such as any Midwest farmer would have. The house which stood a little farther on was typical of the region, a two-story building with a lean-to sloping away at the back. Under construction were wings to the left and right of the main structure. When finished, it would be a dignified country house reminiscent of New England.

No one was about. No one seemed to have heard his car, but as he stepped from it he saw Sam, with Jo on one side and Sally on the other, coming out of the big red barn which stood some distance back from the house.

Jo and Sally were wearing well-cut country clothes. Sam looked oddly at variance walking between the two well-dressed women. He wore a pair of trousers hopelessly out of press, and a shirt with a frayed collar open at the throat.

"You look more like a tramp than a rich doctor with a country estate," Alan chaffed his brother. Then he dutifully gave Jo and Sally the conventional family kiss.

"This is going to be my retreat," Sam answered. "For forty-eight hours every week end I'm going to forget I'm a doctor. Didn't Grandfather use to say he needed his garden to drain off into the soil the misery of so many sick people?"

"Yes, something like that, but I think he did it through his fingers. You know—getting dirt under his nails."

"Wouldn't do for a modern surgeon," Sam answered, leading the way into the house.

"You'd better be thinking about what Grandfather taught you." Alan gave a downward glance at Sam's waistline.

"You're envious of my full figure," Sam responded good-humoredly, enjoying the kind of banter they had indulged in when they were boys. "You look as if there's not much more to you than the sticks Grandmother used in her scarecrows. What have you been doing to yourself?"

"What you need is some good home cooking, Alan. Why don't you spend your week ends with us for a while and catch up on your eating?" Jo asked.

"I haven't any week ends. Won't have until October," Alan answered.

"You sound as if something nice was going to happen then," said Sally. "Is Esther coming home?"

"Yes, I think so." Alan found he didn't want to talk about Esther. He longed for her too poignantly. Only if he didn't think about her coming was he able to hold his heart down to something like its everyday rhythm.

But Sally persisted. "You're saving up all your free time until she gets here. Is that why you haven't any free week ends?"

"Not quite, Sally. A doctor isn't that free, as you should know by this time. Patients sometimes choose week ends to be sick." Sam tweaked his daughter's ear.

Sally smiled, happy somewhere inside her that he treated her like a child, for it gave her the sense of security she needed. Then, abruptly aware of the paradox of her position, she scowled. If he learned of her engagement to his assistant, he would demand of her a childish obedience and to defy it would rob her of that security. He had told her recently he did not wish her to go out with Tom Merton. "He's getting too attentive. You're only eighteen, too young to be going steadily with one man."

"Want to hear what I've been doing this summer?" Alan asked his brother. He had accomplished something at last that would seem important in Sam's eyes.

"I want to show you why I chose this particular farm." Sam led the way to the front of the house and pointed to the west where the sun was about to sink below the flat horizon. Its light, thrown across the plain, had turned the fields into a sea of golden rippling waves.

"Let's hear your news, Alan," said Jo, feeling it too bad that Sam was so absorbed in his own undertaking he had brushed aside what Alan had come to tell him.

"I've been arranging for my own hospital," Alan said.

"You're kidding!" Sam swung around, surprised enough to satisfy the most demanding younger brother.

"Not quite all mine." Alan was willing to qualify his original statement, now that he had actually captured Sam's attention. "Gunsaulus—you know, the industrialist—I've been taking care of his son. He and some of his associates are putting up the money."

"Well, good for you! If you've a man like that behind you, you've sound backing. Now take a last look at this view before it's dark, and then we'll go in and you tell me the details."

"Why, if he's going to have a hospital he's going to need a lot of doctors!" cried Sally.

Sam looked at his daughter. "Why should that interest you?" Sally's eyes fell.

"Come, Sal," said Jo, "let's lead the way." She took Sally's hand. "My dear," she exclaimed, "what are you doing with cold hands on a hot summer day?" She looked anxiously at her daughter. "Anything wrong?"

"Why should there be?" Sally demanded, and then as if to make up for her words, which sounded defiant now that she had spoken them, she squeezed her mother's hand.

For one fleeting moment Alan had the idea that there was a battle going on among these three but never brought to the surface. Just how they were divided on the fighting line he could only guess. He remembered the evening Sally had introduced Sam's new assistant to him in the lobby of the medical building—the light in her eyes and his too. Had they fallen in love? Did Sam object? Where did Jo stand?

"Don't you think this Early American furniture fits in well here?" Sam asked as they entered the house. "I'll show you around after I've heard about your hospital."

Sam sat down in a straight-backed chair, motioned Alan to another. Sally dropped down on the floor. Jo brought forward a rocker of the period.

"If Gunsaulus is setting you up, I don't need to ask you about the business end of it. How about the doctors? Maybe I can help you out there."

"That's what I hoped. I need someone to take Dr. Gertz's place."

"He leaving you? That, I'd say, is all to the good." Sam took his pipe out of his pocket and began filling it.

"He's a distinct loss," Alan answered. "He has the confidence of everyone. It's because of his wife." He turned to Jo. "The shock of the baby's death . . ." He left his sentence hanging.

"Any chance for women on your staff?" Jo asked.

"No minority groups excluded," said Alan with a smile.

Jo laughed and went on with her knitting. How she would have loved the work! When Sally was married and her happiness secure she meant to make Sam consent to her taking up her practice.

"To get down to brass tacks, what's your setup, Alan?" Sam turned slightly in his chair, excluding Jo, so it seemed to Alan. "This means of course you're through with that insurance scheme you were trying out. Naturally a businessman like Gunsaulus wouldn't fall for that."

"On the contrary, it's group practice we're going in for. An insurance plan something on the order of what I've been doing. Doctors on salary."

"You won't get good doctors that way!" Sam exclaimed. "Listen, Alan, I've had more experience than you. Don't wreck yourself on that idea. Right now you've got a grand chance to make a name with men like Gunsaulus backing you. Don't muff it. The kind of doctors you'd get would be the ones who can't make good on their own—the timid, the stupid, a few young ones who'll just use you to get a start."

"You're partially right," Alan conceded. "We'll have to weed out the chiselers and the failures who apply, but I think we can get good men who see it as a profession, not just as a business."

"Take away the initiative of making good on his own and any doctor will deteriorate," said Sam.

"I don't see why he should," Alan answered. "Research men are on salaries. Some of them are outstanding."

Sam stiffened visibly. "I thought I could help you get some good men, but not on that basis. I'd consider doing so unprofessional."

"Well, of course I wouldn't want you to do that. Let's drop it. Suppose you show me the house." Alan followed Sam about, trying to make amends for being such a disappointment by admiring everything. It wasn't hard to do. Everywhere the marks of Sam's efficiency were evident.

"I've something here to show you," said Sam, picking up a sheet of stiff paper that lay on his desk in a room he told Alan was meant to house his collection of books on early American history. "Recognize this?"

"Why, yes," Alan said. "A drawing of the sundial over the door of the old homestead. You didn't use to be interested in that part of the family history. What are you planning to do with this?"

"I'm going to have it cut into the clapboard over the front door. The Massachusetts house now is a historical landmark."

Alan, looking at the drawing in his hand, was filled with sudden emotion. He remembered the day when he had stood with Esther before the old house.

"I should think you'd take pride in her too," Sam said. He took the drawing from Alan and placed it carefully on a shelf.

"I do." Alan gave a short laugh, suddenly conscious of the irony of the moment. "Our ancestress certainly departed from tradition in a big way, didn't she?"

Sam surveyed him somewhat coolly, Alan thought. Then he changed the subject. "Jo must be waiting for us to come to dinner."

ꙮ 39 ꙮ

NEWS of the basis on which the hospital was set up spread quickly. Not only were most of the doctors in the district opposed to it, but doctors all over Athenia were violently against physicians signing contracts limiting their incomes. If you took away the incentive to make money, a poorer grade of men would enter the profession, they insisted. Alan had expected some opposition, but had not anticipated it would be so general or so bitter. He had supposed people recognized that with the rising cost of medicine such hospitals were inevitable in medium-income communities. Now he was beginning to fear that he might be prevented from getting the specialists he wanted.

He had made a preliminary list of the men he'd like to get hold of. He had even approached certain doctors. He was encouraged when Dr. Lambert, the general practitioner he wanted, immediately accepted the offer. Lambert was from another state. Dr. Powell, who had once been in the Public Health Service in that state, recommended him. "I've never worked with any other physician who seemed to understand so well the co-operation needed between the private doctor and Public Health—until I met you, Towne," Powell had said.

His reason for joining the hospital staff, Lambert said quite frankly, was that he was an older man and the regular hours appealed to him. Two young specialists signed up because it gave them hospital privileges. They, too, stated their reason candidly. Three others signed because they liked the financial security that a salary would give them. Soon Alan had enough applicants for two hospitals. Carefully he and Nathan weeded out those they thought would use the hospital merely as a steppingstone to more lucrative private practice and those who were looking for an easy berth.

Meanwhile discussion and argument entered every home and shop of the Southeast District. Was a man who limited his income in order to care for the sick a bad risk? Miss Prentiss, when asked about it by the other women in the ward, asked in return, "I've taught many of your children. My income was limited. Did I do a good job or not?"

"You helped my Billy after school so he'd make his grade," the woman two beds away replied. "But aren't doctors different?"

"They're human beings," said Miss Prentiss, picking up the book she had put down when the discussion began.

These were satisfying days for Alan. Once the business details were settled, Gunsaulus, who had bought, not leased, the school building and made a gift of it to the hospital corporation, moved rapidly to get the building in shape by early fall. He knew every angle of the intricate problems of construction. He secured the best architect to design the addition to the school. He drove sharp bargains with contractors. Then, playing on the humane quality in the workmen by talking about the possibility of an epidemic of polio, he had carpenters and plumbers completing their work in record time. Quite within the rules the union set Gunsaulus knew a considerable speed-up was possible.

Nearly every evening now he brought blueprints or fragments of materials for his son to see. "What did they do today, Dad?" Roger would call out the moment he heard his father's step on the stairs. Soon, to both the father's and Alan's satisfaction the boy was asking it from the head of the stairs. And at last one triumphant evening he met his father at the front door.

Then came the evening in early September when Gunsaulus gained Alan's permission to drive Roger out to see the hospital, which would be ready for occupancy in another two weeks. The light was not yet gone when they reached the school grounds. "There you are!" said Gunsaulus. "There's our hospital, Son."

With pride and happiness in being included in this undertaking of his father but shy of expressing his feelings, Roger said in a flat tone, "It looks nice, doesn't it?"

Gunsaulus was disappointed. He had bought the building outright in order that he might have the right to name it. He expected Roger to show some pleasure in that name. What did the kid want anyway? Maybe it was too dark to see the words over the door.

"I'll be back in a minute," Gunsaulus said, getting out of the car. "I think they've got the electricity connected. Get a better look at the building with it on." Roger lost the squat figure of his father in the darkness, and then all at once the building sprang into light. There above the entrance in illumined letters, he read: THE ROGER GUNSAULUS HOSPITAL.

Gunsaulus switched off the lights and went back to the car.

Under cover of the darkness Roger's adolescent shyness gave way and he blurted out, "I got something to tell you, Dad. I . . . I've been pretending . . . making you believe I'd be . . . you know . . . just as if I hadn't ever had polio. I'll only be almost straight. That old brace, I won't have to wear it, but . . . there'll be a little twist. I should have told you. It's all right if you want to take the sign down. I've been fooling you."

Also under cover of darkness the elder Gunsaulus was able to speak to his son as never before. "You haven't been foolin' me. The sign stays. You're a Gunsaulus to be proud of. You've got the guts to make a first-rate business-man. You've got what it takes." In an offhand voice, he added, "Dr. Towne says you can come home next week."

"Oh, Dad!" It was all Roger could say. And then: "I'm going back to school in the fall."

Gunsaulus maneuvered the long luxurious car cleverly between the piles of debris left by the builders. He glanced once more at the hospital. God help me, he said to himself, Roger won't ever be a patient there! But it would be several months before he'd know for certain. Dr. Towne had been frank with him. "I have every reason to believe the improvement is per-manent," he had said, "but we must wait six months to be sure. In the meantime I'm going to Nevada, where I'll discuss Roger's case with Dr. Carothers."

❧ 40 ❧

THE STAFF was nearly complete. Only one of the men Alan had wanted proved unacceptable to the Board. Just how Gunsaulus and the others had reached their decisions Alan never understood, but he had come to respect the industrialists' shrewd estimate of men. Both of the women doctors Alan had selected had been turned down. This bothered him, for he wanted at least one woman on the staff, and he was beginning to suspect that Gun-saulus did not.

"You'll have to get a woman pediatrician if you are not to have an all-male staff," said Nathan as they were having a late Saturday-night conference just before he was to leave.

"Where'll I get her?" Alan demanded.

"How about your sister-in-law helping you on that? She might know someone."

"It's worth trying," Alan answered a little reluctantly, not wishing to involve Jo, with Sam so opposed to the whole idea. Still, even Sam might be reconciled to doctors on salary when he learned of the kind of men Alan had secured. He'd take along the papers showing their rating if he went out. Tomorrow was Sunday. Why not drive to the country after he'd made his morning calls, see Sam, and talk to Jo about a pediatrician?

It was after five in the afternoon before he finally got away. When he arrived at the farm he found Jo alone. What luck! he thought. "I've a problem, Jo." He went straight to the point, hoping to get her opinion before Sam appeared. "I need a child specialist. I want a woman. I thought you might know of a good one."

Jo dropped her knitting in her lap. "Why, I believe I know just the person. She's good. She has a big practice, but she's just the kind who'd go in for a hospital like yours. I'll see what I can do."

They heard Sam's step in the hall. "Where did you come from?" His voice showed pleasure. "I've an operation on for tomorrow I'd like to talk over with you—a new operation which hastens recovery from a fractured femur."

"I've something to talk over with you too." Alan pulled from his pocket the list of the doctors he had secured. He handed it to his brother. "Don't you think it's a pretty fine setup?"

"I'd like to go along with you, but I can't," said Sam. "Frankly, such a list doesn't prove your plan is good: in fact, as far as I'm concerned, joining on such a basis simply lowers the men professionally. But let's forget about it," he said in a kindly tone. "Now for the operation which I'm going to perform tomorrow morning."

As he described it Alan realized he had been briefed on such an operation in India by a surgeon who had been in the European theater. Captured German prisoners had had it performed on them by German surgeons. Alan had later assisted in performing the same operation and he intended as soon as he had a fracture of this nature to perform it himself. But he did not tell Sam all this, thus spoiling his pleasure in describing it.

After a little Alan rose, saying he must get back to town. "Do stay for dinner," Jo urged.

He made the excuse of evening calls. He'd get a bite before he went to bed.

"Alan's always in a hurry," said Sam after seeing Alan to his car. "I'm afraid he's going to be one of those do-gooders. It's a pity. He could have anything he wants in professional circles if he were a little more normal. I just don't understand him." Sam broke off to ask, "Where's Sally?"

"She asked if she might have my car to go into town for a date. I said yes, I'd drive in with you in the morning. She left while you and Alan were talking."

Sam walked about the room. He was scowling. Jo sighed; Sally's departure had spoiled the evening for him. Happiness for one of them always seemed to mean unhappiness for the other.

"These young people"—he said after a little—"they're too restless. What's wrong with them? We've done everything for Sally, but she hardly stays in the house long enough to eat. . . . Why don't you say something?" he demanded when Jo didn't answer. "Why do you all shut me out?"

"Sam, do sit down. You don't need to be shut out of Sally's life." Should she try again? Jo asked herself. Yes, she must for Sally's sake. "You'd have her full confidence if you'd be willing to let her marry Tom Merton."

"But I can't!" exclaimed Sam. "I can't turn her over to a man like that. How many times do I have to tell you he'll never get very far in the profession? That's why I had to let him out."

"You've let Tom out! You always told me he was good." Jo couldn't believe it. So that was why Sally wanted to get to town this evening.

"I can't have a man who's always dragging his feet," Sam retorted. "I can't have him for my assistant and won't have him for a son-in-law. Sally should marry a man who's my peer—I mean her peer. She'll get over this. If you'd only help me! I can't understand a mother wanting her daughter to marry a man ten years her senior."

"It's not a question of what I want. That has nothing to do with it. Listen —if we break up her engagement to Tom, Sally might never marry. Do you want to take that responsibility?"

"Who said anything about her not marrying?"

"Sally needs to marry," Jo pleaded. "She's actually wanted children since she was a little girl."

"Don't talk nonsense. At eighteen life isn't over." Sam's tone was caustic. Again he began walking back and forth. "Maybe I made a mistake buying this place. I thought you and Sally would get a lot of good out of it. I thought Sally would bring her young folks here. Why don't those goddam crickets, or whatever they are, stop making such an infernal noise? Let's go back to town." The silence of the country, overlaid with the sharp rasping of locusts, seemed suddenly to have turned his retreat into a lonely habitation.

"Tonight!"

"Why not?" Sam's aimless wanderings took direction now.

"If you want to, Sam, but we'd better eat first. I'll have to get a few things together." When she came to think of it Jo was glad to go back. She wanted to be at home when Sally came in this evening. She must steady her. Sally would not take Tom's dismissal lightly.

Sally was well into town now. She was driving fast. She was a little late. Would Tom think she wasn't coming, think she was backing out, as she had twice before? This time she really would go through with it. There was no other way. Once they were married, her father would accept the inevitable. She could make it up to him then. She'd show him she still loved him first— no, not first, second.

A clock on the tower of the courthouse showed her she was fifteen minutes late. She hadn't time to do what she'd planned—park her mother's car in the garage at home and take a taxi to the airport. Barely escaping a collision with another car in her haste, she drove rapidly along the brightly lighted driveway that led up to the entrance of the airport terminal. A red-cap stepped up. "Take your luggage, miss?"

"I'm looking for someone." Sally scanned the people, but she didn't see Tom. "May I leave my car here a minute while I look inside?"

A hand on her shoulder. "Right here! What made you so late? I'd begun to think——"

"That I wouldn't go through with it?"

"Your car, miss. It can't stand here."

Both Sally and Tom were thankful for the interruption. Something normal and natural to do made them forget for a tiny interval that they were ignoring loyalties lived by all their lives. They'd been brought up to accept the responsibilities of family relationships which they were now violating, but if they did not, they would be violating the right of a man and woman to choose whom they would marry.

"The best thing to do is leave the car here and mail the keys in a note to your mother. She'll get it the first thing in the morning—about the time she comes in from the country," said Tom as he occupied himself maneuvering the car into a parking place.

"I left a note for her at the house yesterday morning after she'd gone, so she wouldn't worry. I drove out with Father. Oh, Tom, why do we have to do it this way?" Sally was close to tears.

"We've tried everything else. I can't stick around any longer now your father has fired me. If I go away now——"

"Yes, I know." Sally sighed. In silence they went back to the main building, bought an envelope, enclosed the car keys with a note on paper torn from Tom's notebook, then went and stood at the gate ready to be the first to get on the plane.

"It should be in now," Tom said. "I'll go look at the billboard."

"How late?" Sally asked when he came back.

"Twenty minutes."

"I'd have had time to take Mother's car back. It seems a mean trick to play on her." It's only the car that's bothering me, thought Sally. Centering her remorse on her mother left no room for thoughts of her father, who deep in her heart she knew would be irreparably injured by her act.

"The gate's open." Tom took her hand. They ran. The hot night air flowed around them. Sally was breathless and bathed in perspiration when they reached their seats and again she was close to tears. The plane lifted. The city was below them. There was no turning back now.

Sam drove carefully along the gravel road, for a thick darkness hung over the countryside, but as he reached the highway he pushed his car well over the speed limit, finding relief from his unhappy mood in action. Jo, refreshed in the night air stirred to a breeze by the rushing movement of the car, felt herself relaxing. After all, there was no need to worry over Sally. They'd manage to work something out. The lights of the city cast their glow on the sky, but around them lay the dark fields from which Sam thought he was fleeing. He picked up more speed, held it until he reached the outlying districts of the city. Here the streets were full of people who found their dwelling places too hot to be borne. Stopping for a red light, Jo saw in the glare of their own headlights a man and woman crossing the street, a baby asleep on the man's shoulder—wayfarers in the night. Were they happy? Were they worried? She forgot them when Sam turned the car into the quiet comfort of their own street with its great box-elder trees meeting overhead, an old street dedicated to good living and ordered ways.

"I think I'll go right to bed," Sam said as soon as they entered the house. "I feel sleepy after the drive. And I've that important operation the first thing in the morning. I suppose the country does rest me. Maybe I get the benefit after I've left it."

Jo followed him upstairs, stopped for a moment to look into Sally's room. The closet door stood open. Hooks and shelves seemed unusually empty. They were always crowded, for Sally loved clothes. She must have decided to pack some of them away for the summer.

Jo went on into her room, taking with her a book she had found on the way upstairs, intending to read until Sally came in. When she turned on the lights a large white envelope propped up against the mirror of her dresser caught her attention. How queer! Perhaps the maid had put it there. She picked up the envelope and saw on it in Sally's hand the words, *For Mother*. Fear struck at her heart. Surely Sally wouldn't do anything hasty. The bare closet flashed through her mind. Her hand trembled as she drew out the single sheet.

Forgive me, Mother [it read]. There didn't seem any other way. Perhaps when Tom and I are married Father will accept the accomplished fact. I had to do it, Mother. I can't let Tom go away defeated and alone. I had to choose. It's terrible to have to choose. Please make Father understand. You'll get this in the morning many hours after our plane has left, so there is no use trying to stop us.

There wasn't a clue to the direction in which they were going or what plane they were taking. As Jo stood there, trying to decide what to do, she heard Sam calling to her. At first she had a wild desire to hide the letter—give Sally time to get away, assist her as she often had before to gain independence from her father. Then she was angry with Sally, angry that she had abused the freedom Jo had helped win for her and injured Sam. It was as if the roles of the two had been suddenly reversed, Sally the adult, Sam now the child. But how to protect Sam? No way, for unnoticed by her he had come quietly across the soft-carpeted room in his slippers and was now standing beside her. Startled, she let the letter drop from her hand.

He stooped and picked it up. "May I read it?"

She nodded.

"Why, it's . . . why, it's . . ." With a glance he took in the meaning. "And you stand there wasting precious minutes! My God, are you a fool? We've got to catch her. Go down and get out the car," he commanded. "I'll join you as soon as I'm dressed. The scoundrel! I always knew he was no good. Hurry, Jo!" He took hold of her shoulder and gave her a little shake that woke her from her trancelike immobility.

Never had Jo known him to drive as he did now. He took every privilege given to a doctor, trusting to the sign of the caduceus above his license plate which relieved him from traffic regulations in an emergency. Once they were stopped by a policeman. "Don't you see I'm a physician? It's life and death," he called out. The policeman waved them on.

"She didn't say where she was going, did she?" Sam asked the question for the hundredth time, it seemed to Jo. They were in front of the administration building at the airport now. "Park the car while I look over the passenger lists."

When she came back from the parking lot Sam met her at the entrance looking less distraught. "Two planes have gone in the last hour. Their names weren't on either list. Thank God we've arrived in time." He took her arm and hurried her over to the gate where a crowd was already gathering for the next plane. As group after group passed down the runway to the planes and no Sally appeared, Sam grew more tense. Then, when hours went by, he grew querulous. "All they could think of was themselves. Both of them knew I had that operation tomorrow morning. What will this do to me?" He kept looking at his hands, delicate instruments so skillful, so useful. Jo could scarcely bear it.

After prolonged waiting and watching Jo said, "It's no use, Sam. They must have taken an earlier plane, not given their own names."

"Yes, I guess so." He walked out of the building in a daze.

When they reached home Jo made him lie down. Sitting by his side, she talked to him in low even tones. She tried to make him see that Sally's elopement need not be a catastrophe. She would come home. He had only to ask her. Sally still loved him.

"She knew I had to operate in the morning. Evidently she didn't think that very important."

At these words Jo saw what Sally had done to her father. She had threatened his estimate of himself which he had painstakingly built through the years. All at once Jo's thought went to herself. Sam had shown no concern over what Sally's elopement might mean to her mother. He thought only of his own suffering. The old rebellion rose up in her. Sally, always the contributor to Sam's happiness. Suddenly she saw Sally's elopement could mean new freedom for her. She had achieved her objective. Sally was happily married. She would telephone Alan in the morning and tell him that the pediatrician she had been thinking of was herself. She had kept up with her profession by reading and her visits to Naomi Pratt. Alan would take her into his hospital. "Come, Sam," she said. "If you're going to operate in the morning, you must get to bed."

Jo, lying awake, could hear him turning and shifting. Gradually two things became clear to her. If she defied Sam now, she might break him, he might age rapidly, his hands might really tremble. She could not do this to him. She saw, too, that if Sam broke and Sally came to know it, as she certainly would, her sense of guilt would ruin her marriage. For Sally's sake and for his own Sam must not be destroyed.

She rose and went in to him. "Sam, you must be ready for tomorrow morning's operating. There is not another pair of hands like yours in Athenia. Don't let what a couple of selfish children have done interfere with your work." She felt herself bleeding at the heart as she spoke these words, knowing she was trying to break the ties which bound him to Sally. Deliberately she went about the task of driving Sally out of his life.

At last Sam slept, and when he woke in the morning he was silent and self-contained. He came to the breakfast table at the precise moment he always did when he had operations scheduled. His hands were steady. As he seated himself he said, "I want you to promise me you'll not try to reach her." Jo noticed he avoided using his daughter's name. "Do nothing to help her. She needs to learn about that fellow the hard way."

ᘓ 41 ᘓ

ALAN was drinking a last cup of coffee preparatory to making his morning rounds when the telephone rang. "It's Jo, Alan."

"Well, hello," he answered. "You don't mean you've already got me my pediatrician?"

"I'm going to call Dr. Pratt, but I haven't had time yet. Alan, do you think you could manage to get in town in time to witness that special operation of Sam's he was telling you about yesterday afternoon?"

Alan whistled. "Does it have to be today? I've a full morning. Wouldn't the next time he does it do just as well? What's the hurry, Jo?"

"If you could go this morning——" There was a catch in her voice. "Last night after you left Sam decided he wanted to come into town. We found a note from Sally at the house. She and Tom have taken matters into their own hands." Somehow she couldn't bring herself to say they had eloped.

"Where are they? At home?" asked Alan.

"We don't know where they are. You could mean a lot to Sam just now."

Alan looked at his watch. "There's just a chance I can make it, Jo. I'll have to call a few people first. I'll try to get there." Alan rang off, his own thoughts mixed and disturbed—first anger at the man Merton, trained by Sam, taking such an advantage of him, then anger at Sally. Why, she meant everything to Sam! And then he saw his own part in this. If he'd never left Sam, there wouldn't have been any Merton. Nonsense! he told himself. If it hadn't been Merton, it would have been some other guy wanting to marry Sally. "I don't see why watching him operate will help out very much." And then, quickly, he did see.

When he reached the hospital where once he was so well known Alan told the secretary at the desk, "Dr. Towne asked me to come in and observe him perform an operation scheduled for this morning."

"He left no word here," the girl answered. "I'll check with the operating floor. He said nothing about it there either," she reported, "but the head nurse on the floor says to come up."

Alan found she was one of the older nurses and that she remembered him. "He doesn't like anyone to come in while he's operating, you know, but if you'll take the responsibility——" She was worried that she might be in for the surgeon's censure either way, she decided. To break the rules was a risk, but if his brother missed the operation through her stupidity, that, too, might mean a sharp reprimand for her. By the time he had cap, gown and mask on and was ready to go in, the doors of the operating room were opened. What a futile effort this is! Alan fumed inwardly.

Through the doorway Sam caught sight of his brother. His bleak expression gave way to one of pleasure. "Hello, there," he said, stepping forward. "What a pity," he exclaimed, "you've missed it! Give me a cigarette." Alan lighted one, put it in Sam's mouth. "Thanks." Sam puffed, his hands in rubber gloves hanging at his sides. "I've another operation coming up. It's not a very interesting one." He named it. "You've done it yourself often." His first pleasure over seeing Alan had driven Sally from his mind. Now his daughter and his brother appeared before him in their true light. To each in turn he had given his best, each in turn had let him down. "I wouldn't expect you to stay," he said.

The hurt look that had come into Sam's eyes brought Alan to a realization of what he and Sally together had done to him. Yes, and Jo, too, he thought. He feels we're all against him. A great desire to make amends welled up in Alan. "I'd like to stay," he said. "I haven't had the chance for a long time to watch you operate." Alan stood by while his brother scrubbed, then went into the operating room with him and stood watching.

They left the operating room together.

Now for my own problems, Alan thought as he drove back to the Southeast District, but he found it hard to forget Sam. If he had never left his brother—— Darn it all, why shouldn't I do something on my own? Sally, too —she has a right to her life. . . . But it hurt him that Sam was so hurt.

Not until afternoon did he succeed in pushing Sam out of his mind. Jo had not forgotten her promise. Soon after he reached his office he received a telephone call from Dr. Pratt, asking if he would be free at five to see her.

Alan was not prepared for the kind of woman Naomi Pratt turned out to be. She looked more like a Southern grande dame than a doctor. She was slight and not more than five feet four inches tall. She had large brown eyes and fluffy brown hair, and she wore a fluffy print dress. What on earth was Jo thinking about to recommend such a woman! Alan glanced at Nathan, whom he had asked to sit in on the interview, and wondered what he was thinking. To Dr. Pratt both men were extremely polite, in Alan's case at least in order to hide skepticism. But as he said later, "We didn't know our Naomi, did we?"

It was she who asked the questions, with staccato precision. They found themselves the ones being interrogated. She wanted to know every detail of their insurance plan. Then she brought out her own records. How, they wondered, had one woman been able to carry such a load?

"Why do you want to join us?" Alan asked when he finally had a chance. "You've a big practice."

"I've been a success and against great odds," she answered. "Women haven't had an easy time in the profession. I've won out. That's done. I'd like to get into the fight again. To put over an idea like yours will be exciting. I like obstacles."

"You'll have to be interviewed by Mr. Gunsaulus before any final decision can be given. I hope you won't mind. I'll tell you frankly he thinks of it as a simple matter of hiring an employee, and I fear he's prejudiced against women employees. Do you think you can take that?"

Dr. Pratt's eyes gave off lightninglike points of fire. "He wouldn't be the first man I've had to convince of my ability," she answered. "You arrange an hour."

What went on between Gunsaulus and Naomi Pratt Alan was not told. Gunsaulus called up after the interview, saying he was willing to accept her. "She has a good record," he added in a tone that seemed somewhat grudging, "and I suppose women do know a good deal about kids."

⚬ 42 ⚬

THE DAY the roster of doctors was completed Nathan and Alan were going over some last details before Nathan's departure when Eichel walked in. "Thought I'd drop around and say good-by, Gertz. I heard you were leaving."

"Awfully good of you!" Nathan was too surprised to say more and Alan too surprised to say anything. Eichel had never come into the office since he had given up the partnership. He always insisted on seeing in his own office patients they referred to him. Of late they hadn't happened to need to send anyone.

"Sit down, won't you?" Alan brought forward a chair. He thought, Eichel is not here primarily to bid Nathan Godspeed. He was beginning to develop a sixth sense as to whether a man was an applicant or not, and he believed Eichel was.

"I suppose I ought to congratulate you, Towne, on the success of your scheme," said Eichel. "You took a pretty big gamble. I really didn't think you would win out."

"Thank you. After all, we came darn near failing. It was a tossup. A big risk to take."

Alan had meant only to show Eichel that he didn't hold his leaving against him, for he didn't want bad blood between them, but he immediately saw Eichel had taken his remark as an opening.

"I came around with the idea I might be of a little help to you—that is, if you're in need of a general surgeon," said Eichel.

"I don't know whom you have in mind, but I signed one up a couple of days ago," Alan hastened to put in before Eichel could get any farther. He wanted to save the man the embarrassment of offering his services only to be refused, and in any circumstances Alan would refuse Eichel. A man who had crawled out of a bargain as he had once might do it again.

"I would have come around sooner, but I learned only today that this friend of mine wanted to get started out here. He's young, not much experience yet, but I understand that's the kind of doctors who are taking your salaried jobs." Eichel rose. "I must be getting on. Good luck, Gertz! I suppose you've seen the light and are going in for private practice."

"On the contrary, into group medicine in New York."

"Well, good luck, both of you!"

Before either of them could say more Eichel had gone. As he passed the window they saw him jamming his hat down, as they remembered he used to do when he was angry.

"What about it?" asked Alan. "Do you think he wanted the position? I'm pretty sure he did. Was the young friend a blind?"

"That's what I made of it. You were lucky you didn't have to turn him down directly. He'd have resented that forever. Now for my records," said Nathan, dismissing the little scene. "Our Naomi will be here in a few minutes." Already they were affectionately using Dr. Pratt's first name.

Eichel was not only resentful but worried. His partnership with Corwin had not lasted long. For several months now he had been on his own, a very satisfactory own until he had learned of the Gunsaulus Plan and that the insurance they offered included operations. In this low-income district he would be at a disadvantage with his high fees. He could no longer insist that they were legitimate because he was a specialist, if the staff at the new hospital included a specialist in his field. Worrying over the threat to him in the new hospital, Eichel feared he must relinquish his dream of wealth. Gradually he had come to believe he might even be crowded out of the Southeast District. Today he had felt he could bear it no longer. It was this Dr. Eichel now resentful against his former partners whom Alan had turned down, not the successful Dr. Eichel of a few months ago who had thought somewhat scornfully of his former associates.

The next morning Alan went to the airport to see Nathan off. It had been a good friendship, a stimulating companionship. Each realized that he might never again have such an association in his professional life, also that in the stress of living they might even lose track of each other. "We'll be working along the same lines," Nathan said. "We must exchange information."

"Yours is a larger outfit," Alan replied, hoping even as Nathan was hoping to keep the relationship. "Write me when you get time how the plan's working out. Let's see, it's three years since they started in New York, isn't it? A lot of groups in different parts of the country working along the same line as we are may bring medicine within reach of all the people eventually." They'd said all this to each other many times before, but it was the link which would be most likely to hold in years to come. On Alan's part it was a reaching out for the strength Nathan always gave him.

The two were standing now on the narrow veranda outside the administration building where they could catch the breeze. A plane was rising from the ground. Overhead a great DC-6 was circling for its landing. Following the impersonal movement of the planes, Nathan saw more clearly than he had ever seen before the impersonal pattern of the modern industrial world, and he also saw more clearly than ever before that it was not group medicine, not medical insurance, for which Alan was really working. Rather, it was to preserve the value of the individual. Modern medicine with its necessary emphasis on the mechanical structure of the body and its chemistry tended to lose sight of the individual. Spirit and body were inseparable. If in medicine they ever came into open conflict the battle would be bitter. The night he had decided to cast in his lot with Alan came back to Nathan. Then he had glimpsed the fate that might be Alan's. And now he was leaving him to carry on alone.

"I'm not certain, Alan, whether any of the doctors we've chosen fully understand what you are after—except Naomi; I'll make an exception of her. As for the doctors of the district, sometime they're going to fight you. Don't try to go too fast. Your ideas are frightening to a great many people."

"You think I don't realize sufficiently the hazards in starting a hospital of this kind? I understand perfectly that if I make a mistake, Sam's prestige might not save me as it did once," Alan answered quietly, and added with a smile, "I'll be cautious. I've learned a good deal in the last year—from you. There's your plane coming in. The gates are opening. Give my best to Brenda."

"And mine to Esther."

They gripped each other's hands.

Back at the office Alan was soon absorbed in the problems of moving to the hospital, making a last sorting out of his papers. He was mailing cards today, notifying the insured patients that until the end of the year they would pay at the rate originally agreed on. After that their rates would be raised slightly to cover hospital expenses. He smiled when he came to the name Prentiss, remembering the sharp bargain Agatha Prentiss had driven with him on their first meeting. This afternoon he was taking her home from the hospital. Mrs. Watkins had asked him to stay for dinner—one she would prepare.

Miss Prentiss was standing on the step of the hospital when he drove up. "Don't try it alone," he called out. In a moment he was by her side, and together they went down the steps to his car. It's odd, he thought, how little pleasure she seems to be getting out of her home-coming.

But when they reached the little house and she saw her sister standing in the doorway there was a marked change in Miss Prentiss. She seemed almost gay. The dinner was a great success. Miss Prentiss entertained them with dry sardonic remarks about the women in the ward.

Alan almost forgot that he was meeting with the board that evening. He would have to hurry. He gave the sisters a few last instructions. "You can go it alone now," he said to Miss Prentiss, knowing how fiercely she prized her independence. "But you, Mrs. Watkins, I'd like to see about once a month —at the office," he added.

The question before the board was how much medical aid and hospital service could be included in the insurance. All agreed it must be settled tonight since the hospital was to be formally opened in another week. As at the previous meetings, Alan found himself between the two equally urgent claims. He must suggest nothing that would make it impossible for the hospital to succeed financially; he must suggest nothing that would eat too far into the resources of the middle-income family. Clear in his mind were the statistics that every fourteen years the average family had all its savings exhausted by a major illness.

The board was made up of shrewd businessmen who kept upping the insurance and lowering the benefits. Alan fought hard, afterward he feared too hard, to put over his ideas. A relationship of understanding with the board was as necessary as the doctor-patient relationship.

It was finally agreed that they would offer the members a preliminary examination, doctor's care at the office, operations and a month's free hospital care for every major illness during any calendar year. It was over this last item that Alan had fought so strenuously. As in the case of Miss Prentiss, accidents often meant hospitalization for a long period. He had insisted that two months more should be included at a minimum cost.

ҩ 43 ҩ

It had been Gunsaulus' idea that they have a dedication ceremony when the hospital was formally opened. The role of public benefactor seemed to bring him the importance denied him by the established industrialists who still regarded him as an upstart. To sit on the platform with a group of prominent citizens was a recognition he coveted. It did not trouble him that this recognition might be accorded because of his money. Wealth was his own criterion of worth. Also to feel that from him flowed the bounty which supported the doctors who would staff the hospital, even Dr. Towne who had once lorded it over him, would be a unique satisfaction.

The ceremony was held in the lobby of the hospital. The small rotund Gunsaulus, his son Roger and the other members of the board flanked the improvised lectern on one side. On the other were seated rabbi, priest and Protestant minister and other distinguished citizens of the Southeast District. Alan had hoped that Miss Benninger, self-appointed guardian of the people who lived on the land once owned by her family, would be among the distinguished citizens. He had sent a note asking her to join them, but had had no reply. Absent, too, were the doctors of the district except Judd. In the second row sat the doctors of the group hospital.

"Fool business!" whispered Naomi Pratt to Alan.

"Not if you've seen Roger's face."

Dr. Pratt's expression softened. "I haven't but his back says a great deal." It was so nearly straight that Alan, studying the lad from behind, believed few would ever notice the slight curvature. If I could only have made him perfect! he was thinking. In his mind was the picture of a boy's beautiful figure, the artist's conception, the work of a sculptor—but the human body was more resistant sometimes than the sculptor's clay.

In the space in front of the platform the camp chairs brought in for the occasion were filled, and men and women were standing at the back of the lobby. Alan recognized some of his former patients, but there were many new faces. The babble of voices was punctuated with the crying of babies. The Southeast District was not much given to baby-sitters. It was indeed a neighborhood affair except for the absence of the local doctors and, of course, Miss Benninger.

A hush fell over the room as Gunsaulus rose to present the hospital to the community. He made a surprisingly good speech. The occasion lent him dignity. "I take especial pride in this building," he said in closing. "It is the tribute to my son, who has triumphed over a disease that has entered into many of your homes. I would like to dedicate it to you in the name of my son Roger Gunsaulus." He turned now toward the boy. "He is a symbol of what can be done for your children if stricken." A kind of shiver ran over the room as if Gunsaulus, by his words, had let in the dread enemy. And then at his next words, "Stand up, my son, so all may see what a fighting spirit can do," applause broke over the room.

It was an ultradramatic effort on Gunsaulus' part, but no one minded or even noticed except one of the staff. He shifted uneasily, and the movement attracted Alan's attention. He caught the expression of distaste on the man's face. Before he could evaluate it he heard his own name announced. "And here is Dr. Towne, to whose vision you owe this hospital. I'd like him to tell you a little of what we expect to do here."

Alan, unprepared and thrown off guard by Gunsaulus' tribute to him, stumbled in his first sentences. Deciding that they had had enough of sentiment for one day, he gave them in cold hard figures what the hospital could do and what it couldn't. "It's not the whole answer to your medical problems, but it's a start," he ended. "Whether we'll succeed will depend on you as well as on us."

The ceremony was over. Men and women came forward to speak to Gunsaulus, his son, the members of the board and the members of the staff.

Among them, trying to make her way toward him, Alan saw Jo. She looked tired and strained. They had only a moment with the crowd pressing around them. "It's good of you, Jo. Is Sam here?"

"Sam sent his best to you. He said to tell you he couldn't manage to get away."

Alan wanted to ask about Sally. While he debated whether or not to, the opportunity slipped from him. "There's Naomi!" Jo exclaimed. In a moment Alan lost sight of his sister-in-law in the crowd.

ॐ 44 ॐ

LATER there was another dedication less spectacular than the dedication of the building. No one called it that, but in reality it was the dedication of the staff to their work. It was entirely private and held in Alan's office. He sat on the edge of his desk, one leg dangling over the edge, his foot swinging. "I wanted to get you together so we'd understand one another. I'm not here to lay down rules. I'm as new at this as you are. You are all competent in your work, or you wouldn't be here. However, as you know, it's not the old solo practice all of you until now have been used to. It undoubtedly will take a little time to get ourselves running smoothly. Streamlining ourselves will of necessity mean a subordination sometimes of our individuality to the organization as a whole." He saw immediately that in his mention of subordination he had precipitated a crisis.

"You mean you plan to make a kind of assembly line out of us?" The doctor who asked the question was Beritz, the man who had looked so cynical over Gunsaulus' emotional dedication of the hospital. He was the specialist in gynecology, one of the Jewish doctors on the staff and as unlike Nathan as could be imagined. Because of his professional arrogance, Alan and Nathan had debated long over whether to recommend Beritz to Gunsaulus. But he was highly skilled, and the letters he had presented to them from other doctors had been unusually enthusiastic. They had asked him to have dinner with them after the interview and he had been charmingly simple and natural. It was evidently only in his professional capacity that he displayed his less desirable quality. Before they decided they had asked Dr. Pratt to talk with him. She had given her unqualified approval. So had Gunsaulus when he interviewed him.

"An assembly line may be a poor way to put it," said Alan, "but what we are after certainly means a subordination of the individual doctor to the group."

Alan looked from one to another of the men around him, wondering if so soon he had come up against a wall of opposition. It hardly seemed possible, because these men had already stepped forth from tradition in accepting positions in the hospital. In coming here they had given up the possibility of large fees. All had limited themselves to a stated income. Would they refuse this further step in co-operation?

Dr. Beritz lighted a cigarette, tossed the match into an ash receiver on Alan's desk in the gesture eloquently expressive of dissent. Above the low murmur of men's voices rose Dr. Pratt's clear treble. "Gentlemen, gentlemen," she said, "we all came here with the idea of group practice. Certainly we are not so naïve as to think it doesn't mean some sacrifice of individual initiative. We've all, I imagine, gone into this with Dr. Towne when he interviewed us. Why should we be upset because we have been confronted with the reality of that conception?"

Dr. Lambert—an arresting figure, tall and very erect, "almost too handsome for his own good," had been Naomi's silent reaction when she first met him—now supported her. "I've hesitated to speak because as general practitioner I am to see the patients first. I believe we'll like this streamlining, if you want to call it that, when we get used to it. A preliminary diagnosis made by me and my assistant"—he nodded toward a young blackhaired man at the back of the room—"will, I think you'll find, save the rest of you time. In solo practice, as you know, the patient diagnoses his disease before coming to you. A man has a headache, and he thinks it's his eyes. Maybe it's a brain tumor. I think you'll find we two general physicians are better at diagnosis than the layman. That's all. We'll act as intermediaries, saving you examining patients who don't come under your specialty."

His frankness, his modesty made their appeal. The better judgment of the group took over. Most of them inwardly were a little ashamed that, having accepted positions under group practice, they had been alarmed at the first mention of what it entailed, but most of them were young and jealous of their professional reputations.

Now they settled down to a discussion of details and a planning of the hours each would be on duty. Each was to have his day off and night work was to be rotated.

Alan thought afterward he had said nothing of his concept of the personal relationship of doctor and patient. That was an individual problem to be handled individually. He had discussed it with each doctor before he was selected. He must leave how it should be worked out to each one of them. It must come from real understanding. It could not be laid on from outside.

The month before Alan was to go to Nevada to bring Esther home was crowded with activities and problems. The direction of a hospital, its doctors, its nurses, taxed all his administrative powers. Dr. Lambert was a great help to him, but Alan often longed for Nathan with his sensitive natural understanding of human beings. Especially he missed him when it came to enrolling the original members of the insurance plan. Many of them felt uneasy over trusting doctors they did not know. Alan saw each one himself, leaving the new members to be enrolled by the other doctors.

Everything was in readiness for Esther. He had taken great pains in erasing any evidence of Mrs. Gunsaulus' stay in the house, wanting Esther to find it as she had left it. Only the kitchen was different. Mrs. Gunsaulus had insisted on leaving behind the huge refrigerator and the deep freeze she had installed. But the old-fashioned kitchen was large.

With the last of his inheritance Alan had bought a specially built car with hand controls for Esther. He felt the independence it would give her would be a help in getting back into the world of well people. Now that he was to have a salary he could risk using up the balance of his backlog in this way.

These final days before he left to bring Esther home, full of work as they were, seemed to drag interminably. One evening on an impulse he decided to drop in on Mrs. Watkins. He'd like to see how the sisters were getting on.

When he drove up to the house he noticed there was a child's scooter in the middle of the walk leading up to the steps. There were small muddy footprints on the porch. Somebody had been playing with the hose. The sisters must be having guests. Hard on Miss Prentiss—she's so neat, he thought, ringing the bell.

A young woman with a baby in her arms answered his ring.

"Is Miss Prentiss in?" he asked.

"She doesn't live here any more."

"You mean they've sold the house! I thought they intended——" He stopped. Naturally he didn't know all Miss Prentiss' plans. "Could you give me her address?"

"She didn't leave any. I asked for one, in case there might be mail, but she said there wouldn't be any."

Alan turned away. It was a frustrating moment for any doctor. Miss Prentiss had no business going off like that, taking her sister away from his supervision. She'd drop back into the old habits. She might lose all she had gained. It annoyed him to have a patient snatched away from him. It isn't as if it were costing her something every time she came to see me, he thought. Here was a defeat he had not anticipated. His understanding with the two sisters, more especially with Mrs. Watkins, he had considered an ideal one between patient and doctor. Why had they suddenly ended it without a word of explanation?

Alan had reserved the last afternoon before leaving for the West to see how Roger was getting on at home. Earlier in the day he had turned the hospital over to Dr. Lambert for the period of his absence. He had reached the in-between area of old neglected houses which separated the new development from the factory district when he remembered he had no bread for tomorrow morning's breakfast. The stores would be closed when he came back. He'd better stop at the first grocery store he came to. As he was coming out of the market two women a little farther up the street attracted his attention. There was something oddly familiar about them. Why, they were Miss Prentiss and her sister! But surely they wouldn't be living in this district. . . . It was all nonsense, he told himself. It was his own desire to solve the mystery of their disappearance that had made him see a likeness to them in the two women.

He started his car, easing his way through a group of boys playing ball in the street. "Let me through, please," he called out.

"We were here first," a boy a little larger than the others flung back. Sullenly the group stood its ground. Alan drove slowly, edging the boys away with his fender. Suddenly a well-aimed stone struck the side window, shattering it. There was a hasty scurrying down a near-by alley, leaving the street empty.

Alan drove on, his mind still occupied with the enigma of the sisters' departure. All at once many little details fitted together. Miss Prentiss did not have hospital insurance as she had said. If she had had it, by this time the hospital would have presented him with a form to sign—routine procedure with the insurance company.

The sisters' thin margin of safety had been overstepped. The hospital bill had greatly depleted their savings, so much so that Miss Prentiss had felt it necessary to sell the house, seek a cheaper place to live in. Even if they were living here, there was no need to go without his services. Then he had a vision of Miss Prentiss forced to live in this neighborhood—the hurt to her pride. He could not intrude on their privacy by trying to hunt them out and help them—his first impulse.

That evening took on a special meaning for him. He was in the tangled garden behind the house which he had started to put in order for Esther's sake. He was kneeling among the shrubs and rosebushes he had recently planted and was using a hand tool to loosen the earth around them, grown hard during the recent dry spell. Suddenly he felt an inclination to abandon the tool and work with his hands. Then he experienced for the first time the healing touch of the earth. The burden on him of the sick in mind and body seeped away.

❧ 45 ❧

For most of the time during the flight to Nevada Alan slept. When he awoke, the green, rain-watered plains of the Middle West to which he was so accustomed had given place to the conical, brown, sun-baked hills of Nevada. In that interim of sleep he had at last let go responsibility for the hospital and given himself over to his own personal life—his meeting with Esther.

At the Institute he found the lobby empty except for a clerk at the desk. "I'm Dr. Towne. Is Mrs. Towne ready to see me?" he asked.

"Yes, she is. I think you know the way to her room."

He walked down a wide corridor full of patients, some in wheel chairs, others on crutches, a few with their families around them. It was as if they were all expecting him, for everyone he met gave him a friendly nod.

When he turned into a side corridor he saw Esther at the farther end walking carefully, precisely, using a cane for support. His heart gave a leap. With a few long strides he reached her, took her, cane and all, in his arms. The dear dark head rested on his breast. Then carefully he released her. They looked into each other's eyes and laughed.

"Down there is my room," she said, pointing to an open door. "Now watch—see what I can do."

He followed her slow difficult progress, tried not to see the steel brace on her right leg.

"I meant to do better for you. I can. It takes concentration. It's because I'm too excited," she said ruefully, closing the door to her room behind them. Again he took her in his arms. They kissed—a long moment with his heart and hers beating hard against each other. Then they began the long pent-up conversation that a man and wife under normal conditions would spread through many days—desultory, fragmentary—a bit about the new hospital, a bit about her day-to-day struggle, questions about Nathan and Brenda, Sam, Jo and Sally. Some things placed Alan in Esther's restricted world; some placed Esther in Alan's busy world which she was about to re-enter— two worlds they sought to integrate.

Finally Esther said, "I can't keep you to myself any longer. Everyone wants to see you. I fear I've talked a good deal about you."

In the corridor they came upon a group of men in wheel chairs. "Hello, Esther!" one of them called out. "See you've got your man."

"*This* is Alan," Esther answered, smiling.

As they went on she explained. "Those are miners from West Virginia. You should have seen them when they came—just wrecks. They hadn't had any skilled care since their backs were broken in the mines. One of them said they just lay in bed and rotted. None of them could sit up. Most of them were drunks or dopes. They're grand fellows."

"But weren't they given some compensation by the company?" asked Alan.

"Yes," Esther answered. "So much for a leg, so much for a back. It kept their families going. But until the union gave them sick insurance that brought them here the men themselves were just discards—you know, like broken-down machines."

Alan smiled at her warm defense of them. "You're certainly all for them, aren't you, Esther?"

"I suppose I am. We're like a small town. Everyone knows everyone else's problems."

A small town! The words rang in Alan's ears. One out of every seven in

America was crippled in some way. If gathered together, they would make a vast city. The judgment which had been passed on many of them left them without hope, doomed to helplessness and continual pain. It was men like Dr. Carothers who pushed aside such verdicts and risked their reputations to attempt what was regarded as impossible by the rank and file of best specialists. While Alan stood with Esther at the doorway looking into the gymnasium filled with the afflicted he thought of the infinitesimal advancement each might make in any one day. A battle to be renewed day after day, month after month, possibly year after year. Only the stalwart of heart could endure such demands on the spirit, and Esther was one of them.

Seeing Alan and Esther come into the room, each man, woman or child working with his trainer paused and smiled. A triumph for one was the triumph for all.

They went over to where Dr. Carothers was teaching a young girl to walk. "Hello! It's you, Towne, is it?" Then again he centered his attention on the intricate problem the girl faced.

Esther whispered, "That's how I learned."

When the lesson was over, Carothers turned to Esther and Alan. "Come along to my office. I don't suppose you can stay long, Towne, and I'd like to show you what you can do to help your wife get back the full use of her leg. I've a new technique I think she can use to advantage."

Alan was impressed, as he had been on his first meeting, with the man's probing mind—never satisfied with what he was doing for the handicapped, always in search of new approaches.

When they came out of Carothers' office they found the miners at the door of the gymnasium. They no longer looked like men with the will to get well. Their wheel chairs were huddled together. "When does the train leave, Doc?" one of them asked, his voice bitter with disappointment.

"What's all this about?" asked Dr. Carothers.

A young man with wasted legs tapped a newspaper lying on his lap. "See this—all sick pensions have been suspended! What's the goddam use? They always get us in the end."

Dr. Carothers reached for the paper, read the article, then drew up a chair and sat down among the men. "We're in this thing together," he said. "If you give up now, not only do you lose your chance to get to the place where you can support yourselves and your families, but you lose the battle for all the other fellows who get hurt in the mines. We haven't proved ourselves yet. If you don't make the grade, they'll say the whole experiment is a failure—that what we're doing here isn't any good; that it's all a waste of money."

"That sounds O.K.," one of them broke in, "but how do we do it? We ain't rich men. It takes dough to stay here. You offering to help us?"

"Yes," said Dr. Carothers quietly. "That's what I'm doing. I can't accept any more of your men right now. I'll have to wire your union to that effect, but I'll find the money for you who are here until the union again takes over. It's my gamble." He rose, straightened his shoulders and walked away.

"By golly, he's got guts!" said the miners' spokesman. "We gotta back up a guy like that." With one accord they swung their wheel chairs into motion, marched them into the gymnasium and began their daily routine.

Would there ever be enough money to bring back to usefulness the crippled of the country? Alan asked himself. Then that problem was crowded out of his thoughts as his mind took a leap forward. If what Dr. Carothers outlined would help Esther, might it not help Roger Gunsaulus too? Alan's eyes were alight. New ideas were stimulating him to hard thinking.

∽ 46 ∼

IT WAS very early in the morning when the taxi bringing them from the airport stopped before their house. Esther, Alan beside her, passed through the gate, heard its latch click, went slowly up the steps and across the veranda. She heard Alan shut the house door behind her. Home with its privacy, its quiet was a reality, no longer a far-off memory. Details one by one took shape. The chairs in the living room set stiffly back against the wall, the precision and order, the unused look made manifest Alan's loneliness through the days and weeks she had been away. And yet no word of complaint had crept into his letters.

"Is it all right?" he asked. "I tried to have everything the way you like it." Her throat was too tight with emotion for her to manage more than a nod.

"How about some coffee? You'd be surprised how expert I am at making it." Alan's voice sounded young and happy. Arms around each other, they went into the kitchen.

"What have you been running—a hotel?" asked Esther, and her tone matched his in gaiety.

"No, just my one-patient hospital. Mrs. Gunsaulus left behind the extra refrigerator and the deep freeze—her way of expressing gratitude over Roger, I guess."

Once, twice, three times, four the telephone rang without either of them being aware of it. The fifth ring penetrated Alan's consciousness. He went into the hall and picked up the receiver. Esther heard him say, "Yes, I'll be there in a few minutes.

"They need me at the hospital. Can you manage?" he asked when he came back.

For a long time Esther sat by the kitchen table, trying to bring her life into focus. Brenda was not here. She could not go to the telephone and call her as she used to do. The steadying influence of Nathan was gone. Then the larger aspects of the days ahead swung into the foreground of her thoughts. Much of the success of the hospital lay in the co-operation that could be achieved between him and the staff, Alan had told her. That depended partially on the men's wives and how they adjusted themselves to their new environment. Some of them might resent the limiting of their income. Some whose lives had been more sophisticated might be lonely and bored. Esther figured she might be a help there.

She realized that in the past she had held aloof from the community, not understanding it. All her experience in America until they moved to the Southeast District had been with large cities. Through friendship with the patients of the Institute, most of whom came from small towns, she had learned that not only America's sturdy independence but much of its friendliness was rooted in its towns. In memory these patients trooped before her, all of them handicapped, all of them determined again to become independent human beings, most of them showing a friendly warmth different from anything she had met with before in America. Possibly something of what she had learned could be passed on to those wives who like herself had known only the impersonality of the city.

Then her mind went to the family. She would call Jo. Remembering what Dr. Carothers had taught her about walking, she concentrated her full attention on crossing the kitchen and reaching the telephone. As she dialed the number she thought, Oddly enough my mind remembers the number better than it does the concept of walking. She wondered how long it would be before she could take a step without thinking.

"Hello!" Jo's voice sounded lifeless and flat.

"It's Esther. I'm home."

"How grand! When did you get here?" Eagerness was in Jo's voice now.

"About an hour ago."

"I suppose Alan's spending the day with you. How about my coming out to see you tomorrow?"

Esther laughed. "You, a doctor's wife, saying that! I'm surprised."

"He's gone already?"

"Yes."

"I'll be out."

At first nothing seemed changed about Jo. As before, she appeared the well-dressed, satisfied wife of a prosperous doctor, but after a little Esther noticed that she looked older and that her clear brown eyes clouded over from time to time. Her mouth seemed thinner and more firmly set. She talked a great deal about Sam, of the unusual operations he was performing, of his growing reputation, especially of the time he gave to free patients at the clinic.

Quietly Esther listened, now and then asking a question, hoping Jo eventually might speak of Sally.

Finally Jo rose to go. "Could you and Alan come to dinner tomorrow night?" she asked. "It would do Sam a world of good."

"I'll let you know when Alan gets home," said Esther. Then as they stood at the door an impulse drove her to say, "Jo, dear, do tell me about Sally."

"Everything seems to be going very well. Her husband has taken up general practice in Arizona."

"Does Sally like it?"

"Oh, I think so," Jo answered. "Let me know about coming to dinner. And, Esther, please don't say anything about Sally before Sam. He never mentions her. He refuses to let me tell him anything about her."

How can he be so unforgiving? Esther thought. Did he love his daughter only as long as she bowed to his will?

About four that afternoon while Esther was coming down the stairs after a rest, carefully negotiating each step, her mind concentrated on the undertaking, she heard the doorbell ring. A caller so soon! The door was open, the screen fastened. "I'm coming, but it will take a little time," she called out.

"Don't hurry," a woman's voice called back. "I can wait. I'm a friend of Jo Towne's and a doctor."

At last Esther was down. Outside the screen she saw a small, daintily dressed woman in a flowered hat. "You're Naomi Pratt," she said, unhooking the screen.

"Dr. Towne has been delayed. He asked me if I'd come around and see if you needed anything. Otherwise I wouldn't have intruded on you your first day at home," Dr. Pratt explained as Esther led the way into the living room.

They had talked for only a few moments about the trip from Nevada, the unprecedentedly warm day and other trivialities when Dr. Pratt said, "Mrs. Towne, there's a difficult situation at the hospital. Your husband thinks he should spare you any worry, but now that I've seen you I believe he's wrong."

Esther felt herself emerging from the restricted world of sick people. It was going to be easier than she had thought to be accepted in Alan's busy world.

"Until the hospital is established—I don't mean licensed, of course we have our state license—we'll be constantly under attack. We're not yet approved by the Medical Association as you no doubt know—won't be until we've shown what we can do. We'll be watched for mistakes. We've lost a patient. It wasn't through neglect, nor bungling. The death was inevitable. There are doctors around here who don't want this kind of hospital to succeed. For some time we'll be doing a tightrope performance. I don't mind the acrobatics." Naomi's eyes sparkled. "It's the younger, untried doctors who are likely to become worried about their professional standing."

"And where do I come in?" asked Esther.

"With the wives," was the prompt reply. "You and I know that women are concerned first with the well-being of their families—that's their primary interest. With men it's their work. There's a cleavage. I see both sides, being a doctor and a woman. If we can pull together as a unit, we can win. Just now everybody is standing firm against criticism, but criticism wears away the soul. It's a long-time struggle we have on our hands. . . . There, I've talked too much!" Dr. Pratt rose to go.

After she had gone Esther sat still, her hands folded in her lap. It was thus that Alan, slipping quietly in, found her. "It's so good just to have you at home!" he said, sitting down beside her on the couch. Hands laced together, they sat silently watching the late afternoon shadows creep across the room.

It was not for several days that Alan mentioned the difficulty at the hospital, and then only to say, "A bad situation developed while I was away. I think it's going to work out all right."

So she need not concern herself, thought Esther.

October slipped into November. Indian summer lingered. This year no one wished it to end. There was no dread epidemic lurking in the hot days. There was health in the golden light falling through the yellowing leaves of the trees, stored-up sunshine to counteract the fogs and rains and the snows of the approaching winter. It was as if nature's quietude—days without wind or storm—were communicated to man. The possible attack on the hospital which had loomed so large the day of their home-coming had not materialized. The case against it had been dropped because the evidence was too flimsy, Alan believed, not because of any change of attitude toward the group hospital.

For Esther and Alan it was a serene time in which they gradually grew back into each other's lives. The avenues of communication clogged with piled-up experiences which letters had not cleared away opened one by one between them. Esther gained rapidly.

And then without warning walking again became difficult. A small panic all her own took hold of her. The concentration necessary, the will needed to control muscles still new to their task seemed to leave her. How much strength for her fight had been borrowed from doctors and patients at the Institute she had not realized until now. For a day or two she longed to go back to the shelter she had had among other handicapped people. Then she was ashamed. She was simply meeting what every patient met when he went home.

Dr. Pratt, who came often to see her, shrewdly guessed at the one-man struggle Esther was making and that she was attempting too much. "You won't be letting yourself down, Mrs. Towne, if you take someone to help you with the housework," she advised.

"Do you think so? But then where does one get help in the Southeast District? All the women do their own work," said Esther.

"Don't generalize," Dr. Pratt answered. "There's a young colored girl I can get you."

The woman came next day, a tall handsome Negro about thirty years old.

"It's not permanent. It's only until I'm completely recovered," Esther told her.

"I'd like to come even for a short time," the girl said. So it was that Beatrice Graham came into the family.

Now Esther saw that in the fight to get well there is a delicate balance between independence and reliance on others. She found that giving the house into Beatrice's capable hands did not weaken her. She began to gain again. She was considering asking the doctors' wives to come in some afternoon when she received a telephone call from Mrs. Lambert. "We wives have been getting together once a week," she explained. "We wondered if you felt able to join us."

For a moment Esther hesitated at making this first encounter with the outside world. Then quickly she met the challenge and accepted the invitation.

"Would you like one of the other women to call for you?" asked Mrs. Lambert. "I imagine you are not driving."

"It's kind of you, but it's not necessary. I've my own car, and I know the Southeast District well." Esther's gratitude to Alan recurred to her for his thoughtfulness in having the car fitted to her abilities. However much she might allow Beatrice to help her, and Alan at times, Esther did not intend to recognize her handicap outside the family. To do so was subtly to destroy herself. She must live a normal life in a normal world.

On the day of the luncheon she steeled herself for her first public appearance.

The afternoon held another hazard for her. The Lamberts had taken over Nathan's lease. As she drove up to the house memory of the last time she had been there flooded over her—that rainy afternoon when they brought Nathan and Brenda home after the burial of little Nath. Resolutely she put the thought from her. Her latest letter from Brenda had been a triumphant one. Both she and Nathan were working hard. Esther slid over to the right side of her car. She picked up her cane and managed, deftly she thought, to get herself out.

Mrs. Lambert ran down the steps. "I've been watching for you!" she exclaimed. "Just stay where you are. I'll help you." Reaching Esther's side, she put her hand under her elbow.

"Please. I can manage nicely," said Esther, freeing herself; "better in fact alone. I'm so glad to meet you."

"As you wish," said Mrs. Lambert.

Determined to take attention from the brace supporting her right leg, Esther kept up a lively conversation as they went together up the steps and into the house. I've won the first round, she was thinking, but just then Mrs. Lambert pushed forward a chair, set it apart from others in the room, and said, "I think you'll be most comfortable in this chair, Mrs. Towne." Esther took the chair, not knowing what else to do, but not until she had edged it close to a group who were sitting on the couch. As she did so, she caught the eye of the woman nearest her, and a look of understanding passed between them. The woman seemed hardly more than a girl. She wore her black hair in page-boy fashion, and the collar of her dress was like those worn by choir boys. It needs only a bow under her chin to complete the picture of untouched youth, Esther thought. But her dark eyes belied the impression. They were adult eyes. "I'm Mrs. Beritz, Mimi Beritz," she said.

Glancing about, Esther saw how completely different the room was from what it had been when Brenda lived there. Most of it then had been filled with Brenda's baby grand. Nathan's big chair had been opposite. In every detail the room had been severely plain. Now it was gay with bright curtains and large patterns of chintz on sofa and chairs—definitely smart. Someone exclaimed, "Isn't it wonderful what Inez has been able to do with this little house? If you'd seen it before she redecorated it! And she has made it a kind of meeting place for us. It's been a godsend. You know, not knowing anybody at first."

"I guess we're all here, girls," Mrs. Lambert said, pushing back the screen which shut off the dining room to display a table glittering in silver and glass, with a great bowl in the center full of heavy-headed chrysanthemums.

"How lovely!" everyone cried almost in one breath.

"I thought we'd sit down at the table today in honor of Mrs. Towne's joining us," Mrs. Lambert explained. "Here at my right." She looked at Esther. "The rest of you wherever you please."

With an efficiency at which Esther marveled, Inez, as everyone called her, managed to serve the rather elaborate luncheon and also direct the conversation. First she spoke of the difficulty of getting servants in this low-income area of the city. "They just won't come out here, no matter how much you offer them. How did you manage it?" she asked, turning to Esther.

Esther was hard pressed for an answer. Either she must appear financially better off than the others or she must make a necessity of her handicap. Before she had made up her mind what to say, the young woman with the adult eyes exclaimed, "I'll come and work for you any time, Inez—that is, if you'll teach me your best recipes!"

With a mock bow Inez acknowledged the compliment. She tossed the salad with expert hands and started the bowl down the table. "Can you manage?" she asked in an aside to Esther.

"Oh, yes." Esther quickly brought her left hand to the support of her not too strong right in order to hold the bowl.

The woman at her side reached forward. "I've done this before. It takes a little doing to handle Inez' salad bowl. I'll hold it while you help yourself." The words and the help came from a plump, middle-aged kind-looking woman. Esther tried to place her. Which doctor's wife was she?

"I suppose none of your husbands has heard from the County Medical Association?" Inez addressed the table at large. When no one answered, she added, "I said to Herbert this morning, Hasn't the time come to put up some kind of fight?" She turned quickly to Esther. "Of course I'm too impatient, and Herbert pointed out to me that Dr. Towne was the one to handle the matter, and I'm sure he will when the right time comes."

A number of voices were raised, all expressing degrees of anxiety, and then the older woman spoke who had helped Esther with the salad bowl. "I don't see that we've anything to worry about. It isn't as if we were without a hospital, or without an assured income. Dr. Towne has seen to it that we are protected in every way. We don't need to worry even if we haven't as yet been taken into the Association."

"It's our husbands' reputations we're concerned about," cut in Inez. "Of course, Mrs. Towne, you don't share our anxiety. Your husband already belongs to the Association."

"Oh, yes, I do," Esther hastened to say. "Alan had to go through all this when we first came to the district and were without a hospital here. I'm sure he understands your anxiety." She had been floundering in a sea of conflicting impressions; now she saw that Inez resented her, fearful evidently that she would take over the leadership of the wives, a position Mrs. Lambert had worked hard to attain. She has energy enough to run a factory, Esther was thinking, and it must all be confined now to this small house and these twelve doctors' wives. She may prove a dangerous influence, stirring up dissension and suspicion. Is this the risk Dr. Pratt foresaw? Right now Mrs. Lambert certainly seems bent on creating disunity. Is it possible for me to win the friendship of a woman like that, or will she always consider the wife of the hospital head her rival? Is her sense of rivalry limited to me, or does it include Alan?

But when the conversation passed to less controversial subjects and Mrs. Lambert showed she could be a charming hostess, friendly and almost kind, Esther told herself that she had been too suspicious.

Just as the women were getting ready to go Dr. Lambert came in. His effect on his wife was astonishing. Although he was not a forceful man at his entrance the restless playing for position which had characterized her at times all through the afternoon was abandoned almost as if with relief.

He sat down beside Esther. "It's wonderful to have you home! Alan has a heavy load. I learned something of how heavy when he was away. I can see it doesn't weigh on him so much now you're here."

Later, talking the party over with Alan, Esther found he dismissed Mrs. Lambert's talk as unimportant. "She may stir up a certain amount of discontent among the wives, but the doctors understand the situation. Sure, the hospital isn't approved yet. It's the kind of work we do that will get us our rating eventually. As for the local Association, once we get on the approved list of hospitals, that should take care of itself. To be honest, though, there is real hostility toward us, and it may grow. Our success depends on having a great number of patients all paying a little. If patients leave other doctors to join us, some opposition is bound to arise. There's work enough for every doctor in this district and more too, if the sick are cared for adequately, but the doctors who lose patients to us because we charge less are certainly going to see us as their cut-rate competitors. It's possible a majority would vote to keep our doctors out of the Association."

"But you'd still have your hospital."

"Yes," said Alan, "and it's going to be good."

As the weeks went by the hospital little by little became what Alan wished it to be. The doctors were developing into a team. They met in his office once a week to discuss their common problems. The subscribing families began to take shape as units. The concept began to prevail that as a diseased organ could not be considered apart from the patient, so also it could not be considered apart from the patient's family and his community. A man's sickness and recovery were not related only to his occupation, but to his salary, the number of children he had, the health of the wife, and whether there had been any other major sickness in the family recently.

The preliminary examinations for the purpose of curbing disease in its early stages entailed a great deal of routine, but on the whole the doctors accepted it cheerfully. Patients, too, had to be convinced of the value of such a checkup. It took time for them to come for test after test, bringing samples of urine for analysis, going without breakfast before a basal metabolism. The original group of insured patients returned for their yearly examination. A few revealed diseases that had not appeared a year ago—tuberculosis was the most prevalent. Cancer, the disease especially dreaded by women, had in all but one instance been detected the year before.

The hospital was a friendly and informal place, almost like a community center, Alan thought sometimes. Red tape was at a minimum. During visiting hours members of families were given every possible freedom. One of the things that pleased Alan most was the acceptance of colored people in the waiting room. As soon as the plan had been announced a small group of Negroes had asked to be enrolled. Alan had not segregated them, as was customary in this half-Southern, half-Northern city.

On the whole he was well satisfied with the coverage the hospital was giving to the insured patients. It troubled him that anyone with a chronic disease who wished to enroll had to be willing to accept the fact that it could not be included in the insurance. Because so many of the chronics fell in Alan's department he was particularly aware of this limitation. But the hospital would have gone under if chronic diseases had been included— that he knew.

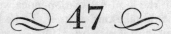

47

ON A COLD January afternoon Esther was completing her home. Before her sickness she had sought to cut herself off from her past, leaving her parents' possessions in storage. She had had no place for them in the apartment she and Alan had first occupied in Athenia. Why she had not sent for them when they bought this house in the Southeast District she hardly knew.

During the last weeks at the Institute she had thought often of the objects connected with her life with her parents—a bas-relief her father had brought back from Greece, a great favorite of his; a couple of paintings he had given to her mother. Then she began to long for his books, remembering the library in England. In looking forward to children she began to think of the rich heritage she as well as Alan could bequeath to them. Continuity now seemed important—continuity through her as well as through Alan. The treasured diary of Alan's grandfather should be augmented with the treasured annotated books of her father—philosophy and medicine, two good heritages to pass on. She had thought often in those last days at the Institute of her mother and father, not separate as she had so often regarded them, but together: evenings in England, their laughter and pleasure in each other, laughter and gaiety—and she a part of it all. One day not long before she left the Institute she had sent to England for the tangible evidence of her life with her parents.

In preparation for the arrival of the books Alan had arranged for a carpenter to build cases to fit the wall spaces in the living room. On this January day, just as he was leaving for the hospital, the packing boxes from England were delivered. Esther and Beatrice set to work, hoping to have everything in place before he got home for dinner.

"Let's unpack the books first," said Esther. When Beatrice unwrapped them and handed them to her and Esther saw their familiar bindings she was carried back to the library in England: the tall windows with their rich red draperies, the coal fire falling to ashes in the grate, her father sitting by his desk with a green shade above his eyes, while she watched him from the hearth. Beatrice, hearing the sudden indrawing of Esther's breath, turned and saw her staring straight ahead. Gently she took the books piled in Esther's lap and put them on the shelves.

After they were in place Beatrice unwrapped the plaque and the two paintings and Esther directed her where to hang them.

Beatrice now set about clearing the room of paper and packing boxes, preparatory to Alan's home-coming. "Well, I never! Here's a crate the man forgot to open," she exclaimed.

"I told him we'd let it wait," said Esther. "He seemed in a hurry. I can't even remember what's in it."

"A jiffy and I'll have it open. You sit down while I do it. You look tired," said Beatrice.

Esther sat watching, wincing a little at the metallic blows of the hammer on the chisel and then at the squeak of the nails as Beatrice pried off the top. "It's another picture!" exclaimed Beatrice. She drew out a flat object from which the paper wrapping was partially torn away, disclosing a gold frame.

Now it came back to Esther what the picture was. "Let me have it," she cried.

Beatrice looked up in surprise, caught by the sudden urgency in Mrs.

Towne's voice. Wondering, she took the package and stood it on Esther's knees, steadying it with her hand.

Carefully Esther drew away the tissue paper that hid the face beneath. "This is my mother when she was a young woman. Isn't she beautiful?"

"Indeed, Mrs. Towne, she is."

"She is a Jew. I am very proud of her."

"I guess yes, but how did you forget about her picture?"

"I don't know," Esther answered.

"Let me hang it over the mantel," Beatrice begged. "I'll move the other picture. She'll look nice up there."

After the portrait was in place the two women stood looking at it. How she graces the room! Esther thought.

"Now you rest right here on the couch. I'll touch a match to this fire, and you just lie here and look at your mother and rest. The doctor'll be in soon." Beatrice went out.

The fire blazed up, sending a flickering light over the familiar bindings of books, up into the face of the young and lovely woman in the portrait. The rich red of her dress glowed in the firelight. The blue-black hair crowned a face filled with vitality—yes, and with tenderness.

❧ 48 ❧

WHEN Alan entered the hospital that January afternoon the secretary at the desk reported that while he had been out for luncheon someone had telephoned that Miss Benninger would like him to come to see her at five. That she had been sick for months and could not live long was common knowledge. It would put Alan in an embarrassing situation if this eccentric but influential woman almost on her deathbed should decide she wanted him for her physician. He was glad that the rules of the group hospital did not allow him to have outside patients. To take so influential a patient away from Corwin would increase his enmity. And yet Alan could not risk refusing to answer her call. If he did so, that, too, could be used against him.

The short afternoon was darkening into twilight as he drove out of the suburban area and onto the Benninger farm through a gate in a wire fence which bordered the bleak winter fields. Tall cottonwood trees edged the well-kept private road that led up to the house. They swayed stiffly in the rising wind. About the fields and roads there was the spinsterish neatness characteristic of Miss Benninger. The tall and narrow house, set in the midst of a group of soft maples now bare of leaves, was primly New England. Three steps gleaming white in the twilight led to a paneled door. Two long windows filled the space to the right. The three windows on the floor above were faintly illumined. The lower floor was completely dark, but when he pulled the old-fashioned bell a bright light sprang up in the fan-shaped panes above the door. Immediately it was opened by an elderly German woman, who pointed to the stairs which led straight up from the narrow hall. "I on the stairs not often go," she said, motioning him upward.

Used to meager instructions when he called on patients in their homes, Alan went along the second-story hall to the front of the house and knocked on a door under which he saw a thin line of light. It was instantly opened by some contrivance worked from within.

The room he entered was large, extending across the whole front. A partition must have been taken out, he thought, remembering that the rooms in New England houses of this type were always small. Set between two windows was a wide colonial bed with fluted posts. The valance across the top obscured the occupant, but Miss Benninger's familiar voice commanded him to take the chair by the side of the bed. "I've a lot to say to you, but first don't think I'm going to ask to become one of your patients."

Relieved but puzzled, Alan seated himself, and this brought Miss Benninger within the range of his vision. The two mahogany fluted columns at the head of the four-poster framed a pile of pillows in freshly ironed pillowcases, against which her head rested. Her hair had been cut very short, revealing the fine modeling of her head. With her short, ill-proportioned body hidden beneath the covers her face was given its true value. The deep-set brown eyes, large and intelligent, were shadowed by the prominent bones of her forehead. The cheeks, once plump, were hollowed now, showing her strong, high cheekbones. The nose was straight, the mouth well shaped and generous. A noble face indeed.

Then as she snapped off her reading lamp, leaving only a central ceiling light to illuminate the room, she was lost to him in the shadow cast by the canopy. The windows were now black spaces, for the night had shut down.

"I'll not beat about the bush," she said. "I've not much longer to live. My family dies out with me, a fate it ill deserves. There have been great and good members of it who have served their country." The last word was a mere whisper. She was silent. He thought her strength was ebbing.

Then she cried out, "Why my family should end in a runt like me only the good God knows." The voice no longer sounded like Miss Benninger's with its ironic overtones; it was the voice of an anguished woman crying out her frustration and longing.

Alan, accustomed as he was to revelation long held back and released at the approach of death, felt he could not bear to have her give over her reserve and expose to him the torment life had been to her. He recognized that this was a cry against sterility, against the celibacy her awkward body had inflicted upon her, a cry against the humiliating years of her woman-hood when no man had offered her his love, a cry against the death of the family through her, something she was not responsible for and yet for which she held herself responsible, a responsibility freighted with bitter rebellion against the cruel fate which had been meted out to her.

In the quiet he heard the rustling of papers and then the familiar sardonic tones characteristic of the eccentric Miss Benninger. "Well, we've been pioneers, and it is fitting that we should end that way. I'm going to make the monument to my family not sterile stone but people, good strong Americans, lots of 'em. I don't want a single weakling living off the land my ancestors cleared. They've got to be kept healthy. Medicine's getting too expensive for families with youngsters. I've been through the mill."

She paused, waiting for strength enough to go on. Finally, when he was beginning to think she had dropped into the exhausted sleep of the very sick, she spoke again. "I know what it costs to be sick a long time. I like what you've done. There's a lot ahead of you before you win, more than you think. You've got to have a club with which to fight your way through. Here it is." She paused, picked up a folded paper.

"I've deeded the farm to your hospital. It can be divided up into suburban lots and sold. But this house is not to be sold. I've stipulated in my will that the head of the hospital is to live here after my death. That's you. If you're dropped from the hospital, the house and two acres in lawn and woods surrounding it go to you personally. That will keep them from ever firing you. After my death you are to take this to my lawyer. I'll leave instructions with him." She pushed the folded paper toward Alan.

Amazement, the instinct to save himself and the hospital from such a gift, held Alan speechless. It was too personal. He could not accept it. He could imagine Corwin's expression when he learned of it and what he might make of such a bequest. Still vivid in Alan's mind was last winter's attack on him. He could even be accused of influencing Miss Benninger on her deathbed to will him her house. He could be accused of exerting undue influence when it became known he had the deed to her property in his possession. It was the most embarrassing position his physician's role had ever placed him in.

"Well, aren't you going to take it?"

Her half-hysterical cry warned him what his refusal would mean to her. Sometimes the innermost longing of a complex personality asserted itself in strange ways when death was not far off. He saw that she had come to envision him as the one whom she trusted to see that sturdy stock be reared on the Benninger land. To protect him satisfied a deep maternal instinct. She had given him the clue when he first entered the room in her cry of protest against her fate. He must not deny so valiant a woman this last thing she asked of life.

"Please let me explain," he said. "You make a gift like this and expect me to act as if such things happened to me every day. This is the finest tribute to me as a doctor I've ever received. It's not only the gift, but the faith you show in me."

"Pshaw!" she said, the rough quality back in her voice. "Don't be mealy-mouthed and act humble. You deserve it, and you know you do."

The next step Alan realized he must take was harder. "All right. We'll just forget about that side of it. As I see it, this farm of yours, if it's to do what you want it to do, cannot help me personally for a good and sufficient reason. The board—they are businessmen—would not be willing to accept your property if you stipulate that they must keep me."

He heard the rasping sound of paper being torn again and again. As the last scrap fell from her hand she murmured, "I'm not so dumb as not to understand."

He was destroying her as he had foreseen he might. He must somehow manage to have her gift carry a personal meaning. But how? Then, with one of those flashes of intuition that always alarmed Sam, he saw a way out. It was his ability to think boldly and constructively in the moment when catastrophe threatened him that brought her need and the need of the community together in his mind. If Miss Benninger's money could be used to provide the care for chronics which the hospital was unable to give, two purposes could be served.

"Don't misunderstand me," he pleaded. "There is something you can do for me. A doctor's specialty means a great deal to him. I think you can understand that better than most women. You would make a dream come true I never expected to see fulfilled, if you willed this property of yours to the group hospital for an addition where the crippled would be treated. The hospital is not able to take on such a burden. Without your help it never could."

He went on to picture for her the handicapped, the hidden away, the lonely, frustrated, useless. "I'm trained to aid such as these, but I've neither a place nor the money to do it. If you added a wing to the hospital you could feel that my work with the handicapped would be your monument. I could realize myself as I never could otherwise."

There was silence in the room. He waited. A gust of wind blew a branch against the windowpane.

She who had always been apart saw even more clearly than he how apart these people were. She would give them their chance, and she would give this man, whom in her imagination she had built to heroic proportions, his opportunity. "If you wish it that way," she said. Her head turned restlessly on the pillow.

Alan saw that pain held in abeyance by drugs was once more taking over. There was a creak of a stair and a heavy tread, the German woman coming to take charge. With a sudden impulse he lifted Miss Benninger's hand to his lips. Then he went out.

Esther heard Alan's car, the click of his key in the lock of the front door. She rose and went toward the hall, switching on the light. He looked unusually tired. As together they entered the living room his eyes traveled from the well-filled bookcases to the portrait over the mantel.

"You look like her," he said. "I am glad." What had taken place in his home during his absence this afternoon was evidence of a new stability in Esther.

As never before it seemed to him he sensed the goodness of his marriage, the goodness of marriage—something which had been denied to the lonely woman he had just left. Again he heard the cry of protest against the disappearance of the family.

❧ 49 ❧

IN THE mail a few days later Alan received a letter from Miss Benninger. In short characteristic sentences she wrote that she had deeded the estate out-right to the hospital association, to be used after her death for a rehabilita-tion center for handicapped members of the Southeast District. She had made her lawyer her executor. She gave no details. Alan could only hope that she had left the board free, not hampered it with difficult restrictions. But that was a problem for the future.

For it was evident to him that as his conception grew of the social role of a doctor, so also grew the demands on him and the hospital. The doctors had barely finished the preliminary examination when Powell of the Public Health Service dropped in to see him about protecting the children of the district.

"We've tried an immunization program giving free inoculations in the public schools, but some of the doctors felt children should come to them for inoculations for smallpox and diphtheria and pay for them. They said the state was encroaching on their practice."

"What rot!" Alan exclaimed. "It's a dog-in-the-manger attitude."

"You're looking at it from a different angle from the others. Your liveli-hood like mine is assured," answered the health officer.

"These doctors who protest—I won't ask who they are—can't have it both ways. They demand to be given the chance at the top to make all the money they can, but they ask to be protected against the chance they're taking if the competition gets too heavy."

"And the kids," said the health officer a little bitterly, "have to pay some-times with their lives as many parents don't take them to the doctors."

"Well, what do you want me to do?"

"Inoculate the children in your plan free."

"Phew! It's another expense. Probably we could manage that, but it means more routine work. I hate to ask it just now, but I'll see what I can do." Here again was a responsibility Alan couldn't refuse to take.

That afternoon he had a consultation with his doctors over handling the inoculations. Most of it would naturally fall in Dr. Pratt's department. "Can we divide up the work?" he asked. To his great satisfaction the staff sup-ported him. Day by day they were being welded into an efficient body. But it worried him that they were protecting only the children of the district whose parents had taken out insurance. He was puzzled over the stand of the local doctors. During the poliomyelitis epidemic, face to face with death, all of them had fought with all the power they had to save the children. Why didn't they have the same spirit toward preventive measures? What was the quality of mind that closed many doctors' minds against this phase of medicine? He did not believe it was entirely mercenary.

His pondering was interrupted by a knock on his office door. "Come in," he called.

The doctor who entered was the ear-nose-and-throat specialist, a very capable young man. Although he had always done more than his share of routine work, Alan had never felt that this youngest member of his staff was entirely in sympathy with the plan. At the weekly meeting of the doctors he had been strangely silent, and he never before had sought Alan out. Pleased and surprised at his coming, Alan pushed forward a chair, saying, "Sit down, Pichard. I've all the time in the world."

"I'll not take much of it. I'll get right to the point." Pichard ignored the invitation to be seated. "I've come to resign."

"But when you came you promised to stay a year!" Alan's quick temper almost got the best of him. "You can't break a promise. I gave you a chance, took you straight from your residency. Now, after getting a footing for yourself at our expense, you want to break your promise."

"I gave my promise in good faith; but now that I have a real chance to better myself, you won't hold me to it, will you?"

"Your leaving right now would put us in a hole. You made a gentleman's agreement. To a gentleman that ought to mean something."

Pichard flushed angrily. "Anyway my resignation stands."

Alan took his own anger in hand. He didn't want bad blood between them. "Let's talk this out. Give me your reason for wanting to leave. You owe both me and yourself an explanation."

"I don't see any use going into that," Pichard answered.

"I do."

There was something in Alan's firm tone that evidently affected Pichard, for he obeyed the command to sit down. "A fellow has to look out for himself," he said, looking unhappy.

"And you don't think you can here?"

"What chance have I to make a name for myself?" he demanded. "Look at the amount of time I spend on this preventive program of yours. Now we have these inoculations to get through with. How much experience in my specialty do I get in that routine stuff?"

"Not much, I suppose," said Alan. "If that's your main objective, you won't be satisfied here. We're not out primarily to give you a reputation." In spite of his determination not to be angry, Alan knew he was. "In such case I imagine you've made the right decision."

Pichard was startled. He hadn't expected Towne would let him go so easily. "I'll stay, of course, until you find someone to take my place," he said. When he had made his plan to resign, he had counted on Towne's being impressed with the obvious fact that if he left it would be to better himself. He had pictured Towne's look of admiration when he presented his resignation. Towne would think he must have a pretty good offer. It would give him a bargaining point to get rid of some of the routine. But Towne was making no effort to keep him. Pichard had a sudden disturbing sense of doubt whether what he was about to do was ethical.

"You shouldn't blame me," he burst out. "I haven't been trained for this sort of thing. All the emphasis at the medical college was on curing the sick. Isn't that what a doctor's for?"

"It depends on how you look at it." Alan was doodling on his desk blotter, trying to think through a new idea. Here, in a way, was the explanation why most of the doctors of the Southeast District wouldn't co-operate with the Health Department. "I think it's a matter of emphasis. Are you interested primarily in human beings or just in throats?"

"Throats, of course, and ears." Pichard's aplomb had come back. Towne was certainly corny. No wonder the doctors who worked under him weren't taken into the County Association. "I need to make good in my specialty to get into the County Medical Association. It's a pretty big handicap not to be in it. It puts a man behind the eight ball." Watching the change of expression in Alan's face, the look of worry that came into his eyes at this remark, Pichard felt his confidence returning. He had scored one against Towne. His thrust had gone home.

"It's hard on all of you, I know," Alan answered, "not to be taken into the Association immediately. But let's get down to your resignation. If you'll give me ten days I think I can make arrangements. It probably will take you that time to complete your records and wind everything up." Alan believed he wouldn't have much trouble filling Pichard's place with another young man. After all, it was a good opportunity for a doctor just getting started. But he didn't intend to have the hospital used again as a springboard. He'd try first to get an older man to take Pichard's place.

"Very well, sir." Pichard turned sharply on his heel and left the room. What would he tell his wife? Marie liked it here . . . the free days they had together. And suppose the thing he had in mind didn't come through. It was a gamble. He should have waited at least until he was a member of the Association. Marie hadn't wanted him to resign. He really had only half intended to when he entered Towne's office.

After Pichard had left Alan sat thinking. It was hard on the doctors, he knew, not to be taken into the Association. Esther had said that at Mrs. Lambert's luncheon party there was a good deal of discussion among the wives over the continued tabling of the doctors' applications. Most of them were standing by the hospital, but one or two were restive, even hinting they wanted their husbands to leave. Esther had urged that she and Alan invite them all to dinner, give the women a chance to know him. For some reason he held back. He was tired at night, and he had not until now discerned any dissatisfaction in the staff.

But wasn't he taking too much for granted? After all, his ideas were not the accepted ideas of the profession. He had come to them by a long and circuitous route, beginning in the mountain valley hidden deep in the Himalayas. He had held the same views that Pichard held—that Sam held. Wasn't he asking too much too soon? Also, if he thought in terms of the family regarding patients, why shouldn't he regarding the doctors? He should make an effort to know the wives. Being united in a group might give them the needed strength to accept the ostracism inflicted on them by the other doctors of the community. Too, if he did nothing, Pichard's resignation might start a kind of landslide. He must rally his forces. He would follow Esther's suggestion.

∽ 50 ∾

To ESTHER the day of the dinner was a mountain peak from which she looked across the stretch of land she had traversed in the last year. Life here in the Southeast District was no longer colorless to her. Its life and her own with its homely details had been given significance by the last year's happenings. The domestic round of duties made monotonous for other married women by repetition was not monotonous for her. Sickness, closeness to death, and months given over to the mere effort to walk had acted as an abrasive cleansing every act of the commonplace.

It was a sparkling day with the wind blowing in great gusts. Esther went into the garden to get some bare branches to put with the chrysanthemums Alan had brought her the evening before. She took pleasure in the sound of dry leaves scurrying across the brown winter grass and the sight of clouds moving swiftly across the sky. A tall box-elder tree swayed in the wind, but the low-growing shrubs were still. Then a rush of wind swept them into motion. Going about the garden, she saw everywhere the intelligent care Alan had given it. She smiled. Preventive measures used with plants as he used them with human beings—splints and braces to help trees and plants grow straight. He had risen early this morning to give support to the frailer inhabitants of his garden against the rising wind.

All at once she remembered Grandfather Towne's garden. He could not tolerate a crooked tree or plant any more than he could a crooked human being. As a college student he had majored in the school of forestry. Making a study of what could be done to help nature produce straight, healthy trees, he had begun to think about what could be done to twisted human beings, and he had decided to become a doctor. Both he and Alan, so different and yet so alike, held each human being in deep respect, recognized the necessity to minister to all human beings at whatever cost to themselves. She felt in the two an affirmation she now felt in herself.

While she arranged the bare branches and the yellow chrysanthemums she looked up often to watch the pattern of clear light cast over the room. A branch had broken loose from a climbing rose trellised to the wall of the house outside the living room. It fell across the window, moving rhythmically with the wind, breaking up the still square of light from the window patterned on the floor. Feeling tireless, more and more certain that life was being created within her, although she hadn't told Alan as yet, she came to the evening.

Alan was late getting home. Esther was already dressed. His surprise and delight as he looked at her lifted him up out of weariness. He had forgotten during the months of her struggle to gain back her health that she had once been beautiful. She had been too thin when he got back from abroad, and then had come her sickness. Until this moment he had been unaware of the physical transformation taking place in her during the last few months. Now she stood before him, a beautiful woman carrying herself almost regally. In the process of rehabilitation her body had been taught a primitive knowledge let slip in this industrial age, the well-balanced erect figure of the primitive woman. She was wearing a simple black dress; the skirt was full and fell to the floor. For a moment he wondered why she had chosen a long dress for so informal a gathering. Then he understood that the long skirt hid her disability, concealed the brace she was still wearing.

There was about her a joyousness and vitality which unconsciously he was beginning to rely on.

Together Esther and Alan went down the stairs.

At the ringing of the bell he opened the door to Dr. Beritz and his tiny, boyish-looking wife. "Are we the first? I told Mimi we'd be," Beritz said.

"You don't mind, do you?" said Mimi, putting her hand trustingly into Alan's. He liked her immediately, as Esther had at their first meeting.

Before Alan had time to close the door the Lamberts arrived, and on their heels the other doctors and their wives. Altogether there were twenty-four. One of the unmarried doctors came with Dr. Pratt, who wore a creation of pink chiffon and black velvet. Others take on color just being near Naomi, thought Alan. Dynamic and forceful as she was, she had also the ability to listen. Young Pichard, at first a little on the defensive, was now telling Dr. Pratt something that appeared to amuse her greatly. Warmed by her laughter and appreciation, he dropped his guard and became friendly.

Talking to the wives of the doctors, Alan realized how wise Esther had been in insisting that he know the women, that only so could he understand the men. These men associated with him took on another dimension in the presence of their wives. Some seemed stronger, some weaker. The plump specialist in internal medicine who was easygoing until a crisis arrived, when he invariably became courageous, Alan saw took at least some of his courage from his wife. Looking into her candid blue eyes, Alan knew she would expect her husband to have courage. Mimi undoubtedly toned down the natural arrogance of Dr. Beritz.

From two of the wives Alan could draw no response. They were evidently followers of Mrs. Lambert. Almost immediately they gravitated into the circle forming around her, demanding that their husbands serve them the buffet supper Beatrice was presiding over at a table at the other end of the long room. Dr. Lambert was very attentive to his wife. Her remarks were less biting when he was within hearing.

As Alan moved among his guests to pass coffee, Mrs. Pichard rose. "Please let me help you, Doctor." Walking by his side down the long room, she whispered, "Dr. Towne, Godfrey doesn't really want to leave. He hasn't anything else. Give him another chance. He'd die if he knew I was asking you for it, and he'd hate me forever."

This gathering wasn't such a good idea after all, Alan thought. Here was a wife interfering in a professional matter. But instinctively he covered for Mrs. Pichard, saying so all could hear, "I could do with a little help." Well, it would have to be thought out later. It was up to Pichard to come to him.

While they stood around the room drinking their after-dinner coffee, the wife of the specialist in general surgery, one of the women who had been in the group about Mrs. Lambert, asked in a voice loud enough for all to hear, "Dr. Towne, won't you tell us what you think is going to happen to us if the County Association doesn't recognize us soon? We feel such orphans."

"Orphans! When we belong to a group like this!" protested the wife of the roly-poly man in internal medicine.

"As long as we stand together I think nothing dreadful is going to happen to any of us," Alan said quietly. "Of course we had our state license before we ever opened. We have a splendid set of men on the Board. Our patients are satisfied, and I have every reason to hope that with the excellent work we have been doing the examining board of the National Medical Association will soon put us on their approved list."

There was a general murmur of assent. Something good was happening here in this room. They were drawing together, feeling support in being together. If no one wavered, no one gave up, they'd win in the end. Co-operation was a stronger force than the competitive forces against them, Alan believed. In a glance around the room he saw that individually none of the men, unless it was Lambert, looked very imposing. Two were bald; one was squat and round-shouldered. Beritz was ungainly, and his expression bordered on the belligerent. There was the nervous, aggressive Pichard. In other words, they were all, including himself, ordinary rank-and-file Americans. It was as a group that they attained stature. They were putting over a new idea in medicine. He would give Pichard a chance to reconsider. He who had brought these men together would not be the one to break them apart.

Alan went over to where Esther stood by the fireplace talking to Dr. Beritz, Mrs. Pichard and Mrs. Lambert. He heard Mrs. Lambert say, "I'm so interested in this painting." She was looking up at the portrait of Esther's mother. "I've been wondering why you chose it. Of course the Jews lend themselves to portraiture." She added, with a little laugh, "I hadn't noticed the likeness to you until you came and stood under it."

Esther looked at her with steady gaze. "I'm delighted if you see in me a resemblance. It's a portrait my mother had done at the time of her marriage."

"She is a most beautiful woman," murmured Mrs. Pichard.

"I wonder if wisdom must always come by way of suffering," Beritz said. He looked directly at Mrs. Lambert, then walked away without explaining his cryptic remark.

Alan rejoiced at Esther's part in the little scene, her poise, her dignity. She had evinced neither superiority nor inferiority. She moved at ease now within her double inheritance. She was well—mind and body. She actually seemed unaware of the cruelty in Mrs. Lambert's remark. For some reason it suited Mrs. Lambert's purposes to foster disunion. Alan could see she enjoyed using the power of a dynamic personality to stir up dissension. But he saw that Esther had power, too.

After they had gone Esther sank down on the couch. "I'll rest a little before climbing the stairs."

He sat down near her, picked up his pipe, content to wait until she was ready. He was thinking how best to handle Pichard when Pichard, the hospital and everything connected with it were driven clear out of his mind by Esther.

"Alan, I want to tell you something. I've been waiting, wanting to be sure. It amounts almost to superstition with me that if I speak out—— But here it is, Alan! I really do believe I'm pregnant."

He had not known until this moment how much he wanted a family. Even now he did not allow himself to rejoice fully. "Are you sure?"

"I . . . you mean you don't think it's so?" He saw a look of apprehension come into her eyes.

"Oh, my dear," he exclaimed, "I didn't mean to doubt you! You know nothing satisfies a doctor except scientific proof. I'll arrange for you to see Beritz."

"You are a doctor. You don't need someone else to tell you," she answered. For a doctor's wife this was an entirely irrational remark made, he felt, because she didn't wish to subject herself to any test.

But he persisted, "You will see Dr. Beritz, won't you, for my sake if for no other reason?"

"If you insist. Then make it for tomorrow. Let's get it over with."

Alan was waiting in his office for Esther to come in after seeing Dr. Beritz. It was not Esther but Beritz who, a few minutes later, opened his door. "Your wife said I was to tell you that she was late for a luncheon engagement."

"Is she right in her supposition?"

"It is impossible for her to be pregnant, but I've told her I'm making certain tests. For her sake it seemed wise to make them. Frankly, I wanted to talk to you before I gave her my verdict." There was nothing arrogant about Beritz now, instead a delicacy of approach as he went on, which

Alan deeply appreciated. "Am I right in thinking if I tell her the truth it might have tragic meaning for her?"

"Yes."

"I must instill hope in her even as I take it from her then?" said Dr. Beritz. "I believe it *is* possible for her to conceive—a slight operation. I do not want to invade your privacy, Towne. I think you understand that. But I need to know a little more about Mrs. Towne if I am to help her. Am I right in thinking that the tragedy which she thinks threatens her is bound up with the fact that she has not always wanted a child? She let slip the word 'retribution.' "

"It might be so," said Alan.

Dr. Beritz rose. "I think I understand. Will you trust me to tell her the truth?"

"Yes," said Alan.

As Beritz went out, he was still revolving one question he felt he could not ask. How had it come about that Towne, a doctor, had not insisted on an examination long before this? It too, he sensed, was tied up in some way with the crisis which Esther Towne must face.

At her next appointment Esther demanded, not giving the gynecologist an opportunity to speak, "Of course the tests were hardly necessary in my case. Didn't you find it so, Dr. Beritz? Certainly you knew I was right when I was here the other day."

He waited for her to finish, realizing that she was unconsciously trying to get him to agree with her, as if by so doing she could make what she desired come to pass regardless of the facts. He had met this in women before, but never in a doctor's wife.

He placed a chair for her, then sat down at his desk, saying, "Mrs. Towne, you are trying to take from me my prerogative as doctor. Stay in your own place, an infinitely more important one than mine. You know it's very important to be a mother."

There was something in his voice that broke through her bravado. "I promise," she said quietly.

"I would have faith in any promise you made, Mrs. Towne. I shall rely on you. You *can* have a child."

"You mean I haven't—I'm not—?"

"No, in fact it's been impossible up to now. *Up to now,*" he repeated, pausing for a moment to let his words sink into her mind. "According to all my findings I believe it is possible for you to become pregnant." He waited, giving her the moment she needed to call up her reserves. "It means a slight operation, and it means you give up the nervous tension you are now under. I want to talk to you and your husband together. Shall I call Alan? Are you ready?"

"Yes," said Esther.

When Alan entered, Esther smiled and held out her hand to him.

But in the night Alan was wakened by her stifled sobs. "Oh, Esther, dear," he pleaded, drawing her to him, "you mustn't despair."

Under cover of darkness, with the comforting sense of his arms around her, in broken sentences she tried to explain. "It's not what you think. . . . It's . . . it's that I've been given absolution."

"Absolution," he exclaimed. "You need no absolution!"

How explain to him the need for it? "During the war when you had not written for weeks I got to thinking you were sorry you had married me—that you shared other people's prejudices. I talked to Grandfather. He warned me not to build the barrier of race between us; I might not be able to break it down when I wished to. I did build it when I decided we should have no children. Then when I wanted them I was afraid it was too late. I had heard that long-continued preventive measures could make a woman sterile. Even if we don't have children I'm in no way to blame. I am absolved."

His arms tightened around her. "We are both absolved," he said humbly, remembering his part in her suffering. Of course what Esther believed about the consequences of using contraceptives had no medical foundation, but the false idea had lost its power to trouble her and now was not the time to explain.

Long after she was asleep he lay awake trying to understand all that had happened to him and Esther in their marriage. Not only as husband but as doctor he had failed her. He had not unraveled for her the crossed strands of body and spirit. Suddenly a question flashed through his mind. Had the sterility of her body been transferred to her mind—the failure of her body placing its burden there?

Once he would have drawn quickly back from such an unscientific flash of intuition. Tonight he ventured farther along the frontiers of thought. Could the body exert that much power over the spirit? Then in another flash he saw the connection between his thinking and the thinking of the profession. Was it not accepted that certain diseases brought personality changes? How much, he now asked himself, did the volume of disease in a nation account for its spirit? If so, the eradication of sickness, as far as it was possible, was a responsibility a democracy must assume for its people. He had one more flash of intuition. Such venturing into revolutionary thinking led down a lonely road.

❧ 51 ❧

ABSORBED in his personal concern over Esther, Alan had let the problem of how to approach Pichard drift. This morning he had made up his mind he would talk to him, but as yet he had no idea what he was going to say.

Certainly he couldn't beg him to stay on. That would give the advantage to the little upstart, for, in spite of his efforts to be fair, in his heart Alan so regarded Pichard. He was cocky and might become more so if he felt that by resigning he had scored a victory over Alan. As Alan was drumming on his desk, trying to think out a feasible approach, there was a knock on his door. "Come in," he called.

To his surprise it was Pichard who walked into the room. Well, thought Alan, I'm up against it now.

"I might as well get right down to business," Pichard said as he came to a halt by the desk. "Have you found anyone yet to fill my place? I want to know because——"

"I was about to ask you to come in. Before I went any farther about getting someone I wanted to be sure you——"

"You don't by any chance mean that——"

"Just a minute," Alan interrupted. "Maybe we're trying to say the same thing. If you haven't anything as yet——"

"Oh, hell," Pichard again interrupted, "I might as well say I haven't and I'd like to reconsider."

"And I was about to say I'd like to have you reconsider."

So there it was. There was no problem after all.

"I'd better get along. I've a patient sitting in my office." Just as he reached the door he turned to say, "Now that I get the idea, I like what you're trying to do. I see there's a good fight ahead, and I like a fight."

Well, that's over, he thought as he went along the hall to his office. I didn't come off too badly.

52

EARLY in February Alan opened the local morning paper and saw in a boxed-in space the announcement of Miss Benninger's death. Large headlines proclaimed her gift to the Gunsaulus Hospital; smaller type mentioned the specific purpose to which the bequest was to be put. This was followed by a long account of the history of the Benninger family.

Throughout the Southeast District there was considerable excitement. The few old residents who were left telephoned one another: "Wasn't it just like Kate Benninger to do a thing like that? I suppose in heaven she'll appoint herself the guardian angel of everyone who ever is to live on land that once belonged to the Benningers."

"Cracked!" said a retired farmer whose property once had adjoined hers.

Her minister went about pointing her out to his flock as the modern Samaritan.

Dr. Corwin shrugged his shoulders and was reported to have said, "Here's an example of the gratitude of a patient! I've endured Miss Benninger's sharp tongue for years. This is my reward." In his heart he blamed Alan Towne for undercutting him.

The hospital telephone was busy all morning. Well-wishers called up to congratulate Alan. Members who held insurance in the hospital wanted to know if it would lower their rates. Bedridden arthritics, polio victims called to ask if they might enroll now for treatment. Finally Gunsaulus phoned Alan to meet with the Board that afternoon.

When Alan walked into Gunsaulus' office he was immediately conscious that the usual cordiality toward him was lacking. Gunsaulus, terse in his greeting, proceeded at once to the business in hand. "We'd like to ask you a few questions about this bequest of Miss Benninger."

"I shall be glad to answer anything I can," said Alan, "but Miss Benninger's lawyer can give you the details and the technical points. I can't."

"Technical points, yes," Gunsaulus answered. "But there was a note with the will suggesting that the executors consult with you about the plan."

Chesterton cleared his throat. Alan had always wondered how Gunsaulus managed to get him to serve on the Board. Everything he had ever said indicated a hard, cold, even suspicious personality. "Miss Benninger has hamstrung us by the restrictions she put on her gift. If her estate had been willed directly to the hospital to use as we deemed advisable, we'd be getting somewhere, for we need endowment. It seems a little queer to us that Miss Benninger should have chosen to support your specialty exclusively. What we want to know is whether you knew of this bequest before it was announced yesterday, Dr. Towne. Were you in the woman's confidence? It would seem so from her request to the executors."

Just how was Alan to answer? The ethics of the profession forbade his divulging a confidence given him by a sick person. Furthermore, to explain he might have to tell what had been in the will she had torn up, reveal that they would have been even more hamstrung had she made her gift contingent on keeping him. It was one of those difficult positions in which a doctor sometimes finds himself. Feeling his way, he sought to clear himself in their eyes and preserve Miss Benninger's confidence. "I think you are laboring under a misconception," he said. "Crippling from various diseases, especially poliomyelitis, is not alone my specialty. Poliomyelitis falls under Dr. Pratt's specialty as well as mine. Not only orthopedists, but pediatricians and neurologists will be needed in such an institution."

"You are hardly answering our original question." The dry, clipped voice of Chesterton ended Alan's explanation. "Did Miss Benninger consult you before making her will?"

"I was coming to that," Alan answered, knowing he now had his back against the wall. "I'll answer you as far as I can. Miss Benninger did consult me about leaving her money to the hospital. For reasons I can't divulge without betraying her confidence, she decided as she did."

"You have us over a barrel." It was evident that Gunsaulus was far more angry even than Chesterton.

But Alan knew better how to deal with Gunsaulus' explosive temperament. "You can refuse the gift if you don't wish to accept the terms on which you get the property. But before you do I'd like to call your attention to the fact that we had an epidemic of polio here two years ago. Any year we may have another. We can't take care of cases except in the acute stage."

"You're not going to frighten me that way into taking on a bad business venture," shouted Gunsaulus. "You can't intimidate me!"

Alan looked directly at the red-faced, angry industrialist. "Do you, sir, of all men wish to take the responsibility of denying help to polio victims?" He knew that Gunsaulus hated any reference, however indirect, to his son's long illness, but he knew also that when it came to a battle with him you had to take off your gloves and fight. "Do you think the chance to be of sound body is a privilege only for the wealthy?" he demanded.

"You needn't try to crawl out of it that way," shouted the little man, pounding on the table with his pudgy, freckled fist. "I don't allow my employees to tell me what my duty is."

"Just a minute," said a man recently come to the Board. "I'm new here, but it seems to me the good doctor did what he thought was best." There was a twinkle in his Irish blue eyes as he turned to Alan. "Doctors aren't supposed to be businessmen, are they? They think, let me say, like doctors."

A general laugh went around, easing the tension. Gunsaulus sputtered and fumed, but with less and less vehemence, like a boiling kettle when taken from the fire. He contented himself finally with the remark, "We've got a white elephant on our hands. We've got just about all we can carry now. How are we going to finance another setup, I'd like to know."

"Another setup!" exclaimed Alan in surprise. "An adjunct to the hospital, a wing perhaps or even a separate building, isn't another setup. From the size of the estate as given in the paper the undertaking is adequately endowed, and of course the patients will have to pay for treatment. We can't work out any insurance to cover these chronic cases."

"Miss Benninger had no such simple ideas," said Chesterton. "She stipulates the institution is to be erected on the three acres of land surrounding her house and the house itself is to be preserved."

So Miss Benninger in the end could not divorce herself from her gift! This institution she was creating must stand as a momument erected on the actual land of her forefathers. The arrangement, Alan saw, meant an entirely separate plant. There would have to be a doctor in charge there. At such a distance Alan could supervise the work, not manage it directly.

"It's very evident Dr. Towne had no conception of the grandiose ideas of his patroness," said Chesterton. "But suppose you give us your own notion how to establish an institution like this."

"The first thing that occurs to me," said Alan, a little piqued at Chesterton's manner and words, "is to make the group hospital more self-sufficient. That would free you for the new undertaking. Single contracts, I fear, will never do it. We need group insurance. I'd like to suggest that you start group insurance in your factories. I simply offer the idea for your consideration," he added, aware now that the board to a man considered such a proposal none of his business.

"And your next suggestion"—asked Gunsaulus—"is it as impractical as the one you've just made?"

"May I first ask you a question?" said Alan. "Do the terms of Miss Benninger's bequest put any restrictions on whether or not the farm itself is to be kept or sold?"

Chesterton eyed him suspiciously. "No."

"Then," said Alan, "I suggest that you sell the major part of the farm to one of the real-estate firms for a new subdivision. It will bring in a very considerable sum of money. For what more is needed I suggest a money-raising campaign in the city—that is, if you intend to accept the gift. Of course you don't have to."

The discussion that followed was heated and lively. In the end they voted to accept. These were men who had risen to wealth because of a certain acquisitiveness; to let valuable property slip through their fingers was against their natures. Property was property, however you looked at it.

They'd have to get the rest of the money somehow, they grumbled, when the meeting broke up. Put on a drive, they supposed, as Dr. Towne had suggested.

Alan slipped away, realizing that though he had succeeded in getting them to take the bequest, he was certain he had lost prestige with some of the men. Gunsaulus, he felt sure, would come around. He was a pretty good gambler and also a good loser. Alan wasn't so sure Chesterton would ever trust him completely again. Nothing he had said had convinced Chesterton that Alan had not deliberately influenced Miss Benninger to his own advantage.

53

Sam believed he had never been so efficient as he was the winter after Merton took Sally away. The movement of patients through his office was swifter than ever before, his operating technique was superb. The book he had been writing for so long was nearly finished. He had taken no partner to fill Merton's place. He was done with trying to pass on his knowledge. He believed that in some way or other each of his partners in turn, even Alan, had used him for his own purposes. What he considered Merton's traitorous act had convinced him he could trust no one.

Out of many long hours of thinking he had finally been able to free

Sally of any responsibility for her ruthless disregard of his place in her life. It was Merton who was entirely to blame. Some day she would see how mistaken her choice of a husband had been. She would see then what a father could be in an emergency.

But when the weeks and the months went by and Sally did not call on him he grew anxious. Sometimes he wished Jo hadn't carried out his orders so conscientiously. He began to picture all kinds of disasters which might have overtaken Sally. Tom was cruel to her. She was sick. She wanted to leave her husband, but didn't dare. She was in need of money. Merton was not capable of supporting her. It was obvious that Merton would not be able to establish himself professionally without help. He would need a recommendation from his father-in-law to get himself placed with another surgeon. Merton knew better than to ask for that. Certainly he was not capable of starting out on his own.

As a matter of fact, Tom Merton was proving himself resourceful. At first he had hoped to get into the office of one of the two specialists who had offered him a partnership at the time he accepted Sam's proposal. One needed no partner now; the other asked for some kind of indorsement from Sam of his efficiency. Tom knew his father-in-law would never give it.

He decided to go West. He had his state license and his specialty-board certificate. He hoped to find some hospital that needed an orthopedist. But he ran up against the same difficulty Alan's partners had encountered when they went to the Southeast District—how to get hospital privileges.

He and Sally were driving back from California when he learned that a certain small Arizona town and the surrounding country had no physician, and that in order to get one they had offered to guarantee a salary to a doctor who would settle there. No doctor so far had wanted to take up practice in so remote an area, on the theory that anyone who tried it would be so out of touch with the medical world he would soon be completely behind the times.

Tom saw that this was his chance. The region was doctor-hungry and would do a good deal to keep a man once it secured him. There was money among the ranchers. Encouraged by Alan's success, Merton intended, after he had gained their confidence, to try to get them to set up a small private hospital. To keep up with advances in medicine he thought he might work out a plan that had been tried in New England's rural districts. There, local doctors carried a case difficult to diagnose right up through established channels to the big specialists in the most advanced city hospitals. All this would take time, but Tom believed he had the patience to see it through. However, he was a cautious man and did not intend to get caught here if the community would not carry out a progressive program. He said he would try it out for a year.

Sally liked the idea. On the edge of the town, which was at the center of the region, they found an unoccupied house, little more than a shed, but in the dry climate they decided it would do. Had Jo been able to look in on them she would have been satisfied with her daughter. Sally was showing a surprising ability to give up without difficulty the easy life she had been used to and to find delight in the almost primitive existence which was now her portion.

Together Sally and Tom in his spare time made adobe bricks for an addition to their house. She learned to care for the chickens when he was away, even to clean their coops. Sewing, too, she learned, making her own house dresses in order to save every penny. Each thing she did had meaning for her, because it was hers. Only at night—and then only when Tom was away—would she lose confidence in the rightness of her act in leaving home. Then a feeling of guilt would blot out everything else. She, to whom her father had looked ever since she was a little girl to carry on the ideals he had set for the family, had let him down. Like her mother she had been untrue to him.

Several times she had the same dream. She was a little girl playing at dressing up. She had put on one of her mother's negligees when in anger her father came in and demanded she take it off. And then all at once the angry man seemed to be Tom. She would wake crying.

Three months after marriage she knew she was to have the child she had so long craved. From then on her love for her father became a maternal yearning over him. She accepted with understanding her mother's letter explaining why she would not be writing to her regularly. "Your father isn't as yet reconciled to your marriage. He has an idea that I would be deserting him if I kept in touch with you. You are capable of living your own life, and I think it good that we let you do it." At the end she wrote, "If there comes a time when we really need you, I promise to let you know. Be at peace, my child, until then."

It had been a hard letter for Jo to write. She wanted to create no sense of obligation in Sally, but the mother in her refused to let her cast her daughter entirely adrift. Her last sentences had been written with the hope of conveying to Sally the fact that she was inextricably bound into the family and that sometime the bond seemingly broken could be renewed.

Tom thought it a pity there had to be this division in the family. He liked families, and he didn't think much of the present arrangement. A family, he believed, needed continuity if each of its members was to be sound in mind and body, the parts independent but also interdependent. His parents had died when he was a young boy; he knew the emptiness that went with any interruption of family life. Sometimes he blamed himself for the drastic step he and Sally had taken. But as the months passed and no further word came, he blamed Sam for this continued punishment of the child he professed to love beyond anyone else in the world. It was especially hard on Sally just now to be separated from her mother. As the process of creation went on she spoke of her often with wistful longing. Tom tried in every way, through gentleness and concern, to fulfill her emotional needs, but he knew in part he failed.

During the period of thawing and freezing which came each year in

March Sam took a hard cold. He had driven himself all winter, and the cold slipped quickly into pneumonia. He was allergic to the usual drugs, or thought he was, and refused to take them. His physician found him a most recalcitrant patient. "I don't know what to do with him," he said to Jo. "I'd rather take care of a dozen spoiled children than one doctor. They're impossible when they're sick." Alan was the only one to whom Sam would listen at this time. Their positions seemed to be reversed. Alan now seemed the older of the two as with unending patience he ministered to Sam.

At last Sam was convalescing and home from the hospital. But he was not gaining as he should. The doctor suggested a trip to a warmer climate. Sam stubbornly refused. He was going back to the office.

Jo, worn down by his continued disregard of his health, certain that his refractory attitude during his sickness and now his obstinate refusal to take a vacation was rooted in his inability to reconcile himself to Sally's absence, began to wonder if this wasn't the time to tell Sally she was needed. By now Tom and Sally must have developed their faith in each other to the point where they would not jeopardize their marriage by yielding some concession to Sam. Sam, she knew, would never make the first advance. Sally and Tom were the winners in the struggle. They could afford to be generous now. After weighing the hazards and the advantages she decided to suggest to Sally that she write her father she would like to come home for a visit.

Jo's letter arrived on a spring day when all the earth and Sally were occupied with the joy of creation. All through the noon meal she had sat in a kind of dreamy state. Tom, watching her, was beginning to think about her confinement. She should be nearer a hospital. He must make arrangements for her somewhere soon.

After luncheon he went down to the post office to get the mail. It was the day for his medical journal to arrive.

"There's a letter here for Mrs. Merton, Doctor. It's registered. I thought you'd be coming by for your paper, so I didn't send it up. It's from Athenia."

Tom walked quickly back to his house at the end of the town's one street. As he opened the screen door he saw Sally still sitting by the table just where he had left her. "I've a real present for you," he said. "A letter from your mother!"

Eagerly Sally stretched out her hand. Poor child, he thought, she has missed her mother more than even I have realized!

"I'll clear the table. You go ahead and enjoy your letter," he said. While he went about his task, he heard the rustle of the sheets as she turned them. When she had finished she held out the pages to him. "Father's been sick. He's better now, but Mother seems to think he needs me."

Carefully Tom read the closely written pages, came to the paragraph:

It would be better than any medicine or any trip for him to see you. Do you think you could manage to come home for a couple of weeks? If you write him suggesting it, I think he would welcome such an overture on your part, although he would never, I fear, make one himself. Couldn't Tom come to get you when you are ready to go home?

For a moment Tom was angry. What kind of man was Sam Towne to be so unforgiving? Well, they could be unforgiving too. But after all why hold a grudge? Why shouldn't he be willing for her family to have her for a few weeks? Perhaps here was the answer to everything. Sally would be in the hands of the very best obstetrician Athenia could provide, and the coming child could be made the reason for her taking the initiative in reuniting herself with her family.

"I think it's just the thing," he said. "Of course you should go."

The light in her eyes told him he had made the right decision. He walked around the table, stood behind her. Gently he ran his fingers through her hair. "You've been an awfully good sport. I'm mighty glad, darling, that it's coming out all right!"

Until Sally arrived Jo was unable to rid herself of the memory of her daughter as she had been through all her adolescent years—resolute and irresolute, a woman and a child, the child so often winning over the woman. She had written her daughter in mingled fear and hope. Would coming home mean the resurgence of the child in Sally so fatal to her growth in the past? Or had the potential woman in her, which Jo had nurtured against the strong and often destroying force of Sam's possessiveness, developed in these months since her marriage to the point where she was secure within herself? Jo felt she had to take the risk, for Sam's sickness might leave him permanently ailing unless its cause was removed.

And then Sally came, a woman indeed! One glance at the full figure, the sweet serenity expressed as their eyes met, and Jo's apprehension left her. Marriage and conception were experiences Sally needed to mature her. Toward her and toward Sam, Sally showed a protectiveness which seemed to Jo a kind of overflow of her mother feeling. In the language of the Psalmist, thought Jo, her "cup runneth over," and she wants to fill ours from hers.

Quite naturally Sally would bring Tom into the conversation, telling about his growing practice. At first Sam was restive when Tom was mentioned, but gradually he accepted references to him, if not enthusiastically, at least graciously.

 54

MAY found the Benninger land sold to a real-estate firm. Much-needed houses were going up in the new division. Around the old Benninger house there was activity, too. The Board, encouraged by the good price the land had brought, raising the value of the bequest to half a million, had hired a good architect to design the main building. Delighted with the simple colonial lines of the old house, he had cleverly duplicated them in the larger building. The house itself, as Miss Benninger had stipulated, was not to be radically altered. It had been a problem what to do with it. Finally it had been decided to use it as the residence of the doctor in charge under Alan, and the doctor would then require a smaller salary.

Alan hoped to have everything ready to open in late July. The reports on poliomyelitis over the state, although not alarming, had set all doctors and hospitals on the alert. Alan, aware of a possible epidemic and anxious to supplement care of patients in the acute stage with prompt rehabilitation care, still did not push and strain as he had last year when the hospital was being built. A certain amount of his freedom from that nervous drive was due to the fact that Esther was at home, but some of it came from a better understanding of himself. He did not forget that at the meeting with the Board over the acceptance of the Benninger gift he had roused a certain amount of antagonism in some of the members. Part of it he knew had been unavoidable, but part of it had sprung from his own lack of appreciation of the Board's problems. Co-operation with the businessmen, as with the doctors at the hospital, meant a discipline of himself. He was learning patience and the value at times of compromise.

In the last year he had had to meet outside criticism, too, take it and profit by it, or else wreck himself in irritation and anger. There had been failures, and he had learned to acknowledge them, and there had been many triumphs which he had learned to take without complacency. They were not his triumphs alone; they belonged to the group.

Doctors and nurses who worked with him sensed a change taking place in him. He consulted them now where once he had pressed an issue through when he believed he was right. The tall man turning gray around the temples, with the blue-gray eyes half hidden under projecting eyebrows, they realized was a wise friend, not a monitor as he had sometimes seemed at first.

Alan took advantage of his day off from the hospital in the first week of July to put in the morning tending his newly planted lilac hedge, which would give the garden the seclusion he wanted. His desire for a child, so long delayed, was at last to be satisfied. Esther was physically stronger than she had ever been. Merely carrying a child seemed to have set loose in her forces of energy she had never before given evidence of possessing. What Alan had thought was a constitutional weakness in her was proving not to be so. She was untiring these days. She was still wearing the brace; the weight of the child made it advisable. But after the birth of the baby she would not need it. Alan was dreaming of the day in late October when he would be bringing her and the baby home from the hospital. Something of his old impatience took hold of him at the thought. It seemed a long time to wait.

It was Beatrice's day off, and Esther had set their luncheon on a table on the back porch. They were too content to talk much.

The telephone rang. Alan from years of training rose instantly, on the instinctive reaction that someone needed his services. "It's probably for me," Esther said. "Remember, it's your day off." He settled back, glad to surrender responsibility for a little.

"It's for you after all. It's Sam. He wants to speak to you," she said when she came back. "He seems excited."

"Why didn't he tell you what he wants?" A little reluctantly Alan went into the house.

Sam's voice came over the wire, exultant and full of pride. "It's a boy, arrived an hour ago! Sally has named him after me."

"Great business!" said Alan. "Samuel what?"

Somewhat diffidently, it seemed to Alan, Sam gave the full name: "Samuel Thomas Merton."

"A good strong New England name," said Alan. "When's Tom due?" He wasn't going to connive in Sam's ignoring of the part Merton had played in giving him a grandson. It was absurd of Sam not to forgive Tom.

"Not at this time. Sally and I thought, since it wouldn't be easy for him to get away from his practice, it would be better to let me take her home when she's ready to go."

"Well, give Sally our congratulations."

Alan went back to Esther. "Sally has a boy. Tom isn't here. I think I'll wire him my congratulations. No, I guess I'll wait till evening and call him long distance. He'll probably be home then. It's pretty hard on him not to be here. Sally's been away from him for months. I thought of course he'd come on for the baby's birth. Sam's going to take Sally home—or so he says."

Alan went back to his garden, to work contentedly until the shadows were long across the grass. Sam's announcement had made him doubly conscious of the continuity of the family—how it reached back to his father, his grandfather, to its beginnings in America, and forward to Sam and to him and to their children. Tragedy and happiness, failure and success, knitting them all together. How the family had spread itself out over the country! Massachusetts, then New York State, then Athenia, and now that Tom and Sally had settled in Arizona it had moved westward again, continually drawing other families into it. His grandmother's family were Quakers come from England. There was Jo's family two generations back come from Germany in protest against conscription and Esther's Jewish and English ancestors. And there were all the other branches of the Towne family. He had never followed their history. Where had the other sons and daughters of the martyred woman of Salem settled? They must be a mighty band by now. In a sense we are America, he thought.

When he looked over his office mail the next morning Alan found a bulletin from the State Health Department. "We are setting up a special division," it said, "in the Bureau of Preventable Diseases. We shall be issuing daily reports giving the latest scientific information about poliomyelitis. The disease is already reaching epidemic proportions in the state." Then followed an account of the distribution of cases and deaths in the various counties. Black dots on a map showed the numbers. It was unbelievable. The county in which Athenia was situated was heavy with dots, yet not a single case had as yet been reported in the Southeast District.

Well, thought Alan, we're equipped this year to handle the acute stage here at the hospital, and the rehabilitation work will start soon at the Benninger Center. The doctor recommended by Dr. Carothers to take charge of the institute would arrive in a few days. Alan had feared the board might object because he was a Negro. The man was exceptionally well fitted for the work, and unless one was looking for Negro characteristics his race would not be suspected. Somewhat to Alan's surprise, the board after considerable discussion had decided to accept him.

That afternoon Alan went to see just what was still to be done at the Benninger Center. He liked the strength and dignity of the building. The wings, one story high, were low; the central section was tall and narrow, an enlarged replica of the Benninger house. Oddly enough, Alan realized, the building resembled Sam's farmhouse. There was little of the institutional look about it. He wondered if Sam had had the same architect. He had never thought to ask Sam whom he had had.

He entered the lobby of the central section. Its tall windows, its high-arched doorways, gave him the same feeling of lofty endeavor a cathedral conveys. It was after working hours, and Alan had the building to himself. He went from lobby to gymnasium, to the dining room, to all the rooms ready for the occupants. The smell of new wood and paint filled his nostrils. Here he would work out his own theories. With gratitude he thought of the woman who had given him this opportunity.

55

WITH July came the usual hot, dry, west winds. They blew along the streets sending up clouds of dust. Day after day the thermometer stood high in the nineties. There were not many in the Southeast District who could afford to send their families to the mountains or the seaside for the summer. Most families took a two weeks' vacation when the man of the house could get away. A few sent their children to summer camps, but that, too, was beyond the average pocketbook. Dooryards and streets resounded to the shouts and cries of games and quarrels until night came and mothers blew whistles to call the children home, and silence fell. Then parents and doctors marked another day off the summer when poliomyelitis, the unidentified enemy, might stalk through the streets, claiming its quota of children.

A child with a cold, a fever, an upset stomach, was kept in bed, and the mother waited anxiously, hoping against hope that it was not polio. July ended, and still there were no cases reported in the district more serious than cramps caused by eating green apples from the trees that had once belonged to the Benninger orchard and been left standing along many of the streets. But parents and doctors did not relax their vigilance. Two months at least to go before the threat would be over! In spite of all the selfless effort of research men the cause of polio was as unknown as it was in ancient Egypt. In the tombs where the pharaohs lay some bore its marks.

Dr. Pratt was as good as a whole vigilante corps, watching her children to see that none, if she could help it, dropped below par. In her office she had printed on the wall in large letters: AN OUNCE OF PREVENTION IS WORTH A POUND OF CURE.

Beritz, coming in to discuss the case of a mother who had to have an operation, grimaced when he saw the inscription. "Going in for mottoes, Naomi?"

"I'm not leaving a stone unturned." Dr. Pratt radiated determination.

"You believe in clichés then?"

"I believe in anything that reaches my mothers. I'm not teaching English."

Beritz laughed. "You're O.K., Naomi. Allow me to say, 'You're all wool and a yard wide.'"

Naomi showed no sign that she grasped his irony. "What's the problem?" she asked.

"Mrs. Eberly needs an operation, but what's to be done with her three children? They mustn't run loose—not at a time like this."

"Can't you postpone the operation till fall when they'll be back in school?"

"No." He explained the case.

"I see." Naomi looked off into space. "I've an idea. I'll talk to one of my mothers. She's a good mother. I think I can get her to help out, take the children while Mrs. Eberly's in the hospital. After all, safety for one is safety for all."

"Naomi, Naomi, I'll never make a master of English out of you, but you're the best pediatrician I ever met."

"Thank you," said Naomi in a demure tone.

In August scattering cases of polio began to appear in the Southeast District. Two little girls, patients of Dr. Judd, were brought into the ward for acute cases at the Gunsaulus Hospital. All the doctors of the district had been informed that it was available to them, but Judd was the only one so far to make use of the privilege. Dr. Corwin reported to the Health Department the case of a teen-age girl very ill indeed. However, he took her to the hospital in the city. He told his son, who was planning to be a doctor and later carry on his father's practice, "I wouldn't take a sick cat to Towne's place."

It was Alan's turn to be on night duty at the hospital. He came in early intending to try to decide whether an all-but-hopeless arthritic was to be admitted to the Center. Glancing out of his office window, which commanded a view of the front door, he noticed a little boy sitting on the steps—waiting for someone, he supposed. But when an hour later the child was still there, Alan went out to discover who the child was and what he was up to. As he came toward him the boy edged away into the shadows. Alan, moving quickly, placed his hand on the child's shoulder. "You waiting for someone?" he asked casually.

"My mother," the boy said.

"It's after visiting hours. You must have missed her. You'd better run along home."

"No," he cried, "they've got her in there!"

Alan noted the break in the boy's voice and that he was near to hysteria. "You mean she's sick?" he asked gently.

The youngster broke down. He sobbed until hiccups took over. Alan put his arm around the narrow shoulders. Remembering his suffering when his own mother had lain sick, the door of her room barred to him, Alan determined to lessen the boy's anguish if he could. "Come along with me, old fellow. I am a doctor here. We'll find out if your mother feels well enough to see you, but I'll have to know your name. . . ."

Tom Eberly. This was Beritz's case. He'd have to get in touch with him first. Fortunately he was still in the building. Leaving Tom in the care of one of the nurses, Alan went along to Beritz's office to explain things.

"I'd hardly like to risk a high-strung child in the room just now, Towne," said Beritz. "We've had hard work keeping her from worrying about her children. But let's go and see if she's asleep. She should be with the sedative we gave her. Perhaps we could let him peek at her. Do you think that would help? We'd have to be sure he'd not burst out crying."

"I think we could make him understand."

They found Mrs. Eberly lying back on her pillows, her eyes closed. In the half-light of the fading day her startling pallor would not be noticed by the boy. "I'll wait here," said Beritz. "You get him, but make him promise to be quiet."

When he reached the lobby Alan found an older girl trying to pull Tommy out of the chair where he had placed him. She had loosened one hand from the chair arm only to have him grasp it tightly again when she tried to loosen his other hand. "You're a bad, naughty boy!" she cried.

"What's the matter?" Alan asked.

"He's got to come home. My mother can't keep running after him all the time."

"If we let you see your mother, will you go along home after that, Tommy?" asked Alan.

"If you keep your promise and really let me see her." Tommy was evidently taking no risks.

"Come along then, pardner." Alan took the boy's hand, and they went down the corridor. What a cold, clammy hand! he thought. "We can only let you look at her from the door. She's asleep. But you can see what good care we're taking of her. Can I trust you to be quiet?"

"Sure." It was the first naturally boyish reply Tommy had made.

When they came to the door Beritz put his finger on his lips. Tommy held his breath in his effort to be quiet. Alan stooped, whispering assurances. "You see how quietly she's sleeping. Will you trust us now to take good care of her?"

Tommy nodded, and then a smile broke across his face. "She looks awful pretty," he whispered.

As Alan led Tommy away the boy began to shiver. The reaction is almost too much for him, thought Alan. "You tell your mother to put him right to bed when you get home," he said to the stern little girl who stood waiting for them.

"Aw, he's only pretending," she retorted. "Come along, you!"

"Wait a minute," Alan said, noticing that Tommy was now shaking violently. "I tell you what. You run along, and I'll take Tommy home when he gets over this chill."

"I was told to bring him." Only when Alan promised to telephone her mother and explain would the girl surrender her charge.

An hour later Alan was fairly certain that Tommy was really sick. Soon after it was evident he had polio. By morning both arms and legs were paralyzed.

In a few days the ward was nearly full of polio victims. The doctors of the area now began to avail themselves of the opportunity to have their patients in the acute stage cared for so close to home. They were surprised to find how efficient the doctors on salary were. No longer able to close their eyes to the splendid record the group hospital was making, the outside doctors one by one opened their minds to this new approach to sickness. They felt less antagonism even toward Dr. Towne, who had started the hospital, especially after they found him as willing to arrange for their patients as for his own to go eventually to the Benninger Center. Alan drew on the fund set up by Gunsaulus for handicapped boys to care for three who were patients of other doctors. There were two badly crippled girls whom Alan admitted on the chance that either he or their physicians would be able to raise the money for the long slow rehabilitation.

"You've simply got to take Jeanie at the Center," Dr. Pratt told Alan.

Jeanie was a Negro child whose parents had not called in a doctor for several days after she had been taken sick. None of the group doctors had thought the child would live, but Jeanie was a fighter. And there was a fighting chance for her to get well.

"We can't let a colored child be crippled if there's any way to prevent it, can we?" said Naomi. "She'll have to earn her living when she grows up."

"We'll get the money somewhere." Alan's jaw set. "We'll just have to take care of her somehow."

"We don't have to worry about Tommy," said Dr. Pratt.

"Right. The Gunsaulus Fund will take care of him," Alan answered.

"No," said Naomi. "The family refuses to accept help. There's a rumor they're mortgaging their home."

✑ 56 ✑

Jo WAS only dimly aware how many weeks had passed since Sally came home. Her young grandson filled the void in her life left years ago by the death of her own baby son, claimed all her attention, wiped out for the time being the need to steady Sally. When she thought of it, it seemed to her that the baby held in his aimless hands the power to draw the broken family together and that Sally in her maturity was wisely allowing time for the process of healing to complete itself.

Sam had actually taken the initiative toward reconciliation and written to Merton, something that not long ago she had believed impossible. He had suggested his taking Sally and the baby home when they were equal to the trip.

Slowly Jo awoke to the realization that as time went by Sally talked less and less of what she and Tom were going to do in Arizona—in fact, less and less about Tom. A day came when Jo's vague feeling of uneasiness crystallized. A letter from Tom, which Sally had received in the morning, in the late afternoon still lay unopened on the hall table where she had dropped it when she heard her baby crying. Jo thought, Sally is becoming more mother than wife.

One evening when Sam had coaxed Sally to go to the country club with him and Jo was at home looking after the baby, the sudden thought struck her that, if Sam still wanted to, now was his chance to break up Sally's marriage. His own distrust of Tom could be a slow poison injected into Sally, in time destroying her trust in Tom's ability to give little Samuel the proper advantages. Hereafter Jo tried to rouse in Sally some concern for her husband, but to no avail. "Tom's quite able to take care of himself," Sally answered whenever her mother spoke of how lonely he must be. Finally, a little on the defensive, Sally asked, "Is it because you don't want me here any more that you talk so much about Tom needing me?"

Jo studied her daughter. "That's hardly worthy of you, Sarah. You're trying to dodge the issue. You have an obligation to your husband as well as to your child. You have no right to deprive Tom of his son, or of his wife any longer. He has been alone for several months—that's a long time."

"I'm not a child, Mother. I'm a mother as much as you are. The living conditions in that little Arizona town Father says aren't fit for a baby." Sally rose and walked out of the room.

She could almost remember the exact number of times in her life when her mother had called her Sarah. The name was connected in her mind with doing things she didn't want to do. Its use now had roused her resentment. That evening at dinner she turned to her father, saying in a tone her mother knew only too well, "Mother thinks it's time I went home."

"I think Tom needs her," said Jo, accepting the challenge. "You know, Sam, it's pretty hard to carry on a doctor's practice and do your own housework. I think Tom has been generous not to press his needs."

"I stand with Sally," Sam answered. "She should wait till the summer is over before she takes the baby back to that hole in the ground. There's no pediatrician there."

Later, when Sally had gone upstairs, Jo, though she had little hope of changing Sam's mind, made the effort.

"There's a very good reason why Sally should stay here, but I didn't want to mention it before her," said Sam. "I'm sure if he's any kind of physician Tom would recognize it. There's an epidemic of poliomyelitis in the state. Traveling with a small baby is too risky."

"Why, I hadn't heard a word about it! It hasn't been in the papers," exclaimed Jo.

"It's being kept out purposely."

"In that case," said Jo, "I think Sally should be told and make her own decision."

"We've no right to ask Sally to make the decision."

"Sally is a grown woman, Sam. We can't protect her as we did when she was little. You explain it to her. She'll stand up to it if we ask her to."

"I prefer not to take that responsibility," said Sam.

Jo spent a wakeful night. What had she done to her child? As she faced it now she had to own that when she had written Sally asking her to come home it had not been all for Sam's sake, but a good deal for her own. I couldn't have foreseen this polio epidemic, Jo told herself. But she could not throw off the burden of responsibility for bringing Sally back into the net from which she had once freed herself.

In the morning Jo went to see her friend Naomi. Dr. Pratt had looked after Sally all through her childhood, and she was a wise woman. Merely looking at the small dynamic Naomi clad in her white doctor's coat brought Jo back to a calmer mood.

"There's no use beating around the bush with you, Naomi," she began. "It's about Sally I've come. You cared for her when she was a child . . . an only child," she added.

Naomi knew many things Jo thought were known only to herself. She had guessed why Jo had not taken up her profession during the war and why she had suddenly abandoned her work at the clinic. "Sally's still here, I take it." Naomi's tone was a little dry.

"That's just it," said Jo, thankful for the lead her friend had given her.

"Sam wants her to stay for the summer. He says there's an epidemic of polio in the state. Of course we know so little of the disease—— I'm confused."

Naomi looked at her quizzically. "No, you aren't, Jo. Sam holds the trump card, doesn't he?"

"Then there *is* an epidemic?"

"No," said Naomi. "There are around thirty thousand cases throughout the country for the year. We are now beginning to call that normal. Once it would have been considered epidemic." She paused, reached out her hand, picked up a paper weight, placed it over some papers rustling in a gust of wind. "It's my advice that you write Tom to come up here. Tell him frankly why."

"But he could probably stay only a few days. He has no one to leave his practice to."

"I don't know that I have any right to tell you this, but I'm going to. The staff for the Benninger Center isn't completely filled yet. Maybe Alan could get him in there."

"You mean ask Tom to give up what he has started in Arizona?"

"Wouldn't it be his only chance with Sally?"

"You mean Sam will always have a reason—and Sally will accept it—for not taking the baby back to Arizona?" Not entirely convinced of the wisdom of Naomi's advice, Jo rose to go. "I wonder if I have the right to interfere," she mused.

"You interfered in getting Sally home, didn't you?"

"How did you know?" exclaimed Jo.

"Mrs. Towne," said Naomi with mock gravity, "I see an awful lot of mothers in the course of my practice."

A week later Alan received a telephone call from Tom. "Hello there! When did you arrive?" he asked with surprise. "The last I heard, the family was to drive Sally home. Thought you couldn't get away."

"A retired doctor took over for me, but I've got to hurry back. He can't stand the strain very long. I wonder if I could come out to see you today. I'd like to consult you about something."

Alan had an impression of Merton as a quiet, not very aggressive fellow, possibly a little lazy. He did not realize it, but his opinion was to a large degree a reflection of Sam's. Sam never said much about Merton. If he had spoken out against him Alan would have been on his guard, but Sam's occasional references to his son-in-law professionally were always reserved, always incidental. Once when the two brothers were discussing a case Sam had said, "That was when Merton was with me . . . an emergency . . . I couldn't be reached. Tom, for some reason, was slow getting there." Another time he had commented, "I never was entirely satisfied with our diagnosis of that case. I shouldn't have left so much to Merton."

When Tom Merton walked into Alan's office his first words after shaking hands were "I know you're busy, so I'll get right to the point."

"Go right ahead." The frank businesslike young man did not fit the image Alan had of him.

"I understand there's one opening at the Benninger Center. Would you consider me for it?" Tom's blue eyes were clear, and they looked directly at Alan.

"How come you're giving up practice in Arizona? The country has need of doctors with the guts to go to rural districts. You're not discouraged already, are you?" So here was the flaw in Merton! He wasn't a fighter. No wonder Sam was a bit concerned over Sally's marriage.

"No, I'm not discouraged," Merton said. "In fact I like living in the country, and I believe there's a future for country doctors. I think I could solve the problem of not getting to be a back number, though as it stands now I'm out of touch with other doctors. Of course I didn't figure it out by myself," he added modestly. "They've done it in New England, you know—city doctors high in the profession giving refresher courses to rural practitioners, with consultation on troublesome cases—a kind of chain diagnosis, I call it." Tom's eyes had lighted up as he talked.

This was no project conceived by a lazy man, thought Alan. Ah, there was the flaw again! No stability. After a few months Tom wanted to try something else. "I'd say the thing for you is to stick to your plans. You've hardly given them a fair trial yet," Alan said.

"I've a family, you know. I must think of them."

"Country's a good place for children," was Alan's laconic rejoinder.

Merton did not answer for a moment. He was engrossed in a talk he'd had with Sally the day he arrived. He'd said he'd come to take her home. He could see her now standing with their son in her arms, that irresolute expression on her face so familiar when he'd been trying to get her to marry him. "I don't know what to do," she'd said. "Father thinks it's no place for a baby. Too far from a pediatrician. I don't know, Tom, when I can come home. You see . . ."

"Yes, I see." Tom had seen with great clarity the possibility that, with him so far away, she might never be able to make up her mind to return to Arizona.

He was brought back to the present by a question from Alan. "By the way, how did you learn I might be needing another doctor here?"

"From Sally's mother," Merton answered frankly.

So that was it! Alan tipped back in his office chair, put his hands behind his head. And how did Jo know about it? Well, his imagination was good enough to work that one out. Just what did Naomi think she was doing anyway?

"I'll be frank with you," said Tom. "I've a pretty powerful adversary. I can't win from a distance of a thousand miles. Sally's father is against taking the baby to a rural community."

Why does Sam have to meddle? Alan asked himself. Why can't Sally grow up and get out from under her father's thumb? But surely it was none of his business. "Taking one of my own family onto my staff has complications, Tom," he said at last. "I don't know that the board would consider it."

I'm hedging, he thought. I, too, don't like to go against Sam. Tom should make a good member of the Center staff. He has the courage to think for himself. Already he's broken with tradition by seeing the possibilities in rural practice. That spirit combined with his training in orthopedics is what I'm looking for. Jo evidently respects Tom's abilities. She's too honest to foist on me an inefficient doctor. Sam's estimate of his old partner is colored by emotion.

"Are you willing to unlearn some of the things you've been taught about paralysis and learn some new ones?" Alan asked, testing him. "We're putting into practice at the Center some of the theories of Carothers, a neurologist. As you know, Esther was in his institution. He believes even where brain cells have been injured others can be trained to carry the message along undamaged nerves. Also he believes that inactivity often increases paralysis. Disease brings atrophy of muscles. We're working out some new ideas of our own too."

Alan was pleased to see no opposition building up in Merton. He asked questions. He was alert and eager and yet fearless when it came to differing with Alan over points he did not immediately accept. They talked for a long time.

Finally Alan summed it all up. "What you need most is an open mind and also a willingness to expend yourself. This treatment demands much of the doctor physically. And it demands patience, for you'll be dealing almost entirely with chronics. One thing more—Dr. Carver, whose assistant you'll be, is a Negro. Now, understanding all this, do you still want the job?"

"Yes," Tom answered simply.

"Come along," said Alan, rising. "I'll show you the setup. Then I'd like you to talk to Esther. She's very intelligent about what was done for her."

When Merton was leaving after seeing the Center and Esther, Alan said, "Think it over and if you find you can't wholeheartedly enter into this work where most of your patients have chronic diseases I'm sure you'll tell me so. In other words, you won't take the position just to be here with Sally."

"I promise you." Tom's eyes met Alan's steadily.

"I'm not certain I can get the appointment for you," Alan cautioned him. "It's not ideal by any means to put a relative of mine in an institution where I'm the head. The board quite naturally may decide against it. Don't take any steps to give up your present work until you hear from me."

"I don't want to hurry you," said Tom, "but my year in Arizona is up in another month."

As Alan turned back into the house Tom seemed suddenly less desirable. Sam didn't think much of him. "Esther," he said, dropping into a chair near her, "I guess I've done for myself this time. I doubt if Sam will ever forgive me if I take Tom on. He let him go for inefficiency."

"You know that wasn't the reason," Esther answered with some heat. "That was only why he thought he dismissed him. You know he let him go because he didn't want Sally to marry him. Sam wants to keep her for himself, and he wants to keep you too."

"Aren't you exaggerating a trifle, Esther?"

"I think not." She studied her husband. The demands on him were constant and heavy. He was tired. His weariness made him vulnerable to the old domination by Sam. She marveled at Sam's power to rule all his family. "As I see it, you've found the right person to work with Dr. Carver. It's a professional matter. I think you should decide it on that basis."

Alan rose, kissed her, and went out to his garden seeking out an old bench still half entangled in vines he had not had time to clear away. Pushing them aside he sat down. For the first time in his life he intended to work out what was his relationship to his brother without the confusing emotion either of gratitude or of anger. Slowly, carefully Alan felt his way behind the façade of strength with which he had always endowed Sam. Why did he want power over them all? What was this hunger in Sam that drove him to exact such allegiance from them all? Did he feel he needed to protect them? Protect himself? How could he? He had wealth, position and recognition in his chosen profession. And to him had been given more love than the ordinary man received. He was surrounded with it right now. But he did not trust those who loved him unless they thought and acted as he wished them to.

Reasons for exacting so much of his family, applicable to other men, did not seem applicable to Sam. Alan was baffled. He would have to give it up. He was too close to his brother to see him clearly. The lines of the picture blurred.

A leaf drifted down touching his hand. Here in the quiet garden he began to think back to their childhood. He remembered how Sam as a little boy had loved order, precision. Change he could not bear. He had built around himself a static world in which he pictured himself living with grace and elegance. But it was his misfortune to be born in one of the most chaotic periods of man's history.

Alan saw he must accept the fact that despite Sam's money and honored standing he felt himself threatened by a hostile world. In Sam's eyes both his wife and his beloved brother had allowed themselves to be drawn into that world. Almost he had lost Sally to it. If he did he would be alone. There lay the tragedy for Sam and for Sally.

For a long time Alan refused to let his thoughts go further. Then unwillingly he faced it. He must go against Sam to save Sally. And yet he lingered in the garden. The fall evening grew chilly. At last he rose, went into the bright kitchen where Esther was getting dinner, on into the hall. He called Gunsaulus, asked for an appointment and explained he thought he'd found the right man to work with Carver at the Center.

Tom said nothing to Sally of his interview with her uncle. He wanted first to be certain that the position was his. Neither did he say anything to Jo, largely because she evinced no interest in the outcome of the visit to Alan although she had suggested it. This puzzled Tom. He did not guess how difficult it had been for her to make the suggestion because she saw in it a conspiracy against her husband; clearly as she visioned what was happening to Sally, she found it distasteful to help her by undercutting Sam.

A week went by. Tom spent his time with his wife and baby, patiently building himself back into Sally's life, getting her to accept his role as father to their son. At the end of the week, when he had heard nothing from Alan, he grew anxious. He must get back to his practice soon. Letters from the retired doctor showed the work was telling on him. Saturday evening Tom was upstairs with Sally, watching her put little Samuel to bed, when the telephone rang. Eagerly he picked up the receiver in the upstairs hall. At the same moment Sam picked up the one downstairs. The two hellos were almost simultaneous. "Whom am I talking to—Sam or Tom?" asked Alan.

There was some irritation in Sam's voice as he answered, "Which of us do you want?"

Tom put down the receiver. He shouldn't have answered the phone. It was not his house. Then he heard his father-in-law calling from the foot of the stairs, "It's for you, Tom."

"It's in the bag," said Alan. "Can you come out and see me at my office tomorrow afternoon? Then I'd like you to go and see Gunsaulus. But he said if I felt you were the man, it was all right with him."

When Tom came back into the room, Sally put her finger on her lips as she whispered, "He's really asleep." Gently she continued rocking; he waited. At last she rose to lay the baby in his crib.

"Come out in the hall, Sally," he whispered. "I've something good to tell you." Together they tiptoed out of the room. "Sally, Alan has offered to take me on at the Center. It means you needn't ever go back to Arizona."

"Oh, Tom, you're good to me!" she exclaimed, clasping her arms around his neck. "I haven't known what to do," she murmured with her head against his shoulder. And then before he could answer she said, "Let's go and tell Mother and Father."

Hand in hand they entered the living room. "We've something good to tell you," Sally cried.

"Yes?" said Sam.

"You tell them." Sally turned to Tom.

"I'm going to give up my practice in Arizona. We don't feel it's the place for the baby." For just a moment Tom felt a pang of regret. He had wanted to work something out there. He didn't know of anyone to take his place. His patients—what would they do? What they'd done before he went there, he supposed—trust they'd be able to reach a doctor in time if they were taken seriously ill.

"Is it wise?" asked Sam. "After all, you have your living to make."

"I'm coming to that," said Tom. "I went to see Alan the other day. I found he needed help at the Center. I asked if he could use me. He thought he could. He called just now to say the board has approved my appointment."

"How fine!" cried Jo, relief in her voice.

"Fine, indeed!" gasped Sam. "First Alan, now you, highly trained surgeons both of you, going in for that kind of quackery!"

"I'm still a surgeon. I shall operate when it's necessary," Tom was stung to retort.

"How good will you be?" his father-in-law demanded. "You'll operate once to my ten."

The bewilderment so recently gone from Sally's eyes came back. Tom saw it, and so did Jo.

57

OCTOBER came. Esther and Alan had only a few days to wait before their baby would be born. Alan was filled with excitement kin to no other excitement he had ever felt. A son? A daughter? Sometimes he wanted one, sometimes the other. With all his knowledge of the functions of birth a mystery hung about the birth of his own child.

Esther seemed only partially aware of what went on around her. "It's 'most time," Beatrice said to Alan as he went into the kitchen one evening just before dinner.

"Well, not tonight surely. It's my night to be on duty at the hospital."

"Women don't look like that for nothing, Dr. Alan!"

"Like what, Beatrice?"

"Like she looks."

When Alan left, Esther sent Beatrice to bed. "I'll call you if I need you," she assured her. She tried to read, but found it impossible. She was close to the fulfillment of her deepest desire. Although most women are impatient as the time draws near to be rid of the weight and discomfort, Esther felt no such haste. Each time she shifted her position in search of a better distribution of her burden the knowledge that she was indeed heavy with child was driven into her mind, and it gave her the assurance she needed. But the years she had determined to be sterile had left their indelible impression, robbing her now of a sense of reality.

When it drew on toward midnight, the house, the street, the whole world grew very still, so still it seemed to Esther she could hear her own heart beat. The pains now came in rhythmical sequence. She went to the telephone and called Alan.

"I'll be there in a few minutes," he said. "You're not frightened, are you?"

"No," she answered; "not now that I've heard your voice."

Her panic had left her, but it returned in the delivery room. She asked for Alan, and when he came she begged him not to let them give her an anesthetic.

"But, Esther, there's no point in your suffering."

"How can I know I've really given birth to my baby if I don't suffer?" she demanded. Then Alan knew, as Beritz did, that her spirit was in more travail than her body and that for Esther unreality was cloaking reality. Quietly Dr. Beritz assured her that no general anesthetic would be given her unless she herself asked for it. "We could give you a spinal injection."

To this Esther consented. And then a strange thing happened: she let go her fear.

"It's going to be a very normal birth," Beritz said to Alan in a low tone.

Early in the morning when the child was born Alan held him up for Esther to see. "It's a boy."

"Yes, I know." There was a triumphant note in Esther's voice.

When she was asleep and her son asleep in a crib at her side—something which was against hospital regulations, but on which Dr. Beritz had insisted, fearing Esther when she wakened might again touch unreality if her baby was not near her—Alan left the room.

His first instinct was to call Sam. Then he remembered. There had been a rift between them ever since he had taken Merton on. Sam had never been bitter before over their differences, but he was now. Still he had to tell his brother. The deep underlying structure that was the family made it necessary for him to communicate to Sam the high emotion of the moment. He looked at his watch. It was ten minutes past five. He'd wait another hour. Sam was an early riser.

The minutes ticked off slowly. At six he picked up the receiver and put in his call. Three, four rings. Perhaps he'd better hang up. If he got Sam out of bed, it wouldn't be so good. Five. He was about to put down the receiver when he heard his brother's voice. "Sam, it's me!" he exclaimed. "I've got a son. He's a dandy!"

"Good enough," said Sam, surprised into cordiality. Then his soreness of heart reasserted itself; his cordiality froze into ultra politeness. "I hope everything is all right. Esther doing well?"

"Yes," said Alan.

Sam rang off.

No go. Alan turned away.

It was evening. Alan was sitting by Esther's side. The baby lay in her arms. She lifted the blanket folded around him, and together they examined the tiny male creature, their son. "He has the Towne chin," said Esther.

"But altogether he's more like you," Alan answered.

Soon Esther drifted off to sleep. The child slept, too.

Unwilling to disturb them, Alan sat there on guard, a little uneasy over the preferential treatment his family was receiving at the hospital. And then, as so often these days, his own experience seemed to him like a tuning fork putting him in harmony with the world around him. If such delicate adjustment was needed between Esther and her child, was it not needed by many mothers?

A street lamp outside threw a faint light on the ceiling. He could barely discern the figures of his wife and child, like half-carved-out sculptured figures—a woman's curved shoulder eloquently expressing protection, the less formed line of the blanket poignantly conveying the helplessness of the newborn.

Had science in its effort to guard mother and child against infection eliminated some necessary close relationship between them? Some doctors thought so. Finally he called the nurse, watched while she placed the baby in his crib.

As Alan went through the corridor, he stopped for a moment at the babies' ward to look through the glass at the rows of infants. Then he went on through the sleeping hospital. Dim lights burned in a few rooms, indicating where pain had ruled out sleep. He knew that death was near in two of the rooms. Life and death jostling each other as always in a hospital. And then an idea struck him. In the modern hospital a baby was born into the atmosphere of sickness, not health. If first impressions were, as now thought possible, indelibly written on the tiny brain—was this good?

I must talk to Beritz, he thought. Too long we've considered women who are having babies sick.

58

ALAN was preparing to leave his office early in order to take Esther and his son home before the short afternoon was over. He had reached the door when his interoffice telephone rang. Reluctantly he went back and picked up the receiver.

"There's a woman here who says she must see you, although I told her you had special business on," the girl at the reception desk explained. "She says to give you her name, and she knows you'll see her. Her name is Prentiss."

"Miss Prentiss?" he asked.

"Yes."

"Send her in." He took off his overcoat, laid it on the corner of his desk, put his hat on top of it. Miss Prentiss, Mrs. Watkins' struggle to get well, the battle almost won when they had done away with his services.

At a knock on his door he called out, "Come in."

"Good afternoon, Dr. Towne," said Miss Prentiss, as distant in her manner as on their first meeting.

"Good afternoon. Won't you sit down?" He placed a chair for her by his desk. "What can I do for you?"

"I believe my insurance with you has a half year to run. My sister needs your professional care."

Alan was taken aback. He had expected some explanation of why she and her sister had left him. Now he realized he would never receive it. He knew also that Mrs. Watkins must be in desperate need or Miss Prentiss would not be here now demanding services on a contract which had really lapsed. He remembered that glimpse he had thought he had of the two sisters over in the poorer section adjoining the Southeast District. He noticed the carefully mended finger tips of the gloves lying in Miss Prentiss' lap.

When he did not immediately answer, Miss Prentiss said in the old belligerent tone he had once known so well, "You promised a cure, did you not?"

"I think you are mistaken. I always carefully avoid the word cure. Such a term cannot be used for arthritis. I promised your sister freedom from the symptoms of the disease—arresting the disease, if you will—if she fulfilled certain conditions. One of them, you may remember, was a monthly checkup."

As he spoke these last words, a hunted look came into her eyes. "As to the insurance, I accept the obligation and will come to see your sister, if you'll give me your address," he said.

She gave it, then rose, the mask of her pride back in place. "When can she expect you?" she asked.

He looked at his desk memoranda, thinking, This will have to be extra-curricular. "Tomorrow about six, if that's convenient."

"Thank you, Dr. Towne." Miss Prentiss started to put on her gloves. Then he saw she could not control the shaking of her hands enough and gave up the attempt. Thinking he didn't like to have her leave like this, he walked with her to the door and down the hall, talking casually about the day, how beautiful it was, and then, remembering how often in the past they had talked about Esther, he told her of his son. "My sister will be so pleased!" she exclaimed. For a moment the barrier between them went down.

The number Miss Prentiss had given him was on the very edge of the depressed area, an old house, shabby but neat, the steps scrubbed, the windowpanes shining. He spoke into the speaking tube hanging by the mailboxes. Immediately he heard the click of the hall door. He went in and along the hall. There was not even a table to break its bareness.

At an open door at the back stood Miss Prentiss. As he reached her she stepped aside, and he entered a room of medium size. His quick eye took in the details—a screen was set across one corner, hiding, he had an idea, their meager kitchen equipment. A double door he suspected hid a wall bed.

Across the room an old woman was sitting, her hands resting on a cane, her back in an almost horizontal position. The bent old woman was Mrs. Watkins! He walked across the room and placed his hand over hers. Pity, then anger, surged up in him. All he had done for her had been destroyed and more, too. This was no recurrence of the form of arthritis for which he had treated her. Here was the spinal type of atrophic arthritis, sometimes called "bamboo spine," which only rarely occurred in older people. Cause unknown. Vitamin deficiency? Worry? Had she been under his care he would have detected the early symptoms. Then he could have used a cast with a good chance of arresting the disease. The chances now were that he would have to operate. There was the new drug cortisone, which might have helped earlier. It was almost prohibitive in price, and sometimes it had bad aftereffects.

"Agatha says you have a son," said Mrs. Watkins.

Her words gave him his lead. If he were to help her, neither by word nor deed must he embarrass Miss Prentiss. There must be no mention now of how seriously ill she was lest it seem to imply he should have been called in earlier. He began telling about Esther's recovery, then of his son. Then he explained how the hospital had been the result of the generosity of Mr. Gunsaulus. "You are really back of it all," he said, turning to Miss Prentiss. "You sent Mrs. Gunsaulus to me with Roger."

"You are too kind." Although Miss Prentiss' tone was not devoid of sarcasm, her cheeks flushed ever so slightly with pleasure.

The story of the Center and how it had come about held Mrs. Watkins enthralled. "What hope for chronics!" she exclaimed.

She is not licked yet, thought Alan. And when at last he felt he had established his position as friend, he said, "I judge you are having some trouble with your back. I think you'd better come into the hospital for a few days of observation."

Mrs. Watkins looked at her sister.

"Does that come under our insurance?" asked Miss Prentiss.

"Yes," he answered. "I'll send for you tomorrow afternoon," he said, looking at Mrs. Watkins. "We'll have to have X rays, you know. Perhaps we'd better keep you for a little rest if Miss Prentiss can spare you." He turned toward Miss Prentiss. He was startled by the bleak tragedy in her face.

"Of course," she answered, knowing in her heart she was accepting charity. She had taken these meager accommodations in order to conserve their meager resources. What she had saved from the sale of the house after the mortgage and her own hospital bills had been paid she had invested, using only the income from it to eke out her pension. The principal must be saved in case she should die and leave her sister alone.

Miss Prentiss had closed her eyes to the steady but slow deterioration in Mariana's health. Sometimes she had spoken sharply to her sister. "Why don't you do what Dr. Towne taught you? Why don't you stand up straight?" she'd say. Remembering Dr. Towne's instructions, she had insisted that her sister exercise, not knowing that a rigidity of the thorax was taking place which lessened the ability to ventilate the lungs sufficiently for exercise. Then had come that day, a week ago, when she had insisted her sister go for a walk. "It will do you good," she had said. "I don't know why you avoid doing so natural a thing." They had started out, Mrs. Watkins walking bent over her cane, her hips rotating outward, feet turned outward, knees flexed—the characteristic walk of people so affected, had Miss Prentiss known it. The pain was intense, but grimly Mariana walked at Agatha's side.

And then the boys, those awful boys, had come out of an alley, giggling and shouting. They had limped ahead of the two women, bent over, pretending to be riding broomsticks. "Witch!" they shouted.

Silently the two sisters had come home. Mariana had made light of it. "They didn't mean to be cruel."

Does she mean me, too? thought Agatha. Still, it was only after several days of struggle with herself that Miss Prentiss had gone to see Dr. Towne.

It was Esther's first day at home. She was sitting by the window in their bedroom. Beatrice had tidied the room against Alan's coming, snapped off the light and gone out. Listening to the faint sounds coming up from below as Beatrice moved about preparing the dinner, Esther experienced a deep sense of security.

She heard Alan at the door, heard his key turn in the lock, heard his step, but how slow it was! He must be very tired from a long, hard day. Her stay at the hospital had given her an insight into the heavy load he was carrying. As he reached the door of the bedroom she switched on the low light at her side. "Why, Alan," she exclaimed, "whatever is the matter?"

"It's Mrs. Watkins," he said in a flat, lifeless voice. "All my work has gone for nothing. She's worse than she ever was."

"Mrs. Watkins?" she said in bewilderment. Then she remembered. He had written so much about Mrs. Watkins while she was in Nevada. "Was there an accident?" she asked.

"No. Well, yes, once to her sister."

"What did happen?"

"It's a lot of things."

As bit by bit Esther learned the story, compassion welled up within her for the two sisters, both broken by adversity. Whole herself for the first time, Esther was seeing life in another dimension. "What are we going to do now?" she asked.

"Going to do now?" Suddenly his anger and sense of frustration were gone. "Go at it again, of course. This time it means an operation. Afterward she'll have to be at the Center probably for some time. But where am I going to get the money?"

"We've got to get it somewhere," said Esther, feeling it was her responsibility as well as Alan's. It was an emotion new to her. Interest she had felt in others, yes, but never before this necessity to help as if all humanity were of one piece. "We must get it. What about Mrs. Gunsaulus?"

257

"I hate to approach her. Gunsaulus has done so much," Alan answered. "And he's expressly said he's helping only handicapped boys."

"This is different," Esther insisted. "Wasn't it through Miss Prentiss that she learned about you? Isn't Roger's recovery in a way due to Miss Prentiss? If you made your appeal through Roger, I think she'd do something."

"Perhaps it'll work. I'm turning into a regular beggar. I expect she's tired of appeals. Imagine the number she must have."

"Let me ask her. I'd like to meet her. She left a number of things here in the house that indicated thoughtfulness. I should have thanked her long ago."

"It seems a little like taking advantage of her—also a little late," Alan answered.

"I doubt if she will feel that way. Besides, what else can you think of to do?" asked Esther.

"Nothing."

From the start Mrs. Gunsaulus and Esther understood each other. "We need your help," Esther had said quite frankly, and then had gone on to explain why. Once she understood the situation, Mrs. Gunsaulus assumed responsibility for Mrs. Watkins' expenses, and furthermore she found opportunities for Miss Prentiss to tutor some of her friends' children. She is full of human kindness once she forgets that she is a rich woman who might be exploited, thought Esther.

Swiftly and skillfully Alan went about the delicate operation. He took a wedge-shaped piece from Mrs. Watkins' spine. Then gently he put her crooked body straight and nailed in a plate that would hold it so. Once he would have felt that as soon as she recovered from the operation his work as surgeon was done. Now he felt he'd only begun the rehabilitation. As soon as she could be moved he took her to the Center. He wanted to teach her how to stand, how to walk, how best to distribute the weight of her body to eliminate the strain.

Mrs. Gunsaulus came often to see Mrs. Watkins, bustling with a proprietary air about the frail and still very pale woman, who met the assault with innate dignity. Alan, watching his patient so that no harm should come to her fighting spirit, saw that she understood the pathetic desire of Mrs. Gunsaulus to be needed. Roger's great improvement, for which his mother was fundamentally responsible, had taken him out of her reach. His childhood, long extended because of his sickness, was over at last, and in his efforts to grow up he brushed off the attentions she longed to shower on him. Mr. Gunsaulus, too, was outgrowing her. She was a lonely woman, and Mrs. Watkins with a smile conveyed to Alan that she understood and was not disturbed by Mrs. Gunsaulus' assumption of ownership.

But it was not so with Miss Prentiss. Her subterfuge of demanding treatment for her sister under the old contract she knew fooled no one, least of all herself. She was accepting charity. She allowed no one to break through the cold and distant demeanor under which her pride burned with a furious heat, consuming her body. She grew thin and angular and bitter of tongue. Only to the children she tutored was she kind. There was a deep and underlying understanding between them and her that seemed indestructible.

Alan, watching both sisters, asked himself if he were rehabilitating Mrs. Watkins only to destroy Miss Prentiss. Pride, the American spirit of independence so much vaunted, was undoubtedly destroying her. Miss Benninger would have called it erosion of the human being. How she herself would have hated charity if she had been forced by circumstances to accept it, as Miss Prentiss was!

‿℘ 59 ℘‿

As ALAN drove about the Southeast District he noticed more and more often "For Sale" signs on houses. It drove home to him a realization of the growing unemployment in the community. Although there was no indication yet of a national depression, a local depression had very evidently set in. A small-income district like this was never too secure, dependent as it was on how busy the near-by factories were. The unemployment in several of the larger plants, caused by a national recession, had already reacted on the Southeast District. Independent groceries, hairdressing salons and small dress shops had begun to close.

It was rumored that the private hospital was feeling the pinch. Private rooms were standing empty. It was well known among medical men that in times of depression people took chances on their health rather than incur debts they could not pay. So far the Gunsaulus Hospital had not been affected, as payments were made three months in advance. But if unemployment continued two months longer, many might not be able to pay their next installment.

No one knew better than Alan's old partner Dr. Eichel that unemployment was eating deeper into the resources of the Southeast District. He had fewer and fewer operations scheduled. There were days when he performed none. That need to operate, always a hunger within him, and the need to earn money for his growing family to keep them from bodily hunger drove him into something approaching frenzy, which was more and more directed toward Alan Towne, who, he now believed, had forced him out of the partnership at a time when they were about to make money. Alan had had the Gunsaulus Hospital up his sleeve all the time, Eichel persuaded himself. He brooded incessantly over such injustice. He looked at his wife working harder than she ought to work, looked at his children deprived of luxuries he considered their right, and cursed Alan in his heart. Five of his children were robust, hearty youngsters, but his eldest son, ten years old, had had a series of strep throats. Fearing rheumatic fever might attack the boy in the cold, damp winter ahead, he determined somehow to get the money to send Mrs. Eichel and the children south for the winter.

Eichel had about decided that he'd have to realize what he could on his insurance policy when a new patient, evidently a woman of some means, came to his office. "I have been sent by my regular physician." She named a general practitioner for whom Eichel had often performed operations. They had divided the fees, a practice some specialists considered unethical, but which others argued arose almost inevitably out of the character of the individual-practice system. After Eichel had asked a few questions he suspected that she was a woman who found escape from the realities of her life in sickness.

"My doctor thinks it's appendicitis." Her eagerness increased as she told him her symptoms.

He saw how great would be her disappointment if he told her there was nothing wrong. Why not, then, perform the operation even if he found she did not need it? It would for the time being give her the importance she craved. He found on questioning her further that her husband had a good position. It might pinch them a little to pay surgeon's fees and the hospital bill, but wasn't he, Dr. Eichel, pinched to the point where disaster might come to his eldest son? Slowly after the examination he gave his answer. "I think your physician has given the correct diagnosis."

He was a little uneasy under the honest eyes of the head nurse in the operating room, but he knew he was safe, for the ethics of the profession forbade her to speak. The operation over and his need to cut and tinker with the human machine satisfied for the moment, he was ashamed. However, when in a few days his patient, surrounded by flowers and the attention of family and friends, gave every sign of being relieved of her despondency, he took a cynical pleasure in her recovery.

Twice more he found reasons for operations on well-to-do people not touched by the depression. Then, after his family had left for the South and he was alone in his house, he began to worry over being discredited among his colleagues, although he told himself not all of them were lily-pure themselves.

On the evening of the monthly meeting of the County Medical Association he was trying to decide whether to attend. He thought he had detected in one or two of the doctors an effort to avoid him. Finally he decided that he had no reason to skulk in the corner. His record was beyond reproach. He had not lost a single patient in the years he had been in the district.

For Alan this was a very important meeting of the Association. Dr. Judd had come to him a few days before, saying, "I have a feeling this is an excellent time to get your doctors into the Association, now while the service the Gunsaulus Hospital rendered to polio victims this summer is fresh in the memory of local doctors. I'd like to make a motion to have all your doctors here taken in."

"You want my approval?" asked Alan with a smile. "You know, Judd, there's nothing that would mean quite so much to me right now as to have that happen."

"What I want to ask you," said Judd, "is not to come to the meeting. To be frank, I think I've a better chance of getting the men in if you're not there. Certain doctors will never forgive you for starting up such an institution as this."

When Eichel came into the meeting a little late Dr. Judd was giving an account of the efficiency of the group hospital as he had seen it in action in the summer. "I would like to recommend that its doctors be taken into the Association."

There was a general murmur of approval. "Will you put it in the form of a motion?" asked the chairman.

With rage and hate for Alan Towne almost choking him Eichel jumped to his feet. "Just a minute, gentlemen," he said in a commanding voice. "Do you really want to give an endorsement to doctors who have lost their initiative or will lose it? What has the profession stood for all these years? A man is kept on his toes when he has to compete; a physician on a salary is a kept man. Such an environment is conducive to making a soft and lazy doctor who finds it unnecessary to advance with the advances in the techniques of his specialty. There's a personal responsibility," Eichel ended, "which can never be passed on to a group without disaster."

Some of the doctors present had heard disquieting rumors about Eichel, but now, listening to his impassioned plea for personal responsibility, they dismissed the rumors as local gossip. They saw Eichel as a man brave enough to fight for the good of the profession. The feeling of friendliness toward the group hospital, pretty general before Eichel had spoken, gave way to a long-established prejudice against doctors engaged in group practice. The doctors in Washington, D. C., who had gone into a group plan, had been refused the use of the hospitals until the Supreme Court had decided in their favor—"restraint of trade" was the verdict. But in the eyes of the profession such a verdict did not mean such doctors were acceptable. When Eichel made the motion to table the applications, several rose to second it. There were only a few who did not vote for it.

For Eichel this defense of the profession brought a surcease of his disquieting guilt over the unnecessary operations he had performed. He had upheld the standards of the profession.

Alan had waited until after the meeting of the Medical Association to talk over with his doctors the matter of the impending reduction in their salaries advocated by the board if the enrollment at the hospital dropped any more, hoping that, rid of their anxiety over their status as doctors, the staff members would not be discouraged by the prospect of a smaller income.

After the doctors learned their application had again been tabled by the Association, Alan sensed a restiveness among them. Through Esther he learned that Mrs. Lambert had told several of the wives that her husband was beginning to feel that his reputation was being seriously damaged by the lack of recognition by the Association. When Alan asked Lambert about it, he was surprised to find that Lambert did not take the situation seriously. "After all, group hospitals are here to stay. They are generally accepted now," Lambert said. "We've just got to be patient. In time we'll be taken into the Association."

But when Alan mentioned salary cuts Lambert was disturbed. "That would be pretty hard on the men, especially those with families. Some might feel they'd have to go into private practice. A man like me without children, of course, can get along."

"I'll have to find some other way to keep us out of the red," said Alan, ending the interview. At least I don't need to be worried about Lambert, he thought, but I wish his wife would hold her tongue.

Alan saw only one way to avoid the drop in salaries. To him it was clear that now was the moment for the industrialists on the board whose factories were not hit by the national recession to take out insurance for their employees with the hospital. It would be a big step forward in employee-employer relationships, it would be partially paid for in the lessening of absenteeism due to sickness and it would give the hospital the backlog it needed just now. But as the board members had refused to take such a step before the recession, there was little hope of their doing it now. What seemed good business to Alan did not to them. With his growing knowledge of these men Alan had to face it that, although they were helping to finance an institution built on the philosophy of better health through insurance, they would consider it a fringe benefit which it was not businesslike to grant to their own men.

There was one exception. The rotund Palosky had played a little with the idea of insuring his employees. His factory produced a nationally distributed product and so had not been affected by the slump in business. Alan's only hope to save the doctors from a salary cut was Palosky. Well, he would go to see him. He called him and secured an appointment for late that afternoon at his office.

As he put down the receiver Alan had a ring from the hospital desk. "A stranger in the city is asking to see you. He says he is a representative of a business planning to locate in the community."

"Show him in," said Alan. His heart gave a leap. Business starting up again!

"I'm making a survey of this district," the man said, once he was seated by Alan's desk. He wore a blue suit with a pronounced stripe. His voice was resonant with good fellowship. "We're trying to decide whether to locate a branch of our business in this district. One of our checkups is with doctors. I've seen the others. Business has been slow with them for six months or more. I understand you are a pretty good barometer of the community. How do you stand? Any falling off? What's your prospect for the next year?"

"I am not prepared to give it to you today," said Alan, hoping that after his interview with Palosky his position would be much improved.

"But can't you give me a rough estimate of how much your enrollment has dropped off? That would give me some idea of our chances here."

"You mean," Alan demanded, "that's one of your yardsticks? If people can't afford to have a doctor, then it isn't a good place for a business?"

"Right."

"I can't answer you now." Alan stalled for time. "Could you come in tomorrow? I think by tomorrow I can give you a pretty accurate picture of what my enrollment will be for the next year."

"Righto," said the man, snapping his brief case shut. "Tomorrow at this hour."

Palosky, unlike Gunsaulus, had set no hour for the appointment. "I'll be in my office all the afternoon. You're a busy man, too," he had said. "Come along when you can." Gay, informal Palosky was not difficult to talk to. He had been a grown man when he left Europe, and he had the European's deep respect for the professions. "You are a goot man," he said simply when Alan explained his errand, "even if not a goot businessman." His eyes twinkled. "You ask me to risk a big expenditure when maybe this little depression become a big one?"

"I ask you," Alan flashed back, "as a good businessman to take a risk with a very big chance of success—for the hospital," he added. "And your men I imagine would even take a cut in wages if you have to ask it from them later—which I hope you won't have to," he added hastily, seeing the inconsistency in talking about cuts when he was working to save his doctors from just such a sacrifice.

"I'm sorry," said Palosky, rising and laying his hand in a kindly gesture on Alan's shoulder. "It's not goot business."

The next day at the appointed hour the man in the striped suit walked into Alan's office. "Ready for me?" he asked.

"As ready as I'll ever be," Alan replied. "We've had about a twenty-five-per-cent nonrenewal of our enrollment."

"You'd say about twenty per cent of your loss is due to unemployment, five to higher costs of living?" the man asked.

"Well, yes," said Alan, "but how did you figure that out?"

"It tallies with all our other findings."

"But look," Alan protested, "don't draw any mistaken conclusions from that—we are not going to fail, and the community is not going on the rocks."

"It isn't whether your hospital will fold up or not—that's not the answer. It's the buying power of the community we're after. If people can't afford to buy doctors when they're sick, it's no place to start a business."

"Your business might make it possible for them to afford doctors."

"We're not philanthropists. We're businessmen." The man stretched himself to his full height, said it proudly. "What's more," he added, "you doctors don't seem to be philanthropists either."

"We are trying to serve the community so far as we can." Alan knew he sounded stuffy, but he couldn't help it. As far as we can. And how far was that? thought Alan. When people can't pay their insurance, we let them go unattended. Solo practice or group medicine, it's just the same. If you haven't the money, you don't get the service—unless you accept charity.

"I guess none of us is in business for his health. We all have to live. Well, thanks a lot." As on the other occasion the man snapped shut his brief case and bowed himself out.

After the man had gone a call came in from Palosky. "I've been thinking things over. Those are goot men you have at the hospital. I make an offer. The board is planning to take a thousand dollars off the salary of each. I pay that for a year."

"But I thought," stammered Alan, "I thought——"

"I know what you tink. Insurance, insurance. Always you talk insurance. Not goot business. I can't afford the risk!" His voice had risen, and its resonant notes banged against Alan's ear.

"But can you afford——" He got no further.

"It is from my other pocket I take this money for the doctors. It iss my gift."

Shall I and the men on the Board ever fully understand one another? Alan wondered as he put down the phone after thanking Palosky. What was the key to personalities so different from his own? Sam understood such men, always had. They seemed shortsighted to Alan.

Although the doctors were a little embarrassed when they learned of the gift (it seemed to smack too much of charity), all agreed that, as Pichard put it, "We're not in a position to look our gift horse in the mouth." They needed the money.

It was a few days later that Alan received an anonymous letter suggesting that he look into the activities of Dr. Beritz. "I think you will find that he is making a comfortable income by taking private patients."

Alan was indignant that one of his doctors should do such a thing. He was about to send for Beritz when his better judgment took over. He picked up the letter and examined it closely. It was a woman's handwriting, he was pretty certain, and from someone who had more than surface knowledge of the hospital. An ugly suspicion came into his mind, but he put it quickly aside. To send an anonymous letter was a cowardly act. He would not doubt one of his doctors on such flimsy evidence. It would be like Beritz to take outside cases at a time like this, but not for money. He touched a match to the letter and let the ash fall into the ash receiver.

The continued exclusion of the doctors from the Medical Association, Alan discovered, acted on them in a way quite contrary to what men like Corwin and Eichel evidently had expected. They'd be darned if they'd let such a dog-in-the-manger act get them down. They'd make the hospital succeed. Then it wouldn't matter whether they were in the Association or not. This hospital just had to succeed. There was desperation in their determination, too, for if the hospital failed, they would be thrown out into solo practice without a place to operate and with the stigma of having been denied membership in one county association. They worked with a singleness of purpose to get for the hospital a reputation for the finest kind of service, hoping that they would attract people of better means from surrounding districts.

To some extent this did happen. From residents in more well-to-do districts came some applications. When Alan questioned the applicants he learned that the burden of sickness was becoming too great for them also. "Although we are insured in one of the voluntary groups," one man told him, "my bills for the year for my family of five have come to twelve hundred dollars, and we've had no major sickness. We've had a baby," he added.

Yet these scattered enrollments did not compensate for those in the district who were dropping out. As the weeks went by the enrollment grew smaller and smaller. They all knew that if something didn't happen soon the hospital was doomed.

A few of the more thoughtful began to take an interest in the research the Federal Security Administration had made preparatory to setting up a National Health Insurance. For a year prominent men in every field had studied the question of how to bring to all the American people the best in medicine. The average doctor had regarded this study as a theoretical approach to the problem. The sickness of a nation was not his concern. If he kept up with the advances in medicine, a heavy assignment in itself, and looked after the sick who sought him out, he had fulfilled his duty to the public.

Now the question had suddenly leaped to the fore. The National Medical Association openly was opposing the plan. Pressed by circumstances, the doctors at the Gunsaulus Hospital were doing some hard thinking. Maladjustments in society which brought about inadequate care of the sick also might jeopardize a doctor's livelihood. It was doing just that right now to them. Possibly the most efficient way to take care of the health of a nation was through taxation. Considerable good-natured discussion went on among the doctors. Some were for the plan, some were not.

❧ 60 ❧

What Alan and the other doctors did not grasp was that the community itself did not want the hospital to close any more than the doctors did. Even Alan did not yet fully understand that medicine was as much the concern of the layman as of the doctor, that the final answer concerning the success of group practice would eventually be decided not by the doctors but by the laymen. Possibly, too, the question of government insurance. Some of the labor people were already expressing themselves in favor of it. It would relieve the men of one of their worst anxieties—fear of sudden illness with the possibility of crippling doctor's bills.

Bill Ackerman, manager of a filling station near the hospital, was one of its most ardent supporters. It had served his family well. He noticed that business was falling off at the hospital. It worried him, and he took it upon himself to advertise the hospital at every possible opportunity. A workman from the railroad shops stopped his battered old car one morning at Bill's station. Usually the two greeted each other with highly insulting remarks meant as pleasantries. But this morning all the man in the car had to say was "Fill her up."

"What's eating you?" asked his friend. "You sore about something, Jim?"

"Why wouldn't I be?" All Jim's sense of injury came to the fore. "The railroad doctor said I'd better get a thorough checkup. I got one. What do you suppose the guy I went to told me? Says I need a vacation." Jim slumped lower in his seat.

"Well, what's wrong with that?" demanded Bill. "Haven't you got some sick leave coming to you?"

"A hundred and eleven bucks to tell a guy he needs a vacation!"

"That what the doc soaked you!"

"That's it. I asked him how did he think I could take a vacation and pay him. Well, so long."

Here was Bill's opportunity. "You got it coming to you," he said. "You talked awful big to your union against taking out insurance at the Gunsaulus Hospital. I told you you were a fool."

"Aw, shut up!" shouted Jim and drove off, mulling over in his mind the items on his bill: X rays, urine test, Wasserman tests, basal metabolism. Imagine, one hundred and eleven dollars! And Jenny wanted a baby. They'd have to put that off. What a boob he'd been, blocking the men in his union's local from taking out group insurance! He had accused them of being traitors to the union. "Just saving our bosses from doing it," he had argued. To back down wasn't exactly to his liking. But a hundred and eleven dollars to be told he needed a vacation!

However, it was the plight of another man that convinced this local of the value of group insurance. The major share of his income had been garnisheed by his creditors, most of whom were doctors. Discouraged and half sick, the man's wife had left him. He told one of the older men he'd half a notion to light out for Mexico. He would if it weren't for his three children. He couldn't desert them.

A delegation from the union, including Jim, came to see Alan. The spokesman, an older man, looked familiar to Alan, but he couldn't place him. "You looked after my boy once." Still Alan did not remember. "Hurt at the yards. Name is Mulligan. He isn't the least bit lame." Then Alan remembered the night he'd operated for Judd.

266

"What's the bottom price you can make us?" Mulligan asked. Alan made a tentative offer.

"Not good enough. We haven't the whole union behind this. It's voluntary, doesn't come out of dues."

This was the backlog Alan was looking for. He'd make every concession he could to get the union. "I'll tell you frankly," he said: "we want a big group like yours. I won't be able to offer any other union the terms I'm going to offer you. We'll be doing it to get started. Now let me figure." He picked up his pencil. "Just you men, not your families?"

"Men and families," Mulligan answered.

Alan did some estimating on costs and the probable number of major sicknesses among the men. "If my board agrees, and I hope it will," he said at last, laying down his pencil, "a dollar a month for each man, fifty cents extra for a wife, twenty-five cents for each child."

"And me paying a hundred and eleven dollars to be told to take a vacation!" mumbled Jim. "If I ain't the dumb one."

"What did you say?" asked Alan.

"Nothin'."

"But," continued Alan, repeating the "but," "it's only if you can guarantee five hundred."

"Five hundred!" the older man gasped. Now they were the ones to figure. It would have to be a very attractive offer to induce as many men as that to join. "How much do we get for our money?"

The bargaining was close now: the men trying to get all they could, Alan gambling against too many major operations, too many sudden illnesses, an epidemic, too many newborn babies. He explained that the hospital couldn't take all the risk. It was a hard-fought battle. Neither side felt able to give a quarter. "But once the agreement is made," Alan said to them, "money between us can be forgotten. You needn't worry when you come to us. We'll want you to consult us whenever there's the least need. I'll arrange a meeting of my Board immediately and telephone you," said Alan in closing. "Then see what you can do."

The members of the Board drove home their satisfaction that the men were paying out of their own pockets. "You see," they said to Alan, "if you had had your way, all this would have been done by management. If we don't give into the men, they come around."

Two weeks went by, and Alan had heard nothing from the union. Then at the end of the third week, when he had given up hope, the committee walked in. "How's this look to you," the chairman asked, laying a paper before Alan. "It totals to six hundred families as we reckon it," he said, unable to keep pride out of his voice.

Alan's relief was so great that he felt giddy for a moment.

"But," said the chairman, emphasizing the "but," "we'd like to get you to make one concession. You insisted anybody having a kid born within ten months after we signed would have to pay regular prices. We got a lot of young married folks. They don't want to wait. Take that out, and you get the six hundred. If you don't negotiations are off. They're pretty determined about it."

"I think we'd better talk that over with our obstetrician. I'll ask him to talk to you," said Alan.

Beritz' face, when he was told, was a mixture of consternation and amusement. Then he burst out laughing. "I'll take the gamble," he said. "You'll keep me up nights a lot, but have a heart, don't make it too heavy."

There was a loud guffaw from the committee, after which the agreement was signed.

And now through the hospital flowed a tide of men in overalls, men in white collars, men and women with dark skins and those with light, a cross section of the neighborhood—the gentle, the brutal, the good, the bad, the indifferent. At last the waiting room took on the look Alan had always desired it to have. The comfortable chairs he had insisted on having placed in the lobby began to show wear.

The doctors in the first weeks felt as if an avalanche were passing over them, but after the semi-idleness they had recently experienced, accompanied by the creeping fear of failure, they took the extra work in their stride. The hospital was over the hump. They were safe. They had made a good record. It had paid off. The Board of the National Medical Association on Hospitals had recently examined the hospital and put it on its approved list. As Alan saw it, there was just one thing to guard against. With the larger enrollment, of necessity they would be forced to give less personal attention. As soon as possible the staff must be increased. For the immediate present he could ease the burden by getting interns, denied to him until the hospital was approved.

Now that his concern over the hospital was less immediate, Alan could give more attention to the Center. He decided to take a step forward. No difficulty had arisen over Dr. Carver as its head. Alan meant to try something he and Esther had long had in mind—give Beatrice the opportunity which her college education warranted. He was in need of another therapist. Beatrice had all the qualities he sought. She was strong enough to give the resistance treatment which was proving so valuable to the half-paralyzed, and she had the warmth and resilience of spirit that inspired the afflicted. She could train under Dr. Carver.

He talked to her that evening. She seemed, as he put the plan up to her, to cast aside resignation he had not before realized was there. "Me!" she exclaimed. "You mean I could make something more of myself?" she asked in a kind of wonderment. In her face was the look of a freed person. Then her expression changed to one of doubt as she looked at Esther. "But I'm needed here." She knew that even yet there were times when Esther looked to her for strength.

"It's just what you offer me," Esther said, "that you can give to the patients at the Center. I can get along."

"I could help you evenings," said Beatrice.

With Beatrice and Tom the staff at the Center was now complete. Tom

268

was proving extraordinarily well fitted for work with chronics. His patience stood him in good stead. He and the more volatile Dr. Carver made a perfect team, and they liked each other.

Alan walked with his shoulders thrown back these days.

❧ 61 ❧

IT WAS a bright spring morning with the sun shining in long shafts of light through the windows of the hospital lobby. The day nurses were coming on duty. The night clerk at the desk was getting ready to leave. Alan, who had come in early to perform an operation, noticed that all the doctors were opening letters handed them by the clerk. "What do you know! After all this time!" someone exclaimed.

"What's up?" asked Alan. The man nearest him handed him his letter. "We've all been elected to the County Medical Association!" he explained.

"Pretty decent of them, as they don't stand for group medicine." Pichard's voice was high-pitched with excitement.

"Were you born yesterday, Pichard?" asked Beritz. "Haven't you figured out why we are suddenly being taken in?"

"Well, why are we?" demanded the younger man.

Beritz shrugged. "It couldn't be that they want our support in the fight against government insurance, could it?"

Lambert answered for Pichard. "You're too cynical, Beritz. Group hospitals are being accepted quite generally. Why impute any ulterior motive to the Association? I'd like to say it seems to me we should forget the past, from now on support the profession in whatever stand it takes."

"Look here," Alan put in: "I am glad, you know, that you've been given membership in the Association, but I hope it won't mean you feel you have to be rubber stamps. Every man is free in this institution to have his own opinions. If you do believe in government insurance, as some of you have been saying, you have the right to say so. If you don't you also have that right. The Federal Government doesn't claim to have the final answer, and I don't think the Association has. There's no point in their shouting that we're the best-cared-for people medically in the world. We're not. In spite of all our scientific advancement, here in the most prosperous country in the world, disease is far from being under control. The war proved that. That's not a popular idea, I know. I think it's a time when every doctor should do some pretty careful thinking. I don't claim to know the answer. When every member was asked to give to a fund to fight the government's plan, I didn't give to it. I didn't think that was the way to go at it. We can't fight a thing blindly. That's been the doctor's weakness always—fighting change blindly."

"Aren't you a little hard on the profession, Towne?" asked Lambert.

Alan didn't want this discussion to develop into a battle between him and Lambert. "I know you're trying to be a mediator here, Lambert," he said, "and I admire you for it."

But Lambert wouldn't let it go at that. "As to doctors being blind—prove it," he demanded.

"How about the way organized medicine fought for years against voluntary medical insurance of any kind?" Alan demanded. "How about what has happened to you right here in the county? How long have we been ostracized because we dared to differ?"

"Do you imply we are a union when you speak of the profession as organized medicine?" Lambert asked, not answering Alan's questions.

"In many ways, yes." Alan looked into the faces of the men grown familiar to him. They were now noncommittal. Did the mere belonging to the County Association make them want to conform?

"All I ask is that you doctors don't close your minds. I believe the doctors and the government together could work out a plan that would adequately care for the sick. Look what co-operation has done in medical research."

His plea went unanswered. The group broke up.

Alan went on to his office, disturbed over what this controversy might lead to.

∽ 62 ∼

ALL WINTER Jo, with alternating hope and fear, watched over her daughter. For weeks Sally appeared to be a well-poised, mature person able to handle her love both for her father and for her husband. After the first evening she had not been upset over Sam's continued disapproval of Tom's work at the Center. "After all, Dad, it means you can have a hand in bringing up your grandson," she told him as she placed little Samuel in his lap and sat down on the arm of his chair. She's learning that loving her father does not mean that she must surrender her will to him, thought Jo.

And then suddenly Sally seemed confused and upset if anything Tom did went contrary to her father's wishes. Often Tom came in late for dinner, delayed at the Center or caught in traffic. Sam, a stickler for routine, insisted that they enter the dining room promptly at seven whether Tom was there or not, and displayed a resigned patience when Tom later took his place, murmuring, "I'm sorry to be late." More and more often Jo noticed that her daughter was close to tears over this small annoyance to her father.

There came an evening when Tom, taking his seat, did not apologize for his lateness. Instead, turning to his father-in-law, he said, "It won't be necessary to upset your dinner hour much longer, sir. I've found a house for us."

"But, Merton," protested Sam, "don't you think you are a little hasty? You don't yet know how your present position is going to come out. After all, you're not on your own. You're working for somebody. Aren't Sally and the baby better off here for the time being? It leaves you freer, too, to make a final decision whether this is the kind of medicine you want to go in for permanently. Besides, this part of the country has a depression on its hands. Alan may not be able to swing the Center, to say nothing of the hospital."

"I thought Tom was really settled!" exclaimed Sally, her voice small and filled with fright.

"The Center isn't like the group hospital," said Tom, trying to reassure her. "A fair share of our patients are paid for by rich people or are rich people themselves."

"A rather precarious setup, isn't it?" said Sam, looking at Sally.

"We'd better think it over, Tom," pleaded Sally, "if there's any doubt."

After dinner Sam detained both Sally and Tom in the living room, telling them of some plans he had for the country house. "I'd thought of arranging one wing for you two. Of course you'd want the babe out of the city during the hot summer months. If you take the house you have in mind, it would hardly do for the summer, certainly not for a child's second summer."

Tom was too tired to bring up any very forceful arguments, Jo could see. To her great relief Sally rose, saying, "Tom, you look dreadfully tired."

"Well, I am a little," he owned.

"Is it the ride back and forth every day?" she asked, once they had reached their own room.

"I do find the ride is pretty hard after a heavy day's work. After we're settled near the Center you'll have a chance to see what I'm doing." It was good to have her as a companion again. He was convinced that once they were by themselves, as they would be in a home of their own, she would be as anxious to share in his work as she had been when they were alone together in Arizona.

"I don't know what to do," she cried. "Of course, as Father says, we must think first of the baby."

"Never mind, darling, don't let's talk about it tonight," he answered. Afterward he wished he had forced her to a decision, made the issues clear to her, made her face it that it wasn't the baby's welfare that was really at stake. It was the old problem of going against her father's wishes that she had had to face when she decided to marry him.

Tom waited for Sally to bring up the question of the house of her own accord, but when the week end passed and she did not, he quietly relinquished his option. The strained look went out of Sally's face for a little, but he realized that every time there was the slightest difference between him and her father, it came back. "You don't seem to understand I can't help being late," he told her one evening a little irritably. "We're under-staffed, and we have some particularly difficult cases just now."

"What can I do?" she cried.

"Forget it," he answered.

But she couldn't seem to forget. "I do wish you and Father could come to a better understanding. Couldn't you make some overture? After all, he's so much older."

"Aren't you a little unfair?" Tom asked. "After all, what about my giving up my wishes to have a home of our own?"

"So you really do resent it," she cried. "I've known it even if you didn't say so in so many words."

"Oh, Sally, don't let's quarrel!" he begged. "It's all right. Whatever you want is all right."

One day in early spring Sam said to Jo, "I've a scheme to draw the family together. We've all been going our own way too much of late. I really believe that Alan, as he grows older and carries more responsibilities, is maturing. His hospital has been approved, you know." Jo did know, but she didn't say so. "And I'm encouraged over Tom. Hard work seems to be mak-ing a man of him. Whatever I think of the Center—and perhaps the less said the better—Tom is working hard. I never thought he had it in him. I've been watching him. I see he comes home worn out. Undoubtedly I was too considerate of him when he was with me. I should have cracked down on him as Alan evidently has. How about inviting Alan's family to the country next Sunday? I was out there today, and it's getting pretty. Call up Esther and see if they're free. You know, I haven't seen Alan's baby yet. I've been so busy."

Was the long wait for Sam to adjust himself to Sally's husband proving the right course after all? Jo asked herself. Had she in the past been too impatient? Perhaps Sally was right in allowing Sam to win out on the house business. Perhaps Sally had been wiser than she.

"I want to draw both Alan and Tom in with me on the fight the profes-sion has ahead of it. Our family standing united against the government's interference in medical matters," Sam explained.

So he was basing all his hopes for a closer union of the family on their views coinciding! That didn't promise too well for better understanding, thought Jo. "Are you certain Alan and Tom see it as you do?" she asked, hoping to guard him against a new disappointment.

"So you're not with me," he said, bitterness creeping into his voice. The knowledge that he could never make her fully accept his way of life, knowledge held dormant in his mind ever since he had almost let her leave him—something he now dared not contemplate—rose to the surface. "I ought to know by this time I couldn't expect help from you."

"Sam, don't jump to conclusions," begged Jo. "It's not that I am against the stand you are taking. I just think it shouldn't be made a family issue."

"I don't agree with you. I'm the head of the family. It's my responsibility to see that both Alan and Tom do their duty when it comes to a threat to the profession. They must understand that we need every doctor in the country in the fight. We've got to present a solid front."

All winter Sam had been bitterly unhappy over what he considered Alan's defiance in taking Tom on. It was a threat to him as head of the family. In this emergency lay his opportunity to reinstate himself, build up his family around him in security. But he must have Jo's support. "Will you, or will you not ask Alan and Esther?" he demanded.

"Yes, I will," said Jo.

Spring was really here in a sudden miraculous burst, or so it seemed to Alan. The slush of melting snow, the winter fog, the short days which brought him home after dark were over. The burden of the sick he could now drain away into the soil. It was light enough for a half hour in his garden at the end of the day, and the ground was no longer too spongy and water-soaked to cultivate. He felt relaxed and at peace. But sometimes in the evening his mood changed. He felt a sense of uneasiness, a feeling that the fine cutting edge achieved by the co-operation of all the doctors at the hospital was blunted of late. I'm tired, he thought; I'm working too hard.

This evening Esther glanced up from her sewing and saw that Alan's book lay unopened on his lap. He had grown older-looking this winter despite the success that was beginning to come to him. There were etched lines fanning out from the corners of his eyes, and the lines around his mouth were more pronounced. His hair at the temples was turning gray. That impulsiveness which had been so marked in him when he first came to the Southeast District she found less and less noticeable in him. Perhaps that belonged to his youth. And yet she didn't want him to lose it. It was, she believed, the part of his mind that made him risk change and kept him moving forward.

He looked up, aware that she was watching him, and smiled. "Well, do I measure up to your standards?" he asked.

"You've never been fearful. I've sensed of late that you are—a little."

He did not answer at once, surprised at the seriousness of her reply. "I think I am—a little."

He had been sitting stretched out in an easy chair, his feet on the hassock in front of him. He sat forward now, put his feet on the floor, fiddled with his pipe, intent on shaking out the burned tobacco. "The climate for independent thinking isn't very favorable. We are in an epoch of fright. It's this way," he said. "Esther, we might as well face it. Anyone is suspect now who believes in social change."

"And you do?"

"Whatever you call it, we've got to find a better way to handle the expense of disease. Odd as it may seem, the more efficient we become in eliminating disease, the more our services are out of reach of the people. Take the new drugs for instance. People often don't get them, partly because many of the drugs are patented and a royalty is included in the cost—

that helps to make them expensive—partly because the drugs are scarce. Private companies are not always interested in mass production. If you could do away with patents, you'd do away with the high price. That's just one problem we doctors ought to face. Then there's government insurance, which the doctors as a whole bitterly oppose. I don't go along with them. A tax on all, as I see it, would equalize the load and would be a democratic solution."

"At Mrs. Lambert's they were arguing about it one day. Inez insisted we shouldn't oppose the stand the national organization has taken on it. What does it mean, Alan, if you do?"

Very slowly, choosing his words, he answered, "Maybe nothing. Maybe a great deal. The National Medical Association is planning to make it compulsory for every doctor to support a fund to fight the government by imposing dues on its members—if you don't pay your dues, naturally you'd be out. That would mean you could lose your staff appointments in most hospitals. It makes it practically necessary for all except the best-established doctors to go along."

"And you?" asked Esther. "You have your hospital."

"If every doctor pays his dues, it means a three-million-dollar fund used blindly to fight the government. The bitterness, suspicion engendered won't die out for years."

"So you aren't going to?"

"Do you want me to? In times like these it's not wise to stand apart from your fellows. It's happened like this in America before—times when it wasn't healthy to differ."

"There's the telephone."

Alan rose. "Probably an emergency at the hospital." He was back in a moment, eagerness in his voice. "It's Jo. Sam wants to know if we'll come to the country next Sunday, bring the baby—a family party. I'd like to go if it's all right with you."

❧ 63 ❧

THEY woke Sunday morning to a cloudy sky. By the time they sat down to breakfast the rain was pelting against the windowpanes. "Do you think we ought to take the baby out in this?" At her question Esther, seeing how disappointed Alan was at the possibility of giving up the visit, said, "You go without us. You haven't seen Sam for a long time." Esther knew that Alan regarded this invitation of Sam's as a gesture of reconciliation. He was ready to forgive his brother for his defiance in giving Tom a position.

"Perhaps it's only a shower. Perhaps it will clear," said Alan hopefully, going to the window and looking at the sky. "The clouds are breaking. There's blue sky."

He was right. By ten o'clock the sun shone down out of a clear sky, the clouds rolled back to the horizon. Esther did not voice her thought that the clouds might drift up again, and when they were in the car and on the road leading to the country, she was glad she hadn't, seeing how happy and relaxed Alan was. After all, she was overstressing her role as mother to be so apprehensive of a little weather. The picnic Jo had planned could be held in the house. She lifted the corner of the blanket and smiled down at her son, then studied her husband's profile. The lines seemed miraculously gone from around his mouth and eyes. The country always did this to him. And today there was an added reason. After many months when there had been no communication between the brothers, it was to begin again.

Alan sighed, settled back in his seat, gave himself over to the great undulating stretch of the prairie. Spring plowing had begun, and the black earth turned by the plows lay in long, straight furrows, smoothed to velvety texture by the plow blades. The fields were empty this Sunday morning, except for flocks of birds swooping down on the newly turned earth, rising and swooping again. Alan stopped the car. "It's so beautifully still," he murmured.

After a little he drove on, but slowly, taking in every detail of the scene. Little ponds so characteristic of this part of the country, filling the hollows here and there, were black agate taking into their clarity the image of the black earth beneath. The willows which edged the streams, full now after melting snow and spring rains, sent flickering shadows down on the rushing water. The trees by the roadside had delicate green buds not yet shaped to leaves. Everywhere the earth was pregnant with life.

Only once was the scene marred. Among the well-tended fields they came to a neglected one. The winter snows and the spring rains had cut gullies, some of them new and shallow, some of them old and deep.

But soon they had passed the neglected farm, and once more the rich productive earth stretched away to the horizon. A wind high above the earth blew scattering clouds, too white and billowy to mean rain, across the blue sky, sending shadows racing over the fields.

As they turned off the main thoroughfare the baby woke and cried. Esther hushed him against her shoulder. And so they came to Sam's place.

The house, the wings finished since Alan had seen it and covered with a brand-new coat of white paint, looked larger than he remembered.

"It's lovely, isn't it?" said Esther. "Why, Alan," she exclaimed, "isn't that the family sundial above the door, the one from the Massachusetts house?"

"A copy," said Alan.

Odd, thought Esther. Alan had told her Sam wanted nobody to know that part of the family history.

Guessing what she was thinking, Alan explained. "He does now. He no longer regards the incident as a disgrace. It places us among old American families. Where is everybody? Shall I honk?"

The door opened, and Sally ran down the steps to greet them. "It's so nice to have you!" she exclaimed. "Tom and I came out last night, but he was called to the Center early this morning. He had to go in, but he said he'd be back before noon. Father and Mother aren't here yet. Oh, there they are! They must have been right behind you."

"There wasn't a car in sight when we turned off the pike," said Alan, taking the baby from Esther.

"Father drives like a demon," said Sally.

"And you, my dear, drive like a snail in the country," Esther put in, laying a hand on Alan's arm. "Shall I take him?"

"I want to show him to Sam first." Alan walked over to his brother, who was just stepping out of his car. "What do you think of this young fellow?" Proudly he lifted his son up so Sam might have a good view of him.

"So this is the great Frederick Francis! He looks like the Townes, has the long face. Two boys in the family. Good! But where's my grandson?" he asked, turning to Sally, who had come up with Esther.

"Asleep, Dad."

"Where's Tom?" asked Jo.

"At the Center, Mother. He'll be back soon. I hear his car now."

"Do you like it out here, Sally?" asked Esther. "Tom tells me you're going to spend the summer here."

"It's very good for the baby, and Mother and Father come often, and Tom will be here nights—I wouldn't want to stay nights alone." No word of the lonely days escaped her. She owed it to her father to do what he considered best for his grandson, who took the place of the son she had known ever since she was a little girl that he had wanted.

A strong hearty cry came from inside the house, and Sally fled up the steps under the sundial, its shadow now on the hour of noon. Presently she came out carrying her son in her arms. The family stood at the foot of the steps, waiting.

"How big he's grown!" cried Esther.

"Plenty of good country air," said Sam, holding out his arms to his grandson, who held out his in return.

"How small Francis looks beside your youngster, Tom!" Thus Alan drew Tom in from the periphery to the center of the family.

"We have several months' edge on you, haven't we, Sally?" answered Tom, unable to conceal pride in his son.

Jo went to the kitchen to get things ready for their picnic luncheon, and soon, carrying the baskets and other paraphernalia, the family straggled along the banks of the stream. "Here's a good place," Sam, in front, called out.

"Let's go a little farther," Jo suggested. "I'm sure we'll find smoother ground."

"Have a heart," cried Tom. "This young fellow is heavy."

"Softie!" said Sally, smiling up at her husband.

Under a great willow that hung over the stream they finally came to agreement. The collapsible carriages Sam had been carrying were opened up, the babies placed in them. Tom built a fire. Jo set the coffeepot on it. The willow cast thin shadows down on them and on the stream flowing swiftly between its banks. The sound of its rushing waters made an accompaniment to their voices.

Sam looks satisfied, thought Jo with a sense of relief.

Sam, glancing around, thought, I haven't lost Alan or Sally. He felt a kind of fierce desire to protect them as his eyes traveled from his brother to his daughter and then to his grandson sitting in his carriage, and finally to Alan's son asleep in Esther's arms. I've always taken care of them, and I always shall. I'm the steady one.

The world, its anxieties, seemed far away. There was a stability in family life that seemed to give the lie to the frightening, changing postwar world. During these hours under the willow tree, with the rushing stream safely held within its embankments, everyone felt secure. Tom and Esther smiled at each other. In spite of occasional upsets we think this is a nice family we've been taken into, their eyes said to each other, but does its head think the same of us? Does he think we're nice members of the family? It didn't worry them much today.

All things promised well here in the spring with the earth just coming into its renewal and the family re-created in the two boys born to them. Even Sally was free of the conflict which so often tormented her. When she felt no guilt in relation to her father, she so often felt guilt toward Tom. And if she gave to one, she took from the other. But today father and husband sat in the same circle, the circle of the family.

Later, when the women and the babies went back to the house, the three men walked about the farm, Sam talking of what he had done to bring the land back. "Scratch the surface of a Towne," he said, "and you get a farmer. Our ancestors would never have allowed the erosion that produced a stream like this, however nice it is to camp by it when it comes to a picnic. Every year when the water is high a bit of good land breaks off and is washed away. I intend to make plantings soon of trees all along the banks—trees with a fast-growing root system. The Agricultural Department is interested in schemes like this, even helping out on them. I think they'll co-operate with me on it."

So Sam does not see the government as his enemy, at least when it comes to farming, thought Alan.

Tom knew nothing about farming, but he was content strolling behind the two brothers, chewing a blade of grass, his mind idling. He was essentially easygoing. It was standing him in good stead now. If he just played along with his father-in-law, it looked as if things would come out all right. As for Alan, he felt real admiration for Alan—admiration not unmixed with gratitude.

It was a long and beautiful day. It's ending happily. Sam isn't going to risk upsetting its tranquillity, Jo reflected.

"It's a ritual here to watch the sun go down," said Sam.

277

In deference to him they were all silent until the sun sank below the far-off horizon.

"I suppose we should be thinking of going." Alan rose reluctantly. "It's been a good day."

"Oh, not yet," said Sam. "You can't go yet. I want to talk over with you two doctors something very important. I suppose I don't need to ask where you stand on this threat to our profession."

Oh, Sam, Jo mourned, why do you do this?

"Threat?" said Alan.

"You mean you don't consider socialized medicine a dangerous doctrine?"

"But look, Sam, if you've studied the plan, you must know it's miles from that. There's no control over doctors. A man like you with plenty of patients who can afford to pay would not be affected at all unless you wanted to be," said Alan.

"I'd have to pay a tax."

"Yes, but not very much, and you'd be collecting more from patients you now operate on free of charge in the hospital clinic than you'd pay out in a health tax."

"However you put it, Alan, we'd have government on our necks. I think a doctor has the right to decide how much he'll charge for his work."

"The plan provides for procedures to be worked out by professional groups, localities and the states, together with the Federal Government. These could be the county medical associations. What's wrong with that?" Alan demanded.

"I'm in this fight up to my neck, and I want you, Alan and Tom, with me. I'm calling you to your responsibilities as doctors," Sam said, ignoring Alan's last remark.

Sally looked anxiously at Tom. If he'd only speak up right now, Father would really accept him.

"I don't know that I can go along with you the whole way, Sam, not if the game is to block the government plans by coercing all doctors."

"Game!" Sam exclaimed in a shocked voice. "Game! What do you mean, game?"

"Look here, Sam. It's this paying of dues I don't like. We've never had any before. Now suddenly when the Association is putting on a big campaign against the government plan, our dues go to support it whether we believe in it or not."

"Dues are legitimate, aren't they?" demanded Sam.

"You've always complained that the labor bosses collected dues and then gave their men no chance to say how the money should be used," Alan countered.

"And so what?" Sam stared at his brother.

Alan shrugged. "If the shoe fits, put it on."

Taken unawares by Sam's sudden demand for his and Tom's allegiance, relaxed and offguard after the harmony of the day, not suspecting that here, now, in the family, he would be called on to take a stand, Alan, unprepared to meet the challenge, spoke angrily. He was upset and thrown off balance. He could see that Tom didn't know what to do either. And then he noticed Sally. A look close to terror had come into her eyes. He didn't like that look. With an effort he got himself under control. If he could only put off the issue for a little! After all, it was a professional matter and had no place getting mixed up with family relationships.

"There's a lot to say on this subject, Sam. I don't believe we can settle it tonight. Suppose we three doctors get together for luncheon someday, Sam, and have a real go at the subject." There was a note of appeal in Alan's voice.

Sam, ignoring him, fastened his eyes on Tom. "You haven't spoken, Merton. Where do you stand?"

"I haven't thought about it much. I've been so busy. I'd like to study it a bit."

"I see." Sam's voice held a tight, cold quality. "You work for Alan. I'd forgotten that."

"Look here," exclaimed Alan, "this is a bit thick. I haven't bought Tom's brains; he has a right to think it through. Why shouldn't he hesitate? You know how short of doctors we were in the last war. You know how the country is threatened with the possibility of another war. Suppose it comes. What are we going to do this time about sufficient doctors? The Association has blocked the Medical School bill in the House of Representatives. They are the one big obstacle in the path of efforts to meet the doctor shortage with Federal aid to medical schools. You know the schools are sadly in need of money and so can't train the doctors we need. It's bad to make the public believe that things like that are steps to a socialized state. If you want to take the responsibility, go ahead. I'm not going to, and you've no right to demand it of Tom."

"You frightened me, Alan, with your alien philosophy." Sam's voice was stern and uncompromising.

"It's as indigenous as you and I," Alan flung back. "It's the same philosophy that gave us our public schools."

"Really we must be going, Alan," said Esther, rising. Relief spread through the little group. The women began talking, Jo saying how nice it was having all the family together.

"Do you need an extra blanket for the baby? These spring evenings get pretty cold." Sally's voice was tense and unnatural.

Sam had not risen, sat withdrawn unto himself, taking no part in the leave-taking. Alan was ashamed that he had let himself go. In his anger he had used his own sense of security to flail Sam. He went over to his brother, put his hand on his shoulder. "Don't take it so hard, Sam. There's no alliance between Tom and me. A difference of opinion doesn't mean anything personal. I don't know yet just what is the solution, and I don't think Tom does. Give us time."

Sam did not answer, but he rose and by so doing shook off Alan's hand. "I'd better turn on the light over the door," he said.

To Alan's relief he saw Esther standing in the hall with the baby in her arms. All he could think of now was getting away as quickly as possible. Leaning out of the car to call a casual good-by, Alan saw Sally go over to her father, put her son in his arms.

Not until Alan had turned into the lane leading to the highway did he speak. "I guess I messed things up, but I just wasn't prepared. Do you suppose Sam invited us today just to see where Tom and I stood?"

"It's Sally I'm thinking about," Esther said.

"Yes, I know. I was trying to keep Tom out of it, but I guess that would have been impossible." After a pause Alan added, "Tom's only chance to become reconciled with Sam is to accept his thinking."

"Oh, don't say that!" exclaimed Esther. "Suppose he feels he can't. What will happen to Sally?"

"I don't know," said Alan.

"She's like a soft little animal caught in a trap. She goes round and round, looking for a way out. Did you notice her eyes during the discussion?"

"At the end I did." For the rest of the way home Alan did not speak. He felt Sam had forced him to take a stronger position on the government proposal then he had intended. He saw weaknesses in the government plan. Only in cool calm discussion could a solution to so gigantic a problem be found. Tonight he and Sam had been in opposite camps with no common meeting ground. And where did that place Tom? Should he say to him, "Look here, for Sally's sake and the safety of your home, you'd better support Sam. What you do isn't going to matter very much one way or the other." But he knew that would be only the first step. Tom could never give enough to make him wholly acceptable as son-in-law. His very youth made him a menace to Sam.

✺ 64 ✺

IN THE days that followed the family picnic Sam hardly noticed Tom. There were times when Tom felt like a ghost in the house of his father-in-law. Is he ignoring me with the idea of paying me off for not taking sides with him against Alan? Tom wondered. Slower to reach conclusions than either of the two brothers, he was honestly puzzled as to what he thought. He saw arguments on both sides. Once or twice he attempted to talk his puzzlement over with Sam, for he valued his opinion, but Sam always replied, "I wouldn't want to interfere between you and your boss—meaning Alan of course."

He didn't have any better luck talking the issues over with Alan. When he'd brought up the subject Alan had said he didn't want to influence him.

"You know when I got you in here I spoke of its not being too good a plan because you are a member of the family," he said in explanation. "You'll have to stand on your own two legs."

And then Tom did have a chance to thrash the issue out with a man he both admired and trusted. Dr. Carothers stopped off on his way east to explain some interesting new techniques he had recently tried out with great success. Dr. Carver was on vacation, so for an absorbing afternoon Tom worked with Dr. Carothers. Tom realized as he never had before the originality of Dr. Carothers' thinking—no rigidity of thought here.

Before leaving Dr. Carothers went over the new approach with Tom, intent on his grasping its full significance. "Do you think you've got it?" he asked finally.

"Yes. There's one question I'd like to ask you. It's a little off the point, but I'd value your opinion."

"Go ahead."

"It's about this government insurance everyone is talking about."

"Is everyone talking about it?" Carothers asked, his slow smile spreading from his mouth to his eyes.

"Well, around here they are," Tom answered. "I'd like to know if you are in favor of it. We certainly need money if we are ever going to care for the crippled."

To Tom it seemed that it was an effort for Carothers to bring his mind back from his own special work. "I haven't thought much about it. Too many immediate problems of my own, I guess, but now that you ask me I am inclined to think I'm against it. I instinctively react against bigness—certainly in my work. The success against diseases such as we handle, where the gain from day to day is slight, depends on the personal relationship we establish with each patient. There is a limit to the number of such relationships any one person can have. Government would tend to establish big units, I imagine."

"Then you are not for government insurance?"

"Government is impersonal. I fear its effect on work like ours, possibly on all medicine." Carothers looked at his watch. "I've just time to make my plane."

Tom felt the neurologist had presented a valid argument swinging him to his father-in-law's side. Certainly the patient-doctor relationship must not be destroyed. Still he felt he must weigh the matter more fully. He came to conclusions slowly.

One evening driving home he was puzzling over the problem of a crippled boy he had been unable to rouse to any effort. Dr. Carothers' phenomenal success with his patients was, Tom believed, due to his ability so to identify himself with the discouraged that his will became theirs. A unique ability, an instant involuntary reaction to suffering. Carothers maligned himself when he said he could lose that close relationship if government assumed through taxation the support of the Institute. He actually implied that his personal interest in the patient could be changed. Nothing could change Carothers' peculiarly warm personal reaction to the crippled. Slowly thinking it through, Tom reached the conclusion that the doctor-patient relationship lay in the personality of the doctor, not in how fees for service were collected, not necessarily on the number of patients treated. Carothers handled a comparatively small number; Alan a much larger number. You had only to go among the sick in Towne's hospital to realize that each patient felt he was personally important to Alan. There was no need to fear government insurance on that score. However, he'd give the matter a little more thought before he decided.

Tom had made one decision. In the fall, when the hot weather was over, he would insist on his own home. His extremely husky son would certainly be hardy enough by then to stand the Southeast District, he thought with wry humor which he knew he must keep to himself. Such a decision, he saw, was one Sally could not make for herself. He would have to make it for them both, relieve her of the responsibility of going counter to her father's wishes. He was worried. Sally had become more child than wife.

65

IN LATE June prosperity fathered by war came back to the Southeast District. Ships leaving the western coast for Korea took much of the surplus man power with them. Soon there was a scarcity of laborers. The factories were booming. Orders were coming in as scare buying became more and more prevalent over the country—scare buying induced by scare thinking. The wide seas no longer shut America off. A chaotic world of revolutions, counterrevolutions and new weapons which left man no place to hide had been created. There developed a general desire to hit back at the inexorable processes of fate, a kind of emotional blood-letting to ease the tension and uncertainty of a world without security.

In this borderline state between North and South where the Negro was the habitual scapegoat, he was again singled out. A few Negro families had in recent years bought homes in streets bordering the district to which they had always heretofore been confined. Suddenly the old prejudices and frights of Negro penetration were being whispered about. Alan remembered his childhood in this city when there had been race riots. Times had so changed, he thought, that the Negro sick need not be penalized. He did not know what to think when Dr. Lambert asked him if it wouldn't be wise to have separate consulting hours for the Negroes and whites. "It could easily be arranged," he said.

"But that's one of the fundamental principles of the hospital," exclaimed

Alan. "From the very beginning we've taken it as a matter of course that all sick should meet on the common ground of their needs."

"I'd think it might be wise." Lambert's tone held almost a fatherly note. "You understand, don't you, Towne, I'm with you one hundred per cent, but I'm naturally more cautious than you are. Possibly that's my value to you. At a time like this it's better to cling to established ways. There seems to be a notion abroad in America just now that change of any kind is suspect. I understand that feeling."

"Your conservatism was one of the reasons I was anxious to get you," said Alan. "I am apt to charge ahead too rapidly, but surely we can't go back on a point like this. It's been won and shouldn't be given up."

"All right," said Lambert. "Of course I will abide by your decision. I only thought under the circumstances—— But forget it."

"Under the circumstances, under the circumstances"—the phrase kept coming back to Alan.

A few days later Dr. Carver at the Center asked to see Alan privately. "I think maybe I'm jeopardizing your position in being here, Dr. Towne. Under the circumstances, I wondered if I hadn't better resign."

"Are things being made that uncomfortable for you here at the Center among the patients, or is there pressure from the outside?" Alan asked.

"I don't know whether it's anything that could be avoided under the circumstances," Carver answered, evading a direct answer.

"What are these circumstances?" Alan was determined to run them down if he could. Were they inside or outside the hospital?

"It has been suggested by one or two of the staff that I am making it harder for you at a critical time," Carver somewhat reluctantly answered.

"I'll not ask you who these men are, Carver," Alan replied. "All I have to say is this: I'd be seriously handicapped if you left just now. You are unusually well qualified for this work. It would take time to find someone to fill your place. In the meantime the burden would be heavy on me and Dr. Merton."

"They say," Carver answered, "even if the patients get less care, it's better that I go."

"I don't agree with that for a moment," Alan answered.

Alan heard no more of the matter. He was beginning to think they were in the clear again until, after he had returned from the hospital one evening, Beatrice came in unannounced at the back door and called from the hall, "Dr. Towne, can I see you a minute?"

"Come on in," Alan called in return. But when there was no response he went to see why she did not come in.

"Don't put on the light, Dr. Towne, please don't!" Beatrice cried.

"What are you scared about?" asked Alan quietly.

"It's about the Center. I got a letter today telling me to get out or I'd be sorry."

"Was it signed?" asked Alan.

"No."

"What about Dr. Carver?" he asked.

"He sent you this."

As Alan took the letter she handed him and moved automatically in the direction of the electric switch Beatrice cried out again, "Don't turn it on!"

"Come back and help me out for a while," said Esther, who had joined them. "Perhaps later——"

"Could I come back?" Beatrice's voice was filled with relief. "It's all right for me to be your servant. They wouldn't bother me here."

Going back into the living room, Alan read Dr. Carver's note. "I'm sorry to leave without giving you notice," it said, "but Dr. Merton, I'm sure, will be able to handle things. I'm afraid for my family. Later perhaps. I'll write you."

Next morning Alan called the doctors together and explained the situation. "Be as careful as you can to avoid trouble. I don't see that we can join in the witch hunt and drop our Negro patients. We may lose a few white patients, but I doubt it. Certainly there'll be no attack on sick people coming to the hospital."

"There won't." Dr. Pratt spoke a little dryly. "The Negroes themselves have decided it. They've taken cover. I've had calls over the telephone from mothers for several days, but none has come to my office." A check at the desk revealed that she was right, not only in her department but in all the others.

Alan realized he was powerless. The hate would have to wear itself out. In the meantime he must find some way to attend the Negro patients at their homes. He'd take that on himself. No one except Judd would want to care for them, and Judd would welcome his help.

"Not the children," said Naomi. "Nobody's going to keep me from my duty as a pediatrician," she declared.

That night Jeanie's father came secretly to Alan's back door and begged Beatrice to ask the doctor please would he come to see his little girl. "Why don't you get Dr. Pratt?"

"She's not at the hospital tonight."

"Then get Dr. Lambert," Beatrice told him, standing like a great statue guarding the doorway, guarding Dr. Towne's few leisure moments.

"You call Dr. Towne," begged the man. "We got trouble. It's black man's trouble. You can't go back on us."

Reluctantly Beatrice took the message.

Alan could not see the man hidden in the darkness outside the door, but he could hear the frightened voice. "It's my little girl Jeanie."

Jeanie had been something of a pet at the Center while she was recovering from polio. She had put up a good fight, always going through the exacting exercises to a rhythmic song she had made up herself. Alan had seen her only today playing near the Center. "What's wrong?" he asked. "I saw her a few hours ago. She was all right then."

"Please come, it's black man's trouble," begged the man.

So Alan went with him. Jeanie's mother opened the door cautiously. "In here," she said, and let him into the bedroom where the child lay moaning.

Alan pulled back the covers, saw great welts across her back. "Who did this?" he demanded, and his voice was stern.

The father fell on his knees. "I didn't mean to. A black child has to learn to stay away from trouble. She wouldn't learn. She'd kept going back to the Center. She'd stick out her tongue at me and say everybody was her friend up there."

The mother spoke now. "Please, Doctor, he just got beside hisself. He's good to his children and me."

Gently Alan went about caring for the child. Then, sitting down beside her, holding her small black hand in his, drawing the mother and father into the group, he talked to the child. "Your daddy was trying to take care of you," he began, trying to think what he could say that would help. "Sometimes we big folks don't know how strong we are. Sometimes we hurt little things."

"I got a cat," she said, still gulping down her sobs. "She boxes her kitten's ears."

"It's like that, Jeanie. I boxed too hard." The tall black man drew nearer, leaned over Alan's shoulder. Then he added, "But you know you got to stay away from where there's trouble."

The white balls of Jeanie's eyes grew big again with fright.

Quietly Alan tried to explain prejudice, how men suffered from it when they were frightened. And men were frightened now in America. It was a disease of the spirit. It lay dormant in everyone. Gradually the other children hiding away in fear crept into the circle. Jeanie dropped off to sleep.

"You won't tell?" begged the man as Alan rose to go.

"No," said Alan. He did not even exact a promise from the man not to whip his children. He knew he would if he were frightened for their safety.

❧ 66 ❧

AT THE next meeting of the Association Dr. Corwin singled Lambert out. "I want your help," he said.

"I have been waiting for some time to have a talk with you," he went on. "I'm frank to say I've fought your hospital in the past, and, as I see it now, it was mostly due to Towne's attitude. He has never shown much desire to co-operate. For instance, he's not here this evening."

"I think there's an explanation for that," said Lambert.

But Corwin didn't allow him to say what it was. "There's his non-segregation of Negroes at the hospital that's an unnecessary affront to the community. I've heard you were against that, tried to prevent it. Your approach interests me. You seem to have an unusual capacity to accomplish a great deal without arousing antagonism."

Lambert was flattered. "I'm glad if you feel I am helping to bring a better understanding. Whatever I can do I'll be glad to do."

"What would help most just now would be to have all your doctors pay their dues. Of course the Medical Association is very generous not to insist it be done before the end of the year," said Corwin. "Perhaps some of us have been too hasty in thinking Towne doesn't intend to. Perhaps you could find out. Maybe persuade him to."

Lambert started to say why he himself was uneasy about the use to which the money was to be put. Instead he found himself saying, "I fear I can't be of help there. I've heard Towne express himself as opposed to the principle, and if he is opposed to a thing on principle, hell or high water won't make him change."

"That's been the trouble always. He doesn't know what the word co-operation means." Corwin fairly spat out his condemnation of Alan.

"Oh, I wouldn't put it that way!" Lambert hastened to answer. His loyalty was to the fore now for the man who had given him an opportunity when he sorely needed it. Lambert's real reason for coming to the hospital only Alan knew and he had never betrayed the confidence. Lambert hastened to give Corwin an elaborate explanation of Towne's stand, ending, "In fact, he's all for co-operation between government and the profession."

"If he's against the principle as you say he is, I can see now why so many of your outfit haven't paid their membership fees," said Corwin. "A man like you, if he had the chance, would probably pull them with you. It's too bad Towne is against the Association."

"He isn't," Lambert protested, but it was too late. He realized he had put ammunition into Corwin's hands. Dr. Corwin, he saw, was no longer interested in what he had to say. He had evidently found out what he wanted to know.

When Lambert reached home Inez was waiting for him, eager as always to know what had gone on at the meeting. He appreciated her interest in the profession. "It makes for companionship between husband and wife," she had often told him. "That is why I stay so energetic mentally—it's your respect for my mind." She knew to a millimeter how much flattery her husband would accept. Too large an amount put him on his guard. He was essentially an honest man, but years of association with her had made him kind to himself, overlaid his honest thinking with expediency.

Instantly alert to the obvious fact that something had gone wrong this evening, she did not bombard him with questions. Silently she ministered to him, brought him a cup of coffee, then sat down near him. When he had finished, she said quietly, "Would you like to talk out what's troubling you? It might clarify your problem."

It was the direct approach, and he welcomed it. "Frankly, I fear I've let

Towne down. It wasn't intentional." As accurately as he could, he repeated his conversation with Corwin.

"Let's see," she said when he had finished. "What I see in this is that you've uncovered a danger to the hospital. Your loyalty is first to the hospital, then to Dr. Towne. As I see it you've confused the two. If co-operating with Corwin will bring better understanding of the hospital's aims you will be performing a real service for Towne as well as for the hospital."

Lambert was not entirely convinced.

In the morning he determined to clear himself with Alan, tell him frankly of the conversation with Corwin. Long trained in the art of smoothing things over, by the time Lambert reached the hospital he thought, Why stir up more animosity? He had always known there was considerable feeling between Towne and Corwin. Better let the matter ride. Things would work out in time. There was one thing Lambert could do—take over the Negro patients. That would keep Towne from working so hard.

Later in the day he went to Alan and in his quiet way suggested that he make the calls on Negroes. Then before Alan could answer he added, "I'm older than you. I hope you won't be offended if I offer you a little advice. You've left yourself open to attack. I admire your courage, but doubt your wisdom in bucking the County Medical Society."

"What's that got to do with your taking care of our Negro patients?" asked Alan, puzzled.

"A doctor who is repudiated by the Society is extra vulnerable. As you have gone against the mores of the profession and the mores of the community by taking on a Negro doctor, why don't you drop the home calls?"

"First, let's take up the dues business. I have to the end of the year to pay," said Alan.

"Your position, I understand, is known to the County Association."

"One of our doctors must have been talking about my views then."

"You didn't ask secrecy of them, did you?"

"No, but I did——" Alan suddenly decided not to say that he did expect loyalty from them. Instead he took up the other issue, saying, "What's wrong with my attitude toward Negro doctors? Negro doctors in 1949 were invited to attend clinical sessions of the national organization. One of them was even put on a committee."

"I'm not talking about national organizations. The doctors here don't like it. It's men like you, Towne, who are proving difficult."

"You don't need to say any more," Alan broke in. "I've committed the unpardonable sin of doing my own thinking."

"Put it that way if you like." Lambert's voice was overlaid with irritation. "If you should lose hospital privileges, perhaps you'd be a little more cautious."

"I hardly think that can happen." Alan's voice was deadly calm.

"Don't be too sure," Lambert shot back.

Alan studied Lambert's face. Was he trying to help him or to undercut him? It was a good face, even kindly, but not strong. But he had no reason to doubt Lambert's loyalty. He really should be grateful to him for offering to take over the Negro patients. He was having to put in extra time at the Center since Carver left. "All right. I'll let you make the outside calls on the colored patients, but," he added, "you must give me your promise that none will be neglected."

"If you don't trust me," said Lambert, "perhaps I'd better not undertake it."

Alan could see Lambert was deeply offended. "It's not that I don't trust you," he hastened to say. "It's that you think in case of trouble we should protect ourselves. Suppose talk starts that we're sacrificing the white patients in order to care for the Negroes. Would you stop going to see them?"

"You're carrying the thing too far," Lambert replied. "I don't face such situations ahead of time."

⟳ 67 ⟳

IN GOOD faith Lambert performed his new duties. He really liked Alan, and he wanted to save him from catastrophe—a catastrophe he honestly believed Towne was bringing on himself. An ideal, as Lambert saw it, should be surrendered if there was any great opposition to it. Life was rooted in compromise. He was worried that any doctor would set himself up against the powerful National Medical Society. It was foolhardy.

Gradually, as Alan gave more and more time to the Center, he surrendered much of the executive work at the hospital to Lambert, who began to enjoy the authority. He found he was executive. He tightened up places in the organization he thought weak, enlarging, as he put it to himself, his field of usefulness. Once or twice it occurred to him that the managing of the hospital fitted his peculiar abilities as a tool fits the hand of a good workman. Ambition to hold Alan's position slowly took shape in Lambert's mind.

Inez, of tougher fiber and without illusions, smiled to herself at her husband's often reiterated expressions of loyalty to Alan Towne. She watched with satisfaction the delight he took in his authority. Now she bombarded the soft underbelly of his mind, down underneath where he did not guard it with conscious protestations of service to his chief. She told him what some of the wives had said to her, how much their husbands liked to work for him, enlarging on insignificant remarks, some made in politeness and some with design, for there were several wives who estimated with a good deal of accuracy their hostess' ambition and their belief in her ability to achieve it. Recently Esther had been absent from Mrs. Lambert's luncheons. Had Inez dared to ignore the wife of the head of the hospital? Several of the wives came to the conclusion that their husbands' interests could be best served by following Inez.

Inez recounted for her husband carefully chosen anecdotes gathered during her attendance at the various organizations to which she belonged. She told them well, for she had a flair for the dramatic. Mostly they illustrated how near to violence the Negroes and whites had come before he took over at the hospital. She made him believe that his diplomatic handling of Negro patients had saved the community from disaster.

She urged him to join Rotary. She made a point of going to church on Sunday and taking him with her whenever he was free. "We are here," she would say to the minister as he shook hands with them after the service, "to represent the hospital. Dr. Towne is so busy these days." But most of all she urged on her husband attendance at the meetings of the County Medical Association. "It's absurd that the other doctors in the community should hold aloof from us. You can do a job there for group medicine. It's an opportunity."

Finally one evening she asked as if it were a sudden idea, "Don't you think, my dear, it would be a great help to Dr. Towne if you went with him to the Board meetings? You are handling so much of the executive work."

The day for Mrs. Lambert's bimonthly luncheon had come around again. The luncheons somehow were well publicized at the hospital. Also the fact that Esther had not attended them of late. Alan knew she hadn't gone during Beatrice's absence because she had been unable to get a sitter for the baby. But why, Alan wondered, hadn't she gone since Beatrice's return?

At breakfast the morning of the luncheon Alan brought up the subject. "I suppose you're going to the Lamberts' today?"

Esther shook her head.

"Couldn't you reconsider? I thought you might be able to explain that racial feeling will die out as it always does—steady the wives a little."

"Tiny Beritz and I aren't invited," Esther answered.

"Aren't invited!" exclaimed Alan.

"I wasn't going to tell you," said Esther. "You've enough to worry you already. We haven't been invited for some time."

An ugly suspicion popped into Alan's mind. Was Lambert trying to make things difficult for him? Was he behind this exclusion of the two wives who were Jews? A number of things seemed to point to it. But certainly not. If he were, he wouldn't be so clumsy as to affront Alan openly by an insult to Esther. The temptation to be suspicious was one he must not yield to. He had yielded to it once—that time they'd tried to pin communism on him, and he had been suspicious even of Sam, his own brother. Sternly Alan took himself to task.

"It's a pretty cheap trick, Esther," he said, "but we've always known Inez was a troublemaker. I think she finds trouble dramatic. It keeps her from being bored. Just now she's trying to sow dissension among the doctors' wives, but I don't think she'll be able to make the devil's brew she'd like to.

I don't think Lambert will let her get away with it. He's loyal to the core. He's a great help to me just now."

After Alan had gone Esther kept asking herself why Alan made such a point of Dr. Lambert's loyalty. As for Inez, Esther believed she could do more harm than Alan gave her credit for.

﹏ 68 ﹏

IN THE fall talk of the threat to the American people that lay in national health insurance seemed to be growing. Patients began to display some anxiety. One man brought to Alan a pamphlet distributed by the National Medical Association which said of compulsory medical insurance:

"It proposes a new tax to support a government-regulated medical system—with doctors, dentists, druggists, nurses, hospitals—*and patients*—in lockstep under it.

"A government agency proposes to: direct doctor and patient participation; dominate every citizen's medical affairs.

"If you value your health—and if you value your liberty and if you agree that compulsory health insurance—political medicine—is bad medicine for America, write your Congressmen and Senators today."

Alan tried to explain to the man what his conception of the plan was. "I think it would take away the fear that lurks in the minds probably of most of the families in the Southeast District that a major sickness might wipe out their savings, even put them in debt for years. You belong to a group hospital, but you get only partial protection. If one of your family had to be in the hospital for several months your bills would be large. We frequently get accident cases that require long periods of hospitalization."

The man was not convinced. "But your Association implies that under the plan I'd lose my liberty. How do you know I won't? That's a greater risk, isn't it?"

"I suppose it depends on how much you feel you can trust your government," Alan replied.

"I guess I'd better play it safe and write my Senator," said the man at leaving.

Alan wondered who had given him the pamphlet. So far he had left his doctors free to decide what they would do with the material sent them by the Association. Now, Alan asked himself, was he dodging a responsibility? As the material bore the imprint of a firm of publicity agents was it not aimed at the emotions of people rather than their reason? Cool, calm discussion could not take place in such an atmosphere.

Alan had had an unusual number of operations of late and he had had no leisure to look over the pile of pamphlets, issued by the Association, which had accumulated on a table in his office. Now he felt he must take the time to go through them.

He called the telephone operator and asked her to see that he was not interrupted unless it was imperative. Then he began reading. He did not like what he read. He pondered long over one of the Association releases. On one side were listed without comment some organizations against federal health insurance. Opposite was a short list of organizations supporting the bill. It read:

"The 'Committee for the Nation's Health,' another propaganda agency organized for the purpose of sponsoring Compulsory Health Insurance.

"Sponsors of Government-controlled medicine deny it is 'socialistic,' or that it constitutes a move toward regimentation. Yet its ardent supporters include: the Communist Party; every left-wing publication and organization in America."

Alan knew many of the members of the Committee for the Nation's Health were men and women of unimpeachable reputation but the public would not, as no names were given. People would naturally be alarmed.

At the bottom of the pile he came upon a comic put out by one of the city medical societies. Wearily he glanced through several pages of pictures —a sick boy, under Compulsory Health Insurance, is trying to get treatment for a sore throat. The doctor, too busy to examine him, says, "No time to have a lengthy talk, friend. Fill out this form for home treatment."

At home the boy waits, growing sicker as the days go by. Finally a doctor rushes in saying, "Can't linger—got twenty more calls today." He leaves a prescription and dashes out.

A following picture shows an old hag knocking at the door of the boy's home. When the boy's mother opens the door the hag mumbles, "They call me Old May. Better let me see if I can't do somepin' for that sick boy of yours. Heh-heh! They put us out of business three hundred years ago. We're back now! My broomstick won't be grounded much longer! Hurray for socialized medicine."

This supposed to be the scientific voice of medicine! Suddenly Alan's anger burst forth in a flame hotter than it had been in his youth. He called in the doctors who were in the building. He gave the comic to the first one who entered. Silently it was passed from one to the other. When the last one had looked at it, Alan spoke, his voice crackling with anger. "So we go back to scaring people with superstition. Broomsticks went out in the days of my great-great-great-grandmother."

He looked around at the doctors. "I try to issue few orders to you, but I issue one now. None of this literature is to be given to any patient of the Gunsaulus Hospital. That is all."

The men filed out. Never had they seen their chief so angry.

Lambert was annoyed. The idea of getting so excited over this type of stuff! It was he who had placed the comic among Alan's papers. He had also distributed it among the other doctors. If it accomplished its purpose of keeping medicine free of government—something Inez had convinced him was necessary—what did it matter? He had lost face with the other doctors by Alan's outburst.

69

CORWIN longed to rid the District of the doctor who had been a menace to him almost since the day of his arrival. The group hospital was a constant danger to him and the other doctors who were in private practice. But need it be, under proper direction? The more he thought about it, the more he believed that under Lambert its rates could be raised. Something must be done to get Towne. Towne's disloyalty to his own profession, shown in many ways and in particular by his failure to pay dues to the Association, damning among the doctors, had not hurt his popularity in the District, even though Corwin had spread the news around when he could.

And then in his hand was placed a real weapon against the man he hated. The Lamberts and the Corwins had become good friends. The four were playing bridge one evening when Lambert was called to the phone. Inez said idly, "Too bad Dr. Carver had to leave so suddenly. It certainly makes it harder for Herby now that Dr. Towne has to spend so much time at the Center. Of course it was unwise to take a Negro doctor."

"Carver a Negro?" exclaimed Corwin, genuinely shocked. He was from the deep South and a Negro doctor caring for white patients was a terrible thing to him.

"Oh, didn't you know?" said Inez. "Please don't say anything before Herby. I thought of course you knew."

Lambert came back into the room. "I overheard what you said. It worries me that Towne does such things."

After the Corwins had gone, Lambert poured out the story of Alan's outburst before the doctors and the embarrassment it had caused him. Inez saw that her husband from now on would be a perfect instrument in her hands.

Early the next morning Corwin called one after another of the people who had been leaders in the drive to push the Negroes back into their district. "To think that Dr. Towne would be guilty of putting a Negro over white patients. I understand he actually operated on some of them."

No man weakened by anxiety is immune to the virus of panic. Hate and suspicion lurk in the bloodstream of the spirit awaiting a moment when an individual or community can no longer bear anxiety. Then panic takes over. That moment had come to the Southeast District. War, high prices, a threat to their sick—it was too much. Many in the community had suspected that Dr. Carver had some Negro blood but until now had let it pass.

It was Inez Lambert who had quietly engineered the sending of the letter which had brought about his flight. Now she and Dr. Corwin fanned the flames of hatred. Dr. Carver was out of the people's reach, but Dr. Towne was an acceptable scapegoat.

Why, it was he, of course, who had destroyed the well-established lines between Negro and white and almost brought the community to violence last summer. Such experiments in the care of the sick as Dr. Towne had started at his hospital smacked of alien philosophies. They were dangerous!

Evening after evening Beatrice came in, as Alan and Esther were at dinner, with the same message. "Doctor, there's a man at the telephone who wants to speak to you. I told him you were at dinner. He says he has to speak to you."

Alan, true to his training as a doctor, would answer the call. Esther and Beatrice would keep very still listening, night after night hearing Alan say, "This is a cowardly attack you are making. Come out into the open and tell your name."

"It's as I thought, it's just some fanatic," was his customary remark when he came back to the table. "The moment I asked for his name, the man hung up. Let's get on with dinner."

Finally Alan went to the telephone office, asked for a private number. Anyone needing him professionally could reach him through the hospital. Friends were given his private number. Still an occasional threat came through and nothing could stop the letters which arrived day after day. Almost every evening the doorbell was rung several times. When Beatrice opened the door no one was there but always a letter lay on the porch. To stop this nuisance Alan oiled the old lock on the gate in the high iron fence which surrounded the house and garden. At dusk every evening the gate was locked.

The trite accusations of nigger-lover, Communist, so general, so often hurled at Alan, glanced off the armor he had gradually developed during the years he had worked in the Southeast District. He clung to his belief that the attack on him was simply a manifestation of the tension in the community. He was a doctor who had always tried to consider the mind as well as the body. He knew what fear could do to people. The Southeast District was afraid. They were afraid of their own shadows. Humanitarian ideas once believed in were now looked upon as subversive.

Esther and Beatrice drew close together these days. Beatrice went out very little. She followed her race's instinct to take cover at such a time. And Esther, knowing she belonged in part to a minority group often made the scapegoat, had her own reasons for withdrawal, an instinct as deeply imbedded in her as it was in Beatrice.

Alan realized the strain Esther was under but felt powerless to do anything about it, other than to reassure her. "If we can only stand these attacks a little longer, I'm sure it will come out all right," he would say to her. "Our patients still believe in what we are doing, the Board has made no sign of disapproval, and the doctors at both the hospital and Center are with us, I'm sure. Several of them have made a point of saying so. Nothing can really happen so long as there is that kind of loyalty, so long as we stand together. And attacks like this do in time wear themselves out."

Of one thing Alan was certain: There would be no use ever attempting to bring Carver back. Until now Tom had been acting head at the Center. Alan had not asked the Board to appoint him head because of the relationship between them. Now he came to the conclusion that it was unfair to deny Tom the position he had well earned. He was relieved when he did present the matter to the Board to find they did not consider the personal relationship between Tom and him an insurmountable difficulty. Unanimously they voted to appoint him.

After the meeting Alan went directly to the Center to tell Tom what he would be formally told later in a letter. He found him in his office finishing up some last details before going home.

"I came in to speak to the new head of the Center," he said.

Tom looked puzzled.

"Wake up, Tom. You're it." Nothing had happened all fall, thought Alan, so nice as the light that came into Tom's face. He hadn't realized it would mean quite so much to Merton. He knew it was not only the recognition that had brought that light to Tom's eyes. It solved a personal problem growing more urgent as the weeks went by—the problem of a home of his own. So far Tom had not been able to get Sally to consent to leave her father's house. Now the decision would be taken from her. If Tom was to take the position, he would have to move to the Benninger place.

"It'll help me an awful lot to have you here on the grounds," Alan went on. "I'm too busy as it is. I'd like you to move as soon as you can arrange it."

"You don't know what it's going to mean to me." Tom had found his voice. "I can't thank you enough, Alan, for everything."

Suddenly the expression of happiness in Tom's face changed to one of doubt. "Look here," he said. "I don't know that you'll want me after all."

"Don't be foolish," said Alan.

"It's like this," said Tom. "It's taken me a long time to make up my mind but I have come to the decision that I am not for government insurance. Now do you still want me in this position?"

"Yes," said Alan a little wearily. Why did this problem always have to crop up? Didn't Tom understand that he, Alan, was not prejudiced against those who did not agree with him? It seemed impossible these days not to be regarded as either violently for or violently against the government. "Your beliefs are your own," he said. "However, I'd be interested in your reasons for the conclusions you have come to."

"Well, first I think we are too big a nation to make it work. I know it does in a country like Sweden, but Sweden is small. Also I'm fearful that the people may hand over too many of our prerogatives to the government."

The two talked for a long time, each presenting his arguments. It was a stimulating conversation in which each profited by the outlook of the other. This was the give and take Alan had so longed for. He saw that this man who was so different from him in temperament and in point of view might be the honest and understanding friend he had lost when Gertz left.

"It's all right, Tom," he said, rising. "I still want you."

"I'd like to say," said Tom, "that all the doctors under you believe in you—and I honor you," he added a little shyly.

⋘ 70 ⋙

CHRISTMAS week was a brief interlude of peace. There was a lessening of tension, an upsurge of good will in the community which crowded out resentments. Alan, whose faith in his fellows was not easily shaken, found it not too difficult to believe that the people's good sense had come to the rescue. His mind rushed ahead again, planning how to enlarge the usefulness of the hospital.

As he came home after dark from the hospital or Center he saw on the lawns and in the windows lighted Christmas trees. Under many of them figures of the Wise Men were grouped around the Child in the manger. No one gave thought in their joy to the bold words that same Christ Child had later uttered which had brought him to crucifixion. Not until spring need they think of the Cross.

Alan and Esther were planning their son's first tree. One thing marred their happiness. There was to be no family party this year. Jo had come out bringing an armful of brightly wrapped packages, gifts from herself and from Sam. She tried in every way to make it seem natural that the two families should not join in the ancient festival. It was then that Alan knew for a surety that Sam had not forgiven him for holding views so different from his.

How complex, he thought in wonder, is the web of the family which is woven so tightly about its members! What were the strands of heredity and family association that bound Sam? Had the same strands woven around Alan made in some mysterious way for freedom? Was the independence of his grandfather which seemed to strengthen him destroying Sam? How could a man know whether breaking away from conformity would prove to be too hard on his family—too much a burden for some of them to bear? How would the present attack of the community on him react on his own son? Whatever Alan did would not necessarily guarantee a good life for Francis. In part that good life lay buried in the intricate filaments of the family and, he reflected, in the infinitely more intricate web of the nation.

Two days before Christmas they received a wire from Nathan Gertz, stating that he and Brenda were planning to leave for California and would stop off for Christmas Eve if it was convenient for the Townes.

With delight Esther went about preparing the house for their coming. In memory going back to Brenda's last days in Athenia she found more and more present in her mind the image of Brenda that day of cold, falling rain when they had stood outside the Shelter and Brenda had gazed on her dying child—a broken, distraught Brenda. Would her loss in all its poignancy be brought back to her when she entered this house so closely associated in her mind with her son? Would the memory of him be made unbearably vivid when Brenda saw Esther's son? Esther's and Brenda's positions were reversed now. When they had been together in this house, Esther had mourned the son she thought she would never have; Brenda had rejoiced in her lovely laughing boy. Now Esther rejoiced, and Brenda . . .

Alan went to the airport to meet them. Esther waited at home. She was sitting on the rug before the open fire playing with Francis when she heard Alan's car. Some impulse led her to snatch up her son and take him to Beatrice. "Keep him for a little," she said. Then she went into the hall to greet her guests.

The front door opened. And Brenda crossed its threshold. The men stood back, the two women faced each other. They looked into each other's eyes, each asking the question of the other, "How is it with you?" Each had known despair and the frightening loneliness of the human heart. Each now knew the other had won the lonely struggle to get back into the world of human love.

"How beautiful you are!" exclaimed Esther, seeing the tall splendid woman standing before her—vibrantly alive and, yes, heavy with child.

"And you are, too"—meaning how beautiful in spirit also—said Brenda, a slight catch in her voice as she surveyed the new Esther she had never known before, an Esther without fear.

Then the greeting became general and the four, happy to be together again, moved on into the living room, talking almost at random it seemed in an effort to express the long train of experiences that lay between them and their last meeting. Brenda was to sing in grand opera later in the season. They were on the way to California to stay until their baby was born. Nathan was taking a well-earned vacation.

Alan was struck with how completely Esther stepped out of herself into the lives of her friends. Seeing her against this background he realized how far she had traveled. He need not worry about her even if the attacks on them began again. She was strong in her own right.

Finally Alan said, "Nathan, if you're to see the hospital before dinner we'd better be getting along."

When they were gone Brenda said, "Esther, I can't wait longer to see your son."

With his old friend at his side Alan entered the hospital with its lobby decked with Christmas greens. Then Alan took him about and introduced him to the doctors who were still in the building although the introduction was hardly necessary for together they had chosen these men. Nurses passing down the corridors were stopped to meet a man they had often heard talked about.

All the time Alan watched the sensitive face of his friend. In it could be registered what he thought of the outward manifestation of the dream they had together given its first tangible expression.

"You've done it," at last quite simply Nathan said and Alan was satisfied.

Then Alan hurried Nathan away in order that he might catch a glimpse of the Center before dinner.

As they left the building where the patients were finishing the last preparations for tomorrow's Christmas party and drove down the wintry road between the cottonwoods, Nathan asked, "This is all accepted now? There is no further opposition to what you are doing?" He was probing the cause of the anxiety he had sensed in Alan ever since he had arrived.

And Alan, realizing how much he had missed his friend, gratefully accepted the opportunity rarely given a man to unburden his soul, told of the antagonism to him that had grown up of late and of his own deeper puzzlement over the defensive position he was being forced into on the matter of government insurance. "You're either for or against it around here," he ended. "A gulf lies between the two ways of thinking and I have no bridge to cross it." Alan did not mention Sam but Nathan remembering the differences of opinion between them in the past guessed that Alan was talking of the gulf that had come between the brothers.

"You're not alone," Nathan said. "There are plenty of doctors who know that the tremendous task of care for the sick must eventually interlock all the separate units working to that end. It's too haphazard at present. In time the government's part will be recognized. In a big city like New York I have a chance to meet many doctors. A lot of them don't like the lobbying the Medical Association is carrying on. You're not the only one that's troubled about whether to pay the dues. These men are experimenting to see how best to make their voices heard. Some are paying the dues but under protest, and some are risking not paying. A revolution is going on in medicine as in everything else these days. Some good men, I fear, will be sacrificed in the struggle, but in the end sanity will win out."

Neither Nathan nor Alan declared how they would assert their right in a democratic country to speak out freely, but each knew in his heart what the other would do.

When they reached the house Alan parked the car in the garage, then shoulder to shoulder the two friends walked the short distance to the door and quietly entered. At the far end of the living room they saw their wives standing before the fireplace. Esther was talking in animated fashion to Brenda, who was holding Francis. Above them the pictured face of Esther's mother smiled down on them. All were framed between the heirloom candlesticks now holding red Christmas candles, their flames pointing upward.

⮑ 71 ⮐

IN JANUARY the Board met at the hospital—Lambert had suggested it at the last meeting. "It would give you a chance to see our work more intimately," he had said. Alan was pleased with the idea.

Later Lambert asked Towne if he didn't think it would be a good scheme to have a get-together after the meeting. "It would give the other doctors a chance to know the Board members personally. Have the wives serve refreshments. Inez isn't busy and will be glad to take the burden off Mrs. Towne."

Alan wasn't certain he liked this second suggestion. He felt it would be better if the Board spent what time there was after the meeting in going over the hospital.

However, he didn't like to discourage Lambert. So he gave his consent.

Through her husband Inez had acquainted herself with the characteristics of the various members of the Board. She was reasonably certain that Mr. Chesterton could be influenced to consider a more conservative head of the hospital than it now had. Gursaulus she had brushed off as unimportant to her purposes—a good fellow who was completely taken in by Towne.

At the informal gathering she watched for her opportunity to maneuver Mr. Chesterton out of the general group. In the course of her conversation with him she managed to hint that living so far from the Southeast District he could not know of the tumult stirred up over many of Dr. Towne's unconventional ideas and how the staff, having a deep affection for Dr. Towne, tried to protect him from his own warmhearted acts. Dr. Lambert was especially alert to guard the man placed over him.

January, February, March, gray months of fog and rain, depleted both body and spirit of vigor, laying the members of the Southeast District open to growing anxiety. The outburst of spending at Christmas was followed by financial worry. High prices and general prosperity did not compensate for inflation which increased week by week. Fathers found themselves going into debt; mothers found themselves unable to give their children the meat and milk they needed. Some of the mothers scrimped on their own food in order to augment that of their children. Such denials lowered the women's vitality and left them doubly vulnerable to anxiety. Some of the older women were facing the first grief come upon the announcement of their sons' deaths in Korea. Over everyone lay the fear engendered by newspapers and radio telling them of traitors within the government. Accumulating, too, in the minds of patients of Corwin and those of some of the other doctors was the threat to their liberty in plans the government was making in regard to their health.

Early in January Dr. Corwin suggested to his wife that she, through the Parent-Teacher Association, should rouse the mothers to a realization of what compulsory health insurance would mean to their children and that Dr. Towne was implicated in the scheme.

Antagonism again began to center around Alan. The trumped-up story by Martha Green that he had associated with Communists in India and had been discharged from the Army on that account was again being passed from mouth to mouth. Some of the Townes' friends dropped them. Acquaintances whom they met on the street turned away without speaking. Letters were hurled over their fence, telling them they'd better get out of town.

Under the continual, unrelenting attacks Alan learned to be on the alert, guarding himself and the hospital, watching that there was no vulnerable spot where attack would be fatal—some slip in the hospital that could be interpreted as malpractice or neglect, some patient who felt aggrieved or neglected.

But none of these things happened. The patients showed no signs of discontent. Now and then encouragement came to Alan which strengthened the will to endure. People went out of their way to show their faith in him. The manager of the filling station near the hospital greeted Alan, each time he stopped for gas, with warm friendliness and tales of patients at the hospital who had expressed to him their enthusiasm for the service given them. Alan suspected occasionally the tales were greatly exaggerated, but he went away with a warm feeling that he had the man's support.

The owner of the small grocery store where Alan often stopped on his way to purchase something Esther needed was outspoken in his approval for Alan's stand on government insurance. "Stick to it, Doc," he said. "I'm all for a compulsory health tax. People bellyache about paying this small sum to protect them against a big bill. But I don't. How many times a year am I asked to give to this fund, to that fund? I bet if there's been one there's been a dozen pretty girls coming around to get me to give money for the children's hospital in the city, polio victims, the chronics, and so on and so on. You did it yourself on that drive for the Benninger Center." Alan smiled and acknowledged they had pressed the community pretty hard for donations.

"It's a kind of blackmail," the man went on. "The sweet girls make it plain if I don't give I'll be looked upon as a tightwad—you know what good will means. I'm a small independent. I can't afford to give to all the drives, but I'd have to close up shop if I didn't."

And then there was the support of the doctors at the hospital. Alan asked all the doctors to his house one evening. From the very start everyone seemed at ease. It was a stag affair, for Naomi had refused his invitation. "I don't drink beer," she said. "Let me take over the hospital that evening. You'll need someone." Just as she was leaving she added with mock humility, "The minorities should be retiring, don't you think?"

"Come on out in the kitchen," called Alan as the doctors began gathering. As he looked around at them he had a sense of pride. He knew the work of each man. It was good.

The kitchen was unfashionably large, but ultramodern in equipment, the only reminder of the Gunsaulus occupancy. It held an extra frigidaire, two large white enamel tables, and the deep freeze which Mrs. Gunsaulus had insisted on leaving. It was a comfortable place for a group of men to gather.

Lambert, the first to arrive, exclaimed, "Good business place; nothing we can hurt here. Set your glass anywhere you want to." He settled down comfortably at one of the tables.

Tom followed Alan when he went into the dining room for some more glasses, asked if he could bring Sally to visit them for a few days. "I thought maybe if she were out here we could get her to see how nice it would be at the Benninger house. She's got some idea a small child shouldn't be near so many cripples."

"Why, sure, as far as I'm concerned," Alan told him. "Esther's upstairs. Better go up and talk it over with her. I hope you can arrange something pretty soon," Alan added.

Except for the problem Tom had introduced, it was a carefree evening. The men "let down their hair" as Talbert, the internal-medicine man, put it. It was good shop talk and they enjoyed it.

But as Alan stood at the door watching the last of the doctors go down the walk to their cars, he remembered things that had been said. Should I have been more cautious? he suddenly found he was asking himself. He had spoken freely, feeling safe among them. He would protect any man on his staff who spoke out freely. Certainly they'd do the same for him.

With the first warm days of spring Alan experienced the apathy which everyone who has ever been under attack at some time experiences. The spirit was demanding a respite in order to recharge its batteries.

In this mood Alan one morning came upon a group of the doctors in the cubicle at the end of the first-floor hall which they used to lounge in. "Of all the crazy tales this is the limit!" Pichard was saying. "When you think we've all given up making big incomes to be accused of a thing like this."

"I'm glad you think we could make fortunes. It's gratifying," Beritz, his face deadpan, answered. "But it's not your skin they're after."

"Oh, well, let that go," Pichard flung back. "It's a nasty story however you look at it, and it will affect us all in the end."

"What's the story?" The men were startled. Nobody had seen Towne enter the room.

Pichard swung round, evidently embarrassed. "All the time we call ourselves a nonprofit institution we are giving inferior medical care in order to stack away the money for ourselves."

"Who's stacking away the money?" asked Alan.

"Oh, I don't know, maybe all of us."

"I don't suppose you have any idea where the tale started," said Alan, ignoring the evasive answer Pichard had given. There was no doubt in Alan's mind that he was the one accused. There had been a number of unavoidable deaths at the hospital recently. They could have been used to start stories that something had been missing in the treatment provided. Without a word he turned and left the room.

Pichard, catching a glimpse of his face as he left, exclaimed, "Do you suppose the guy is going to lose his nerve, now? The crackup will be a beaut if it comes! He doesn't do things by halves."

Little things which had happened came back to Alan. Were they all against him? Did the men who worked with him believe that he had misused the funds of the hospital?

He left the hospital early. The school children were shouting with glee as they raced down the streets, school over for the day. White handbills flapped from their hands. As he stopped his car at a red light, a woman pulled up alongside him and called out, "Dr. Towne, I've something for you." She reached across, handing him a bill which seemed to be the same as those the children were carrying. "It's a message for you from the mothers of the community." When he reached his own gate he stopped his car and picked up the leaflet. It read:

"Mothers, keep government out of your children's lives if you want them to be free and to receive good medical care. Those who advocate anything else are your enemies. They are traitors to the great American principles. They are dishonest. They are all under the influence of other countries."

He did not take advantage of the lengthened spring day to work in his garden. He went into the living room and sat down in a chair, his long legs twisted around its legs, his knees almost under his chin, staring straight ahead. Even today, after he had learned about the accusation of his misuse of funds he had believed the people trusted him. He had watched the men, women and children going in and out of the hospital as usual, and he had put his trust in them. But this leaflet had shattered his hope of support from the Southeast District. Now to him had come that frightening loneliness when a man feels communication with those around him has been broken, cries out and there is no one to hear.

So Esther found him. "Why are you sitting here?" she was about to exclaim. "Why not in your own comfortable chair if you're so tired?" Instead she went over, put her hand under his chin, made him look directly into her eyes. She saw his eyes held a bleak expression she had never seen in them before. "Can you tell me?" she asked gently. He shook his head.

Despite Alan's efforts to appear unchanged, the doctors at the hospital were aware of the difference in him. Is the chief going to break under the pressure? they began asking themselves. Most of them, although Alan didn't know it, had not yielded to Lambert's very logical arguments that they fall in line with the policy of the national organization. "We are the ones to stand on principle. We can afford it. We are not going to lose our positions." These had been Alan's sustaining words. But now the doctors began to wonder. Perhaps Towne wasn't so strong as he seemed. Maybe their wives were right. Inez Lambert had hinted to her coterie at such a possibility. Too, Towne didn't look well these days.

It was the moment Inez had instinctively waited for. Surely no man could endure indefinitely. He would break. She persuaded her husband that he, the man next to Dr. Towne in responsibility, should advise the Board of how serious the situation was becoming. Finally she induced him to call Mr. Chesterton.

Beritz, of the arrogant manner and the hurt eyes, was rudely shaken. He had come here disillusioned and bitter to find his faith slowly rebuilt. He had come to trust this man so undaunted by attack, so creative in his work. He was willing to follow him wherever he led. Was that man breaking? He had had enough to break him—overwork and worry. Beritz determined to do something about it. Not the kind to resort to roundabout approach, he went directly to Alan. "You ought to take a vacation, Towne. Let Lambert carry the burden for a while. We'll all help him."

Alan was sitting at his desk. Beritz was standing. "Thanks," said Alan, not looking up. Beritz waited, at last went out.

Alan was thinking, Even Beritz, whom I have relied on, wants to shelve me.

So did suspicion spread. The structure of faith built so painstakingly began to crumble. Stone by stone, it threatened to fall away. Independence of thought, respect for opinions other than one's own, the open mind—sifting, discarding, standing firm in the face of opposition—began to seem dangerous. Expediency was a better principle.

Naomi Pratt, like Beritz, believed in Alan. He had put up a splendid fight, and she did not intend to have him lose it now. "Here's for it," she said to herself and sauntered into Alan's office. Seating herself on the wide window sill, she began, "It's been quite a winter, hasn't it?"

"Yes," said Alan, swinging his chair around so that he faced her. "Quite a winter," he echoed.

"I'm tired," she told him.

"You don't show it," he answered, noticing her well-groomed appearance.

"You look as if you were just off to a party. All you need to do is take off your doctor's coat."

"It's what you should be doing," she retorted.

"So you, too, want me to take a vacation. Why are you all so anxious to get rid of me?" he demanded.

"Cynicism doesn't suit you, Dr. Towne," she answered calmly, swinging one well-shod foot and looking away from him out of the window.

"Just why should I be denied it?" he asked.

"I say again it does not fit you," she retorted. "Why do you deliberately go about destroying the devotion we have for you?"

"Deliberately? You're crazy! It wasn't I who started the story that I was milking the hospital. That was inside stuff."

"Just a minute. Let the lady get in a word. We're with you almost to a man whether you believe it or not."

"Almost—?"

"Ignore the almost." Now her voice softened. "Alan Towne, you've put up a magnificent fight. All we ask is that you see it through." She jumped down lightly from her seat in the window. As she passed him on the way to the door, she let her hand rest for a moment on his shoulder. "Alan, we all lose our way at times."

"You're impossible, Naomi," he cried. "You think everyone's about eight years old. You ought to have been married long ago."

"And if I had been I'd be saying the same things to you, Alan Towne. I'm offering you the best a woman has to give to a man. It is not necessary to have borne children to know that any man who fights for ideals—I hope you don't mind the word, idealism has a bad connotation these days—comes to the moment when he thinks himself alone."

"I'm sorry I spoke as I did," said Alan simply.

When she was gone he took out his watch. He was overdue at the Center. Getting out of the car at its door, he stood for a little facing the Benninger house. It stood on the rise of ground above the main building. It was still empty. But there were signs of life about it today. A man was washing the windows. The front ones were as clean and bright as Miss Benninger would have had them. Tom was moving in very soon.

Suddenly Alan's thoughts jumped to the evening he had sat at Miss Benninger's bedside. He saw the room, the canopied bed, her strong-featured face against the white pillows, the deed to the property lying on the coverlet. Now he realized that she had had a deeper knowledge than his of human nature. She had known a fight against him would be waged sometime. Humbly now he realized that Miss Benninger had understood what no man knew about himself until the moment came—whether he had so wrought out his inner life that he would be strong enough for the crisis. She had meant to help him when that moment came.

As he stood there looking up at the uncurtained windows, he heard someone calling him. Turning, he saw Roger Gunsaulus coming out of the Center. This was his afternoon to work with the therapist. He was running with free and easy movements. He came to a stop beside Alan. "Look," he said, "anybody is nuts to say things against you. That's what I told Dad." With that he was gone.

Alan saw suddenly that he who had so often advocated the open mind had been closing his to the forces of sanity and courage that were all around him. The depression which had fallen over him, like a collapsed tent, was being lifted now at the moment when he had not the strength to do it for himself.

He was again in communication with a goodly company of men and women, no longer alone. But feeling he needed a moment's respite to get his bearings, he walked up the knoll to the Benninger house, ascended the steps. From here he had a commanding view of the city spread out over the prairie. The pioneer spirit wrought this, he thought, and I am a part of it.

When he entered the Benninger Center he stopped to look about. In front of the great windows stood tall vases of flowers for the Easter service to be held in the morning. He thought, Probably Mrs. Gunsaulus sent them. The girl at the desk told him that Gunsaulus had left word that the Board wanted him to meet them in the morning. Easter Sunday morning! Did the Board with whom he had worked give credence to the tale of his dishonesty? I'm through with that kind of thinking, he said to himself and straightened his shoulders. I have no reason to doubt them. They probably want to plan how best to weather this assault on the hospital, for that in reality is what it is.

"And there's another message," the girl added, as he was turning away. "Your brother has been trying to telephone you. He left word he'd like to have you drive out to his place in the country this evening. He said it was urgent."

So Sam had heard. There it was again, support when he needed it. The love the brothers bore each other transcending difference in philosophy. Sam's word would be of value just now but it was not a very good time to drive out to the country. He needed the evening to get together some statistics to take to the Board meeting. He called Beritz asking if he would compile the records for him. Beritz hearing the old quality in Alan's voice was content.

Then Alan called Esther and asked her if she'd go with him to see Sam. "I'll drop by for you in a few minutes."

He's himself again, she thought. With a light heart she went about getting ready. She'd leave Francis with Beatrice. She wanted to be alone with Alan just now.

~~⚬~~ 72 ~~⚬~~

SAM felt that he had matters well in hand this afternoon. Until a few days ago he had seen no way of keeping Sally from going to live at the Benninger Center. It was inconceivable to him that Sally would consent to live in the midst of the crippled, day after day subjecting her growing son, his grandson, to the sight of the handicapped. He had thought he had convinced her that it was no environment for a child, but then Tom said he was going to move as soon after Easter as he could get the house furnished. He had said that he could no longer delay. He had been given the position at the Center with the understanding that he live on the grounds. "The house is all in order," he had said. "I've had it cleaned. It's all ready. I thought we might make a family event out of buying furniture."

Tom, slow and somewhat phlegmatic, of course couldn't be expected to see what a more sensitive person would have seen immediately. But Alan— what was Alan thinking of? He should know that it would tend to make a child different to live in such an environment. But now Sam believed even Alan would listen to him. How many years he had waited for the time when the crazy course Alan had embarked upon would bring him to defeat. All winter Sam had watched the net tightening around his brother. He had done nothing to stop the talk. Alan would have to learn. Now that his honesty had been questioned, Sam felt Alan would at last acknowledge that he was beaten. He could now say to Alan, "I am willing to let bygones be bygones. Take you back as my partner. We'll forget the Southeast District and all that has happened."

The shadows lay long across the green meadows. The birds were settling down for the night in the trees as Alan turned his car into the main highway. Now that that terrifying sense of being out of communication with everyone, even Esther, had gone, he was able to explain to her the crisis that lay ahead of him.

"You can't turn back now," said Esther. "I wouldn't want you to." And she knew despite her own moments of doubt and suffering—and she had had them during the long winter months—she was honest in saying this.

"I suppose Sam is offering me his help but I don't know on what terms," said Alan.

The sun set, and as the twilight fell, they came to Sam's house. It gleamed white in the oncoming darkness, its lights shining out across the lawn. Alan put out his hand and took Esther's and together they went up the steps.

Opening the door Alan gave the whistle which had been the signal between the two brothers when they were boys.

Quickly the family converged on them. Jo came in from the kitchen. She had not known of Sam's call to Alan. This was indeed a surprise. Sally ran down the stairs. And behind her came Tom. Sally flitted among them, first to Esther, then to Alan, and then, seeing her father who had come from the living room standing a little apart, she went over and kissed him.

"We're going to have dinner in a few minutes," said Jo. "Sally, you and Esther can help me." Once in the kitchen Jo began talking about her errand to town that afternoon. "I thought it would help us all, Sally, and not delay your father if I looked up what would be the best buys in furniture for your house." Jo, anxiously watching her daughter, hoped to bring the idea of a home of her own to seem right and natural to her by leading Sally's thought away from her troubling sense of responsibility to her father.

Esther had not seen Sally for some time and it seemed to her there was a change. She looked oddly immature, and at her mother's words she backed away from them crying, "Don't let's talk about it. It's hard enough leaving Father. It seems cruel taking his grandson away from him." Sally stood there a moment as if at bay, then rushed out of the room.

During the dinner Sam looked often at Alan, thinking, He looks completely worn out. The best thing I can do for him after he joins me is to see that he has a vacation.

The meal was over. As they left the dining room, Sam put his hand on his younger brother's shoulder saying, "I want to talk to you, Alan." Together they walked across the living room to the great fireplace. "It's a little chilly these spring evenings." Sam bent and touched a match to the nicely laid kindling. "I know you are in trouble, Al," he said, seating himself on the sofa next to his brother. "I've known it for a long time. Now that the crisis has come, I'm going to act."

"It's swell of you, Sam, to offer to help me out. I realize we don't look at everything professionally just alike. You know sometimes I think we're just a replica of the American people," said Alan. "Differ like hell between ourselves, but let anyone else attack us——"

"What are you getting at, Alan?" There was a note of suspicion in Sam's voice.

"Well, what you are talking about. I supposed that you wanted to help me clear my name of the accusation of dishonesty."

"Clear our name," said Sam. "You've brought us all pretty near to ruin, Alan, with your crazy ideas. But I intend to help you. In fact, I'm ready to take you back into my office!"

"You mean give up all I've done on my own! I thought you wanted to vouch for my honesty, stand back of me," Alan answered.

"Do you realize what you are asking?" Sam's face was stern. "You are asking me, when the high quality of the medical profession is about to be destroyed by government interference, to give you, who have been disloyal to the profession, my endorsement. Oh, Alan, you don't know what you ask."

"Sam, let me ask you. However you may disagree with me in theory, you do trust me, don't you? You know I am an honest man and skillful surgeon, don't you? I don't see that saying so means supporting my theories."

"Doesn't it amount to the same thing? If I vouch for you, you'll go on doing the things I don't approve of." It was incredible that Alan would refuse his generous offer. Alan—who was condemned by his own profession, who was without friends.

"All right," said Alan, rising. "I'll fight it out alone. I'll collect Esther and we'll be going."

The women had come into the hall from the kitchen, Tom from upstairs where he'd gone to see that everything was all right with little Samuel. Together they went into the living room. The two brothers walked toward them.

They heard Sam say, "We've reached the end, Alan. You've condemned yourself. It's not I who am condemning you. It was bound to come, I suppose. I think I've always known it would come ever since we were children," he said bitterly.

The group in the doorway moved forward, each drawn by his own involvement in the issue, each desirous of making some kind of peace between the two men. But before any of them could speak, Sam, seeing Tom standing with his arm around Sally, centered his attention on his son-in-law. "Alan and I have come to the parting of the ways, Tom. I understand your views are the same as mine. At least Sally says so. I think I have the right to demand that you leave Alan. A daughter of mine cannot be subjected to the ignominy of being associated with the discredited. You can come back into my office."

Jo, knowing Sam better than any of the others, felt pity for him. He who is so secure, revered by the top men in his profession, whom he honors, rich and powerful, is frightened. Then she was frightened for Sally.

Tom tried to decide what to answer. Even for Sally's sake, he could not take Sam's offer at the expense of the man who had actually saved his marriage from disaster. Desert Alan now when he was under fire. To leave now would lend credence to the tale of Alan's dishonesty.

Loosening his protective hold on Sally, he drew a long breath, then said calmly, trying to play down the dangerously emotional quality of the moment, "Although I don't agree with Alan in all his views, I think he has a good deal on his side too. He's under fire. If I left him now, it might end his usefulness. Thanks for the offer but I can't accept it."

"Then Sally's got to decide between us."

"Sam, you must leave Sally out of this." Jo spoke with a note of authority, seeking to control him as she often had of late.

Sally, unnoticed, slipped quietly out of the group, moved stealthily through the hall and out the veranda door. She could not bear another clash between husband and father. She could not bear once more to stand between them. She longed for peace. She would look at the serene stars, then go up the back stairs to her son who was sleeping peacefully.

Her father's voice raised in anger reached her, demanding her allegiance. I never can satisfy Father, never, never give enough, her heart cried out. Suddenly panic seized her. She started to run.

Back in the house Sam cried, "I will not have Sally's life ruined. Sally, do you stand with me or don't you?"

Suddenly they all realized that Sally was not there. "Where is she?" Jo cried.

Tom, catching the note of alarm in her voice, stepped to the stairs, calling, "Sally." There was no answer.

Sam was angry—Jo defeating him again, not letting him come to grips with his son-in-law whom he now thoroughly distrusted. With a gesture of frustration he said, "Why all this fuss? She has probably gone for a quiet walk. I should think she'd want to get away."

Tom saw the door of the veranda was open, and he hurried out on the lawn calling, "Sally, where are you? I'm coming." There was fear in his heart. There was no answer. He ran back into the house and asked Jo for a flashlight. She pointed to the hall table.

Then she went over to her husband. "Why did you do it, Sam?" She could not be kind to him just now.

"Come on, Sam," said Alan. "I've a flash in my car."

Over the fields and down the road the lights flickered. Their shouts rang out again and again. There was no answer, only the darkness and the sound of the rushing stream, so turbulent now in the spring. Tom ran along its banks directing the powerful rays here, there, looking for Sally in her white sweater. He saw the delicate green fronds of the willow tree moving in the wind. The embankment was freshly broken away, leaving the roots of the trees on the stream's side bare, dangling over the stream. Then his heart was tight with fear. Had Sally missed her footing, had her weight been just enough to carry the earth away? He ran on, reached the spot, and directed his light into the blackness below. For an instant he thought the white speck on the black water was white foam. No! Sally's white sweater! He ran along the bank until he came to a place where he could slide down. He waded upstream to where she lay face down amid the crumbling earth, half buried in it. Carefully with all the strength he had he worked to free her.

Lights converged on the bank's edge. "She's fallen. Fix up some kind of stretcher," Alan called out to his brother.

Sam and Alan ran back to the house. "Come on," cried Sam. "There's a canvas cot on the upstairs veranda."

Down the stairs, past Jo they carried it and out the door, running along the bank to where there was a place down which the two could carry the cot.

"There isn't any hope," said Tom, his voice breaking. "Her chest is crushed."

Sam knelt by his daughter, his delicate fingers moving with precision, making his own examination, his own diagnosis, his heart refusing to accept what his mind told him. A sob escaped him, then steadying himself he took over, giving the commands.

Alan at the head, Tom at the foot with Sam walking at the side of the improvised stretcher, they made their way along the stream. Sometimes one of them would lose his footing in the slippery mud, sometimes they walked knee-deep in the stream. Finally they came to where the bank was low enough for them to ascend.

And then they came to the house. In the wide front door Jo stood listening to the men's tread on the steps, holding the screen open for them to enter. As they passed into the house with their burden she moved forward. Gently she smoothed the tangled wet masses of hair back from Sally's face, straightened the torn and rumpled dress as she had so often done when her child was little and helpless. No holding back of the knowledge from Jo's honest mind.

When they set down the cot, Tom knelt on one side, Sam on the other, murmuring over and over, "My lamb, my lamb."

Jo stood frozen in trancelike numbness.

At last Sam could no longer refuse the truth and rose from his knees and looked vaguely about. Alan moved to his side, put his hand on his shoulder. Sam backed away. A shiver passed over him.

73

DURING the early morning hours of Easter Sunday while the Southeast District rejoiced, as did all Christendom, that He whom they had thought dead on Friday was alive among them this beautiful spring morning, Alan tried to give proof to the Board of his efficiency and honesty. There was no single accusation that had been brought against him that they did not raise. These were businessmen, and they meant business. One by one Alan answered their questions, pushing back the weariness accumulating within him, pushing back his grief—grief over the tragedy come to the family and over Sam's hatred of him growing more poignant as the hours went on and he recovered from his first numbness over Sally's death.

Two things he was able to prove to their satisfaction—that the hospital had been efficiently run and that there had been no misappropriation of funds. "You have only demonstrated what I already knew," said Gunsaulus when Alan had finished presenting the details vindicating himself. "I consider myself too good a businessman not to have found out long ago if you were dishonest."

"The real issue is that you have been supporting a position exactly opposite to what we take as businessmen. We don't want the government interfering in our business. Why should we keep you when you advocate the government interfering in the doctors' business?" Chesterton demanded.

There was fear and suspicion in his eyes as he went on, "Why don't you say you are discredited because you are in for socialization of the country?" The hated words had been spoken. Alan felt hostility toward him sweep over the office full of men but he was not daunted. His tiredness fell from him. He was fighting now for all he held dear.

"Gentlemen, to work out how best to handle the sick is a problem not easily solved. It will take the best brains of the country to solve it. Many things have been tried. We have tried one—the group hospital. It hasn't proved the whole answer by a long shot. I beg you not to close your minds before you've heard my views, which I know are contrary to yours. Some of you look on government as your enemy. I think that is the old aristocratic idea left over from the days when kings governed from the top. The American revolution started something new—government by the people for the people. I no more believe in the socialization of the country than you do. But I do believe our forefathers meant government should be concerned with the welfare of the people. We are fast moving toward an aristocracy of health.

"We have made the government an instrument of the people long ago when by taxes we supported public schools. Some of you in this room came to this country because of just this opportunity. Poorly cared for brains and bodies are an equal threat to democracy. Taxation of us all for those who need education and medical care is not socialization."

"More taxation!" almost to one man the Board members exclaimed. A babble of voices rose in which each of them expressed his horror of more taxation.

"But a compulsory health tax would lessen the burden you carry for the hospital and Center," exclaimed Alan.

"This is philanthropy," Palosky answered.

Then Alan knew as he had often before that he would never entirely understand these men, nor they him. But he went on, hoping in vain to make them understand his position. "Decide what you want to do about retaining me. I personally believe we'll never get sickness under control until we have compulsory insurance. Now there are many that honestly believe there are better ways to handle the problem. What I have been advocating is a chance to discuss things frankly. All I'm asking for is that we be free men not controlled by the Medical Association any more than by government, allowed to think for ourselves."

"So you insist on jeopardizing the hospital to satisfy your intellectual pride," said Chesterton.

Weariness such as only those who have been long under continued questioning know, combined with his grief, had brought Alan to the point of exhaustion. He rose. "I think I should leave you to decide whether or not you wish to retain me. I cannot recant," he said. The last word came oddly to his tongue. It was not a word he ever used, an old-fashioned word. Far back he had heard it.

"We have Dr. Towne's justification of his actions," said Gunsaulus.

Alan went out.

Hour after hour the men of the Board went on with their deliberations. They were equally divided on the question of firing Alan. Gunsaulus put up a stiff fight to prevent it. "It's not Towne's views that have brought discredit upon the hospital," he insisted. "It's those who want to keep things as they are. We can afford to charge less than the private doctors. Let's face it. You as businessmen should understand. Machines crowded out the one-man shop. Machines and modern equipment in medicine are crowding out the one-man medicine shop."

Chesterton touched his upper lip with his well-manicured forefinger, smoothing the ends of his close-clipped mustache. Then with just the slightest overtone of sarcasm in his voice, he said, "But you go to one of our solo doctors, do you not, Gunsaulus?"

Ignoring Chesterton's remark, Gunsaulus said, "I bet you it's a few malcontents stirring up all this trouble against Towne."

"You are dodging the real point raised before," said one of Mr. Chesterton's supporters. "Socialization is socialization."

"I've heard that till it's stale. We have government subsidies for beesiness, subsidies for farmers. Why not for sick folks?" Palosky said. "They found it goot."

"What about the tale about Towne's being a Communist? Doesn't what he advocates follow their line?" said Chesterton.

"Can't a man believe in help to train doctors without being tarred with that brush?" shouted Gunsaulus.

Hour after hour through the Sunday peace the fight went on. All of them were tired, cross and hungry. It was then that Chesterton offered his solution.

"Why not put Lambert in Towne's place?" he said blandly. "He stands in well with the Medical Association as well as with the town. He's active in church work. His wife is a civic-minded woman."

"It iss goot beesiness," said Palosky. "I like Dr. Towne, but beesiness is beesiness."

And now the third man, who had been on Gunsaulus' side until Palosky spoke, said, "I'll join you."

Gunsaulus was beaten, but he wouldn't vote to drop Towne. No, he wouldn't make it unanimous. He pointed his finger at Palosky. "You're the one that's got him out. You hadn't the guts to stand by what you really believed. I'll not be party to such an act. I refuse to make it unanimous."

Roger Gunsaulus, who had come with his father, had listened outside the door of the room where the meeting was being held. He had darted into a dark corner when Alan left. Now when he heard the verdict pronounced, he ran from the building. He thumbed his way out of the factory district where the Board was meeting, crossed the depressed area and the new section cut from the Benninger farm. On foot he ran swiftly up the road between the tall cottonwood trees. Sobbing, he came to the Center and told his story.

At his home through the long afternoon Alan waited, too tired even to feel anxiety over the decision. He fell into troubled sleep and was caught back with the happenings of last night. Anguish gripped him and he woke. Children's voices drifted down to him from upstairs. Early in the morning Tom had brought little Samuel, asking Esther to care for him. The two children were laughing and chattering.

Alan waited at his home for the verdict, but it was not until four o'clock that Gunsaulus came bringing the news that he had been relieved of his position as head of the hospital. "But it wasn't unanimous," said Gunsaulus. "You bet your bottom dollar I wouldn't vote for a thing like that. I would have won if Palosky had stood with me, but he said it was good business to let you go. I could spit on Palosky.

"But why did you give your enemies a chance to take a pot shot at you?" he demanded. Without giving Alan a chance to answer he went on. "The others didn't see that somebody had got next to Chesterton. He was dead set on getting Dr. Lambert in your place. He fooled the others. But I could have saved you if you weren't such a stubborn old goat, standing up for what you believe."

With these words Gunsaulus wrung Alan's hand, then started toward the hall only to find himself face to face with Esther. He brushed her aside. To Esther's astonishment she saw he was crying.

After the door closed behind him the room was very quiet. How can a man ever know whether he has acted for the best? he asked himself in anguish. Have I let the doctors at the hospital down? Have I hurt my family? This house he so loved, in which he had planned to bring up his family, must be given up. He must start over again in a new place.

Dusk fell. All at once something hit the veranda with a little thud, another, another. Hidden from view by the folds of the curtains Alan looked out. Scarcely discernible in the gathering darkness he saw a straggling line of men, women, and children standing outside his gate—some of his old patients, among them Miss Prentiss. They, too, he thought.

He turned away, sat down, his head bowed in his hands, counting the stones as they fell. Some hit the porch floor; some, better aimed, hit the door.

At last, when no more stones fell, accepting his complete defeat, Alan went to the door and opened it. He saw that each stone weighted a single flower. "Only a woman would think of a thing like that," he said, choking a little. He had suddenly realized Esther was at his side.

He stooped, picked up an Easter lily—a little wilted as if it might have been used at a church service—and a red rose with a vigorous stem, sharp with thorns.

A Final Word to my Readers:

If you have a moment's time I should like to speak to you directly. May I ask of you that you do not try to pick out the city in which this story is laid? For it is no particular city—you will find it neither north nor south nor east nor west. I have placed it as nearly as possible in the middle of America that it might take on attributes of all America.

Please do not try to identify any character in this book, for if you do you might make someone great who is not great, or someone evil who is not evil. Little by little the people of this book have come to life formed out of many human beings.

This is not a true story and yet there is no one incident in it which is not true. So of course it is not my story, except as it is the story of those who must face life under the handicap of a chronic ailment as I have had to do. I wish here to pay tribute to Dr. Joel E. Goldthwait, the specialist to whom I owe many useful happy years. Nor is it the story of my family although I have made the first American generation of the family of this story the first generation of mine. I have done this so that I might superimpose the hysteria of today on the hysteria of witchcraft when Rebecca Nourse, my ancestress, died refuting hysteria.

It is the story, too, of the marriage of people come together in their youth being welded together through suffering and struggle into an inseparable union.

And it is the story of Medicine caught in the maelstrom of world revolution.

It is the story of the human heart under stress.

Alice (Nourse) Tisdale Hobart